Human Rights Litigation against Multinationals in Practice

Human Rights Litigation against Multinationals in Practice

Edited by
RICHARD MEERAN
and
Assistant Editor
JAHAN MEERAN

OXFORD
UNIVERSITY PRESS

OXFORD
UNIVERSITY PRESS

Great Clarendon Street, Oxford, OX2 6DP,
United Kingdom

Oxford University Press is a department of the University of Oxford.
It furthers the University's objective of excellence in research, scholarship,
and education by publishing worldwide. Oxford is a registered trade mark of
Oxford University Press in the UK and in certain other countries

First Edition published in 2021

Impression: 1

Published in the United States of America by Oxford University Press
198 Madison Avenue, New York, NY 10016, United States of America

British Library Cataloguing in Publication Data

Data available

Library of Congress Control Number: 2021935991

ISBN 978–0–19–886622–0

DOI: 10.1093/oso/9780198866220.001.0001

Printed and bound by
CPI Group (UK) Ltd, Croydon, CR0 4YY

Foreword

This edited volume, *Human Rights Litigation against Multinationals in Practice* is a welcome addition to the body of scholarship focused on issues of liability of multinational corporations for human rights abuses committed in connection with their transnational business operations – be it via a subsidiary or through a global supply or value chain. This comprehensive book is a critical contribution to the literature as it includes chapters from leading lawyers who have been on the front lines of corporate human rights litigation over the past two decades and beyond. Having their perspectives on how the law works not only "on the books", but in action is critical to understanding the realities of transnational human rights litigation against corporate defendants. It is a vital and unique resource for practitioners, researchers, students, and policymakers alike.

When I first met Richard Meeran, the editor of and creative force behind this book, more than 20 years ago, the field of business and human rights was not in existence. At that time, a small band of brave lawyers were focused on trying to provide redress for victims of human rights abuses connected to the actions of multinational corporations and their subsidiaries, using civil litigation as a tool. There was Richard and his firm Leigh Day, based in the United Kingdom (UK) , and other lawyers in the United States (US) who were litigating cases against corporations under the Alien Tort Statute. The promise of the UK and US as possible venues for transnational tort cases to provide victims with access to remedy and redress for corporate harms was a long time coming, especially after the failure of victims of the Bhopal tragedy to receive justice in litigation against Union Carbide.[1]

There was no roadmap or guidebook for these lawyers. Their work was novel and courageous. Richard's groundbreaking work paved the way in the UK with theories focused on foreign direct liability as a way of achieving legal accountability of a parent for its conduct when a subsidiary was the more likely defendant. He represented South African miners and local residents in the pivotal asbestos-related diseases case of *Cape v. Lubbe plc*, which opened the door to the possibility of a direct duty of care from a parent company towards employees of a subsidiary and local residents based on acts and omissions of the parent[2]. The Cape Case went to the House of Lords, and in 2000court not only recognized the possibility of a

[1] Baxi, U. (2016). Human Rights Responsibility of Multinational Corporations, Political Ecology of Injustice: Learning from Bhopal Thirty Plus? *Business and Human Rights Journal, 1*(1), 21-40. doi:10.1017/bhj.2015.7

[2] *Lubbe and Others v Cape Plc and Related Appeals* [2000] UKHL 41.

parent's direct liability in tort, but also recognized the likelihood of denial of justice if the case were dismissed on the grounds of forum non conveniens. South African plaintiffs would not at that time have had access to legal aid and legal representation in South Africa.

In the United States, a series of cases were filed against companies in the extractive sector in the late 1990s. Royal Dutch Shell was sued in federal court in New York for its activities in the Ogoni Oil region of Nigeria and the execution of environmental activist Ken Saro Wiwa[3], Texaco was sued for alleged human rights harms arising from oil pollution in the Amazon[4], and Unocal for its alleged involvement in the use of forced labor to clear the way for an oil pipeline in Myanmar[5]. Ultimately two of these lawsuits, those against Shell and Unoca, settled after much procedural wrangling in the court – but more than a decade after the lawsuits had been brought. The suit against Texaco was dismissed on forum non conveniens grounds, with the court sending plaintiffs to Ecuador to seek justice[6]. While seen as a success in larger terms, the fact that it took nearly a decade for two cases to settle is a stark reality about the difficulty of civil litigation against multinational corporations.

Over the past two decades much has changed. As an academic researcher, I worked with a small but growing group of lawyers, to examine how multiple jurisdictions might be providing grounds for civil lawsuits relating to corporate human rights cases.[7] I have had the privilege of watching the universe of practitioners grow, with lawyers like Richard at the forefront. Richard and his firm have partnered with lawyers and law firms across the globe – from Australia to Africa, to bring more cases against multinational corporations. While there are still only a small number of lawyers able to take forward important yet at times daunting cases, there has been an expansion in the field.

We now have a community of practice – of lawyers from a variety of jurisdictions both civil and common law, who are bringing these cases. The book examines a mix of these different fora and examines the litigation hurdles and opportunities across these different countries. There is a cadre of corporate accountability case lawyers who are working to seek justice for victims and access to effective remedy. These lawyers work collectively and collaboratively across the globe, spurred on by their commitment to victims of corporate wrongdoing.

[3] Complaint in Wiwa v. Royal Dutch Petroleum, https://ccrjustice.org/sites/default/files/assets/11.8.96%20%20Wiwa%20Complaint.pdf

[4] Aguinda v. Texaco, Inc., 142 F. Supp. 2d 534 (S.D.N.Y. 2001)

[5] Doe v. Unocal litigation documents https://earthrights.org/case/doe-v-unocal/

[6] This case has led to an epic battle involving Texaco's successor corporation Chevron . Sara Randazzao, Litigation Without End: Chevron Battles on in 28-Year-Old Ecuador Lawsuit, Wall Street Journal (May 22, 2021). https://www.wsj.com/articles/litigation-without-end-chevron-battles-on-in-28-year-old-ecuador-lawsuit-11619975500

[7] Anita Ramasastry and Robert Thompson, Commerce, Crime and Conflict: Legal Remedies for Private Sector Liability for Grave Breaches of International Law: A survey of Sixteen Countries (Favor Report 596 2006) https://www.fafo.no/en/publications/fafo-reports/item/commerce-crime-and-conflict

The litigation landscape itself has changed. The United States, which was one of the more promising litigation fora in the late 1990s, has over the past two decades closed its doors to most transnational corporate human rights cases, through a series of Supreme Court cases including *Kiobel v. Royal Dutch Petroleum*[8], *Jesner v. Arab Bank*[9] and most recently *Nestle v. Doe*[10] which have limited the ability of foreign victims to sue non-US corporations for harms committed extraterritorially.

While doors have closed in the US, the UK remains a potential avenue for redress. The UK Supreme Court has in both *Okpabi v Shell* and *Lungowe v Vedanta, Resources*emphasized that in a number of circumstances a parent may owe a duty of care towards the victims of tort arising from its subsidiary operations. Similarly, recent litigation victories in the Netherlands and Canada[11] demonstrate that other jurisdictions may well be suitable avenues for civil corporate human rights litigation. France is another jurisdiction where civil society has been active in pursuing claims under the new French "Loi de Vigilance" (Duty of Vigilance Law).[12]

That being said, lawyers and civil society groups and victims are still focused on just getting the vast majority of cases into court and being allowed to proceed, numerous procedural hurdles mounted by defense counsel having to be cleared before cases can reach the merits stage. . Thus, while some court rooms may be open to victims, the corporate accountability and business and human rights community still has a long way to go in terms of holding corporations to account. This volume looks at the key challenges that still remain for litigators and victims – from issues of parent versus subsidiary liability, issues of conflicts of law, to the challenge of funding.

This book reminds me very much of another seminal book from the early days of the corporate accountability movement, which explored how tort litigation might in theory be used to pursue claims of torture using civil litigation as a tool for redress for transnational torture claims.[13] The current volume continues by providing a comprehensive guidebook looking at the potential for tort and other civil claims against multinationals in in practice.

[8] 569 U.S. 108 (2013), slip opinion available at https://www.supremecourt.gov/opinions/12pdf/10-1491_l6gn.pdf

[9] 38 S. Court 1386 (2018). Slip opinion available at https://www.supremecourt.gov/opinions/17pdf/16-499_1a7d.pdf

[10] Nestle v. Doe, 593 U.S. __ (2021) slip opinion available at https://www.supremecourt.gov/opinions/20pdf/19-416_i4dj.pdf

[11] In May 2021, the District Court of The Hague ordered Royal Dutch Shell (RDS) to reduce the CO2 emissions of the entire Shell group by 45 per cent by 2030, compared to 2019 levels. See Milieudefensie et al v. Royal Dutch Shell plc

https://uitspraken.rechtspraak.nl/inziendocument?id=ECLI:NL:RBDHA:2021:5339 Nevsun Resources Ltd v Araya, a landmark case in which the Supreme Court of Canada held, in a 5–4 decision, that a private corporation may be liable under Canadian law for breaches of customary international law committed in other countries 2020 SCC 5

[12] https://www.business-humanrights.org/en/latest-news/france-analysis-on-first-legal-cases-filed-under-enforcement-mechanism-set-out-in-duty-of-vigilance-law/

[13] Craig Scott (ed), , Torture as Tort: Comparative Perspectives on the Development of Transnational Human Rights Litigation (Oxford: Hart Publishing, 2001),

As the book goes to press, we are also commemorating the tenth anniversary of the UN Guiding Principles on Business and Human Rights.[14] We have experienced a decade with this international framework, endorsed by States at the Human Rights Council. The UN Guiding Principles, via Pillar III focuses on the need for States and companies to provide victims of corporate human rights abuses with access to effective remedy. Yet after a decade of the UN Guiding Principles, remedy remains elusive and Pillar III has been referred to as the "forgotten" Pillar. We also have negotiations underway in the Human Rights Council about a possible treaty focused on corporate accountability and human rights, which might provide for clearer grounds for civil lawsuits against transnational companies for human rights abuses.[15] The European Union is also considering a new mandatory directive focused on human rights due diligence, building on the concept outlined in the UN Guiding Principles, but which would possibly provide ways for plaintiffs to seek redress for companies who failed to properly prevent harm, via the courts.[16] The French law of vigilance, one of the earliest human rights due diligence laws, does provide an avenue for civil claims, and French lawyers are now testing the ability of this law to provide a road to remedy.[17]

We are entering a new phase where more lawyers are engaging in civil litigation, more jurisdictions are being tested, and corporations are now becoming subject to mandatory requirement to identify the harms connected to or arising from their business operations, and to prevent and mitigate them. This book explores the contemporary experiences of lawyers who are in the trenches, daily testing the boundaries and promise of the law in courtrooms across the globe with one goal – to seek justice and redress for victims of transnational corporate human rights abuses. Importantly, in addition, the book considers multinational human rights litigation from the perspective of business, in detail.

Richard Meeran continues to be a pioneer litigator as well as a mentor and leader in forging a global community of practice. I congratulate him for his vision and his contributing authors for sharing their knowledge and expertise with readers.

Professor Anita Ramasastry
University of Washington, Seattle

[14] UN Working Group on Business and Human Rights Guiding Principles on Business and Human Rights at 10: taking stock of the first decade (report to UN Human Rights Council) A/HRC/47/39 (2021). https://undocs.org/A/HRC/47/39 see also https://www.ohchr.org/EN/Issues/Business/Pages/UNGPsBizHRsnext10.aspx

[15] At its 26th session, on 26 June 2014, the Human Rights Council adopted **resolution 26/9** by which it decided "to establish an open-ended intergovernmental working group on transnational corporations and other business enterprises with respect to human rights, whose mandate shall be to elaborate an international legally binding instrument to regulate, in international human rights law, the activities of transnational corporations and other business enterprises." https://www.ohchr.org/en/hrbodies/hrc/wgtranscorp/pages/igwgontnc.aspx

[16] https://www.business-humanrights.org/en/latest-news/eu-commissioner-for-justice-commits-to-legislation-on-mandatory-due-diligence-for-companies/

[17] Cosssart S, Chaplier J, and Beau de Lomenie T., S (2017). The French Law on Duty of Care: A Historic Step Towards Making Globalization Work for All. *Business and Human Rights Journal*, 2(2), 317-323.

Contents

List of Contributors

Jason Brickhill, Doctoral candidate and tutor, Faculty of Law, University of Oxford; Advocate, Johannesburg Bar; Honorary Research Associate, University of Cape Town

Peter Cashman, Barrister; Adjunct Professor of Law, University of New South Wales

Lucie Chatelain, Advocacy and Litigation Officer, Sherpa

Sandra Cossart, Executive Director, Sherpa

Felix Curtis, Trainee Solicitor, Harbour Litigation Funding

Susan Dunn, Founder, Harbour Litigation Funding

Paul Hoffman, Partner, Schonbrun Seplow Harris Hoffman & Zeldes LLP

Bruce Johnston, Founding Partner, Trudel Johnston & Lespérance

Daniel Leader, Partner, Leigh Day

Rae Lindsay, Partner, Clifford Chance LLP

Zanele Mbuyisa, Director, Mbuyisa Moleele Attorneys

Robert McCorquodale, Professor of International Law and Human Rights, University of Nottingham; Barrister and Mediator at Brick Court Chambers London; Founder of Inclusive Law

Richard Meeran, Partner and Head of International Department, Leigh Day

Miriam Saage-Maaβ, Vice Legal Director/Director Business Human Rights Programme, European Center for Constitutional and Human Rights

Channa Samkalden, Partner, Prakken d' Oliveira Human Rights Lawyers

1

The Litigation Landscape of Business and Human Rights

Robert McCorquodale

I. Introduction

> It is one thing to embark on and fund a heavy group action where the procedures governing the conduct of the proceedings are known to and understood by experienced judges and practitioners. It may be quite another where the exercise is novel and untried ... It cannot be assumed that all judges will respond to this new procedural challenge in the same innovative spirit.
>
> Lord Bingham, *Lubbe v. Cape plc*[1]

The litigation landscape for actions concerning the legal responsibilities of business for human rights harm is constantly changing. In 2000, when Lord Bingham made his statement, cited above, in the UK House of Lords, there were very few cases in this area other than some under the US Alien Tort Claims Act.[2] Two decades later, there is litigation across the globe, as is seen in the excellent chapters in this book. However, as Lord Bingham noted, not all judges (and legal practitioners) have risen to 'the challenge in the same innovative spirit'. The global litigation landscape today is thus muddy, with some shafts of sunlight.

What has remained a constant part of this landscape over this period has been the increase in the number of corporations operating across territorial boundaries. Corporations have had significant economic power in relation to States for centuries, with the actions of the English and Dutch East India Companies in the 17th and 18th centuries an example which extended to considerable military, political, and social power.[3] More recently, the evidence shows that the economic power of multinational

[1] *Lubbe v. Cape plc* [2000] 1 WLR 1545 (HL) 1560.
[2] See Chapter 4 by Brickhill and Mbuyisa.
[3] See, for example, A. Angie, *Imperialism, Sovereignty and the Making of International Law* (2005) and W. Dalrymple, *The Anarchy: The Relentless Rise of the East India Company* (2019).

Robert McCorquodale, *The Litigation Landscape of Business and Human Rights* In: *Human Rights Litigation against Multinationals in Practice*. Edited by: Richard Meeran, Oxford University Press. © The Several Contributors 2021.
DOI: 10.1093/oso/9780198866220.003.0001

corporations (MNCs)[4] is significantly greater than many States.[5] This has a consequence in terms of the lack of power of many States in relation to corporations.[6]

The growth of corporations has been accompanied by the rise of awareness of the consequences of that part of corporate activity which can cause or contribute to human rights harms. Parts of civil society have been very active in alerting the wider public, and the corporations themselves, to these harms.[7] Many of the cases which this book records have arisen due to the concerted actions of individuals, communities, groups, academic, and non-governmental organisations (NGOs), amongst others, as well as concerned legal practitioners.

Indeed, the idea of social responsibilities of corporations has come a long way. In 1970, Milton Friedman, one of the founders of neoliberal economic thinking, claimed that the only social responsibility of business is to increase its profits (provided in so doing it engaged in open and free competition without deception or fraud).[8] However, 50 years later, while many corporations may appear still to accept this approach, there is strong pressure on corporations to consider, in addition to profits, the impact of their activities on stakeholders such as workers, local communities, and consumers.[9] A few corporations act on this and some assert that they will do so. Indeed, in 2019 the chief executive officers (CEOs) of 181 companies promised to deliver value to all their stakeholders including customers, employees, suppliers, and communities.[10] The outcome of this on actual corporate activity and on litigation is yet to be seen.

[4] Note that sometimes this is referred to as transnational corporations, yet the terms are today largely synonymous or used interchangeably.

[5] Z. Rodionova, 'World's Largest Corporations Make More Money than Most Countries on Earth Combined' *The Independent* (London, 13 September 2016) <https://www.independent.co.uk/news/business/news/worlds-largest-corporations-more-money-countries-world-combined-apple-walmart-shell-global-justice-a7245991.html> accessed 13 June 2020.

[6] See *Gagarimabu v. Broken Hill Proprietary Co Ltd* [2001] VSC 517, para. 34 (Victoria, Australia) and *BHP v. Dagi* [1996] 2 VR 117 (Victorian Court of Appeal) on the situation of an economically powerful corporation and the State of Papua New Guinea, which restricted the ability of Papua New Guinea landowners to bring a claim. For other examples see ITT, a US-based corporation, which was involved in the overthrow of the Allende Government in Chile, and the United Fruit Co. which allegedly masterminded a coup in Guatemala, and see T. Reid, 'Banana Company, Chiquita, "Armed Guerrillas"' *The Times* (Washington, DC, 16 November 2007) 50 in relation to the activities of the US company Chiquita in Colombia.

[7] See, for example, the excellent information provided by the Business and Human Rights Resource Centre: <https://www.business-humanrights.org> accessed 16 April 2021.

[8] M. Friedman, 'The Social Responsibility of Business is to Increase Its Profits' *The New York Times Magazine* (New York, NY, 13 September 1970) <http://www.umich.edu/~thecore/doc/Friedman.pdf> accessed 20 February 2020.

[9] See C. Mayer, *Prosperity: Better Business Makes the Greater Good* (2018) and the British Academy Project on the Future of the Corporation <https://www.thebritishacademy.ac.uk/programmes/future-of-the-corporation> accessed 20 February 2020.

[10] 'Business Roundtable Redefines the Purpose of a Corporation to Promote "An Economy That Serves All Americans"' (Business Roundtable, 19 August 2019) <https://www.businessroundtable.org/business-roundtable-redefines-the-purpose-of-a-corporation-to-promote-an-economy-that-serves-all-americans> accessed 20 February 2020.

This chapter aims to provide some legal context to the other chapters by clarifying the landscape in which the litigation against MNCs is conducted. It will briefly explain the difference between the civil law and the common law legal systems, the difference between a criminal law and a civil law claim, and explain a few key terms, such as jurisdiction, *forum non-conveniens*, and applicable law. It also will provide an introduction to the development of business and human rights within the international contexts and how that is relevant to MNC litigation.

II. Litigating in civil law and common law legal systems

The ability to bring a claim against an MNC, the nature of the claim, and the procedure for taking the claim forward all depend to a large extent on the particular legal system in which the claim is brought. There is a range of legal systems, and mixtures of legal systems, worldwide but this chapter will focus on the civil law and common law legal systems as they are the two legal systems in which the significant majority of litigation against MNCs has occurred to date. While this section will attempt to summarise the relevant core structural comparisons between these two legal systems,[11] it is acknowledged that there are many differences in national applications within these two legal systems and these systems also evolve over time.[12]

In civil law legal systems, generally the main source of the law is legislation, which includes specific codes which regulate various areas of society. In civil law, a code is a body of general principles intended to be comprehensive and to encompass the entire subject matter rather than a special law for specific situations. There is also some importance given to the preparatory works and relevant discussions in parliament prior to the passing of the code. Courts do have a role in interpreting the codes, though their decisions do not always create binding precedent unless considered to be so by practice or by Constitutional provisions.[13]

In common law legal systems, most legislation is specific law for particular circumstances, with only a few intended to codify an entire subject matter. The role of the courts is to interpret the law and also to clarify the law to factual situations where legislation was absent or incomplete, with the latter leading to the judicial decisions being a source of the law. Stability and continuity are obtained using the doctrine of precedent, in which judges in lower courts followed the core reasoning of decisions made previously by higher courts with, on rare occasions, an earlier

[11] For a more detailed examination of different legal systems, see, for example, J. Dainow, 'The Civil Law and the Common Law: Some Points of Comparison' (1966) 15 *American Journal of Comparative Law* 419, on which some of this section relies.

[12] See, for example, the comparison of common law legal systems in relation to parent company liability by G. Skinner, 'Rethinking Limited Liability of Parent Corporations for Foreign Subsidiaries' Violations of International Human Rights Law' (2015) 72 *Washington and Lee Law Review* 1179.

[13] See Dainow (n. 11).

decision not being followed due to changes in societal expectations or factual situations.[14]

One of the consequences of these different legal systems arises when dealing with a legal issue in terms of litigation against an MNC, as there may be differences in approaches:

> In the civil law system, inquiry usually begins with the codes and other legislation, then it seeks out the commentators and the treatises, and only in third place do cases come in for consideration and evaluation… In the common law … research is focused essentially on prior judicial decisions, as a result of the very nature of the system. Of course, legislation is controlling where applicable, and it has to be examined to determine questions of applicability, but here again the judicial interpretations become the binding authority whereas in the civil law tradition, each case is related back essentially to the legislative authority.[15]

There are also specific procedural differences in each legal system. For example, claims in a common law system tend to be based on a limited number of specific causes of action under legislation or case law, with novel causes of action difficult to bring, while civil law systems rely on the broader principles in the codes, though usually with only compensatory damages provisions.[16] In the common law system judges tend to focus more on facts and precedents to determine the case between the parties to the case than civil law judges, whose role has a more inquisitorial character where the judges are expected to seek to ascertain the truth more generally.[17] In addition, rules to obtain discovery vary between legal systems and, as noted below, between criminal and civil claims. The *forum non conveniens* doctrine is a common law doctrine only.[18]

These legal system differences can have an impact on litigation against MNCs. As Philipp Wesche and Miriam Saage-Maaß note in relation to the lack of German tort cases against MNCs:

> In fact, the most problematic aspects of litigation [in Germany] are of a practical and procedural nature. Given the absence of pretrial discovery and of effective mechanisms of court ordered disclosure, claimants encounter great difficulties in proving their cases, which are characterized through a structural asymmetry in information. Moreover, there are no collective actions [in Germany], which

[14] See Skinner (n. 12).

[15] Dainow (n. 11) 430.

[16] See C. van Dam, *European Tort Law* (2nd edn, 2014), especially 9–10.

[17] See L. Enneking, *Foreign Direct Liability and Beyond: Exploring the Role of Tort Law in Promoting International Corporate Social Responsibility and Accountability* (2012).

[18] See J. Zerk, 'Corporate Liability for Gross Human Rights Abuses' (2014) Report for the Office of the UN High Commissioner for Human Rights <https://www.ohchr.org/Documents/Issues/Business/DomesticLawRemedies/StudyDomesticeLawRemedies.pdf> accessed 20 February 2020, p. 68.

> would allow lawyers to litigate on behalf of larger groups of claimants in a cost-efficient manner, and significant shortcomings with regard to legal aid. Together with the low profitability of these complex cases, this means that lawyers have little incentive to undertake litigation.[19]

Therefore, when considering litigation against an MNC, both the claimant and the defendant company will be affected by the particular legal system within which the claim is brought. The structure of the legal system, the core elements of it, and the procedures within it will all affect the claim. A legal system can also 'exacerbate inequalities in the extent to which victims will have access to remedy, create legal uncertainty for both victims and companies, reinforce concerns about impunity and place obstacles in the way of future international cooperation'.[20] Nevertheless, there can be a significant degree of similarity with each legal system once the case proceeds, with courts open to consideration of cases from other jurisdictions, as seen in the interaction between Dutch and English court decisions in MNC litigation.[21]

The other major aspect of the claim, and which is also affected by the particular legal system, is whether it is brought as a criminal or civil claim. Indeed, in a survey of almost 50 sets of legal proceedings against MNCs it was found that:

> [A]round 30 [sets of legal proceedings] were commenced in common law jurisdictions and around 17 in civil law jurisdictions. Of the cases commenced in common law jurisdictions, all but one are private law (i.e. tort-based) actions for compensation. On the other hand, of the legal proceedings that have been commenced in civil law jurisdictions, well over half were commenced as criminal law complaints.[22]

Therefore, the type of legal system does appear to have an impact on the type of claim brought against MNCs.

III. Litigating criminal claims and civil claims

The UN Guiding Principles on Business and Human Rights (UNGPs) confirmed that the activities of companies can potentially impact 'virtually the entire spectrum

[19] P. Wesche and M. Saage-Maaß, 'Holding Companies Liable for Human Rights Abuses Related to Foreign Subsidiaries and Suppliers before German Civil Courts: Lessons from *Jabir and Others v KiK*' (2016) 16 *Human Rights Law Review* 370, 384.

[20] Zerk (n. 18) 7.

[21] See, for example, *Eric Barizaa Dooh of Goi and others v. Royal Dutch Shell Plc and others*, Court of Appeal, The Hague, 200.126.843 (case c) and 200.126.848 (case d), 18 December 2015, <https://uitspraken.rechtspraak.nl/inziendocument?id=ECLI:NL:GHDHA:2015:3586> accessed 20 February 2020. See further Chapter 2 by Meeran and Chapter 3 by Leader.

[22] Zerk (n. 18) 91.

of internationally recognized human rights.'[23] However, while some human rights are part of criminal law (such as the prohibition on torture), many human rights are not normally within criminal law, and some fall outside both types of claim (as discussed below).[24] So there is often a decision to be made by claimants about whether to commence litigation against an MNC through a criminal law or a civil law route.

In making such litigation decisions, Paul Robinson argues:

> Conventional lay wisdom holds that criminal liability and criminal commitment are different from civil liability and civil commitment in that the former generally reflect moral blameworthiness deserving condemnation and punishment, while this is not necessarily so for the latter. The notion that the distinctiveness of criminal law is its focus on moral blameworthiness, is supported by the traditional requirements for criminal liability, which as a group are not characteristic of civil liability.[25]

Hence, it is often the sense of 'moral blameworthiness', or what sociologists term 'the stigma',[26] of having a criminal conviction, which can be seen as a possible reason for choosing the path of commencing a criminal law claim. In addition, some claims may be civil in one jurisdiction and criminal in another.[27]

A. Criminal claims

In order to commence a criminal claim against an MNC, it is necessary to establish the elements of the crime. This normally has two key aspects: the actions were prohibited by law; and there was the necessary mental element, such as intent or recklessness. If the offence is of a strict or no-fault liability, then evidence of the act or the outcome is sufficient. In addition, to persuade the court, a high standard of proof is needed, which is defined in some jurisdictions as 'beyond reasonable doubt'.[28] There is an additional aspect in bringing a claim against an MNC, which

[23] Guiding Principles on Business and Human Rights, Implementing the United Nations 'Protect, Respect and Remedy' Framework (2011) HR/PUB/11/04 <https://www.ohchr.org/Documents/Publications/GuidingPrinciplesBusinessHR_EN.pdf> accessed 20 February 2020, Guiding Principle 12 Commentary.

[24] There may also be administrative law claims but these are not considered in this chapter.

[25] P.H. Robinson, 'The Civil-Criminal Distinction and Dangerous Blameless Offenders' (1993) 83 *Journal of Criminal Law and Criminology* 693, 693–4.

[26] See E. Goffman, *Stigma: Notes on the Management of Spoiled Identity* (1963).

[27] See, for example, the misleading advertising case (which is usually a civil claim in common law States), which was initiated by Sherpa against Samsung, was a criminal case under French law: Sherpa, 'Samsung's indictment: Fighting transnational corporation's human right's violations through consumer law' <https://www.asso-sherpa.org/samsungs-indictment-in-france-fighting-transnational-corporations-human-rights-violations-trhough-consumer-law> accessed 20 February 2020.

[28] See Zerk (n. 18) 32.

is not the situation with most criminal claims, which is to determine if it is possible for a corporation to commit a crime within the jurisdiction. The position is that 'most jurisdictions appear to recognise the possibility of corporate criminal responsibility (if not as a general concept then at least in relation to specific offences or types of offences) ... [though] some jurisdictions, for constitutional or doctrinal reasons, do not'.[29] However, even those jurisdictions which may have corporate criminal responsibility may limit these offences to ones committed within the territory of the State. This narrows the situation for bringing a criminal claim against an MNC, as the facts are generally based on some form of corporate complicity for actions outside the territory of the forum State.[30]

Accordingly, a criminal claim against an MNC will depend on the jurisdiction. One jurisdiction where criminal claims have been used is in France. For example, in October 2011, two NGOs filed a criminal complaint in France against a French company, Amesys, alleging that the company provided software to the Gaddafi government in Libya, which was then used by that regime to intercept private Internet communications and to identify dissidents who were then arrested and tortured. Although Amesys admitted that its 'contract was related to the making available of analysis hardware' to the Libyan government in 2007, it 'very strongly denie[d] the accusation of 'complicity in torture'.[31] The French courts initially refused to bring charges and it was only after a successful appeal forced the prosecutor to commence investigation did it begin, though the process is ongoing.[32] Indeed, as this case shows, one of the major obstacles in bringing a criminal case against an MNC is the need to persuade a prosecutor to commence the action, as normally only a prosecutor can bring a criminal charge. Some comparative research on this issue concluded that:

> For a number of reasons, linked either to the legal systems concerned or to the attitude of the prosecuting authorities, and because of the complexity of these cases, lack of resources and know-how, as well as lack of mandate, public prosecutors do not pursue cases involving corporate complicity in human rights violations that occur abroad.[33]

[29] Zerk (n. 18) 32–3. For more detail see J.L. Černič, 'Corporate Accountability of Human Rights' in J. Martin and K. Bravo (eds), *The Business and Human Rights Framework* (2016) 193–218.

[30] See Report of the International Commission of Jurists Expert Legal Panel on Corporate Complicity in International Crimes, *Volume 2: Criminal Law and International Crimes*, 'Corporate Complicity and Legal Accountability' (2008).

[31] See G. Skinner, R. McCorquodale, O. De Schutter, et al., 'The Third Pillar: Access to Judicial Remedies for Human Rights Violations by Transnational Business' (2013) <http://corporatejustice.org/documents/publications/eccj/the_third_pillar_-access_to_judicial_remedies_for_human_rights_violation.-1-2.pdf> accessed 20 February 2020, Case Study, p. 77.

[32] See FIDH, 'The Amesys Case' (2015) <https://www.fidh.org/IMG/pdf/report_amesys_case_eng.pdf> accessed 20 February 2020, pp. 9–10.

[33] Skinner, McCorquodale, De Schutter, et al. (n. 31) 76.

Therefore, even if a criminal claim is the choice made, it still requires a prosecutor to commence the action and take it forward.

There are two other matters which are relevant for a criminal case: documents and remedies. A criminal claim will often lead to the prosecutor compelling the MNC to provide all relevant documents to the court, without the difficulties that usually arise in a civil claim.[34] In relation to remedies, the sanction against an MNC if found guilty of a criminal offence is normally a substantial fine. The victims do not normally receive compensation or any other direct remedy in a criminal case. There are a few States, such as France, where the victims can join the criminal case as *parties civile*, which gives the victims the right to be consulted in the course of the investigation and to make submissions as to liability and sentencing, and they might be awarded compensation directly by the criminal court.[35] In other States the prosecutor can, in some circumstances, decide to request the court to make a compensation order for the victims.

B. Civil claims

As noted above, the vast majority of litigation against MNCs have been commenced by a civil claim. This is possibly because a civil claim, if successful, normally has a significant focus on remedies for the victims, and/or because there is a different (and lower) standard of proof applicable for civil claims than criminal claims.[36] Furthermore, as noted above, enforcement authorities tend not to prosecute MNCs for these matters. Almost all the civil claims against MNCs worldwide have been based on what is called 'tort' in the common law legal systems and the law of 'non-contractual obligations' or 'delicts' in the civil law legal systems. The term 'tort' claim will be used here for all of these claims because, as Liesbeth Enneking has noted:

> Despite the theoretical differences between the tort systems in different societies, the way they operate in practice is often rather similar, although different standards, legal cultures and policy approaches may still make for different outcomes in similar cases. Thus, regardless of whether they are brought in common law or in civil law legal systems, most of these [civil claims against MNCs] are likely to revolve around alleged violations of unwritten norms pertaining to proper

[34] See, for example, the criminal trial against senior executives of ENI and Shell in Italy: C. Albanese, S. Di Pasquale, and K. Gilblom, 'Eni, Shell to Face Trial in Italy in $1 Billion Bribery Case' (*Bloomberg*, 20 December 2017) <https://www.bloomberg.com/news/articles/2017-12-20/eni-shell-to-face-trial-in-italy-over-1-billion-bribery-case> accessed 20 February 2020.

[35] See Chapter 6 by Cashman.

[36] See A. Marx, C. Bright, J. Wouters, et al., *Access to Legal Remedies for Victims of Corporate Human Rights Abuses in Third Countries* (2019) (Study requested by the European Parliament's Sub-Committee on Human Rights) 12.

> societal conduct, as reflected in the duties of care allegedly violated by the corporate defendants.[37]

There have also been civil claims which are legislative or constitution based, such as the Alien Tort Claims Act in the United States,[38] and there are a few which are claims in contract, for unjust enrichment, or on some other civil claim bases.[39]

In relation to civil claims under tort law, most claims are primarily based on negligence in which a claimant must show first, the existence of a duty of care owed to them by the defendant MNC; second, that such a duty of care was breached by the defendant MNC (which may include issues of foreseeability); and third, that the breach of the duty of care has caused damage to the claimants. All of these raise difficulties for a civil claim against an MNC; for example, in order to prove whether there has been a breach of the duty of care it will normally depend on having access to the internal documents of the MNC, which, unsurprisingly, the MNC will be unlikely to disclose without a court order. Indeed, in one of the earliest English cases on the duty of care of a parent company, *Lubbe v. Cape*, which is quoted at the beginning of this chapter, it was stated:

> Resolution of this issue [of a duty of care] will be likely to involve an inquiry into what part the defendant played in controlling the operations of the group, what its directors and employees knew or ought to have known, what action was taken and not taken, whether the defendant owed a duty of care to employees of group companies overseas and whether, if so, that duty was broken. Much of the evidence material to this inquiry would, in the ordinary way, be documentary and much of it would be found in the offices of the parent company, including minutes of meetings, reports by directors and employees on visits overseas and correspondence.[40]

So, access to documents in the hands of an MNC is not easy at the initial stages of commencing a civil claim.[41]

As the decision on these issues are determined by the judges in both common law and civil law legal systems, it is inevitable that there may be different outcomes

[37] Enneking (n. 17) 172–3.

[38] See Chapter 4 by Brickhill and Mbuyisa.

[39] See, A. Beckers, *Enforcing Corporate Social Responsibility Codes: On Global Self-Regulation and National Private Law* (2015) 47–148. See also, for example, the case brought by Malawian tobacco farmers against British American Tobacco: Leigh Day, 'Malawi tobacco farmers in landmark legal fight against British American Tobacco' (*Leigh Day*, 31 October 2009) <https://www.leighday.co.uk/News/2019/October-2019/%E2%80%8BMalawi-tobacco-farmers-in-landmark-legal-fight-ag> accessed 20 February 2020.

[40] *Lubbe v. Cape* (n. 1) p. 1555.

[41] See R. Meeran, 'Access to Remedy: The United Kingdom Experience of MNC Tort Litigation for Human Rights Violations' in S. Deva and D. Bilchitz (eds), *Human Rights Obligations of Business* (2013) 378, 393.

in different jurisdictions, as there will be different procedural rules and principles in each jurisdiction.[42] Many of these place considerable barriers for bringing a civil claim, as discussed in later chapters. A recent important study for the European Commission on due diligence requirements in the supply chain summarised some of these barriers are follows:

Examples of such barriers to access to remedies include:

- Difficulties and costs for claimants to secure legal representation
- Resources and time required to prove claimants' onus and issues related to access to information
- Restrictive time limits on bringing claims
- Immunities and non-justiciability doctrines
- Jurisdictional challenges
- Issues relating to the applicable law
- The complexity of corporate structures and the attribution of legal responsibility among the members of a corporate group
- Proving human rights violations
- The reach and enforcement of remedies[43]

There is an additional barrier which arises in these civil claims: the general lack of a civil claim based explicitly on a violation of a human right. Because these civil claims must be brought within the tort law framework, it forces claimants to fit their claims within certain restrictive legal parameters, and it privileges only those violations that can be expressed in tort claim terminology.[44] This can make it very puzzling and exclusionary for the claimants who consider that their human rights have been infringed but see the civil claim expressed in a language which is not expressed as a human right. It also means that some human rights violations, such as denial of access to education and infringing cultural rights of indigenous communities, may not be able to be brought as a civil claim without some legislative basis in domestic law. This lack of legal expression diminishes the potential significance of the UNGPs clear statement quoted above that businesses can violate the full range of human rights and restricts the possible claims that can be brought to court in MNC litigation.

[42] For example, the Dutch cases discussed above, where the Dutch court did not follow all aspects of the English court's decision. See Chapter 2 by Meeran and Chapter 3 by Leader.

[43] BIICL, LSE, Civic, 'Study on Due Diligence in the Supply Chain' (2020) Study for the European Commission <https://op.europa.eu/en/publication-detail/-/publication/8ba0a8fd-4c83-11ea-b8b7-01aa75ed71a1/language-en> accessed 20 February 2020, p. 229 (footnotes omitted) The author was one of the co-authors of this Study.

[44] See Skinner, McCorquodale, De Schutter, et al. (n. 31) 37.

IV. Litigating across the intersection of laws

Litigation against MNCs on business and human rights matters requires a knowledge of a wide range of areas of laws by lawyers for all parties. Beyond knowledge of the areas referred to above, being domestic criminal, tort and contract law, human rights and constitutional law, and comparative law, there are other areas of law which are relevant. These include domestic corporate law, public international law, international human rights law, international investment law, international humanitarian law, international criminal law, domestic and international environmental law, and private international law, as well as business management, business ethics, financial decision-making, and organisational studies. Therefore it is an area which demands a breadth of expertise which is unusual and makes litigation against MNCs even more demanding. Three examples of the intersection of laws in this area will be considered here: domestic corporate law, private international law, and public international law, as they arise in a large number of types of litigation against MNCs.

A. Corporate law

In relation to domestic corporate law, there is a core doctrine of company law of separate legal personality which is found in almost all jurisdictions.

> Under the doctrine of separate legal personality, a parent company and its subsidiaries are treated as separate legal entities. The result is that parent companies are not automatically treated as being responsible for the acts of their subsidiaries, even subsidiaries that are wholly owned.[45]

As a consequence of this company law doctrine, parent companies and their subsidiaries of an MNC are separate and distinct legal entities, each with their own assets and liabilities, and with separate legal obligations. Public international law (see further below) reinforces this distinction as the State where a corporation is incorporated or registered is considered to determine the 'nationality' of the corporation, and as a result, '[a] subsidiary is a separate legal entity and therefore necessarily distinct from its parent ... as a matter of international law, parent and subsidiary are each subject to the exclusive jurisdiction of their respective [States]'.[46]

[45] Zerk (n. 18) 37. See also Office of the High Commissioner for Human Rights (OHCHR), 'Improving Accountability and Access to Remedy for Victims of Business-Related Human Rights Abuse' (2016) A/HRC/32/19.

[46] F.A. Mann, *The Doctrine of International Jurisdiction Revisited After Twenty Years* (1984) 56.

In addition, each corporate entity has limited legal liability, so that the investors in the company—and parents of subsidiaries, even if wholly owned—are normally not liable for the actions of the company. As MNCs are often very complex legal structures of multiple legal entities, it can make any claim difficult to bring. Any claim against a parent company for an action by a subsidiary can give rise, understandably, to an argument by the MNC that the separate corporate personality doctrine operates and that to bring the claim against a parent company would be contrary to 'the corporate veil' between corporate legal entities. Whether or not the 'corporate veil' can be lifted (or 'pierced'), and whether or not a parent company can be held liable for the conduct of the subsidiaries that it controls or ought to control—and whether the subsidiary can also be included in the claim—will depend on the law applicable to the case and how it is applied by the court in each jurisdiction.

Accordingly, in order to avoid this corporate veil argument, some claims have been commenced on the basis that the parent company itself directly owed a duty of care to those affected by the actions of the subsidiary, and so technically not piercing the corporate veil. For example, in the important case of *Chandler v. Cape Industries*, before the UK Court of Appeal, Lady Justice Arden stated:

> I would emphatically reject any suggestion that this court is in any way concerned with what is usually referred to as piercing the corporate veil. A subsidiary and its company are separate entities. There is no imposition or assumption of responsibility by reason only that a company is the parent company of another company. The question is simply whether what the parent company did amounted to taking on a direct duty to the subsidiary's employees [who alleged that they were harmed].[47]

In other cases, the courts have indicated that they may be prepared to pierce the corporate veil if it is shown that the subsidiary was acting as the agent of the parent company, which is one of the few exceptions to the separate corporate legal personalities doctrine.[48] While this core corporate law doctrine is an element in most litigation against MNCs, it may also open the possibility of litigation against MNCs under corporate law where that law provides that corporations must consider human rights in their decision-making.[49]

[47] *Chandler v. Cape Industries* [2012] EWCA (Civ) 525 [2012] 1 WLR 3111, paras 69–70.

[48] See *Choc v. Hudbay Minerals, Inc.*, 2013 ONSC 1414, Superior Court of Ontario, Canada, para. 49.

[49] See, for example, the obligations in domestic law for corporations in the European Union under the EU Non-Financial Reporting Directive (Directive 2014/95/EU of the European Parliament and of the Council of 22 October 2014 amending Directive 2013/34/EU as regards disclosure of non-financial and diversity information by certain large undertakings and groups Text with EEA relevance OJ L 330, 15.11.2014, pp. 1–9), where they must report on human rights, labour, environmental, and community issues: Alliance for Corporate Transparency, 'The State of Corporate Sustainability Disclosure under the EU Non-Financial Reporting Directive' (2018 Research Report, 2019): <http://www.allianceforcorporatetransparency.org/assets/2018_Research_Report_Alliance_Corporate_

B. Private international law

In claims against an MNC there are usually issues concerning which procedural rules apply because there are likely to be different nationalities of the victims and of the companies involved, including of the parent company and their subsidiaries. As Jennifer Zerk noted:

> There are many reasons why claimants might favour an alternative jurisdiction over the one with the closest territorial connections to the claim, including concerns about lack of impartiality or the capacity of the local courts to hear the claim in a timely fashion. Alternative jurisdictions may also be more advantageous to claimants in terms of sources of funding, access to public interest lawyers and pro bono help, procedural advantages and the prospect of greater damages awards.[50]

Therefore, when courts consider cases for harm arising in another jurisdiction, they engage in an analysis to determine which law applies to the case. Two key matters of transnational procedural rules of private international law (which is sometimes called conflict of laws) are likely to be relevant for most cases: jurisdiction and applicable law. In each instance, the decision will be determined by the relevant rules of the court which is hearing the claim, being the rules of the forum State (which is generally the home State of the parent company).

Jurisdictional issues refer to whether the court in the forum State has jurisdiction in relation to a case with transnational (or extraterritorial) elements. In most common law legal systems, there is a jurisdictional rule that the court must consider if the forum State is not the appropriate or most convenient forum for the matter (called *forum non conveniens*), taking into account the location of the parties, witnesses, evidence, and where the harm occurred. The argument is that the case should be brought in the host State and not the forum State. While this argument does make sense in theory, often the reality is that a claim in the host State may not be possible:

> [T]he host State may not have [an effective rule of law and] a judicial system that is as independent, functional, or stable as the forum State; may have not have remedies that sufficiently compensate the victims for the harm they have suffered; or the government may be unwilling or unable to allow the case to proceed, sometimes due to corruption or complicity. In addition, it may be riskier for victims to file cases in the host State, either because their identity will become better known

Transparency-66d0af6a05f153119e7cffe6df2f11b094affe9aaf4b13ae14db04e395c54a84.pdf> accessed 20 February 2020.

[50] Zerk (n. 18) 48.

> than it would if the case was filed elsewhere or because of the lack of a rule of law. One reason that this issue is so critical is that statistics suggest that 'ninety-nine percent of cases dismissed on forum non conveniens grounds in the United States, are, for one reason or another, never refiled' in the alternate forum and the victims are therefore left without any remedy.[51]

In addition, there may be aspects of international investment law which make bringing a case against an MNC in the host State's courts very unlikely even if the parent company indicates to the forum State that it would consent to a host State's legal system.[52]

The procedural rule of *forum non conveniens* has been removed within the European Union (EU). Under the Brussels I Regulation (Brussels I—now Brussels 1 Recast) the national courts within the EU Member States have jurisdiction over all who are domiciled in their jurisdiction.[53] For corporations, Brussels I defines domicile as the location of a corporation's 'statutory seat', 'central administration', or 'principal place of business'. This definition applies to all EU-domiciled corporations, and so the courts of EU Member States are obliged to accept jurisdiction over claims against corporations domiciled in their State for violations committed entirely or partly outside Europe. In the national law of several European States and in Canada there are also some developments towards an approach of *forum necessitatis*, or forum of necessity, which would allow a court to assert jurisdiction over a case when there is no other available forum.[54]

The second issue of private international law is that of applicable law, which refers to which law would apply to the claim, being the law of the forum (home) State or the law where the harm occurred (the host State). In most situations, the court will decide that the law which applies to the claim, and the law relating to the assessment of damages, is the law where the harm occurred.[55] This has been confirmed in the European Union under the Rome II Regulation,[56] though there are limited exceptions to this rule.[57] Taking this applicable law approach requires

[51] Skinner, McCorquodale, De Schutter, et al. (n. 31) 39 (footnotes omitted).

[52] On this interaction between investment and human rights disputes, see R. McCorquodale and M. Mangan, 'Combating Haze Pollution Through the Enforcement of Investment Treaties and Human Rights' in C. Brown and M. Mohan (eds) *The Asian Turn in Foreign Investment* (2021).

[53] Council Regulation (EC) No. 44/2001 of 22December 2000 on Jurisdiction and the Recognition and Enforcement of Judgments in Civil and Commercial Matters, Art. 2(1), 2001 OJ (L 12) 16.1.2001, pp. 1–23, now Regulation (EU) No. 1215/2012 of 12 December 2012 of the European Parliament and of the Council of 12 December 2012 on jurisdiction and the recognition and enforcement of judgments in civil and commercial matters OJ L 351, 20.12.2012, pp. 1–32 ('Recast Brussels Regulation'), Art. 4.1.

[54] See M. Goldhaber, 'Corporate Human Rights Litigation in Non-U.S. Courts: A Comparative Scorecard' (2013) 3 *University of California Irvine Law Review* 127, 135.

[55] See D. Palombo, 'The Duty of Care of the Parent Company: A Comparison between French Law, UK Precedents and the Swiss Proposals' (2019) 4 *Business and Human Rights Journal* 265.

[56] Regulation (EC) 864/2007 of the European Parliament and of the Council of 11 July 2007 on the Law Applicable to Non-Contractual Obligations (Rome II Regulation).

[57] The exceptions include: where a claimant and the business share a common 'habitual residence' (Article 4(2)); where the event is manifestly more closely connected with another State (Article 4(3));

an investigation as to the particular relevant law in another State, which may not always be easy to ascertain.

The use of applicable law can mean that a claim which would normally be able to proceed against an MNC in the forum State is not able to proceed due to the applicable law. For example, in *Jabir v. KiK*, the German court dismissed the claim on the basis that the claims were time barred under Pakistani law, being the law where the harm occurred.[58] Indeed, it has been argued that 'the outcome of choice of law [private international law] analysis is often directly relevant to the outcome of the dispute'.[59]

C. Public international law

Public international law issues are usually relevant to litigation against MNCs, even if sometimes overlooked. Issues of the sovereignty and jurisdiction of States are at the heart of matters of application of laws across territorial boundaries, and the application of international law in domestic courts is also relevant, as are the developments at the international level discussed below. For example, where a State's laws—whether based on legislation or not—aim to regulate the conduct of corporate nationals operating transnationally (or extraterritorially) through foreign subsidiaries, or where courts may rely on the public international law principle of universality to assert jurisdiction over certain very serious human rights violations, other States may object on the basis that these laws infringe their own sovereignty. Thus South Africa initially objected to the application of claims under the US Alien Torts Claims Act to actions in its territory and Zambia sought to resist the UK courts having jurisdiction over a claim where the harm occurred in its territory.[60] Similarly, the use of *forum non conveniens* (discussed above) is often based on an idea of not infringing the sovereignty or territorial jurisdiction of another State by extending the territorial reach of the laws of the forum State. In addition, in a few instances a court has been asked to limit its decision-making powers in

and or where the application of that law would conflict with mandatory laws or public policy of the State in which the claim is brought (Articles 16 and 26). There is also a special exception for environmental damage, where the law will be that of the State where the damage occurred unless the claimant chooses the law of the State where the event giving rise to the damage occurred (Article 7). See further Marx, Bright, Wouters, et al. (n. 36) 34–5.

[58] *Jabir and others v. KiK Textilien und Non-Food GmbH* Case No. 7 O 95/15, Regional Court (*Landgericht*) of Dortmund.

[59] G. Born and P. Rutledge, *International Civil Litigation in United States Courts* (4th edn, 2007), Part 3—Legislative Jurisdiction and Choice of Law.

[60] See C. Gowar, 'The Alien Tort Claims Act and the South African Apartheid Litigation: Is the End Nigh?' [2012] *Speculum Juris* 4 <http://www.saflii.org/za/journals/SPECJU/2012/4.pdf> accessed 20 February 2020; and the Intervention of the Minister for Justice of the Republic of Zambia in *Vedanta Resources plc v. Lungowe*, [2019] UKSC 20, [2019] 2 WLR 1051, para. 92. Some might argue that cases brought before home States for harm done in host States are a form of neo-colonialism.

order to defer to its own government's foreign relations activities, such as in the use of a defence of act of State.[61]

In contrast, reliance on public international law can assist in a claim. Some States, such as the Netherlands, apply public international law directly into their domestic law, and many other States can and do have regard to matters of public international law, especially treaties. While these treaties are usually about obligations between States, they can be relevant to domestic claims against MNCs, as seen in the statement by the UN Committee on Economic, Social and Cultural Rights:

> The extraterritorial obligation to protect requires States Parties to take steps to prevent and redress infringements of Covenant rights that occur outside their territories due to the activities of business entities over which they can exercise control, especially in cases where the remedies available to victims before the domestic courts of the State where the harm occurs are unavailable or ineffective.[62]

This statement is also linked to developments in public international law considered in the next section. In addition, in *Nevsun v. Araya*, the Supreme Court of Canada directly applied customary international law to a claim against an MNC. The majority of the court held that customary international law's prohibitions against slavery, forced labour, crimes against humanity, and cruel, inhuman, and degrading treatment are automatically adopted into Canadian law.[63] They went further to decide that:

> Since these claims [against an MNC] are based on [customary international law] norms that already form part of our common law, it is not 'plain and obvious' to me that our domestic common law cannot recognize a direct remedy for their breach. Requiring the development of new torts to found a remedy for breaches of customary international law norms automatically incorporated into the common law may not only dilute the doctrine of adoption, it could negate its application.[64]

Accordingly, the court allowed the claim to proceed without needing a new tort to be determined. This is an interesting development and one that could be considered in claims in other jurisdictions.

[61] See the clarification of foreign act of State by the English courts in *Belhaj & Rahmatullah v. Straw & Ors (No. 1)* [2017] UKSC 3 and *Nevsun Resources Ltd. v. Araya*, 2020 SCC 5, Supreme Court of Canada (see below).

[62] United Nations Committee on Economic, Social and Cultural Rights (CESCR), *General Comment No. 24 (2017) on State Obligations under the International Covenant on Economic, Social and Cultural Rights in the Context of Business Activities*, 10 August 2017, E/C. 12/GC/24, para. 30.

[63] *Nevsun Resources Ltd. v. Araya*, 2020 SCC 5, Supreme Court of Canada, para. 116.

[64] *Nevsun* (n. 63) para. 128.

V. Litigating in the context of international developments

While there has been some litigation against MNCs for human rights abuses for many decades, there has been some significant recent developments at the international level which have placed this litigation in a new context and given it new impetus. The turning point in these international developments, after many attempts, was the publication of the UNGPs on 16 June 2011, when they were unanimously endorsed by the United Nations Human Rights Council.[65]

The UNGPs are founded on three 'pillars': the State's duty to protect human rights, including from abuses by companies; the corporate responsibility to respect human rights; and the need for effective access to remedies. While not a treaty, and thus not legally binding, the UNGPs have had a strong influence in the development of international standards in this area, some of which are legally binding. For example, it has directly influenced the revisions to the Organisation for Economic Co-operation and Development Guidelines for Multinational Enterprises 2011 (OECD Guidelines),[66] the International Labour Organization's Tripartite Declaration of Principles concerning Multinational Enterprises and Social Policy 2017,[67] the Equator Principles on project finance,[68] and the International Finance Company (part of the World Bank) Performance Standards,[69] as well as influencing the EU Directive on Non-Financial Reporting,[70] and the Council of Europe's Recommendations on Human Rights and Business.[71] It has also been directly referred to (along with the OECD Guidelines) in national legislation, such as the French Duty of Vigilance Act 2017.[72]

The UNGPs, the OECD Guidelines, and these other international standards set out that corporations have responsibilities concerning human rights impacts. There is a two-part responsibility on corporations (including MNCs):

[65] United Nations Human Rights Council, Seventeenth Session 'Human rights and transnational corporations and other business enterprises' (16 June 2011) UN Doc A/HRC/RES/17/4, 2 <http://www.unglobalcompact.org/docs/issues_doc/human_rights/A.HRC.17.RES.17.4.pdf> accessed 20 February 2020.

[66] OECD Guidelines, <http://www.oecd.org/daf/inv/mne/48004323.pdf> accessed 20 February 2020.

[67] ILO Tripartite Declaration 1977, amended at 329th (March 2017) Session.

[68] Equator Principles 2017, <https://equator-principles.com/wp-content/uploads/2017/03/equator_principles_III.pdf> accessed 20 February 2020.

[69] International Finance Company 'Environmental and Social Performance Standards' (2012) and '2012 Guidance Notes' <http://www.ifc.org/wps/wcm/connect/topics_ext_content/ifc_external_corporate_site/ifc+sustainability/our+approach/risk+management/performance+standards/environmental+and+social+performance+standards+and+guidance+notes> accessed 20 February 2020.

[70] Directive 2014/95/EU of the European Parliament and of the Council of 22 October 2014 amending Directive 2013/34/EU as regards disclosure of non-financial and diversity information by certain large undertakings and groups Text with EEA relevance OJ L 330, 15.11.2014, pp. 1–9.

[71] Council of Europe, Recommendation CM/Rec (2016) 3 of the Committee of Ministers to members States on human rights and business, adopted on 2 March 2016.

[72] Duty of Vigilance Act 2017, being Art. L. 225-102-4 and L.225-102-5 of the French Commercial Code.

The responsibility to respect human rights requires that business enterprises:

(1) Avoid *causing or contributing* to adverse human rights impacts through their own activities, and address such impacts when they occur;
(2) Seek to *prevent or mitigate* adverse human rights impacts that are directly linked to their operations, products or services by their business relationships, even if they have not contributed to those impacts.[73]

This two-part responsibility means that a corporation that causes or contributes to a human rights impact through its own actions has responsibility. A corporation would also be responsible where it fails to use its 'leverage', being an ability to influence, over a third party with which it has a business relationship and which is engaging in practices which have adverse human rights impacts.[74] The action that a corporation should take, according to the UNGPs and the OECD Guidelines, is to undertake human rights due diligence. This requires corporations to identify the human rights impacts (usually through a human rights impact assessment), integrate and apply these into their operations, track and communicate their actions,[75] and then remediate for any adverse human rights impacts. The UNGPs provide that human rights due diligence 'should be ongoing, recognising that the human rights risks may change over time as the business enterprise's operations and operating context evolve',[76] and not just be a once-off process. The UNGPs also make clear that 'business enterprises conducting such [human rights] due diligence should not assume that, by itself, this will automatically and fully absolve them from liability for causing or contributing to human rights abuses'.[77] However, it might be that undertaking reasonable human rights due diligence could be a possible defence.[78]

This responsibility on a company to undertake human rights due diligence does not seem to be limited to actions within its own jurisdiction:

> Corporations domiciled in the territory and/or jurisdiction of States Parties should be required to act with due diligence to identify, prevent and address abuses to Covenant rights by such subsidiaries and business partners, wherever they may be located. The Committee underlines that, although the imposition of such due diligence obligations does have impacts on situations located

[73] UNGPs (n. 23), Guiding Principle 13 (emphasis added).
[74] Commentary to UNGPs (n. 23), Guiding Principle 19.
[75] UNGPs (n. 23), Guiding Principle 17.
[76] UNGPs (n. 23), Guiding Principle 17(c). The Commentary to UNGPs, Guiding Principle 12 notes that 'situations may change, so all human rights should be the subject of periodic review'.
[77] Commentary to UNGPs (n. 23), Guiding Principle 17. For a fuller discussion, *see* J. Bonnitcha and R. McCorquodale, 'The Concept of "Due Diligence" in the UN Guiding Principles on Business and Human Rights' (2017) 28(3) *European Journal of International Law* 921.
[78] See, for example, *Barber v. Nestlé USA Inc* No. 8:2015cv01364 (C.D. Cal. December 14, 2015).

> outside these States' national territories since potential violations of Covenant rights in global supply chains or in multinational groups of companies should be prevented or addressed, this does not imply the exercise of extraterritorial jurisdiction by the States concerned. Appropriate monitoring and accountability procedures must be put in place to ensure effective prevention and enforcement. Such procedures may include imposing a duty on companies to report on their policies and procedures to ensure respect for human rights and providing effective means of accountability and redress for abuses to Covenant rights.[79]

Indeed, the OECD Guidelines, which have National Contact Points (NCPs) in every OECD State to supervise compliance with them, accept complaints against corporations located in an OECD State about actions which that MNC or one of its subsidiaries or a business relationship, took in another State. For example, *Fivas v. Norconsult*[80] was a complaint filed with the Norwegian NCP arising from human rights impacts on indigenous peoples in Malaysia, who had been forced to relocate due to construction of some dams, as a result of the technical assistance provided to the construction companies by Norconsult and its affiliated companies. In a settlement, the corporation agreed to respect the human rights of indigenous people in future and to implement a full human rights due diligence process.[81] These processes can also encompass the protection of human rights to environmental protection and climate change, as seen in a case before the Dutch NCP, which mediated an agreed settlement of an action by claimants against ING, a financial institution, in which ING agreed to measure, set targets for, and steer their indirect climate impact.[82]

While these international standards generally do not impose a legal obligation on corporations, that does not mean that they are not relevant for domestic courts, as they can be 'a useful tool for human rights victims to argue for a progressive interpretation of domestic tort and company laws'.[83] For example, in *Vilca v. Xstrata Ltd*[84] an issue arose as to the relevance of the defendant MNC

[79] CESR Committee (n. 62), General Comment, op. cit., para. 33 (emphasis added).

[80] *Fivas v. Norconsult AS/NorPower Sdn Bhd*, available at: <http://www.oecdwatch.org/cases/Case_429≥ accessed 25 April 2017.

[81] Joint statement by Norconsult AS/NorPower Sdn Bhd and FIVAS available at: <https://www.responsiblebusiness.no/files/2015/11/150622-Joint-Statement-by-Norconsult-AS-and-FIVAS_FINAL.pdf> accessed 25 April 2017.

[82] The Ministry of Foreign Affairs (Netherlands), National Contact Point for the OECD Guidelines for Multinational Enterprises, *Final Statement, Oxfam Novib, Greenpeace Netherlands, BankTrack and Friends of the Earth Netherlands (Milieudefensie) versus ING* (19 April 2019) <https://www.oecdguidelines.nl/binaries/oecd-guidelines/documents/publication/2019/04/19/ncp-final-statement-4-ngos-vs-ing/190419-Final+Statement+NGOs-vs-ING.pdf> accessed 20 February 2020.

[83] D. Palombo, *Business and Human Rights: The Obligations of the European Home States* (2020) 58. She also argues that cases could be brought before regional human rights courts based on a State not acting to protect victims from MNC activity.

[84] *Vilca & ors v. Xstrata Ltd* [2016] EWHC 389 (QB).

supporting the Voluntary Principles on Security and Human Rights, which are intended to guide companies in maintaining the safety and security of their operations within a human rights respecting framework. The court noted that, even those these Voluntary Principles were clearly voluntary, 'something more than lip-service to those principles is demanded'.[85] In addition, amicus briefs and interventions before domestic courts increasingly refer to international standards, and MNCs themselves do as well.[86] The latter is important, as the UK Supreme Court in *Vedanta v. Lungowe* specifically referred to the published statements of an MNC as being relevant when considering a duty of care,[87] and these public statements could be considered to include corporate statements relating to these international standards. While there can be a significant gap between corporate statements and corporate action, this can change, as seen in the number of MNCs which make positive changes to their corporate policies and conduct after litigation.[88]

It is also evident that these international standards are directly influencing national laws, such as the French Duty of Vigilance Act 2017 and the Dutch Child Labour Due Diligence Act 2019.[89] Further, in April 2020, the EU Commissioner for Justice committed the European Union to begin drafting legislation in 2021 on mandatory due diligence laws on corporations.[90] These will have direct impacts on the law which will apply for claims against MNCs and, arguably, can assist in the clarification of claims, such as whether there has been a breach of a duty of care, what is a 'reasonable and prudent' corporate standard, and the level of remediation sought.[91]

One other consequence of these international developments is that the whole area of law, including litigation against MNCs—which was once known as 'transnational tort litigation' by one of the innovative creators of these claims, Richard

[85] Ibid., para. 25.

[86] See, for example, Shell's corporate website lists a series of 'external voluntary codes' that it supports, including the UNGPs, the Compact, and the OECD Guidelines: <https://www.shell.com/sustainability/transparency/external-voluntary-codes.html> accessed 20 February 2020.

[87] *Vedanta* (n. 60), para. 61. See Chapter 2 by Meeran.

[88] See J. Schrempf-Stirling and F. Wettstein, 'Beyond Guilty Verdicts: Human Rights Litigation and its Impact on Corporations Human Rights Policies' (2017) 145(3) *Journal of Business Ethics* 545–62.

[89] Netherlands Kamerstukken I, 2016/17, 34 506, A.

[90] European Parliament Working Group on Responsible Business Conduct, 'Statement by [EU] Commissioner Reynders in RBC webinar on due diligence' (European Parliament Working Group on Responsible Business Conduct, 30 April 2020) <https://responsiblebusinessconduct.eu/wp/2020/04/30/speech-by-commissioner-reynders-in-rbc-webinar-on-due-diligence> accessed 20 February 2020. This statement was made as a direct result of the Study on due diligence in the supply chain commissioned by the European Commission and referred to in note 43 above.

[91] See A. Sanders, 'The Impact of the Ruggie Framework and the UNGPs on Transnational Human Rights Litigation' in J. Martin and K. Bravo (eds) (n. 29), especially 313. See also D. Cassel, 'Outlining the Case for a Common Law Duty of Care of Business to Exercise Human Rights Due Diligence' (2016) 1 *Business and Human Rights Journal* 179 and C. Van Dam 'Tort Law and Human Rights: Brothers in Arms—On the Role of Tort Law in the Area of Business and Human Rights' (2011) 2(3) *Journal of European Tort Law* 221–54.

Meeran[92]—are now included within the field known as 'business and human rights'. This has led to an acknowledgement that the terminology of 'corporate social responsibility', which was how corporations used to refer to environmental, human rights, and other 'social' issues,[93] is no longer appropriate. Having CSR policies, which are primarily management-driven and corporate-determined for protecting the business interests, and are voluntary,[94] is not the same as providing protection for all human rights. Human rights protections are person-centred and have legitimate compliance mechanisms, they are not voluntary and are not one-off. As Michael Addo and Jena Martin comment:

> The human rights approach ... [is] attractive for its ambition to prevent as well as redress harm by drawing on existing mechanisms such as corporate due diligence, as well as formal and informal redress mechanisms, in an integrated strategy for responding to the challenges posed by business in society.[95]

An approach based on business and human rights changes the focus towards those who are rights-holders and away from a business-centred, self-regulated, voluntary basis. This should be in the interests of both victims and MNCs.[96]

VI. Conclusion

The landscape of litigation against MNCs has boundaries of the different legal systems and the types of claims within those systems. These must be recognised in any survey of the field, as they place procedural and substantive constraints on the ability to bring claims against MNCs and affect the arguments made by all parties to a claim. As one commentator noted:

> As a corollary of being tethered to the past, a lawyer [bringing a claim] has to jump with feet of clay. He [or she] cannot approach the conflict or problem in front of him [or her] with a free and open mind. He [or she] is expected to qualify

[92] For example, R. Meeran, 'Process Liability of Multinationals: Overcoming the Forum Hurdle' (November 1995) 169(256) *Journal of Personal Injury Litigation*, 170–84 and R. Meeran, 'The Unveiling of Transnational Corporations' in M. Addo (ed.), *Human Rights Standards and the Responsibility of Transnational Corporations* (1999) 161.

[93] See, for example, M. Addo and J. Martin, 'The Evolving Business and Society Landscape: Can Human Rights Make a Difference?' in J. Martin and K. Bravo (eds) (n. 29) 348–84.

[94] See, for example, K. Buhmann, 'Public Regulators and CSR: The "Social Licence to Operate" in Recent United Nations Instruments on Business and Human Rights and the Juridification of CSR' (2016) 136 *Journal of Business Ethics* 699.

[95] Addo and Martin (n. 93) 382.

[96] See R. McCorquodale, L. Smit, S. Neely, et al., 'Human Rights Due Diligence in Law and Practice: Good Practices and Challenges for Business Enterprises' (2017) 2 *Business and Human Rights Law Journal* 195.

> it in terms of existing law, within which he [or she] shapes the story he [or she] is told into a legal case for which he [or she] has to find a solution. The number of solutions that are available is also limited. Creativity and innovation are not impossible, but they are limited by the existing system.[97]

This makes Lord Bingham's call (as quoted at the beginning of the chapter) for an innovative spirit of all judges and legal practitioners even more apt. In addition, the breadth of areas of law involved in this litigation, including corporate law, private international law, and public international law, adds a considerable burden on all those involved, and reduces the number of effective practitioners and academics with expertise in the field.

Yet this litigation is also changing. While the litigation against MNCs have been affected negatively recently in some jurisdictions, such as the United States, others are increasing, such as in the Netherlands and the United Kingdom.[98] Developments of law and policy at the international, regional, and national levels have begun to show a movement towards protecting victims of corporate activity and placing some corporate accountability for adverse human rights impacts of their activities. These should begin to have an effect on litigation and on other forms of remediation, as well as, hopefully, corporate responses in this area.

There is also a demand that there should be a 'level playing field' in this litigation landscape. This demand comes from all the parties to this litigation, not just victims:

> A problem that arises directly out of differences between domestic legal systems—and one which may also have a bearing on the lack of public/criminal law enforcement discussed immediately above—is the problem of lack of 'level playing field' for companies. At present, companies domiciled in some jurisdictions face far greater risks of being subject to private law proceedings than others... This not only places the former group at a potential commercial disadvantage, it also makes it difficult for domestic policy-makers to move ahead with reforms that might tilt the playing field yet further.[99]

This demand for a level playing field or harmonisation is understandable in terms of the need for clarity in the law, clearer regulation, and the applicability of it to all companies. However, it must be questioned whether there can ever be a 'level playing field' landscape in a diverse world in which the so-called playing fields are

[97] J.B.M. Vranken, *Exploring the Jurist's Frame of Mind* (2006) 16, quoted in Enneking (n. 17) 51.
[98] See R. McCorquodale, 'Waving Not Drowning: *Kiobel* Outside the United States' (2013) 107 *American Journal of International Law* 846.
[99] Zerk (n. 18) 102.

very different in shape, height, depth, and location, and those playing are by no means equal in power and abilities. There are also very many who are not even able to get on—or are not allowed on—the playing field. So one major benefit of litigation against MNCs is that by seeking to resolve issues between MNCs and victims, it at least allows some people no longer to be passive spectators.

2

Perspectives on the Development and Significance of Tort Litigation against Multinational Parent Companies

Richard Meeran

I. Introduction

> Key management personnel of multi-nationals exercise a closely held power which is neither restricted by national boundaries nor effectively controlled by international law. The complex corporate structure of the multi-national, with networks of subsidiaries and division, makes it exceedingly difficult or even impossible to pinpoint responsibility for the damage caused by the enterprise to discrete corporate units or individuals. In reality, there is but one entity, the monolithic multinational, which is responsible for the design, development and dissemination of information and technology world-wide, acting through a forged network of interlocking directors, common operating systems, financial and other controls.
>
> In this matter, the multinational carries out its global distribution and marketing systems, financial and other controls. Persons harmed by the acts of a multinational corporation are not in a position to isolate which unit of the enterprise caused the harm, yet it is evident that the multinational enterprise that caused the harm is liable for such harm.
>
> The multinational must necessarily assume this responsibility. For it alone has the resources to discover and guard against hazards and to provide warnings of potential hazards.

The 1984 explosion at the chemical plant in Bhopal, India of US-headquartered Union Carbide resulted in a massive leak of methyl isocyanate gas which killed 5,000 people and injured hundreds of thousands more. The above quotation is an extract from the submissions of the government of India (before it reversed its position) in support of the victims' opposition to the company's application to dismiss the claim brought in the US District Court for the Southern District of New York.[1]

[1] Union Carbide Corporation Gas Plant Disaster at Bhopal (1986) 634 F Supp 842 and *Piper Aircraft Company v. Reyno* (1981) 454 US 235.

Richard Meeran, *Perspectives on the Development and Significance of Tort Litigation against Multinational Parent Companies* In: *Human Rights Litigation against Multinationals in Practice.* Edited by: Richard Meeran, Oxford University Press.
 DOI: 10.1093/oso/9780198866220.003.0002

The statement and the court application to which it related encapsulate the key challenges for victims in multinational human rights litigation over the past quarter of a century. During this period, probably the most significant, enduring developments have been in cases against parent companies in the English courts.[2] This has occurred in the context of increasing acceptance of the responsibility of business to respect human rights, to which the litigation has made an important contribution.

This chapter will consider the genesis and development and some important features and experiences arising from these parent company cases, which are of practical and strategic, as well as legal, significance. The interrelationship between the legal cases and field of Business and Human Rights (BHR) will be discussed. The potential for cross-border collaboration between lawyers in pursuing human rights litigation in multinational host State courts will also be considered, based on the experience of class action litigation in South Africa (SA). Repetition of the contents of the excellent chapters reviewing the position in the United Kingdom and South Africa by Robert McCorquodale and Dan Leader (United Kingdom) and Jason Brickhill and Zanele Mbuyisa (South Africa) will be avoided as far as possible.

II. Genesis of the UK litigation

Nearly all the UK cases in this area, from 1994 to 2020, have been brought by Leigh Day. The first three cases to be initiated were against: RTZ (now Rio Tinto) plc, by Edward Connelly, a Scottish throat cancer victim who had been employed at the Rossing Uranium Mine in Namibia (referred by the Mineworkers' Union of Namibia); Thor Chemicals Holdings Plc, by 21 mercury poisoning victims employed at a factory in Kwa Zulu Natal (referred to Leigh Day by the Chemical Workers industrial Union of South Africa in 1994); and Cape plc, ultimately by 7,500 South African asbestos miners and community members (referred by the National Union of Mineworkers in 1995).

All three cases involved parent companies incorporated and domiciled in England with local operations being by subsidiary companies incorporated and domiciled in Namibia and South Africa. In none of the cases would it have been possible in practice at the time for the victims to secure access to justice locally. As the harm in question occurred in Namibia and South Africa, the only basis for

[2] In the landmark decision of the US Supreme Court in *Kiobel v. Royal Dutch Petroleum* 133 S. Ct. 1659 (2013) the Supreme Court held that the presumption against the extraterritorial application of US law applies to claims under the Alien Tort Statute. Prior to then, claims in the United States under the Alien Tort Statute (ATS) were widely viewed as the legal route with the most promise, however Kiobel and subsequent ATS judgments seem to have drastically reduced its potential. See Chapter 7 by Hoffman.

the English courts to exercise jurisdiction was by suing the UK-domiciled parent companies. It was recognised from the outset that this presented two formidable legal obstacles: *forum non conveniens* (fnc), the doctrine enabling a court to decline jurisdiction on the grounds of a more appropriate forum elsewhere;[3] and the *corporate veil*, which prevents the legal liability of a corporate entity extending beyond its boundaries, in particular to the conduct of companies in which it invests, save where those other companies are a sham or in the event of fraud.[4]

Leigh Day being accustomed to bringing cases on the basis of tort law, the idea was conceived of claims based around a legal duty of care owed to the victims by the parent company on the grounds of control over aspects of subsidiary operations which were deficient and thereby posed a foreseeable risk of harm which the parent company had failed to ensure was prevented.[5] The point was to focus on the direct negligence of the parent, for its own acts and omissions rather than its liability for the negligence of its subsidiaries. The approach was canvassed with a senior Queen's Counsel and a retired appeal court judge, both of whom agreed that it was an interesting and novel idea that would never succeed. Fortunately, this advice was not heeded.

Importantly, bearing in mind the magnitude, novelty, and complexity of the cases, and the risk that they entailed, UK legal aid (which was available to foreign claimants) was obtained in all three cases. But for this, it is doubtful whether this area of law would have progressed as it has in the United Kingdom; Leigh Day would probably have switched its focus to a completely different area. In addition to establishing important legal precedents that have paved the way for subsequent multinational human rights cases, the three cases were eventful and illuminating in relation to a range of strategic considerations.

III. *Connelly v. RTZ*

Predictably, RTZ applied to stay the proceedings on the grounds that Namibia was a 'clearly and distinctly more appropriate forum', that being the place where alleged wrongdoing and harm occurred and where the bulk of the evidence was located. Whilst there were contrary arguments, based on alleged control exercised by the parent company in England, it was difficult to contest that Namibia was the 'natural forum'. Instead, it was argued for Mr Connelly that the ends of justice could not be met in Namibia because legal and expert medical and scientific representation

3 N.B. this was before the European Court of Justice (ECJ) decision in *Owusu v. Jackson* [Case C-281/02) [2005] ECR I-1383 The ECJ ruled that there is no fnc power in claims against EU domiciled persons. See further below.

4 *Adams v. Cape Industries plc* [1990] Ch 433.

5 R. Meeran, 'Process Liability of Multinationals: Overcoming the Forum Hurdle' (November 1995) *Journal of Personal Injury Litigation*, 170–85.

would be required for a case of such complexity but that whereas legal aid funding for this was available for a case in England, there was no prospect of any funding for a case in Namibia. The following plea was made on Mr Connelly's behalf:

> Mr Connelly is a victim in every sense of the word. He has suffered appalling ill health; he has faced death; he cannot care for his family in the way he would wish and his claim has so far been lost in a system of bewildering complexity which may occasionally make sense to some of the professionals involved but one must have serious doubts whether it would make sense to those who are intended to benefit from the protection of the law. He has had to comprehend the interplay between Namibian law, South African law, Scottish law and the law of England and Wales. He has followed professional advice and waited for law, medicine and public administration to communicate sufficiently clearly to give him compensation. He remains without any compensation whatsoever. At the very least, every effort should be made to give the plaintiff the simple satisfaction of having his claim heard.

RTZ accepted that there was no funding in Namibia but argued that the absence of funding was not a ground for refusal of the fnc application, that is that the court should stay the claim in favour of Namibia even though Mr Connelly had no real prospect in practice of being able to pursue his claim there. Specifically, RTZ relied on a provision of the Legal Aid Act 1988 (s. 31(1)(b)) which precluded the taking into account, in any court application, of the fact that a party was legally aided. The purpose of this provision was to ensure that the legal aid status of an individual did not result in him/her being treated better or worse than a non-legally aided party. This argument succeeded in February 1995 and was upheld by the Court of Appeal in August 1995.[6] The senior counsel wanted to appeal to the House of Lords (now the Supreme Court) but Leigh Day felt that as the argument involved relying on UK legal aid for foreign claimants, it was destined to fail.

At this point, an alternative strategy was contemplated, entailing the jettisoning of legal aid and representation of Mr Connelly on a 'no win, no fee' basis (such fee arrangements having been made lawful in July 1995) and to return to court to request that the stay on the proceedings be lifted. The same argument could be run that no funding was available in Namibia—there being no legal aid available in Namibia and contingency fee representation being unlawful there—but this time the Legal Aid Act could not operate against Mr Connelly because he would not be legally aided. Moreover, if that argument succeeded it was anticipated that RTZ would appeal and in that case, Mr Connelly could cross-appeal the original decision because by allowing the argument to succeed when Mr Connelly was on a no

[6] *Connelly v. RTZ Corporation Plc (No. 2)* [1996] QB 361.

win, no fee basis but not when he was on legal aid would itself be discriminating against legally aided parties and thus contravening section 31.

The new approach failed at first instance (as anticipated) in October 1995, however in May 1996 it succeeded in the Court of Appeal with the judge making specific reference to the right to a fair trial:[7]

> Faced with the stark choice between one jurisdiction, albeit not the most appropriate in which there could in fact be a trial, and another jurisdiction, the most appropriate in which there never could, in my judgment, the interests of justice would tend to weigh, and weigh strongly, in favour of that forum in which the plaintiff could assert his rights.[8]

RTZ appealed to the House of Lords and Mr Connelly cross-appealed the original legal aid decision.

In 1997, in a landmark judgment, Mr Connelly succeeded in both appeals before the House of Lords.[9] The ratio of the judgment was as follows:

> Even so, the availability of financial assistance in this country, coupled with its non-availability in the appropriate forum, may exceptionally be a relevant factor in this context. The question, however, remains whether the plaintiff can establish that substantial justice will not in the particular circumstances of the case be done if the plaintiff has to proceed in the appropriate forum where no financial assistance is available.[10]

In the dissenting judgment, Lord Hoffmann stated:

> If the presence of the defendants, as parent company and local subsidiary of a multinational, can enable them to be sued here, any multinational with its parent company in England will be liable to be sued here in respect of its activities anywhere in the world.[11]

This negative theme was enthusiastically taken up by the financial media, including in the *Financial Times* under the headline 'The Risks of Being a Multinational'.[12] It was always an irrational concern because lawyers would be most unlikely to take on the huge financial risk of cases, if they were unmeritorious, just because they could secure jurisdiction. Indeed, this has been demonstrated in the

[7] *Connelly v. RTZ* The Times, July 12, 1996.
[8] Per Bingham MR para. 8 pdf p. 4, *Connelly v. RTZ Corporation Plc* [1998] AC 854.
[9] *Connelly v. RTZ Corporation Plc* [1998] A.C 854.
[10] Per Lord Goff para. 30 pdf p. 13.
[11] Per Lord Hoffmann para. 41 pdf p. 16.
[12] *Financial Times* (25 July 1997).

ensuing 27 years, during which time although there have been some major multinational human rights cases in England this has hardly been a deluge. Nevertheless, so concerned were those in the commercial world that they successfully lobbied the Lord Chancellor (Minister of Justice) to propose legislation to reverse the effect of the Connelly decision.[13] However, this proposal was not accepted.

Following his jurisdiction victory, RTZ applied to strike out Mr Connelly's claim on the grounds of 'failure to disclose a reasonable cause of action' and that it was time barred. In its judgment in December 1998[14] the court dismissed the strike out, concluding that:

> On a fair reading of this pleading, it seems to me that ... [RTZ] had taken into its own hands the responsibility for devising an appropriate policy for health and safety to be operated at the Rossing mine, and that either... [RTZ] or one or other of its English subsidiaries implemented that policy and supervised the precautions necessary to ensure so far as was reasonably possible, the health and safety of the Rossing employees through the RTZ supervisors. Such an allegation, if true, seems to me to impose a duty of care upon those defendants who undertook those responsibilities, whatever contribution Rossing itself may have made towards the safety procedures in the mine. The situation would be an unusual one; but if the pleading represents the actuality then, as it seems to me, the situation is likely to ... give rise to a duty of care

Sadly, however, having battled over fnc for three years, Mr Connelly's claim was struck out on limitation grounds in 1998.

The precedent set in his case in the House of Lords did benefit thousands of South African asbestos miners three years later and has been endorsed twice subsequently by the House of Lords/Supreme Court.[15] To date, however, it does not appear that this decision has been followed by the courts of other States that apply the fnc doctrine.

IV. *Thor Chemicals*

Thor had a factory in Margate England which was under investigation by the regulator, the Health & Safety Executive ('HSE'), for high levels of lead in the blood and urine of workers. Thor then shifted its operations, including plant, process, technology, and senior personnel to Cato Ridge (KwaZulu Natal (KZN)). There,

[13] Letter from Lord Chancellor's Department dated 15 September 1998 headed 'Connelly v RTZ Corporation'.

[14] *Connelly v. RTZ* [1999] CLC 533 pp. 6–7.

[15] *Lubbe v. Cape Plc* [2000] 1 WLR 1545; *Vedanta Resources plc & another v. Lungowe & others* [2019] UKSC 20.

the working practices were even worse. Unfortunately, the HSE did not warn the Department of Manpower (South Africa) about the company's record. Workers whose mercury levels reached the maximum were sent to work in the garden and advised to have a beer or a glass of orange juice, or simply dismissed and replaced by workers who queued at the gate each day for work. Mercury exposure was controlled by spreading the burden across the community rather than by effective safety measures. Three workers died and many others were poisoned.

A prosecution of the operating subsidiary, Thor Chemicals SA, in the local magistrates' court resulted in Thor pleading guilty to breaches of occupational health and safety regulations and receiving a fine of R13,500, a wholly ineffective deterrent.[16]

The claim in England against the parent company and its Chairman, Mr Cowley, focused on their role in negligently designing hazardous technology, exporting it to South Africa, and negligently supervising the local factory. Incidentally, this is the only case of this type in England where a court has held that English law is likely to apply, no doubt due to the especially strong links with the Margate operation. The first hearing was memorable for several reasons, one of which was the judge querying why a group of South African residents was suing in England, a question that would not be asked today as the phenomenon is now widely accepted. Another was the judge's palpable anger at the mistreatment of the workers, particularly when he saw a photograph of Engelbert Ngcobo who had been in a coma for three years.[17]

In April 1995 Thor's fnc application was dismissed, with the court ruling that South Africa was not a more appropriate forum. This was the very first fnc success in this area. Thor's appeal was struck out because it erroneously filed a defence which was deemed inconsistent with contesting jurisdiction.[18]

Thor then tried unsuccessfully to strike out the claims against the parent and Desmond Cowley, with the court ruling in November 1996 that there was:

> 'a clear evidential basis upon which the Plaintiffs could argue their case to establish the liability of [the parent company]' and that it was 'arguable that Mr. Cowley could be found liable at trial either on the basis that he has personally directed and procured a company of which he was a director to commit a tort or on the basis that the circumstances of this case were such as to impose a duty of care upon him personally, breach of which is actionable at the suit of the Plaintiffs' the latter on the basis of a personal assumption of responsibility.[19]

[16] 'Thor bosses acquitted, but firm fined R13,500' *Daily News* (SA, 17 February 1995).

[17] 'S. African workers sue British firm over poisoning' *The Guardian* (29 September 1994).

[18] *Ngcobo and Others v. Thor Chemicals Holdings Ltd and Others* (Times Law Report 10 November 1995).

[19] *Ngcobo v. Thor Chemicals Holdings Ltd v. Others*, January 1996 Maurice Kay J unreported.

Thus, by 1996 it was becoming clear that, given the right facts, a claim based on a parent company duty of care had a reasonable prospect of being upheld.

The *Ngcobo* case was settled in 1997 for £1.3 million[20] and was followed by a second group of cases (*Sithole & Others v. Thor*) which had almost reached trial in 2000 when Thor announced to the legal aid authorities that it had undergone a financial restructuring which had left the parent company with insufficient assets and that consequently legal aid funding should be terminated to avoid wasting taxpayers' money. It transpired that the parent company had transferred its assets to an overseas subsidiary and changed its name to Guernica plc, supposedly, according to its Chairman, 'in view of the fascist nature of the attacks on Thor'.[21] The claimants sought a declaration under section 423 of the Insolvency Act 1986 that the transfer of assets was unlawful in that its 'dominant purpose' was to defeat their interests as creditors.[22]

As indicated below, financial rearrangements that potentially prejudiced claimants' rights can result in the freezing of assets before they are dissipated.[23] The *Sithole* case was settled in 2000.

V. *Cape plc*

A detailed account of the facts and legal proceedings can be found elsewhere.[24] In summary, Cape plc[25] orchestrated a worldwide asbestos business from London, which included the world's largest blue and brown asbestos mines in the Northern Cape and Limpopo provinces of South Africa respectively. The asbestos was imported to England and the United States where it was made into a variety of fire proofing products. The demand in Europe and the US drove the mining in South Africa. Workers in the mines and factories contracted asbestos-related disease in droves.

The mining stopped in South Africa in the late 1970s due to a fall in demand for asbestos caused by fears for the safety of American and European consumers, not for the well-being of South African workers. In South Africa, Black mine workers were subjected to huge dust exposures, unprotected. Employment of women and small children as 'cobbers', breaking open rock to expose asbestos fibres, was

[20] I. Burrell, 'Mercury poisoning victims win £1.3m in landmark case' *The Independent* (12 April 1997).

[21] 'Thor Point' *Private Eye* (October 2000).

[22] *Sithole & Others v. Thor Chemicals Holdings Ltd and Another* [2000] WL 14211830.

[23] *Guerrero & Others v. Monterrico Metals PLC & Another* [2009] EWHC 2475 (QB); *Bravo & Others v. Amerisur Resources PLC* [2020] EWHC 125 (QB).

[24] R. Meeran, 'Cape Plc: South African Mineworkers' Quest for Justice' (2003) 9(3) *International Journal of Occupational and Environmental Health* 218–29.

[25] The original name of the case—*Lubbe & Others v. Cape plc*—changed after the House of Lords' judgment in 2000.

widespread. Around 6 per cent of the 7,500 claimants in the case were employed under the age of seven. Teenagers were employed as 'chissa boys' whose job was to light the fuses of the dynamite in the mine and then to run away as quickly as possible. Not surprisingly, the incidence of asbestos-related disease, including mesothelioma, at and around Cape's South African operations, was massive. Due to widespread environmental contamination—in the town of Prieska for example, a mill located in the middle of the town spewed blue asbestos dust across the community—these diseases affected white as well as Black residents. Whole communities were decimated.

Cape's South African subsidiaries were defunct. The proceedings in England began in 1995 and alleged a duty of care owed towards mineworkers and local residents essentially on the grounds that the parent company exercised effective control over the subsidiaries and that the harm was caused by its failure to take reasonable steps to ensure that dust exposures were minimised.

Cape's fnc application succeeded before the court at first instance. Since an fnc judgment entails the exercise of discretion it is usually hard to overturn unless the court has made an error of law. In appealing, the claimants therefore faced an uphill struggle. Strategically it was decided that, rather than arguing that the lower judge had weighed the facts incorrectly, the best approach was to focus on an argument under European law[26] that the UK courts could not invoke fnc in respect of claims against UK-domiciled defendants. This depended on the interpretation of the provision in question and was an argument that had been left open in an earlier commercial case.[27] As an aside, it should be noted that the fnc doctrine is not applied elsewhere in the European Union or between EU States. Hence English proceedings on similar grounds against Cape plc by four Italian asbestos victims of Cape's Capamianto factory in Turin could not be stayed: they were brought by claimants resident in a State (Italy) which is party to the Brussels Regulation against a defendant domiciled in another contracting State (United Kingdom).[28]

There was a strong argument that the court would be obliged to refer this issue for determination to the European Court of Justice (ECJ). It was concluded that the court might be inclined to allow the fnc appeal rather than refer the matter to the ECJ (which the English courts were known to be averse to doing). At the appeal hearing, a known specialist in European law instructed to argue the appeal was almost immediately interrupted by the judges who said they would only need to consider the European law point if they were against the claimants on the fnc issue and that accordingly they wanted to address the fnc issue. They never requested submissions on European law. In this way, the claimants gained the upper hand in what should

[26] Article 2 Brussels Regulation, now Article 4 of the Brussels Regulation on jurisdiction and the recognition and enforcement of judgments in civil and commercial matters (recast).

[27] *Re Harrods (Buenos Aires) Ltd (No. 2)* [1992] Ch 72.

[28] *Lubbe & Others v. Cape* [1998] CLC 1559 pdf p. 7.

have been a very difficult appeal. Of course, in 2005 the issue was referred to the ECJ, which ruled that fnc could not be invoked against an EU domiciled defendant.

The Court of Appeal allowed the appeal, deciding, by reason of the mechanisms of Cape's alleged control of South African operations from England, that South Africa was not a clearly more appropriate forum.[29] For the first time by a court there was also an attempt to formulate the question to be answered in relation to parent company duty of care as follows:

> Whether a parent company which is proved to exercise de facto control over the operations of a (foreign) subsidiary and which knows, through its directors, that those operations involve risks to the health of workers employed by the subsidiary and/or persons in the vicinity of its factory or other business premises, owes a duty of care to those workers and/or other persons in relation to the control which it exercises over and the advice which it gives to the subsidiary company?

However, following the introduction of almost 2,000 further claimants, Cape successfully obtained an fnc stay of the proceedings. When the case returned to the Court of Appeal, the debate revolved around the same issue as in the Connelly case, specifically whether the claimants could obtain legal representation, either through South African legal aid or lawyers willing and able to act for them on a no win, no fee basis. Legal aid in South Africa had just been withdrawn for civil claims on 1 November 1999, however the court was unable to conclude that lawyers would be unwilling to act on a no win, no fee basis or that it would not be feasible for the claimants, members of impoverished communities with very limited education, to utilise the available, scientific, medical, and technical evidence in support of their claims. The court also introduced into English fnc law the 'public interest factor' in US fnc law,[30] concluding that the public interest of South Africa in trying the case was greater than the public interest of England. Interestingly, this public interest factor analysis was a factor in the fnc dismissal by the New York District Court in 1986 of claims by the Indian victims of the Bhopal explosion against Union Carbide.

But for the introduction of this public interest factor into English law, the Cape claimants might not have obtained permission to appeal to the House of Lords. Permission was however granted and on this point the appeal was also supported by an intervention by the Republic of South Africa, which submitted inter alia as follows:

> The South African public interest is in the speedy and fair determination of these proceedings, not their being determined in its courts... The allegations against

[29] Ibid., p. 13.

[30] Union Carbide Corporation Gas Plant Disaster at Bhopal (1986) 634 F. Supp. 842 and *Piper Aircraft Company v. Reyno* (1981) 454 US 235.

Cape did not take place in a legitimate legal system, and the new South African government cannot afford to determine every wrong of the old regime through its judicial system. The discriminatory health and safety laws, which left South African workers unprotected, or significantly under-represented, against known risks as a matter of South African law were against the common law of humanity. They should have no part to play in determining the scope of the negligence liability of a foreign multi-national which operated under those laws.[31]

In the *Apartheid Reparations* litigation filed in the United States, the South African government made representations arguing that the issues to be determined were uniquely a matter for the South African courts.[32] The difference in approach however seems entirely understandable. The initial antagonism of the SA government towards the prospect of gold miners' silicosis litigation many years later was however far more disappointing (see further below).

In its July 2000 judgment the House of Lords allowed the claimants' appeal.[33] Regarding parent company liability, Lord Bingham stated:

The issues in the present cases fall into two segments. The first segment concerns the responsibility of the defendant as a parent company for ensuring the observance of proper standards of health and safety by its overseas subsidiaries. Resolution of this issue will be likely to involve an inquiry into what part the defendant played in controlling the operations of the group, what its directors and employees knew or ought to have known, what action was taken and not taken, whether the defendant owed a duty of care to employees of group companies overseas and whether, if so, that duty was broken. Much of the evidence material to this inquiry would, in the ordinary way, be documentary and much of it would be found in the offices of the parent company, including minutes of meetings, reports by directors and employees on visits overseas and correspondence.[34]

The five judges endorsed and applied the principle laid down by the House of Lords in *Connelly* in 1997. They unanimously disagreed with the Court of Appeal about the claimants' prospects of obtaining access to justice in South Africa:

I do, however think that the absence, as yet, of developed procedures for handling group actions [in] Africa reinforces the submissions made by the plaintiffs

[31] *Lubbe v. Cape plc*, Statement of Case on behalf of the Republic of South Africa 26 May 2000.

[32] South African Foreign Minister Nkosazana Dlamini Zuma to US Secretary of State Colin Powell (*National Foreign Trade Council*, May 2002) <http://www.nftc.org/default/ussabc/DAE8515.pdf> accessed 25 November 2020.

[33] *Lubbe v. Cape Plc* [2000] 1 WLR 1545.

[34] Ibid., p. 7.

> on the funding issue. It is one thing to embark on and fund a heavy group action where the procedures governing the conduct of the proceedings are known to and understood by experienced judges and practitioners. It may be quite another where the exercise is novel and untried. There must then be an increased likelihood of interlocutory decisions which are contentious, with the likelihood of appeals and delay. It cannot be assumed that all judges will respond to this new procedural challenge in the same innovative spirit. The exercise of jurisdiction by the South African High Court through separate territorial divisions, while not a potent obstacle in itself, could contribute to delay, uncertainty and cost. The procedural novelty of these proceedings, if pursued in South Africa, must in my view act as a further disincentive to any person or body considering whether or not to finance the proceedings.[35]

The judgment prompted a leading journalist to question, rhetorically, how, on a factual issue based on the same factual evidence, diametrically opposite unanimous conclusions could have been reached by the two highest courts in the country.[36]

The House of Lords deflected the dispute as to whether England or South Africa had the greater public interest in hearing the case by deciding that the 'principles on which the doctrine of forum non conveniens rest leave no room for considerations of public interest or public policy which cannot be related to the private interests of any the parties or the ends of justice in the case which is before the court'. Whilst the intervention of the South African government made no difference to the terms of the judgment it does not follow that it made no difference to the outcome.

The fnc dispute lasted three years before it was resolved. During this period, it was estimated that 1,000 of the 7,500 claimants had died. On every visit to the various communities, it would be discovered that people who had attended the previous meeting had died. Moreover, having asserted in the fnc hearings that the case needed to be tried in South Africa because all the evidence and investigations would be conducted there, including for example Cape's intention to re-create the conditions of an asbestos mine there, it was not so long afterwards that Cape effectively caved in, thereby highlighting the artificiality and injustice of the fnc doctrine in human rights cases. Cape announced to the UK legal aid authority that it was able to settle for a limited amount of compensation but that if this was not accepted the company would run out of money by time the trial was concluded. It described the claimants as being in a 'lose–lose' situation. Since the money being offered would have been wiped out by the amount that legal aid had incurred and was required to recoup the offer was rejected. Due to Cape's purported financial

[35] Ibid., p. 11.
[36] D. Pallister 'Poor Law' *The Guardian* (28 July 2000).

position, legal aid was withdrawn and thereafter the case proceeded for a further two years without any funding.

In 2001, negotiations with a Cape investor that took control of the company led to a settlement of £21 million for the 7,500 claimants and future victims. The mechanism was to be the payment of a lump sum and then annual payments into the *Hendrik Afrika Trust* established for the purpose. The amount of the settlement reflected Cape's precarious financial position and was therefore significantly lower than the true value of the claims.[37] It was, however, welcomed by victims' supporters.[38] Cyril (now President) Ramaphosa was the Chair of the Trust, which also included Cape's Chairman and the National Union of Mineworkers (NUM) Deputy President. Ultimately however, Cape reneged on its side of the bargain, the settlement collapsed, and the case returned to court.[39]

The case was finally settled in 2003 for a payment of £10.5 million just to the 7,500 claimants. Another mining company, Gencor, whose asbestos mining subsidiaries had also employed many of the Cape claimants, paid £3 million of that total. To secure this additional payment Leigh Day had intervened, on behalf of the Cape claimants in injunction proceedings against Gencor in South Africa.[40]

Whilst the Cape settlement constituted a victory in the quest for greater multinational accountability, subsequent research indicated that at least one of the more isolated communities involved in the case had not found the experience so empowering.[41] No doubt this was because the compensation paid to each individual (which reflected the amount of the overall settlement and Cape's parlous financial position) were spent relatively quickly. Although the deterrent objective of a tort claim had been achieved the objective of redress for victims had not been fully satisfied.

[37] R. Meeran, 'Cape pays the price as justice prevails' *The Times* (15 January 2002).

[38] 'That this House welcomes the agreement, by Cape plc, a British company who mined asbestos in South Africa for several decades, to pay £21 million in compensation to South African asbestos victims; congratulates the 7,500 claimants, the communities of Northern Cape and Northern Province and the National Union of Mineworkers in South Africa, as well as national and regional political leaders in South Africa for the perseverance and dignity of their long struggle for justice; commends the actions of those in the United Kingdom who have worked tirelessly to support the claimants, including the lawyers of Leigh, Day and Co and John Pickering and Partners, and the staff and activists of pressure group Action for Southern Africa, as well as many trade union members in the United Kingdom; believes that this settlement represents a contribution to the ongoing process of truth and reconciliation in South Africa, particularly through the recognition of the role of United Kingdom based businesses in the injustices of the past; notes with concern that many multinational companies continue to neglect the health and safety of their workers; and welcomes the signals given by this case that the British public now demands concrete action to back up the warm words of corporate social responsibility.' K. McNamara, EDM 661 *Victory for South African Asbestos Claimants*, 2001–02 (House of Commons, 15 January 2002).

[39] 'Payment setback for asbestos victims' *Business Day* (SA, 21 June 2002).

[40] 'UK law firm adds a new twist in South Africa asbestos case' *Financial Times* (28 September 2002).

[41] L. Waldman, 'When Social Movements Bypass the Poor: Asbestos Pollution, International Litigation and Griqua Cultural Identity' (2007) 33 *Journal of Southern African Studies* 577.

This was a high-profile case in South Africa for several years, attracting vocal support from the media, trade unions, government, politicians, and sustained campaigning non-governmental organisations such as Action for Southern Africa (successor to the Anti-Apartheid Movement) and anti-asbestos groups. A photographic exhibition graphically illustrated the plight of the victims.[42] Racism was a central element in the public discourse around the case mainly, though not exclusively, in support of the victims. For example, in 1999 it emerged that public relations advisers and political lobbyists had been instructed by Cape. Referring to a piece about the case on the BBC Newsnight programme, they expressed the view that '[p]erhaps most damaging were the pictures of the orphaned children of Amanda Berger, the (white) 30-year old who died of mesothelioma'. They proposed a campaign in the right-wing British media to discredit the granting of UK legal aid to the claimants: 'The political ironies are so delicious for a paper like the Mail (a Labour Lord Chancellor having to chose (sic) between black workers and multinationals) that the detail of the claims are likely to be of secondary interest'. The lobbyists recommended attacking the House of Lords judgment in *Connelly* and legal cases that undermined the corporate veil protection of multinationals.[43] The lobbyists' proposals were criticised by members of parliament.[44]

VI. The wider significance of *Connelly*, *Thor Chemicals*, and *Cape plc*

A. A foundation for the development of a parent company duty of care

With hindsight two decades on, it is clear that the three cases were each important in changing the legal environment and progressing multinational accountability, and that they remain relevant. Although none of the cases went to trial, or even preliminary trial on the issue of parent company liability, there were rulings in all three cases confirming that imposition of parent company duty of care was in principle arguable.[45] The wider implications in international relations of what was described as the 'foreign direct liability' principle raised in the three cases was noted in a Chatham House Briefing paper in 2002.[46]

42 H. du Plessis, 'Cape Dust' (*LabourNet UK*) <http://www.labournet.net/images/cape/layout4.htm> accessed 25 November 2020.

43 'Mining firm tries to change law to block £100m claims' *The Guardian* (19 March 1999).

44 Ken Livingston MP, EDM 449 *Cape PLC*, 1998–1999 (18 March 1999).

45 *Ngcobo v. Thor Chemicals Holdings Ltd v. others*, Maurice Kay November 1996 unreported; *Connelly v. RTZ Corporation*, (1999) CLC 533; *Lubbe & Others v. Cape* [1998] CLC 1559; *Lubbe v. Cape plc* [2000] 1 WLR 1545.

46 H. Ward, 'Corporate accountability in search of a treaty? Some insights from foreign direct liability' (May 2002) *The Royal Institute of International Affairs Sustainable Development Programme Briefing Paper No. 4*.

The first judgment establishing the principle and circumstances for the imposition of liability on a parent company for breach of a duty of care was in 2012 in *Chandler v. Cape plc*,[47] a case making similar allegations to those in *Lubbe* albeit on behalf of an English worker albeit employed by a UK subsidiary. The Court of Appeal in *Chandler* cited the three cases. Liability was imposed on the parent company based on its negligent omission to advise on precautionary measures to protect the health of workers at its subsidiary. A duty of care to provide such advice stemmed particularly from the parent company's awareness of the risks to the workers, its superior knowledge of health and safety, and its awareness that the subsidiary was relying on the parent to provide that superior knowledge.

The wider significance of the Chandler was recognised in the financial world.[48]

The three cases were also expressly cited by the Court of Appeal in the *Vedanta* case[49] when it concluded that Vedanta owed a duty of care to communities living in the vicinity of its Zambian copper mine. In the judgment which constitutes the current pinnacle of the English law judgments in this area, this decision was upheld by the Supreme Court which confirmed and elaborated the principles relating to parent company duty of care. The core test is that

> [e]verything depends on the extent to which, and the way in which, the parent availed itself of the opportunity to take over, intervene in, control, supervise or advise the management of the relevant operations (including land use) of the subsidiary. All that the existence of a parent subsidiary relationship demonstrates that the parent had such an opportunity.

The judgment confirmed that there is no specific category of negligence that applies to MNC parent companies but that the question of whether a duty of care should be imposed depends on the fact in accordance with the general tort law principles.[50]

In February 2021, the UK Supreme Court delivered a further blow to MNC impunity in *Okpabi v. Royal Dutch Shell.* The claim was based *inter alia* on an alleged duty of care on the part of Royal Dutch Shell arising from its significant control over its Nigerian subsidiary and its assumption of responsibility of subsidiary operations through RDS' group-wide mandatory policies. Consistent with its judgment in *Vedanta*, the court reversed the decision of the Court of Appeal, ruling that the lower court had applied too much focus to the issue of control of the subsidiary rather than management of aspects of its activities; was wrong to decide

[47] [2012] EWCA Civ 525.

[48] 'The sins of the sons—A little-noticed court case with big implications' *The Economist* (26 May 2012).

[49] *Vedanta Resources plc & another v. Lungowe & others* [2018] WLR 3575.

[50] *Vedanta Resources plc & another v. Lungowe & others* [2019] UKSC 20.

that group-wide policies could not give rise to a duty of care; and should not have treated the issue of parent company liability as a special category.[51]

In March 2021, the Court of Appeal ruled that a UK company that had sold a ship to a third party which had arranged for the ship to be beached in Bangladesh, owed a duty of care to a worker who suffered fatal injuries breaking up the ship. In doing so, it applied an established exception to the principle that a defendant is not liable for the acts of a third party, in circumstances where the defendant has created the danger.[52]

It should be emphasised that the English parent company decisions reflect the position in English law whereas under EU law (which, prior to the UK's exit from the European Union, took precedence in English law too), the applicable substantive law will, unless a claim has a *manifestly closer connection* with another country, be that of the place where the damage occurred, that is the host State.[53]

Determination of the position under English law is, however, relevant in former British colonies that have retained English law-based systems, which follow English law, and have no case precedents in this area. It is for this reason that English law has been relevant in the Zambian claims against Vedanta, claims by villagers shot at a gold mine in Tanzania,[54] and the Nigerian oil pollution claims against Royal Dutch Shell.[55] For the same reason, the Nigerian oil pollution claim against Shell in the Netherlands is also effectively governed by English law,[56] as will be so in the *Kabwe & Others* Zambian lead poisoning class action filed in South Africa,[57] provided it is certified.

Regarding legal developments in MNC home States with English-law based systems, the case of *Choc v. Hudbay Minerals*, instituted in 2012, in the Superior Court of Justice of Ontario, Canada, by members of the Mayan community in Guatemala, alleging serious human rights abuses (including killing, shooting, and gang rapes by mine security personnel, police, and military) during forced removals from around the Fenix nickel mine, is noteworthy. An allegation of negligence, arising from the breach of a duty owed by the parent company to the victims on the basis of alleged control and supervision by the parent company of subsidiary operations including mine security and foreseeability of harm. The *Thor Chemicals* and *Cape*

51 *Okpabi & Others v. Royal Dutch Shell plc & Anor* [2021] UKSC 3.

52 *Begum v. Maran* [2021] EWCA Civ 326.

53 Article 4 of the Rome II Regulation on the Law Applicable to Non-contractual Obligations. The indication of the fnc judge in *Ngcobo v. Thor Chemicals*, that English law would probably apply, reflected the somewhat unique circumstances of a case involving the export of hazardous technology and working methods and personnel from an English factory to South Africa.

54 *Kesabo v. African Barrick Gold Plc & NMGML* [2013] EWHC 4045.

55 *Okpabi & Others v. Royal Dutch Shell PLC and SPDC* [2018] WLR(D) 9.

56 *Akpan v. Royal Dutch Shell & SPDC.*

57 See below.

plc cases clearly had an influence on initial the formulation of the claim. The defendant applied to strike out the claim *inter alia* on the grounds that:

> there is no recognized duty of care owed by a parent company to ensure that the commercial activities carried on by its subsidiary in a foreign country are conducted in a manner designed to protect those people with whom the subsidiary interacts.

The court dismissed the application, deciding that the claimants had 'properly pleaded the elements necessary to recognize a novel duty of care'.[58]

By contrast, English law has little relevance to claims entailing damage in civil law countries. Perhaps unsurprisingly, the laws of other countries do seem potentially to cater for the possibility of parent company liability. Consequently, the claims against Monterrico Metals[59] and Xstrata Ltd,[60] relating to alleged corporate complicity in perpetrating injuries to environmental protesters in Peru, were subject to the provisions of the Peruvian Civil Code.[61]

It was alleged, under the 1984 Peruvian Civil Code, that the parent company was vicarious liable, in its capacity as a principal giving for the conduct of its subsidiary and mine security employees, acting under its orders, who committed the human rights abuses.

With regard to jurisdiction, the House of Lords in *Lubbe* had indicated that it would have referred the Article 2 Brussels Regulation issue to the ECJ for determination if it had not found in the claimants' favour on fnc. However, it was not long before the issue was referred to the ECJ in the case *Owusu v. Jackson and Others*,[62] which effectively seemed to lay to rest the application of fnc in respect of UK-domiciled companies after 2005. Consequently, the later cases, for example against Trafigura over toxic waste dumping in Cote D'Ivoire[63] and Monterrico Metals for Peruvian torture victims, were not plagued by fnc tactics and delays. *Forum non conveniens* has, however, remained an issue in relation to claims where a foreign subsidiary is joined as a co-defendant. In those circumstances the benefit of the House of Lords rulings in *Connelly* and *Lubbe* comes into play.[64]

Post Brexit, the United Kingdom has left the Brussels Regulation system, with the result that the mandatory rule, pursuant to Article 4 of the Brussels Recast, that a defendant shall be sued in the courts of its domicile, no longer applies and consequently proceedings brought against UK-domiciled companies are once again subject to dismissal on fnc grounds. This will remain the position unless and until the

[58] *Choc v. Hudbay Minerals Inc* [2013] ONSC 1414.

[59] *Guerrero & Others v. Monterrico Metals PLC & Another* [2009] EWHC 2475 (QB).

[60] *Vilca & Others v. Xstrata Ltd & Another* [2017] Med LR Plus 32.

[61] For example, it was alleged, that under Article 1981 of the 1984 Peruvian Civil Code, that the parent company was vicarious liable, in its capacity as a principal giving for the conduct of its subsidiary and mine security employees, acting under its orders, who committed the human rights abuses.

[62] Case C-281/02 [2005] ECR I-1383.

[63] *Motto & Others v. Trafigura.*

[64] Vedanta Resources plc & Another v. Lungowe & Others [2019] UKSC 20.

UK joins the Lugano Convention—Article 2 of which mirrors Article 4 of Brussels Recast—.[65] Such circumstances would undoubtedly result in a return to costly and protracted fnc litigation and injustice for victims of corporate human rights abuse. Fortunately, victims will be able to benefit from the *Connelly* and *Lubbe* precedents where the absence of funding to secure substantial justice in multinational host State courts can be demonstrated.

B. Some observations for strategic litigation

As far as possible it is important to develop the law through the right cases, in the right sequence, in particular cases that are more likely to attract sympathy and indignation from the public and the courts such that judges want to find in the victims' favour.

The argument that a claim should be allowed to proceed in England due to the availability of UK legal aid was obviously controversial in some quarters, however the fact that Mr Connelly was Scottish, had paid UK taxes, and had returned to live there dampened the volume of the criticism that would undoubtedly have been expressed if he had been a foreigner. One can only speculate as to whether this principle, which was upheld and applied three years later in the *Cape plc* case, would reflect the position under English law today if the *Cape plc* case, for 7,500 South African miners, had come first. The facts of the *Cape plc* and *Thor Chemicals* cases were so gross that one of their lawyers even said they wished they had been on our side. If other cases had been run instead, it is unlikely that English law would have developed as positively from the victims' perspective.

Another important factor, that is impossible to control and which has a strong element of chance, is the attitude of the judges hearing the cases. The experience of the English courts in these cases was that in general, judges were open minded and willing to develop the law to ensure that victims obtained justice. This is not necessarily the position in certain other jurisdictions.

As discussed in the section below on barriers to justice, representation of victims on a contingency no win, no fee basis, in complex multinational human rights litigation, is a risky proposition, financially. The greater the number of legal barriers, the greater the risk. The *Connelly*, *Thor Chemicals*, and *Cape plc* cases were largely supported by legal aid. It would not have been feasible to undertake all three of these cases without legal aid. However, the success achieved in the cases resulted in a reduction in legal barriers, making it possible, when legal aid was no longer available in practice, to undertake subsequent cases on a contingency no win, no

[65] See notification to the Parties of the Convention on Jurisdiction and the Recognition and Enforcement of Judgments in Civil and Commercial Matters, concluded at Lugano on 30 October 2007 Communication by the depositary with respect to the application of accession by the United Kingdom of Great Britain and Northern Ireland. With reference to its notification of 14 April 2020, the depositary informs that, by communication received on 28 June 2021, the European Union notified not to be in a position to give its consent to invite the United Kingdom to accede to the Lugano Convention.

fee basis. The coincidence in the timing of the three cases with the availability of legal aid was fortunate for human rights victims.

A further observation concerns the strategic value of cases that do not go to trial, an issue about which legal academics and campaigners frequently express concern. It is evident, however, from the three cases, none of which reached trial, that principles can be established in cases during the course of litigation which have important long-term value for victims.

The *Connelly* case is a striking example. The House of Lords decision in 1997 ultimately did not assist Mr Connelly, however it enabled 7,500 miners to secure access to justice against Cape plc and enabled the *Vedanta* claimants successfully to resist an fnc motion to prevent the joinder of the Zambian subsidiary to the English claim.[66]

The same point applies in relation to settlement of cases, which occurs in the vast majority of MNC human rights cases that are not dismissed or discontinued. As indicated above, the *Chandler* and *Vedanta* judgments were strongly influenced by the three cases, all of which had alluded to the possibility of a duty of care but two of which (*Thor Chemicals* and *Cape plc*) settled before trial. The *Monterrico* case was also settled before trial but the freezing injunction judgment obtained in the case was relevant 11 years later in the granting of the freezing injunction in the *Amerisur* case.[67] The *Monterrico* decision has also been referred to in decisions in MNC human rights cases of other courts.[68] The antisuit injunction obtained in the case against African Barrick Gold, referred to as the 'Tanzanian Torpedo', has generally deterred MNCs from attempting the same tactic in other cases.[69] Of course, whilst settlement can be frustrating in that it does not entail a trial or finding of liability, it is an important process for securing redress for victims. In that regard, victims are frequently impoverished and the opportunity to secure compensation for human rights abuse speedily and without having to go through the stress of a trial and the risk of losing at trial and not being compensated is crucial.

A further concern often expressed by campaigners and academics relates to the lack of transparency around settlements which are subject to confidentiality. Whilst confidentiality is clearly in one sense contrary to the public interest, the ability to secure confidentiality can facilitate the payment of compensation to victims that a company might otherwise be prepared to make, and it may also encourage such payment at an earlier stage and in a higher amount. The situation can be viewed as a tension between the wider public interest and victims' private interests, although proper redress for victims and mechanisms that enhance this, such as confidential settlements, are also important public interest objectives.

[66] *Vedanta Resources plc & Another v. Lungowe & Others* [2019] UKSC 20 pdf paras 88–101.
[67] *Bravo & Others v. Amerisur Resources PLC* [2020] EWHC 125 (QB).
[68] *US Supreme Court Kiobel v. Royal Dutch Petroleum Co* 621 F 3d 111 (2d Cir 2010).
[69] *Kesabo v. African Barrick Gold Plc & NMGML* [2013] EWHC 4045.

In view of Cape's financial position, in order to secure compensation for the victims, the South African government agreed to release Cape from its environmental liabilities. It did so to facilitate payment of compensation to sick and impoverished workers and their families and because Cape's financial position was such that any hope of the company being able to pay for environmental rehabilitation was entirely unrealistic Yet understandably, this sparked fierce criticism from activists concerned about the principle and the precedent this had set. Ultimately, due to the collapse of the first settlement, the environmental release was also cancelled, however this example illustrates tensions that can arise between the public interest and the interests of litigants and specific interest groups (in this case workers) in private litigation.

Also, in relation to settlement, perhaps one of the most controversial and common agreed restrictions are non-acting clauses by which, in return for settlement, the claimants' lawyers agree not to sue the defendant (and possibly its affiliates) in respect of the same operations (or geographical region) for a specified or unlimited period. In the same way as above, this may secure compensation where a company would not otherwise have sufficient incentive to settle and from that perspective, if claimants' lawyers are willing to agree to restrictions to their future business, the possibility of such clauses can be viewed as a potential benefit to victims. On the other hand, tying the hands of lawyers who might otherwise be willing to represent further victims can result in a denial of victims' access to justice, especially when the number of lawyers willing and able to take cases on is already so limited. On that basis, non-acting clauses are contrary to the public interest. Legal systems (including England and Wales) that do not outlaw such clauses as contrary to the public interest can be viewed as providing a benefit to companies to insist routinely on non-acting clauses. In difficult or financially unviable cases, the pressure on claimants' lawyers to make such concessions will be higher.

Finally, a frequently expressed criticism is that the language of negligence in tort law diminishes the gravity of harm or conduct that has occurred. This point was made in the landmark judgment of the Supreme Court of Canada in *Nevsun* where, in addition to negligence, allegations of violations of customary international law including crimes against humanity, slavery, forced labour, and inhuman and degrading treatment were made.[70] Moreover, MNCs and their investors are likely to take greater heed of alleged human rights abuse than alleged negligence. These criticisms have force and validity, but overlook important factors.

The key objective of claimants is usually to obtain redress. Consequently, claimants opt for the simplest route to success. Creating unnecessary legal hurdles will reduce the prospects of success. Even if legal allegations are expressed in the language negligence, the severity of the abuse will be clear. The case against Cape plc was based on negligence but the facts of what had occurred were graphically

[70] *Nevsun Resources Ltd v. Araya* 2020 SCC 5.

portrayed in legal documents and in public and no-one would surely contest that this was a case entailing serious human rights abuses.

VII. Barriers to justice

Save for notable exceptions, victims' access to justice is rarely realistic in multinational host State courts. This may sometimes be for reasons of corruption and fear of persecution or severe delays in court processes. In the *Monterrico* case, for example,[71] environmental protesters who were unlawfully detained and tortured by an elite unit of the Peruvian police, allegedly assisted by the company, were themselves prosecuted whereas no charges were brought against the police. The inability to obtain effective legal representation due to the absence of funding is, however, an almost ubiquitous obstacle to justice in the Global South. In this regard, the complexity and scale of multinational human rights litigation and power imbalance between the victims and the corporations is the critical issue. Victims cannot afford to pay for lawyers, and public funding, certainly at the level required for such cases, is unavailable and unrealistic. The duration, cost, and uncertain outcome means that public interest lawyers are unable to provide *pro bono* representation or to act on a contingency basis, assuming this is lawful (which it presently is not in States such as Zambia and Namibia), due to the financial cash flow risk that these cases entail. Large commercial law firms that would have the capacity to undertake these cases are invariably conflicted by their corporate client bases.

Whilst problems of persecution, corruption, and severe delay may not apply, these financial risks also affect the ability and inclination of lawyers to represent victims in claims against multinational parent companies in their home State courts. Here, there are key related legal, procedural, and practical barriers.[72]

A. *Forum non conveniens*

Whilst in a commercial context, fnc entails a zero-sum game between businesses trying to have the dispute heard in the forum which is likely to produce the best outcome for them, in a human rights context fnc for victims is generally all or nothing, that is access to justice is only available in practice in the MNC home courts. *Forum non conveniens* is a serious hurdle before the US courts[73] where, for

[71] *Guerrero & Others v. Monterrico Metals PLC & Another* [2009] EWHC 2475 (QB).

[72] R. Meeran, 'The "Zero Draft": Access to judicial remedy for victims of multinationals' ("MNCs") abuse' (8 October 2019) *Business & Human Rights Resource Centre Opinion Blog* <https://www.business-humanrights.org/en/blog/the-zero-draft-access-to-judicial-remedy-for-victims-of-multinationals-mncs-abuse/> accessed 25 November 2020.

[73] See Chapter 7 by Hoffman.

example, it was applied to the detriment of the Indian victims of the 1984 Bhopal chemical explosion[74] and the Ecuadorian claimants who sued Texaco for oil pollution.[75] It is also an issue in Canada[76] and Australia, although there the onus is on the defendant to show that Australia is an inappropriate forum.[77] The fnc availability of funding principle, laid down in the *Connelly* case, and confirmed and applied in the *Cape plc* and *Vedanta* cases, has not as yet been adopted in Canada, Australia, or the United States.

B. Discovery/disclosure

In States where principles enabling the imposition of a parent company duty of care have not developed, limited liability may present a barrier that is too daunting for a victim's lawyer, acting on a contingency basis, to contemplate. But even in England, or other home States that may apply the *Vedanta* principles (e.g. Canada, Australia, and South Africa), whether or not a duty will be imposed depends entirely on the factual circumstances in question, in particular whether the nature and extent of a parent company's involvement in the business of its subsidiary is sufficient to impose a duty. Evidence relating to this involvement is only likely to be publicly available to a limited extent—and increasingly less, given that MNCs (and their lawyers) are acutely aware of the risks of human rights litigation. Further, it is dependent on the extent of litigation discovery/disclosure procedures in the State in question. Therefore, pursuing a parent company case requires effective access to internal corporate documents.

Common law jurisdictions tend to have relatively generous procedures.[78] For example, in England, sophisticated procedures and protocols for e-disclosure are in place. These enable complex word search combinations to be applied to elicit relevant documents, speedily and cost-effectively from vast amounts of documents stored on an array of devices held by many individuals often located in different countries.[79] In this way, past practices of defendants deluging claimants with millions of pages of hardcopy documents, made legendary in US tobacco litigation, can be avoided. By contrast, discovery in civil law jurisdictions such as Germany, the Netherlands, and France, is generally very restricted in comparison.[80]

[74] Union Carbide Corporation Gas Plant Disaster at Bhopal (1986) 634 F. Supp. 842.

[75] *Aguinda v. Texaco, Inc.*, 142 F Supp 2d 534, 554 (SDNY 2001); *Aguinda v. Texaco, Inc.*, 303 F 3d 470, 480 (2d Cir. 2002).

[76] See Chapter 5 by Johnston.

[77] See Chapter 6 by Cashman.

[78] See Chapter 3 by Leader, Chapter 4 by Brickhill and Mbuyisa, Chapter 5 by Johnston, Chapter 6 by Cashman, and Chapter 7 by Hoffman.

[79] See, for example, *Vilca & 21 Others v. Xstrata Limited & another* [2016] EWHC 389(QB) pdf paras 32–82.

[80] See Chapter 8 by Samkalden, Chapter 9 by Cossart and Chatelain, and Chapter 10 by Saage-Maasz.

C. Class actions

The ability of human rights victims to bring class actions, with procedures to ensure that these are case-managed efficiently and cost-effectively, is essential for access to justice, as was emphasised by the House of Lords in *Lubbe*.[81] The key to resolving the issues in dispute in such a claim is to identify and litigate the legal and factual issues that are common to a group of victims through the trial of test or lead cases. Having to institute and plead every individual claim where the number of victims is large, and the value of an individual claim is low, is not constructive, is time-consuming and is prohibitively expensive to an extent that renders claims in States without effective class action mechanisms financially unviable.

In addition, to avoid the need for institution of proceedings by every victim, procedures or laws are required to interrupt limitation/prescription and prevent time barring of claims. In England, which has group actions (i.e. opt-in class action), this is achieved by a system of registration of individual claims.[82] Opt-out class actions that enable claims to be filed by class representatives on behalf of a class of individuals, as is the case in South Africa, Canada, Australia, and the United States, achieve this objective without the need for individuals to come forward, although there are procedures to enable class members to opt out if they do not wish to participate and be bound by orders and judgments in the action.[83]

D. Funding

Victims are invariably unable to pay lawyers to represent them. Assuming representation on a contingency or no win, no fee basis is permissible, clearly, in view of the financial risks involved, a lawyer's decision on whether to act will depend crucially on an assessment of the legal merits of the case, the cash flow risks to the lawyer (often for an uncertain period) and the likelihood of being paid if the case succeeds. Consequently, the legality of legal representation of victims on a contingency basis and the rules on costs recovery are critical. As indicated above, in some States (such as Zambia and Namibia) contingency fee arrangements are unlawful. This is a total barrier to justice because it would require lawyers to act on a *pro bono* basis.

[81] *Lubbe v. Cape* Plc [2000] 1 WLR 1545 pdf p. 11.
[82] Civil Procedure Rule (CPR) Practice Direction 19B—Group Litigation.
[83] See below regarding the Kabwe case and Chapter 4 by Brickhill and Mbuyisa, Chapter 5 by Johnston, Chapter 6 by Cashman, and Chapter 7 by Hoffman.

In States such as the United Kingdom, Australia, and South Africa, the general rule is that the loser pays the winner's costs. No win, no fee arrangements enable claimants' lawyers, in return for the risks they are accepting, to recover their costs from the defendant if the case succeeds, plus an uplift on their fees of potentially 100 per cent, provided this does not exceed 25 per cent of the damages recovered. Consequently, whether the prospect of this uplift provides an incentive for lawyers to act depends on the amount of the damages. If the damages are low compared with the level of costs, the maximum percentage uplift on costs will be low. Whilst the 'loser pays' costs rule is an essential incentive for claimants' lawyers, the downside is that it may deter a victim from pursuing a claim, although the risk in practice to an impoverished individual is minimal. In England, 'qualified one-way costs shifting' ensures that an individual pursuing an injury claim will recover costs if the claim is successful but will not generally be liable to pay the defendant's costs if the claim fails.[84]

In the United States and Canada, claimants' lawyers may act on a contingency under which they may charge a fee corresponding to a percentage of damages, typically 25 to 33 per cent. The viability of a case will therefore depend on its overall value in comparison with the cost of lawyers' time that is likely to be spent on the case and the expense to be incurred on experts, etc.

In terms of the disincentive on lawyers to represent victims, the abovementioned barriers are all part of the equation. The more barriers and the higher they are, the greater the disincentive. In England, development of the law on parent company duty of care and the elimination of fnc has significantly reduced the risks. Conversely, in States that do not have developed group or class action procedures or generous discovery procedures, the disincentives will be greater. Limitations on costs recovery, as is the case in some EU States, will be a significant disincentive.

Third party litigation funding by venture capital firms, which is lawful in many countries, is becoming increasingly common in mass human rights/tort claims. Here the funder agrees to fund the legal fees and expenses, or a proportion of them, in return for a share of the damages, typically 25 to 33 per cent.[85] For example, Harbour Litigation funded an Australian class action for Indonesian seaweed farmers. Augusta Ventures has agreed to pay the expenses and 62 per cent of the legal fees of the Zambian lead poisoning class action (see below) in return for 25 per cent of the damages. To secure a significant return on investment, third party litigation funders will only fund cases that are valued several-fold or higher than the costs outlay. It is for this reason that litigation funding is only usually available in very large cases. Clearly, the involvement of a litigation funder increases the incentive for lawyers to represent victims.

[84] Part 44.14 CPR.

[85] See Chapter 12 by Dunn and Curtis.

E. Damages levels

Related to the issue of funding, the level of damages is important not just to ensure adequate redress for victims but also because, as indicated above, the amount of damages affects the viability of the claim from the perspective of lawyers who might represent the victims and third party litigation funders who might fund their case. Under EU law, assessment of damages will be under the applicable law, that is (unless the claim has a manifestly closer connection with another State) the law of the place where the damage occurred.[86]

F. Fear of reprisals

Victims may be fearful that pursuing a claim will put their lives in danger. Where this is made out, the Civil Procedure Rules in England provide, as an exception to the general rule that hearings should be in public, for anonymity of such individuals.[87] In certain instances, the victims' fear stems from their identity being disclosed to the company. This is problematic as withholding a claimant's identity from the defendant may prejudice the defendant's right to a fair trial. To address this problem, English Civil Procedure Rules allows for a 'confidentiality club' order which limits disclosure to named individuals within the company.[88]

G. MNC financial rearrangements

Financial rearrangements within a multinational can place assets beyond the reach of claimants, denying access to justice by rendering their claims pointless. The example of what occurred in the *Thor Chemicals* case is described above. That was an example of a rearrangement made by a company in the knowledge of outstanding claims. More commonly, however, financial rearrangements are made for genuine commercial reasons unconnected with claims. Here, urgent injunctive relief may be required to prevent the dissipation of assets that it would be impossible to reverse once they had occurred and therefore would frustrate a remedy if they went ahead. Under English law, a freezing injunction over an amount of a defendant's assets corresponding to the estimated value of the claim

[86] Article 15 Regulation (EC) No. 864/2007 on the law applicable to non-contractual obligations (Rome II).

[87] Part 39.2 CPR.

[88] *Kadie Kalma & Others v. African Minerals and others* [2018] EWHC 120 (QB).

may be granted provided the claimant can demonstrate a *real risk of dissipation* of assets and a *good arguable case.*

In 2009, after Monterrico relocated its corporate headquarters to Hong Kong and announced an intention to delist from the UK AIM Stock Exchange, the claimants succeeded in obtaining a worldwide freezing injunction in the English High Court over £5 million of the company's assets.[89] An ancillary freezing injunction in aid of the UK injunction was obtained in the High Court of Hong Kong.

In January 2020, a group of Colombian subsistence farmers from Putumayo province succeeded in obtaining a freezing injunction over £3 million of the assets of English-based parent company, Amerisur Resources plc.[90] A claim for oil contamination of water had been instituted but the claimants were concerned that a proposed takeover by Geopark was a prelude to the dissipation of assets of Amerisur. In granting the injunction, the judge concluded, *inter alia*, that:

> Geopark already had an existing Colombian operation with a headquarters and staff and its intention was to fold the defendant's business into its own. Geopark's purchase plan would likely result in the closing of a number of the defendant's offices. The transaction had all the hallmarks of one that would leave the defendant without a role and there was no evidence to the contrary. The risk of dissipation had been established.

H. MNC instituting legal action in the host State courts

A tactic that has been attempted on more than one occasion by multinationals is to have the key issues in a claim against the parent company determined in the host State courts. For example, in the claim against African Barrick Gold for alleged complicity in shootings of villagers at the North Mara Mine in Tanzania, the subsidiary company applied to a Tanzanian court, after the institution of the English proceedings, for a ruling that the company could not be held liable for the conduct of the police. The English High Court granted an anti-suit injunction against the defendant prohibiting it from continuing with the Tanzanian proceedings.[91]

Many of the above-mentioned barriers are specifically alluded to in Pillar 3 Access to Remedy of the United Nations Guiding Principles on Business & Human Rights (UNGPs).

[89] *Guerrero & Others v. Monterrico Metals PLC & Another* [2009] EWHC 2475 (QB).

[90] *Bravo & ORS v. Amerisur Resources PLC* [2020] EWHC 125 (QB).

[91] *Kesabo & 11 Others v. (1) African Barrick Gold PLC (2) North Mara Gold Mine LTD* [2013] EWHC 4045 (QB).

VIII. Multinational human rights litigation and Business and Human Rights (BHR)

BHR and multinational human rights litigation have developed over broadly the same time frame, from the mid-1990s to the present, and have increasingly converged. In the first few years there was some scepticism as to whether business could have human rights obligations and also whether cases which, notwithstanding their subject matter, were based on tort and made allegations in the language of negligence, could be characterised as human rights cases. By around 2000, however, there was growing recognition and commentary about these cases by human rights organisations and academics, including sustained campaigning, for example by Action for Southern Africa in the *Cape plc* case. As time went on these cases became an integral focus of the BHR movement. For example, a 2002 Briefing Paper from Chatham House reviewed the legal accountability and access to justice issues raised by the *Connelly*, *Thor Chemicals*, and *Cape plc* cases, and proposed an intergovernmental debate on a corporate accountability convention.[92] In later years, the cases *Trafigura* and *Royal Dutch Shell*, in respect of Cote D'Ivoire and Nigeria became central in BHR discussions.

With regard to the United Nations Guiding Principles on Business & Human Rights (UNGPs), there is a striking similarity between the Human Rights Due Diligence duty (which is the central element of the Corporate Duty to Respect human rights) and a tort law duty of care.[93] Thus, under the UNGPs, business enterprises have a duty to 'identify, prevent and mitigate adverse human rights impacts that the enterprise may cause or contribute to through its own activities, or which may be directly linked to its operations, products or services by its business relationships'. The UNGPs were endorsed by the UN Human Rights Council in June 2011 (before the *Chandler* decision). It therefore seems very likely that the cases against Cape plc, Thor Chemicals, and Rio Tinto were directly considered in the formulation of Human Rights Due Diligence (HRDD). Since then, the *Chandler* and *Vedanta* precedents have strengthened the argument for the imposition of tort-style duty of care on business entitles.

Even though the UNGPs are described as voluntary on the part of business, non-compliance with HRDD by a business that adopts the UNGPs could give rise to legal liability. How this may occur can be illustrated by a ruling in the *Xstrata* case:

> It is, I understand, common ground that there can be considerable tension between members of the local community, the operators of the mine and local security forces in areas where a mine is set. Police suppression of protests occurs

[92] Ward (n. 46).

[93] D. Cassel, 'Outlining the Case for a Common Law Duty of Care of Business to Exercise Human Rights Due Diligence' (2016) 1(2) *Business and Human Rights Journal* 179–202.

> and again it is not unknown for that to involve considerable violence. As a result the 'Voluntary Principles on Security and Human Rights', which is a set of principles designed to guide companies in maintaining the safety and security of their operations within an operating framework that encourages respect for human rights, have been adopted by many mining companies over the years including Xstrata. The principles have the backing of the United Nations
>
> ... the very fact that lives were lost and serious injuries occurred is enough to weigh heavily in the balance even if the damages recoverable are relatively modest. Mr Béar is right to say in this connection that the defendants subscribe to the Voluntary Principles to which I have referred and (not his words, but mine) something more than lip-service to those principles is demanded.[94]

The imposition arising from *Vedanta* of a duty of care under English law in respect of public commitments by parent companies would seem of further significance to the UNGPs.[95] Thus, a business which is obliged by stakeholders to support and endorse the UNGPs could find itself subject to legally binding duties of care in respect of the resulting public commitments that it makes.

As indicated above, English law decisions like *Vedanta* can only be relied on where harm occurred in States whose laws correspond to English law. Thus, in the case of *Choc v. Hudbay Minerals Inc*, brought in the Ontario Superior Court of Justice by members of the Mayan community in Guatemala, an amendment to the statement of claim alleged a duty and breach of duty of care based on the company's publicly stated commitment to the Voluntary Principles on Security and Human Rights.[96] The amendment post-dated and was undoubtedly motivated by the *Vedanta* judgment. As the UNGPs are classified as voluntary, there has been a lively debate around the possibility of a legally binding international instrument on BHR. In June 2014, the Human Rights Council adopted resolution 26/9 by which it decided 'to establish an open-ended intergovernmental working group on transnational corporations and other business enterprises with respect to human rights, whose mandate shall be to elaborate an international legally binding instrument to regulate, in international human rights law, the activities of transnational corporations and other business enterprises'. In terms of legal liability, proposals have again been formulated on a tort law basis for parent company liability, namely in

[94] *Vilca & 21 Others v. (1) Xstrata ltd & Another* [2016] EWHC 389 QB pdf para. 12.

[95] 'Similarly, it seems to me that the parent may incur the relevant responsibility to third parties if, in published materials, it holds itself out as exercising that degree of supervision and control of its subsidiaries, even if it does not in fact do so. In such circumstances its very omission may constitute the abdication of a responsibility which it has publicly undertaken' *Vedanta Resources plc & Another v. Lungowe & Others* [2019] UKSC 20.

[96] *Caal v. Hudbay Minerals Inc.* [2018] CV-11-423077 <http://www.chocversushudbay.com/wp-content/uploads/2019/07/2-Caal-v.-HudBay-Proposed-Second-Amended-Statement-of-Claim.pdf> accessed 25 November 2020.

circumstances where there has been a failure to prevent foreseeable human rights abuses from activities over which there was control or supervision.[97] Whether anything comes from this process remains to be seen.

The convergence of multinational human rights litigation and BHR has provided greater scrutiny and a focus for pressure to be applied by civil society on business, on investors in business, and on governments to ensure that compliance with standards of behaviour by business is real and not simply lip service. For example, discovery of documents during litigation may elicit insights to an internal decision-making and even attitudes within a multinational group. Below is an example referred to in a ruling in the *Xstrata* litigation:[98]

> The Spanish expression 'hormigas en acción' translates into 'ants in action' which has recently been acknowledged to be an expression used by some within the defendants' organisation to refer to the protesters. The significance of the expression emerged on or about 19 February, a few days before the hearing. It certainly has a derogatory sound to it (arguably at odds with the approach foreshadowed in the Voluntary Principles) and, in my judgment, is plainly a proper addition to the keyword search given the nature of the case advanced.

Being implicated in human rights abuse can have serious reputational and financial ramifications for a business whose supply chains involve consumers, an obvious case being shoppers at clothing retailers that are supplied by sweatshops in Asia. A graphic example of this is the suspension by UK supermarkets of purchases of avocados from plantations in Kenya. This stemmed from evidence in a claim against parent company Camelia plc and its subsidiary, Kakuzi plc, by 79 individuals alleging serious human rights abuse by security guards employed by Kakuzi.[99] A speedy settlement ensued.[100]

The public flotation of Deliveroo illustrates the potential financial impact of court decisions on human rights issues. In March 2021 the UK ruled that Uber drivers were entitled to statutory employment protection as workers, rather than as Uber had contended, as independent contractors.[101] The ruling was widely interpreted as signalling a recognition of the exploitation of gig economy workers and

[97] UN Human Rights Council OEIGWG 'Legally binding instrument to regulate, in international human rights law, the activities of transnational corporations and other business enterprises' (16 July 2019) *OEIGWG chairmanship revised draft* <https://www.ohchr.org/Documents/HRBodies/HRCouncil/WGTransCorp/OEIGWG_RevisedDraft_LBI.pdf> accessed 25 November 2020.

[98] *Vilca & 21 Others v. (1) Xstrata ltd & Another* [2016] EWHC 389 (QB) pdf para. 54.

[99] E. Dugan, '"Rape, beatings and death" at Kakuzi, the Kenyan farm that helps feed the UK's avocado habit. Court papers allege guards at a British estate in Kenya that supplies Tesco, Sainsbury's and Lidl have committed human rights abuse' *Sunday Times* (11 October 2020); Patricia Nilsson, 'Tesco drops avocado supplier after allegations of rights abuse' *Financial Times* (11 October 2020).

[100] 'UK firm pays £4.6m to settle claims of "rape and murder" at Kakuzi avocado farm', *Sunday Times* (14 February 2021).

[101] *Uber BV & Others v. Aslam & Others* [2021] UKSC 5.

the need for them to have legal protection. Institutional investors stated publicly that they would refrain from taking up the share offering on the grounds that they considered the Deliveroo model to be risky legally as well as ethically.[102]

Multinationals operating in the extractive sector are generally less vulnerable to reputational damage, but this is not necessarily so. Anglo American for example, an organisation that has gone out of its way to emphasise its commitment to human rights, must have been stung by the exposure the silicosis litigation brought on behalf of thousands of South African gold miners and the class action launched on behalf of thousands of children poisoned by a lead at its former mine in Zambia.[103]

IX. Multinational human rights litigation in South African: cross-border collaboration between lawyers

As outlined above, the barriers to justice in multinational home States are significant but the barriers in host States are even more so. Ideally victims should nevertheless be able to secure justice at home and multinationals which commit or are involved in the commission of human rights abuses should be held to account legally by the courts where the harm occurred. Consequently, developing and building the capacity of host State legal systems to enable justice to be obtained locally is an important objective.

Whilst there may be other fundamental barriers to justice in some developing countries, representation by lawyers with sufficient resources and expertise to undertake large scale complex, expensive, and risky litigation on a contingency fee basis (assuming this is lawful) is a ubiquitous impediment. In July 2000, the House of Lords concluded that the Cape plc asbestos victims could not obtain justice in South Africa. Legal aid in South Africa had been withdrawn and local lawyers were unlikely to take on the case.[104]

In the following years, however, with regard to this type of litigation, the position improved in South Africa. The legal aid funding was made available for 'impact litigation' and lawyers in South Africa obtained legal and financial support from English and American class action lawyers.[105] Then in 2013, the South

[102] 'Aviva and Aberdeen Standard spurn Deliveroo flotation over riders' rights' *Money Marketing* (25 March 2021); 'Deliveroo stumbles to London float with pricing at bottom end' *City AM* (30 March 2021).

[103] J. Cotterill, 'Anglo American faces huge class-action lawsuit over Zambia mine' *Financial Times* (21 October 2020); see section IX and Chapter 4 by Brickhill and Mbuyisa.

[104] *Lubbe v. Cape Plc* [2000] 1 WLR 1545.

[105] R. Meeran, 'Open Letter to the Special Representative of the UN Secretary-General on Business and Human Rights: The genesis and development of MNC litigation in South Africa and a possible model for the future' (16 January 2009) <https://www.business-humanrights.org/en/latest-news/doc-open-letter-to-the-special-representative-of-the-un-secretary-general-on-business-and-human-rights-the-genesis-and-development-of-mnc-litigation-in-south-africa-and-a-possible-model-for-the-future/> accessed 25 November 2020; J. Ruggie, 'SRSG's Statement on Open Letter from Mr

African Supreme Court of Appeal laid the foundation for procedures for certifying opt-out class actions.[106]

The cases in which the cross-border collaboration occurred comprised gold miners' silicosis litigation (from 2004–2018) and more recently Zambian lead poisoning litigation, both of which are described in Chapter 4 by Jason Brickhill and Zanele Mbuyisa.

In 2004, following the *Cape plc* litigation in England, Leigh Day was approached by a victims' support group in the Free State to assist former South African gold miners. It was clear from published studies that dust levels in the mines had been high and uncontrolled and that more than 20 per cent of all the long-term gold miners had contracted silicosis, a lung disease which significantly increases the risk of contracting tuberculosis (TB). Hundreds of thousands had contracted silicosis. Whilst silicosis alone may be mild, silico-tuberculosis is a serious disease which has often proved fatal, especially among ex-miners living in remote rural communities where diagnostic and treatment facilities were rudimentary or non-existent. One renowned occupational health expert, Professor Tony Davies, had explained the phenomenon of a 'river of disease flowing out of the gold mines' into rural communities. What was happening was that miners exposed to excessive dust had contracted silicosis, which had made them vulnerable to TB, which due to the fact that they worked and lived in close proximity in mine hostels for nine months of the year was being passed between miners. Miners returning home at the end of the years were then spreading TB in their communities.

In 2004, however, Leigh Day was expressly requested by a senior South African government officer not to pursue litigation on the grounds that the industry had informed government it was operating on the margins of profitability and that litigation would jeopardise the economy of the industry and jobs. Thus, the rights of silicosis victims and their families were considered to be of secondary importance.

The South African Legal Resources Centre, assisted by Leigh Day, represented 23 miners in test case litigation instituted in the Johannesburg High court against Anglo American South Africa Ltd, the South African parent of operating companies that had employed the miners.[107] These cases were subject to protracted litigation and were settled in 2013.

A larger group of 4,500 silicosis miners' claims against Anglo American South Africa Ltd and AngloGold Ashanti Ltd were settled in 2016 by Mbuyisa Neale

Richard Meeran' (19 January 2009) <https://www.business-humanrights.org/en/latest-news/pdf-srsgs-statement-on-open-letter-from-mr-richard-meeran/> accessed 25 November 2020.

[106] *Children's Resources Centre Trust v. Pioneer Foods (Pty) Ltd. and Others* 2013(2) SA213 (SCA).

[107] *Alpheos Blom & Others v. Anglo American South Africa Ltd* Case no. 18267/04, Witwatersrand Local Division of the High Court of South Africa.

Attorneys assisted by Leigh Day.[108] The Q(h)beka Trust[109] was established to administer the settlement, which entailed assessing whether claimants satisfied the agreed settlement qualifying criteria, arranging for medical evaluation of the claimants, determining the precise amounts payable to individuals based on the settlement criteria, and ensuring payment of money.

It is worth noting that although the Blom and Qubeka cases were commenced in court, both were ultimately arbitrated by consent pursuant to a modified version of rules utilised in South African commercial disputes.[110] Importantly, it was stipulated that hearings would be open to the public and that arbitration awards (judgments) would also be public. In both instances, the arbitrators nominated by the parties were mainly retired appellate judges, including former Chief Justice Sandile Ngcobo and the arbitrators' fees were paid by the companies.

In 2016, in a landmark judgment, a larger opt-out class action for victims of silicosis and TB was certified by the Johannesburg High Court against 32 gold mining companies.[111] The main class action lawyers were Richard Spoor Inc, assisted by US law firm, Motley Rice, and Abrahams Kiewitz, assisted by US law firm Hausfeld LLP. This class action was settled in 2018 *Ex Parte Nkala and Others* (2018/44060) [2018] ZAGPJHC 657 (13 December 2018) reportedly for R5 billion. The *Tshiamiso* settlement trust mechanism is modelled on the Q(h)beka Trust.[112]

Despite having many talented and able lawyers and an effective legal system, limitations of money, capacity, and resources mean that these cases would not have been practically feasible without the involvement of foreign lawyers. It was feasible for Leigh Day and Motley Rice to assist local lawyers in bringing these cases for several reasons, as follows:

(1) An effective legal system that has much in common with England and the United States, in terms of the relevant laws and procedures, as well as language. In terms of laws, South African judges were receptive to the notion of a legal duty in delict on the part of parent companies. Regarding procedures, the rules on discovery are similar and there is also case management of group litigation.
(2) The Internet allows for long-distance transmission of communications and documents, which would in the past have made such collaborations unworkable logistically.

[108] *Quebeka & others v. Anglo American and Anglo Gold Ashanti Ltd* Case no. 2012/44831 Witwatersrand Local Division of the High Court of South Africa; <https://www.leighday.co.uk/News/News-2016/March-2016/Victory-at-last-for-South-African-gold-miners-as-A> accessed 25 November 2020.

[109] <https://www.qhubekatrust.co.za/> accessed 25 November 2020.

[110] https://arbitration.co.za/domestic-arbitration/commercial-rules/

[111] *Nkala and Others v. Harmony Gold Mining Company Limited and Others* [2016] ZAGPJHC 97; 2016 (7) BCLR 881 (GJ); 2016 (5) SA 240 (GJ) ('Silicosis Certification').

[112] <https://www.tshiamisotrust.com/about/trustees-advisory-board/> accessed 25 November 2020.

(3) Opt-out class action dramatically reduce the costs of mass tort claims and enable the rights of all class members to be protected against expiry of the statute of limitations without the need for claims to be filed in court on behalf of each individual claimant.

(4) Recovery of the costs of foreign lawyers is possible provided their involvement was necessary. The absence of this possibility would deter foreign lawyers from providing significant assistance.

Third party litigation funding has been sanctioned in South Africa as not necessarily being champertous or contrary to public policy since 2004.[113] The class action filed in South Africa against Anglo American South Africa Ltd on behalf of Zambian lead poisoning victims has the benefit of third party litigation funding.[114]

X. Conclusion

There is a global consensus that business has a responsibility to avoid causing human rights abuse and environmental damage and to provide appropriate redress when they cause or contribute to such harm. Business cannot, however, simply be relied upon to ensure that these objectives and met. Policies and public statements are not sufficient either. Neither can regulators be depended upon to take enforcement action, and even if they do so, the penalties that are imposed rarely constitute a meaningful deterrent.

Over the past quarter of a century significant progress has been made in human rights litigation against multinationals. Developments in English law relating to tort law parent company duty of care and fnc mean that multinationals headquartered in the United Kingdom are likely to be especially mindful of the potential legal, financial, and reputational consequences of failing to ensure that effective standards are in place at their overseas operations. Many of the cases that have been brought have placed MNCs under a degree of legal and public scrutiny that would not otherwise have occurred. Cases have been costly, financially and reputationally. Holding MNCs to account legally is therefore vital to providing adequate redress for victims but also in terms of prevention by deterring bad practices and double standards.

The legal cases against multinationals have been an integral part of the area of BHR, which has mushroomed during this same period, with pressure from civil society on companies and investors, coalescing around campaigns for legal accountability and access to justice and redress for victims. The fact that the central

[113] *Price Waterhouse Coopers Inc and Others v. National Potato Co-operative Ltd* [2004] (6) SA 66 (SCA).

[114] <http://www.childrenofkabwe.com> accessed 25 November 2020.

concept in the corporate duty to respect human rights in the UNGPs is based on a tort-based duty of care emphasises the symbiosis of the litigation and BHR.

At the same time, formidable barriers to justice for victims persist in multinational home States, including in England. As a result, legal cases that are pursued represent only the tip of the iceberg of the actual harm that is done. It is no accident that so few lawyers do these cases. The importance of effective legal representation for victims in cases that are so hard fought and complex cannot be underestimated and depends on national costs and funding regimes enabling proper recovery of costs by victims' lawyers who will otherwise be deterred from acting. The emerging interest of third party litigation funders is likely to be a game changer in big cases of high overall value.

There is scope for greater cross-border collaboration between lawyers in bringing human rights cases in multinational host State courts, in South Africa and other States that are conducive to this, in terms of legal systems, laws, and procedures. Building capacity to deliver justice locally is an important goal, but the MNC host States in which this is likely to be feasible in the near future seem limited. Locally held arbitration of business and human rights disputes, as occurred in some of the gold miners' silicosis cases, could potentially be used more widely. The Hague Rules on Business and Human Rights Arbitration, launched in December 2019, were designed with this purpose in mind.[115]

The principle of a parent company duty of care has not yet been followed by other States and it is only where human rights abuse has occurred in States with English law-based systems, that are strongly influenced by English law, that the English law principle is likely to apply. A legally binding international instrument, including mandatory HRDD, would potentially provide a remedy to victims across the globe, provided other procedural and practical barriers to justice are also lowered. Holding MNCs to account legally is vital to providing adequate redress for victims and in providing a deterrent against bad practices and human rights abuse.

[115] https://www.cilc.nl/project/the-hague-rules-on-business-and-human-rights-arbitration/. The Hague Rules on Business and Human Rights Arbitration significantly modify the UNCITRAL arbitration rules to cater for BHR disputes. The Rules are not intended as substitute for judicial remedies, but as an alternative mechanism that in certain circumstances serve the interests of both businesses and victims and fill the judicial remedy gap in the UNGPs.

3

Human Rights Litigation against Multinationals in Practice

Lessons from the United Kingdom

Daniel Leader

I. Introduction

One of the more promising avenues for remedy against corporations who commit human rights and environmental abuses in the developing world is transnational tort litigation. Over the past 25 years, a series of novel cases have been successfully brought against parent companies domiciled in the United Kingdom with respect to harms committed by their foreign subsidiaries.[1] The overall rate of success of these claims has been relatively high. The jurisprudence those cases has generated is now substantial, culminating in the recent unanimous decisions in the Supreme Court in *Lungowe v. Vedanta Resources* [2019] UKSC 20 and *Okpabi v. Royal Dutch Shell plc* [2021] UKSC 3. Significantly, this case law is increasingly relied upon by lawyers who seek to bring similar cases in other jurisdictions around the world.[2]

The cases which have been brought broadly fall into three categories: (i) personal injury and occupational disease; (ii) environmental harms; and (iii) human rights and security. Such cases are brought on the basis of the *de facto* control, direction, and oversight the parent company exercises over its foreign subsidiary which, it is argued, give rise to a separate and distinct duty of care. This chapter offers an overview of legal developments in the United Kingdom. I explain the relevant case law on parent company liability in the United Kingdom and identify the procedural and legal challenges inherent in these complex claims.

Section II of this chapter examines the nature of corporate impunity, with particular reference to the widespread pollution by oil and gas companies in the Niger Delta. Section III examines the role of transnational tort litigation in the United Kingdom by reference to the novel parent company liability cases, the security and

[1] The case law and statutory law referred to in this analysis is current as of 1 July 2020.
[2] See R. Meeran, 'Tort Litigation Against Multinational Corporations for Violations of Human Rights: An Overview of the Position Outside the United States' (2011) 3 *City University of Hong Kong Law Review*, 1–41.

Daniel Leader, *Human Rights Litigation against Multinationals in Practice* In: *Human Rights Litigation against Multinationals in Practice*. Edited by: Richard Meeran, Oxford University Press. © The Several Contributors 2021.
DOI: 10.1093/oso/9780198866220.003.0003.

human rights cases, and supply/value chain cases which have been brought or are currently being litigated. Section IV considers the complex range of practical procedural and practical factors relevant to such claims, including the relevant rules on jurisdiction; procedural rules on discovery/disclosure; group and class actions; the challenges of litigating on behalf of remote communities in the developing world and the scope for witness protection; and practical issues of costs and funding of complex group litigation.

II. Understanding corporate impunity: the example of the Niger Delta

Few situations exemplify the business and human rights challenge as starkly as the widespread and systematic pollution of the oil rich Niger Delta. Most of the pollution emanates from the oil pipelines and infrastructure operated by subsidiaries of Western domiciled parent companies such as Shell, Total, Exxon Mobil, and ENI. The facts are stark: in 2006 a team of international experts estimated that between 9 million and 13 million barrels of oil (1.5 million tons) had spilt into the Niger Delta over the past 50 years.[3] It is estimated that the inhabitants of the Niger Delta have experienced oil spills on a par with the 1989 Exxon Valdez disaster in Alaska every year for the past 50 years.[4] The causes of this systematic pollution are multiple but include a lack of investment in pipeline maintenance and technology and third party -bunkering' by criminal gangs who siphon off oil. Whatever the cause of the pollution, oil companies are required by Nigerian law to ensure that any oil spill is cleaned up within 30 days.[5] This basic legal requirement is, however, largely ignored and unenforced.

In 2011, the United Nations Environment Programme's (UNEP) published a comprehensive Environmental Assessment of Ogoniland, an area of the Niger Delta, based on two years of field work during which 4,000 samples were collected from over 200 sites.[6] It reported that the Ogoni people were exposed to severe oil contamination on a daily basis, which impacts their water sources, air quality, and farmland. In a number of locations public health was significantly at risk. Some water wells tested by experts showed 1,000 times higher concentrations of oil contamination than permitted under Nigerian drinking water standards.[7] UNEP

[3] Federal Ministry of Environment, 'Niger Delta Natural Resource Damage Assessment and Restoration Project' (2006) Abuja.

[4] Amnesty International, 'Petroleum, Pollution and Poverty in the Niger Delta' (Report) (30 June 2009) AI-Index AFR 44/017/2009, 16.

[5] Sections VIII B.4.1 and VIII B.2.11.1 of the Environmental Guidelines and Standards for the Petroleum Industry in Nigeria (2002).

[6] United National Environment Programme, 'Environmental Assessment of Ogoniland' (2011), <http://postconflict.unep.ch/publications/OEA/UNEP_OEA.pdf> accessed 31 March 2017.

[7] Ibid., 11.

urgently recommended 'the largest terrestrial clean-up operation in history' but ten years later no effective clean-up has taken place.[8]

Communities affected by years of systematic pollution have been provided with little assistance by the Nigerian courts or regulators. There are numerous barriers to justice, including the inefficiency of the litigation process.[9] Victims face decades of delays as cases work their way through the court system. Oil companies invariably resist civil claims and tend to appeal adverse decisions all the way to the Nigerian Supreme Court. The subsequent delays in the determination of cases are dramatic and litigation can often last for 20 years.[10] Furthermore, oil spill litigation requires specialist technical expert evidence to respond to complex evidential disputes, which is unavailable and unaffordable to most claimant lawyers in Nigeria.[11]

There are no reported cases where a Nigerian court has ordered the clean-up of an oil spill by an oil company. There is one example of injunctive relief being granted to a community in 2005 with regard to gas flaring, a widespread and controversial practice in the Niger Delta. However, the injunction was ignored by the oil companies and the judge was ultimately transferred to another State.[12] The position is no better with the regulator. The Director General of National Oil Spill Detention and Response Agency (NOSDRA), the official regulator of the Nigerian oil industry, observed in 2012 that it is unable to enforce compliance because it has no power to sanction polluters.[13] In view of the multiple barriers to obtaining any remedy at a national level against local subsidiaries of oil companies, Nigerian communities are increasingly seeking redress internationally in the jurisdictions in which the parent companies of the Nigerian subsidiaries are domiciled.

[8] United National Environment Programme, <http://web.unep.org/newscentre/un-environments-ogoniland-assessment-back-spotlight> accessed 31 March 2017. See, for example, Amnesty International, 'No Progress: An evaluation of the Implementation UNEP's Environmental Assessment of Ogoniland' (Report) (4 August 2014) AI-Index AFR 44/013/2014.

[9] J. Frynas, *Oil in Nigeria: Conflict and Litigation between Oil Companies and Village Communities* (2000).

[10] In recent litigation in the English High Court concerning the enforcement of arbitration awards the Court of Appeal observed that the extreme delay 'result[ed] from the workings of the Nigerian legal system' and has 'gone beyond the "catastrophic" description adopted by Tomlinson J in 2008; *IPCO (Nigeria) Limited v. NNPC* [2015] EWCA Civ 114, [166]. For example, in the case of *Tiebo and ors v. Shell Petroleum Development Company Ltd* (SPDC), a community sought damages arising out of an oil spill in 1988 and it was 17 years before the Supreme Court handed down its final judgment.

[11] Section 83(3) of the Evidence Act 2011 prevents claimants from instructing experts on a contingency basis.

[12] *Gbemre v. Shell Petroleum Development Co.* Suit No FHC/CS/B/153/2005, 25 July 2005. See also H. Osofsky 'Climate Change and Environmental Justice: Reflections on Litigation over Oil Extraction and Rights Violations in Nigeria' (2010) 1 *Journal of Human Rights and the Environment* 189–210, 191.

[13] Energy Mix Report, 'Laws against oil spillage weak, says NOSDRA' (12 November 2013) <http://energymixreport.com/laws-against-oil-spillage-weak-says-nosdra/> accessed 15 November 2020.

III. Corporate accountability cases: the English case law

A. Parent company liability

Over the past 25 years numerous transnational tort claims against parent companies have been brought in the English courts by relying upon the principle of parent company liability.[14] Two cases reached the House of Lords; *Connelly v. RTZ*[15] and *Lubbe v. Cape*[16] in the late 1990s/2000s. More recently, three cases have been the subject of extensive litigation (against *Vedanta*, *Shell*, and *Unilever* respectively), and two of these cases have reached the Supreme Court, culminating in the landmark Supreme Court judgments in *Vedanta Resources plc v. Lungowe & others* [2019] UKSC 20 and *Okpabi v. Royal Dutch Shell plc* [2021] UKSC 3. These, and other corporate accountability cases which have been brought in the English courts, are explained later in this chapter.

Tort claims are arguably a blunt accountability instrument to deploy in the face of grave violations of human rights. Some commentators argue that such litigation strategies are inappropriate because they cannot be framed in terms of human rights and only a narrow range of cases can be brought. The claims are, in common with all tort claims, *ex post facto* and cannot prevent abuses from taking place. In addition, such cases are slow, costly, and organised on a fragmented case-by-case basis.[17] Whilst these criticisms highlight significant imperfections, many of which are inherent in any tort claim, the reality is that for many victims of human rights abuses by businesses, transnational tort litigation is an important route (often the only route) to effective remedy and a wider function of these claims is that the prospect of litigation can deter corporate misconduct.

In broad terms transnational tort claims are brought against a parent company (which is domiciled in the United Kingdom) on the grounds that the parent company exercises *de facto* control, direction, or oversight over the foreign subsidiary and/or provides relevant advice in a manner which was directly related to the tortious acts/omissions of that subsidiary. Rather than seeking to pierce the corporate veil, the focus of claimant lawyers in England has been on the direct tortious liability of parent companies arising out of the nature of their corporate relationship with their subsidiaries. This principle requires careful explanation because of its centrality to transnational tort litigation in England and its potential to improve access to judicial remedy in other jurisdictions. The concept builds on basic

[14] For a list of some of the key cases see U. Grusic, 'International Environmental Litigation in EU Courts: A Regulatory Perspective' (2016) 35 *Yearbook of European Law* 180–228, 196.

[15] *Connelly v. RTZ Corporation Plc* [1998] AC 854.

[16] *Lubbe & Ors v. Cape plc* [2000] 1WLR 1545, p. 1555.

[17] R. Chambers, 'Is Home State Litigation the Way to Fill the Lacuna in Corporate Legal Accountability for Human Rights Violations Perpetrated in Host States?' (2009) 4(133) *Journal of Comparative Law* 138–9.

principles of tortious liability. English law deploys a three-stage test to determine whether a duty of care arises in any given situation, known as the 'Caparo test': (i) the foreseeability of the damage or loss; (ii) whether there is there sufficient 'proximity' between the parties; and (iii) whether it is fair, just, and reasonable to impose a duty of care.[18]

Whether a duty of care arises in a specific case is fact sensitive and the development of the law of negligence is incremental by reference to decided categories of liability in case law. There is no general duty to intervene to prevent a third party causing damage, but third party liability can arise where there is 'a relationship between the parties which gives rise to an imposition or assumption of responsibility' on the part of the defendant.[19] Parent company liability is, in effect, a class of third party liability, namely a duty of care arises if there has been an assumption of responsibility by the parent company arising out of the nature of its corporate relationship with its subsidiary. In particular, liability can arise if the parent company exercises de facto control over or provides relevant advice in a manner that is directly connected to the commission of the relevant tort by the subsidiary.

B. *Thor Chemicals*, *Connelly v. RTZ*, and *Lubbe v. Cape Plc* [1995–2003]

The principle of parent company liability was first postulated in a trio of groundbreaking cases which were brought in the late 1990s by Richard Meeran.[20] The first, *Ngcobo v. Thor Chemicals Holdings Ltd & Desmond Cowley*,[21] concerned the mercury poisoning of South African workers. It was alleged that the parent company was responsible for the negligent design and transfer of hazardous chemical technology to its South African subsidiary. Thor Chemicals UK factory was closed due to health and safety concerns and it then moved its mercury operations 'lock, stock, and barrel' to South Africa and failed to take effective measures to reduce exposure to mercury in the working environment. As a result, three workers died and many others were poisoned. The parent company was sued in the United Kingdom and the High Court rejected Thor's jurisdiction challenge on *forum non conveniens* grounds and refused to strike out the claims against the parent company case, resulting in a settlement in 1997.

The second case, *Connelly v. RTZ Corporation Plc*,[22] concerned a claim for compensation by a Scottish worker who had contracted cancer after working at

[18] *Caparo Industries Plc v. Dickman* [1990] 1 All ER 568 (HL).

[19] *Smith v. Littlewoods Organisation Ltd* [1987] AC 241, [272].

[20] Head of the International Department at Leigh Day.

[21] '*Ngcobo v Thor Chemicals Holdings Ltd & Desmond Cowley*' (Times Law Report, 10 November 1995).

[22] *Connelly v. RTZ Corporation Plc* [1998] AC 854.

Rio Tinto's Rossing uranium mine in Namibia. A case was brought against the parent company on the basis that it had negligently devised and implemented the subsidiary's policy on health, safety, and the environment. The High Court refused to strike out the negligence claims against the parent company and in a landmark decision the House of Lords ruled that the case should proceed in the United Kingdom given that the litigation could not be funded in Namibia. Ultimately, the case failed on limitation grounds, but it further cemented the principle of parent company liability in English common law and the importance of access to funding in determining the appropriate forum for litigation became known as the *Connelly principle*.

The third case, *Lubbe & Ors v. Cape plc* [2000] concerned more than 7,500 plaintiffs (both ex-employees of the subsidiary and individuals who lived in the vicinity of the mine) who brought claims against an English parent company alleging negligent control of health and safety of its South African subsidiary's asbestos mining operations. The Court of Appeal summarised the key issue as

> whether a parent company which is proved to exercise de facto control over the operations of a subsidiary and which knows . . . that those operations involve risks to the health of workers . . . owes a duty of care in relation to the control which it exercises over and the advice which it gives to the subsidiary.[23]

A clear statement of the nature of the intrusive judicial inquiry a parent company could be subjected to in such cases was provided by Lord Bingham when the litigation reached the House of Lords as follows:

> The first segment concerns the responsibility of the defendant as a parent company for ensuring the observance of proper standards of health and safety by its overseas subsidiaries. Resolution of this issue will be likely to involve an inquiry into what part the defendant played in controlling the operations of the group, what its directors and employees knew or ought to have known, what action was taken and not taken, whether the defendant owed a duty of care to employees of group companies overseas and whether, if so, that duty was broken. Much of the evidence material to this inquiry would, in the ordinary way, be documentary and much of it would be found in the offices of the parent company, including minutes of meetings, reports by directors and employees on visits overseas and correspondence.[24]

Again, in determining jurisdiction, the House of Lords applied the *Connelly* principle and held that the United Kingdom should retain jurisdiction because such

[23] *Lubbe & Ors v. Cape plc* [2000] 1WLR 1545, p. 1551.
[24] Ibid.

complex group litigation could not be funded in South Africa. The claims were ultimately settled in 2001.

In short, by 2001 the English courts had considered parent company liability in three cases and ruled in all three that the legal principle was uncontroversial and, significantly, that jurisdiction in the United Kingdom should be retained on *forum non conveniens* grounds because there was a real risk that justice could not be accessed in the foreign jurisdiction.

C. *Chandler v. Cape plc* [2012]

Both *Ngcobo* and *Lubbe* were settled prior to trial and, therefore, there was no ultimate finding by a court of parent company liability. The first case in which an English court has imposed a duty of care on a parent company was the Court of Appeal decision in *Chandler v. Cape plc*.[25] Although this was not a case of parent company liability with respect to a foreign subsidiary, the case merits careful analysis. The claimant, Mr Chandler, contracted asbestosis at work and by the time of diagnosis the subsidiary that had directly employed and exposed him to asbestos had been dissolved. There was no dispute that the system of work was unsafe and had caused the asbestosis. He chose, therefore, to sue the parent company, Cape plc, on the basis that it directly owed him a duty of care due to its close involvement in the health and safety policies of its subsidiary.

There was a number of important findings of the Court that drove it to the conclusion that the parent company was liable. These included that:

- Cape plc was 'fully aware of the systemic failure' of its subsidiary to prevent the migration of asbestos dust and had previously run the defective factory;
- Cape plc appointed a group medical officer and scientific officer who was involved in relevant research on the link between asbestos dust and related diseases;
- Many aspects of the subsidiary's production process had been discussed and authorized by the Caple plc's Board;
- Although health and safety were dealt with at both parent company and subsidiary level, Cape plc had 'superior knowledge' about the nature and management of asbestos risk, and its resources far exceeded that of its subsidiary;
- Therefore, 'Cape assumed a duty of care either to advise Cape Products on what steps it had to take . . . or to ensure the steps were taken'.[26]

[25] *Chandler v. Cape plc* [2012] 1 WLR 3111. The Australian courts have also made findings of parent company liability in *CSR Ltd v. Wren* (1998) 44 NSWLR 463. This was a mesothelioma case and liability arose by virtue of the complete overlap between the parent's and subsidiary's management and the control and direction CSR exercised over its subsidiary's operations.

[26] Ibid., [57], [75], and [78].

The Court 'emphatically rejected any suggestion' that it was in any way seeking to pierce the corporate veil; liability did not arise simply by virtue of the fact that a company is a parent of another company. The question was simply whether what the parent company did gave rise to a direct duty of care to the subsidiary's employees.[27] Further, the Court was clear that such liability does not arise only in unusual parent/subsidiary relationships or in situations where the parent company excises 'absolute control' of the subsidiary.[28] Indeed, it is not necessary to demonstrate that the parent actively intervenes in the relevant policies of its subsidiary; the court will look at the relationship between the companies more widely (e.g. whether the parent intervenes in its subsidiary's production and funding) and liability could still arise with regard to 'high level advice and strategy'.[29]

The Court provided guidance as to appropriate circumstances where the law *may* impose liability upon a parent company. These include where:

(1) the businesses of the parent and subsidiary are in a relevant respect the same;
(2) the parent has, or ought to have, superior knowledge on some relevant aspect of health and safety in the particular industry;
(3) the subsidiary's system of work is unsafe and the parent company knew, or ought to have known; and
(4) the parent knew or ought to have foreseen that the subsidiary or its employees would rely on that superior knowledge for the employees' protection.[30]

This guidance is not exhaustive and it should not be elevated to the status of a legal test since it is simply descriptive of factual circumstances which could give rise to liability.

There are a number of important implications of this judgment which have been the subject of academic debate.[31] First, the Chandler guidance places significant weight on relevant 'superior knowledge' or expertise by the parent company upon which the subsidiary is reliant. Second, the 'control' test is broadly stated. There is no need to demonstrate absolute control or even active interference in relevant policy or operations, influence on high level policy and strategy may suffice. Indeed, Chandler was a case of omissions liability which arose by virtue of *a failure to act* in response to known health and safety failures. Third, the emphasis on 'knew

[27] Ibid., [69].
[28] Ibid., [66]–[67].
[29] Ibid., [66].
[30] Ibid., [80].
[31] For a critique of Chandler see M. Petrin, 'Assumption of Responsibility in Corporate Groups: Chandler v Cape plc' (2013) 76(3) *The Modern Law Review* 603–19. For an opposing view see C. Witting and J. Rankin, 'Tortious Liability of Corporate Groups: From Control to Coordination' (2014) 22 *Tort Law Review* 91–104.

or ought to have known' creates the prospect of liability for constructive as opposed to actual knowledge, based on the nature of the relationship between parent and subsidiary. The suggestion appears to be that once a parent company excises sufficient control or oversight over a subsidiary it is not enough to claim ignorance. The assumption of responsibility places the parent under an obligation to inform itself as to the safety its subsidiaries operations and, if necessary, to intervene.[32]

D. *Thompson v. Renwick Group plc* [2014]

It is important to understand that whether liability arises is entirely dependent on whether there has been an assumption of responsibility by the parent. Each case will turn on its own facts. For example, in the subsequent case of *Thompson v. Renwick Group plc*[33] the Court of Appeal found that there had been no assumption of responsibility. In *Thompson* the claimant contracted pleural thickening and an increased risk of mesothelioma due to working conditions which were 'really quite shocking and should be a cause for shame'.[34] Neither of his employers was solvent so he sued the parent company on the basis that it had appointed a director of the subsidiary with responsibility for health and safety. However, that was plainly insufficient to give rise to liability. There was no evidence of control or direction by the parent company beyond the appointment of the director and there was no basis to conclude that he was acting on behalf of the parent. Further, there was no evidence that the parent carried on any business at all apart from holding shares in other companies. As the Lord Justice Tomlinson put it succinctly: 'what one is looking for here is a situation in which the parent company is better placed, because of its superior knowledge or expertise, to protect the employees of subsidiary companies against the risk of injury'.[35] *Thompson* was 'far removed' from the facts in *Chandler* and there was no evidence the parent had any knowledge of the risk that was superior to that which the subsidiaries could be expected to have.

E. Developments in parent company liability since 2015

Since 2015 three parent company liability cases have been the subject of robust jurisdiction challenges by the Defendant companies. They are:

[32] A. Sanger, 'Crossing the Corporate Veil: the Duty of Care owed by a parent company to the employees of its subsidiary' (2012) 71(03) *The Cambridge Law Journal* 478–81, 480.
[33] *Thompson v. Renwick Group plc* [2014] BCLC 97.
[34] Ibid., [1].
[35] Ibid., [37].

(1) *Lungowe and others v. Vedanta Resources plc* [2019] UKSC 20[36] (*Vedanta*)
(2) *AAA & Ors v. Unilever plc* [2018] EWCA Civ 1532 (*Unilever*)
(3) *Okpabi v. Royal Dutch Shell plc* [2021] UKSC 3 (*Shell*)

All three cases were considered by the Court of Appeal and two (*Vedanta* and *Shell*) have now been considered by the Supreme Court. The various judgments are instructive since they demonstrate an inconsistency of approach to parent company liability which has now been resolved by the Supreme Court in *Vedanta and Shell*. In all three cases, the defendants argument essentially followed the same pattern:

(i) The case against the parent company domiciled in the United Kingdom is a fiction and device engineered in order to secure jurisdiction in England, in reality the parent company does not intervene in the affairs of its wholly autonomous foreign subsidiary;
(ii) The company's global policy framework is simply in place to meet stock exchange listing requirements and good governance guidance and, therefore, cannot give rise to a duty of care. In such circumstances, liability for global policy frameworks would give rise to indeterminate liability;
(iii) The litigation concerns a foreign jurisdiction and the case should be heard in that jurisdiction; any access to justice concerns expressed by the claimants are without merit.

i. *Lungowe and others v. Vedanta Resources plc* (2019)

Vedanta requires careful analysis since, together with *Shell*, it provides the most authoritative analysis of parent company liability by the Supreme Court to date. The case concerns claims by 1,826 Zambian farmers whose lands and waterways were polluted by a copper mine operated by Vedanta's Zambian subsidiary. The claimants contended that Vedanta assumed responsibility to ensure its subsidiary's mining operations did not harm the local environment and relied on public statements by Vedanta in which it asserted its responsibility for the establishment of appropriate group-wide environmental control and sustainability standards, for their implementation throughout the group by training, and for monitoring and enforcement. At first instance, the judge found that the claim against the parent company was arguable and joined the foreign subsidiary to the proceedings, rejecting the defendants' argument that Vedanta plc was merely a holding company.[37]

[36] *Lungowe and others v. Vedanta Resources Plc and another* [2016] EWHC 975 (TCC) (for an analysis see V.G. Curran, 'Harmonizing Multinational Parent Company Liability for Foreign Subsidiary Human Rights Violations' (2016) 17(2) *Chicago Journal of International Law* 406–46, 437).
[37] Ibid., [117].

The defendants appealed unsuccessfully to the Court of Appeal and then onto the Supreme Court.

The Supreme Court, in a unanimous decision, clarified the law on parent company liability. Lord Briggs (with whom the other members of the Court all agreed) rejected Vedanta's contention that that parent company liability represented a 'novel and controversial extension of the boundaries of the tort of negligence'. He explained at paragraph 49 that, 'the liability of parent companies in relation to the activities of their subsidiaries is not, of itself, a distinct category of liability in common law negligence'. Instead:

> Everything depends on the extent to which, and the way in which, the parent availed itself of the opportunity to *take over, intervene in, control, supervise or advise* the management of the relevant operations (including land use) of the subsidiary.

Although Lord Briggs was at pains to emphasise that there is no single overarching test for determining whether a parent company owes a duty of care in respect of harm caused by the operations of a subsidiary, his judgment identified at least four different possible routes by which such a duty of care may arise:

- **First Route: Taking over the management or joint management of the relevant activity of the subsidiary**—a duty of care may arise 'where the parent has in substance taken over the management of the relevant activity of the subsidiary in place of or jointly with the subsidiary's own management' (paragraph 51).
- **Second Route: Providing defective advice and/or promulgating defective group-wide safety/environmental policies which are implemented as a matter of course by the subsidiary**—a duty of care may arise where 'the parent has given relevant advice to the subsidiary about how it should manage a particular risk'. Further, '*Group guidelines* about minimising the environmental impact of inherently dangerous activities, such as mining, may be shown to contain systemic errors which, when implemented as of course by a particular subsidiary, then cause harm to third parties.' Lord Briggs cited *Chandler v. Cape Plc* [2012] 1 WLR 3111 as authority for the proposition that a parent company's promulgation of such deficient 'guidelines' would be capable of establishing a duty of care (paragraph 52).
- **Third Route: Promulgating group-wide safety/environmental policies and taking active steps to ensure their implementation by subsidiaries**—Lord Briggs explained that, '[e]ven where group-wide policies do not of themselves give rise to such a duty of care to third parties, they may do so if the parent does not merely proclaim them, but *takes active steps, by training, supervision*

and enforcement, to see that they are implemented by relevant subsidiaries' (paragraph 53).
- **Fourth Route: Parent company holding out that it exercises a particular degree of supervision and control of its subsidiaries**—Lord Briggs explained that, '[s]imilarly, it seems to me that the parent may incur the relevant responsibility to third parties if, in published materials, it *holds itself out as exercising that degree of supervision and control of its subsidiaries, even if it does not in fact do so.* In such circumstances *its very omission* may constitute the abdication of a responsibility which it has publicly undertaken' (paragraph 53).

Applying those principles to the facts of the case, Lord Briggs held that the corporate materials published by the parent company—in which it 'may fairly be said to have asserted its own assumption of responsibility for the maintenance of proper standards of environmental control over the activities of its subsidiaries'—were 'sufficient on their own' to establish that it was 'well arguable' that 'a sufficient level of intervention by [the parent] in the conduct of operations at the Mine may be demonstrable at trial, after full disclosure of the relevant internal documents of [the parent] and [the subsidiary], and of communications passing between them' (paragraph 61).

The Supreme Court in *Vedanta*, therefore, made it clear that the scope of parent company liability is broad, including by virtue of the global policy framework, and that liability can arise where the parent holds itself out as exercising a degree of supervision and control of its subsidiaries but fails to do so. That represents a significant extension of the boundaries of parent company liability and one that will profoundly concern multinational companies, who fear that voluntary steps taken to respect human rights within a corporate group, as required by the United Nations Guiding Principles on Business and Human Rights (UNGPs), could now give rise to a duty of care. In that sense, *Vedanta*, represents for the first time a bridge between the soft law business and human rights framework which has developed over the past 20 years, and the common law of negligence.

ii. *Okpabi v. Royal Dutch Shell plc* (2018–2020)

An illustration of the potential but also the significant limits of parent company liability as a means of effective judicial remedy can be found in recent transnational litigation against Royal Dutch Shell plc (RDS) and its Nigerian Subsidiary (SPDC) in the Netherlands and in England.

In 2011 the Bodo community, a fishing community situated in the heart of Ogoniland, sued Royal Dutch Shell in the English courts with regard to two vast operational oil spills which destroyed their creeks and livelihoods. The oil spilled caused unprecedented environmental damage to some 9,000 hectares of mangrove habitat which belonged to the community and which it depended on for its livelihood. Shell Nigeria agreed to submit to the jurisdiction of the English courts and conceded liability with respect to the two oil spills that were the result of equipment failure in order to avoid litigation with respect to Royal Dutch Shell plc's potential liability. Shell had initially offered to settle the claim for $4,000, behind the backs of their then Nigerian lawyers. In January 2015, because of the expert evidence that Leigh Day obtained to rebut Shell's factual case, the claims settled for £55 million, which was paid directly to each of the 15,000 claimants. This represented the largest damages settlement in the history of Nigerian oil spill litigation and has enabled the Bodo Community to rebuild economically. The pressure of the litigation also resulted in an international clean-up operation which was sponsored by the Dutch Government, the first of its kind in Nigeria. Since then, Shell has robustly fought all further international litigation related to Nigerian oil pollution.

In *Four Nigerian Farmers and Stichting Milieudefensie v. Shell*,[38] the Dutch Court of Appeal considered negligence claims brought by Nigerian claimants arising out of oil damage caused by SPDC's operations in the Niger Delta. The parent company case against RDS was premised upon Chandler and Vedanta principles, given the alleged control RDS' Executive Committee exercises over SPDC and its global policy for Health, Security, Safety, and Environment (HSSE) which applies to its subsidiaries around the world and which is established, controlled, and monitored centrally by RDS. The defendants sought to strike out the litigation at the jurisdiction stage on the grounds that the parent company case against RDS was unarguable and a device to anchor the claims in the Netherlands. In December 2015, the Dutch Court of Appeal rejected Shell's application and held that:

> it cannot be ruled out from the outset that the parent company may be expected in such a case to take an interest in preventing spills ... the more so if it has made the prevention of environmental damage by the activities of group companies a spearhead and is, to a certain degree, actively involved in and managing the business operation of such companies.[39]

The Dutch court, therefore, held that it had jurisdiction over both RDS and its Nigerian subsidiary since the claims were closely related and should be heard together. At trial the Court of Appeal ruled in favour of the claimants and that SPDC was strictly liable for the pollution of two communities and further that RDS had a legal duty to ensure the installation of a leak detection system on one of the pipelines. At the time of writing the case had been appealed by Shell to the Dutch Supreme Court.[40]

[38] *Four Nigerian Farmers and Stichting Milieudefensie v Royal Dutch Shell Plc and another* [2021] ECLI:NL:GHDHA:2021:132 (*Oruma*), ECLI:NL:GHDHA:2021:133 (Goi) and ECLI:NL:GHDHA:2021:134 (*Ikot Ada Udo*). This is subject to detailed analysis in Chapter 8 by Channa Samkalden.

[39] Ibid., para. 3.2.

[40] See Chapter 3 by Leader for further information on the development of business and human rights in the Netherlands.

Parallel litigation has been brought in the United Kingdom on behalf of the Ogale and the Bille communities which are seeking redress against Shell in the English courts arising out of oil pollution by SPDC (*Okpabi v. Royal Dutch Shell plc*).[41] Shell robustly contested jurisdiction in both claims. As in the Dutch litigation, Shell contended that the parent company liability case against RDS is a device to anchor the cases in England as opposed to Nigeria. At first instance, the High Court found that the case against RDS was not reasonably arguable on the grounds that the judge found that RDS was a pure holding company which did not engage in any operational activity and had no superior or specialist knowledge.[42] The Court of Appeal unanimously held that the High Court had fallen into error since it had wrongly excluded critical evidence and failed to appreciate the legal status of the RDS Executive Committee, which actively sets group-wide guidelines and monitors the activities of its subsidiaries and acts on behalf of the RDS Board.[43] However, by a majority the Court of Appeal went on to reject the appeal on the grounds that (i) in principle a global policy framework could not give rise to liability in itself and (ii) the claimants had been unable to provide sufficient evidence of *operational control* of SPDC's day-to-day activities by RDS. The Supreme Court subsequently and unanimously overturned the Court of Appeal's judgement and ruled that there is 'a good arguable case' that RDS is legally responsible for the systemic pollution of the communities. A number of important points emerge from the judgment:

1. The Court rejected the limiting principle and the narrow prism through which the parent company case was evaluated. The approach of the majority in the Court of Appeal could not be reconciled with the guidance the Supreme Court had subsequently provided in *Vedanta* which rejects the bold proposition that global policies cannot give rise to liability. The Supreme Court also asserts that 'control' is merely one potential route to liability, it cannot be the sole prism through which the evidence of a parent company case is evaluated. The Court stated:

> 'to the extent that the Court of Appeal indicated that the promulgation by a parent company of group wide policies or standards can never in itself give rise to a duty of care, that is inconsistent with Vedanta' (paragraph 143).

[41] *Okpabi and others v. Royal Dutch Shell plc and another* [2017] EWHC 89 (TCC) and *Alame and others v. Royal Dutch Shell plc and another* [2017] EWHC 89 (TCC). See E.M. Blanco and B. Pontin, 'Litigation Extraterritorial Nuisances under English Common Law and UK Statute' (Jul 2017) 6(2) *Transnational Environmental Law* 285–308.

[42] Ibid., [116].

[43] Ibid., [101].

2. The Court reaffirmed the four routes to potential parent company liability as set out in Vedanta.
3. It cautioned against making determinations and striking out a case against a parent company prior to disclosure (particularly of internal documents) and a full trial. Courts should not be drawn into an evaluation of the weight of the evidence at an interlocutory stage and a pleaded case should only be struck out if it is 'demonstrably untrue or unsupportable'.
4. Finally, the Supreme Court rejected the proposition that parent company cases can be approached by reference to any generalised assumption or presumptions of liability. There is no special doctrine in the law of parent company liability and no limit to the models of management and control which may be put in place within a multinational group of companies. Indeed, Shell's structure in fact militated in favour of liability:

> 'it is of significance that the Shell group is organised along Business and Functional lines rather than simply according to corporate status. This vertical structure involves significant delegation' (paragraph 156).

At the time of writing, Shell had abandoned its remaining objections to jurisdiction and the litigation is progressing to trial, which is expected to take place in 2022. Overall the judgment in Okpabi further clarifies the broad scope of parent company liability by expressly rejecting the restrictive approach of the majority in the Court of Appeal. Further, it makes it plain that the evidential burden on claimants at the outset of a parent company liability case cannot be set too high when so much turns on the disclosure of internal corporate documents. As such, the case represents a significant victory for victims of corporate abuse who are seeking redress in British courts..

iii. *AAA & Ors v. Unilever plc* (2018)

The Supreme Court's decisions in *Vedanta* and *Shell* stand in stark contrast to the earlier Court of Appeal's judgment in *AAA & Ors v. Unilever plc. Unilever* was a claim on behalf of 218 Kenyan tea pickers who, it was alleged, both Unilever plc and its Kenyan subsidiary failed to protect from the foreseeable risk of ethnic violence during national elections in Kenya in 2007.

It was contended that Unilever placed the Kenyan tea workers in a position of significant risk given that they migrated 100,000 workers and their families on to a plantation that was surrounded by a hostile community and so were potential targets at times of heightened ethnic tension. Put simply, this was the most significant political risk faced by the largest concentration of Unilever workers anywhere in the world and yet no reasonable steps were taken to protect them for the heightened risk of violence in which Unilever had placed them. The evidence showed that Unilever plc, the parent company, was the repository for crisis management expertise within the corporate group, but that they had failed to deploy that expertise until well after the crisis had hit. The allegation against Unilever plc was premised on *a failure to act*, as in *Chandler*.

The judge at first instance held that the claim against the parent company was arguable on the basis that on paper Unilever had assumed apparent control of the content and auditing of the relevant policies.[44] The Court of Appeal overturned the High Court's evidential assessment on the basis that the claimants had failed to provide evidence that the subsidiary had been subject to 'direction or any specific detailed advice from Unilever' with regard to the relevant policies or training. In so doing, the Court of Appeal conducted a mini-trial and chose to ignore the evidence of five former Unilever managers who stated that Unilever Kenya was the subject of close supervision by the parent company. The claimants sought leave to appeal to the Supreme Court on the grounds that the Court of Appeal had considered proximity through the restrictive prism of 'proactive advice' whereas the allegation was that Unilever had failed to provide such advice, that it possessed superior crisis management expertise, and had failed to act to ensure its Kenyan subsidiary was properly prepared. Although the approach of the Court of Appeal was starkly at variance with that of the Supreme Court in *Vedanta* and *Chandler* in that there was no consideration of omissions liability, the Supreme Court declined leave to appeal on the grounds that the law had already been clarified by the Supreme Court *Vedanta*. Clearly, allowing a wrongly decided judgment to stand has provided little comfort the victims in *Unilever* who have now filed a case with the United Nations Working Group on Business and Human Rights.[45]

iv. *Rihan v. Ernst & Young Global Ltd & others* [2020] EWHC 901

The parent company liability principles have been applied in a recent case against Ernst & Young (EY). The case was brought by a former EY partner who blew the whistle on an unethical EY audit. He had been charged with undertaking a sustainability audit of a major gold trader in Dubai which was to be relied upon by gold purchasers and the wider public. In the course of the audit his team uncovered serious incidences of non-compliance with relevant industry-wide standards. The audit findings included billions of dollars' worth of cash transactions, importing large quantities of gold from Moroccan suppliers which had been coated with silver to avoid gold export restrictions, and transactions with high-risk countries such as Sudan, Democratic Republic of Congo, and Iran without proper due diligence. The concern was that the gold trader may have been trading in conflict minerals and that they were being used as a vehicle for large-scale money laundering. The claimant

[44] *AAA & Ors v. Unilever Plc & Anor* [2017] EWHC 371 (QB).

[45] See G. Hervey, 'Kenyan tea workers file UN complaint against Unilever over 2007 ethnic violence' *The Guardian* (1 August 2020) <https://www.theguardian.com/global-development/2020/aug/01/kenyan-tea-workers-file-un-complaint-against-unilever-over-2007-ethnic-violence> accessed 15 November 2020.

escalated his concerns to senior managers within EY's corporate group and instead of transparently reporting the findings, they engaged in a cover up with the Dubai regulatory authorities and ultimately published a sanitised version of the audit which made no reference to the findings. Mr Rihan felt he had no choice but to resign and go public.

Mr Rihan brought legal proceedings against four UK-based companies within the EY global network to whom he had escalated his complaint. The defendants argued that they were merely global service companies and since Mr Rihan had been employed by EY Dubai, they could not be held liable. However, the High Court ruled that the defendants had taken responsibility for investigating his concerns and managing the audit. Further, relying on the principles in *Vedanta*, the Judge held that those entities owed Mr Rihan a duty of care to act ethically, and they had failed to do so. The case represents an important application of parent company principles to entities within the EY network who had responsibility for risk management and compliance despite the clear delineation of responsibilities in the corporate group. The Court expressly rejected the contention that there was no higher authority than a national regulator and stipulates that global corporations are expected to adhere to international codes of conduct. As such, group-wide risk management and compliance departments of corporate groups and partnerships could be held liable for their advice to their subsidiaries in the future.

v. Conclusion

Overall, the jurisprudence of the English courts demonstrates a judicial receptiveness to holding parent companies to account for the harms perpetrated by their foreign subsidiaries, provided there is clear evidence of relevant involvement by the parent in the affairs of the subsidiary. The High Court and the Court of Appeal have demonstrated a much more conservative approach to the potential scope of parent company liability, but that restrictive approach has now been overruled by the Supreme Court in *Vedanta* and *Shell*, which has set an expansive path for future parent company liability cases.

F. Human rights and security cases

A number of other cases have been brought which focus on human rights and security. Serious human rights are routinely perpetrated around mines, plantations, and other installations by company guards, security companies, and/or local police against local communities and artisanal miners. Such abuses include the excessive use of force, assaults, rapes, torture, and arbitrary killings.

Governments are often closely connected to the corporations that operate in their countries and, in many cases, hold shares in form of a joint venture agreement and so have a financial stake in the company in question. As a result, governments routinely prioritise the interests of companies over those of the local population. The Voluntary Principles on Security and Human Rights provide guidance to companies on how to minimise the risk of human rights abuses, but without an enforcement mechanism human rights abuses abound.

The cases which have been brought fall broadly into two categories: (i) corporate complicity and (ii) direct abuses by the companies' security guards or contractors. The case law suggests that corporate complicity cases are significantly more difficult to prove. Due to the range and quantity of security and human rights claims which have been brought in recent years the summaries below of four of the leading cases are necessarily cursory.

The first case concerns a claim in 2009 by a group of 33 indigenous Peruvians against Monterrico Metals plc.[46] The claimants alleged that, following a protest about environmental issues, they were tortured, beaten, and sexually abused by the Peruvian police assisted by mine employees at Monterrico's Rio Blanco mine in August 2005. In June 2009, the UK High Court granted a worldwide freezing injunction over Monterrico's assets to protect against the financial impact of Monterrico's decision to relocate to Hong Kong. A freezing injunction in aid of the UK injunction was subsequently granted by the Hong Kong High Court. The case ultimately settled in 2011 a few months before trial.

A similar case was brought in 2013 by a group of 12 Tanzanians against African Barrick Gold and North Mara Gold Mine Limited (NMGML). The claimants alleged that the companies were complicit in the killings and injuries of villagers by police at the North Mara Mine in Tanzania and that the police were an integral part of the mine's security operation. Subsequently, the foreign subsidiary initiated legal proceedings in Tanzania, asking a local court to declare that the company could not be held liable for the actions of the police. After learning of the Tanzanian legal proceeding, the plaintiffs sought and obtained an anti-suit injunction from the UK court barring the defendants from continuing the legal action in Tanzania on matters being litigated before the UK court.[47] In 2015, the defendants reached an out of court settlement with the claimants.

A third case concerned 273 Mozambicans who alleged that they were the victims of serious human rights abuses at a ruby mine in Northern Mozambique owed by Gemfields Limited, the owners of Farbegé. The case was one of *direct* abuses by the mines guards and security operatives working under the supervision of their security function. The claimants alleged that they had been shot, beaten, raped and/or sexually abused, subjected to cruel and degrading treatment, unlawfully detained, and/or forced to carry out menial labour. The claimants included families

[46] *Guerrero & Others v. Monterrico Metals Plc* [2009] EWHC 247.

[47] *Kesabo v. African Barrick Gold Plc* [2013] EWHC 4045. Referred to by the court as the 'Tanzanian Torpedo' case, the 'Italian torpedo', being a name given to a common tactical abuse of process in cross-border disputes to defeat jurisdiction.

of artisanal miners who were allegedly killed on the mine including by being shot, beaten to death, or buried alive in mine shafts. It was alleged that on one occasion an entire village was burned down by representatives from the mining company. In 2019, the parties agreed to settle the claims for compensation. As part of the settlement, Gemfields agreed to establish an independent Operational Grievance Mechanism to ensure that any individual who wished to raise a grievance in relation to the mine would be able to obtain appropriate remedy promptly. The implementation of the Grievance Mechanism will be overseen by international experts.

The final case *Kadie Kalma & Ors v. (1) African Minerals Ltd,* was brought on behalf of 142 villagers against the mining firm Tonkolili Iron Ore Ltd and its parent company African Minerals, alleging complicity in police crackdowns in Sierra Leone in 2010 and 2012.[48] It was alleged that the company participated in assaults, false imprisonment, rape, and murder against local villagers. It was alleged that the defendants were complicit by calling on the police whom they knew had the reputation of using disproportionate force and providing them with significant support including vehicles, food, and financial support. The company denied any liability for the actions of the police.

The matter went to trial and the judge travelled to Sierra Leone to take the evidence of victims who had been unable to obtain visas for the United Kingdom. In 2018 the High Court ruled that African Minerals was not liable for its complicity in the police's actions although it noted that the company should have done more to engage with the local police to reduce the risk of excessive force and mistreatment. In 2020 the Court of Appeal upheld the High Court's verdict and held that although it was foreseeable that the police might use excessive force that was insufficient to give rise to liability since evidence of actual intention was required. The Court stated bluntly that:

> a party who calls on the services of the police to restore law and order cannot be liable in tort for the actions of the police simply because it is foreseeable that the police may use excessive force to achieve that result... That is not the law.[49]

Leave to appeal to the Supreme Court was refused. To draw the threads of these cases together, it would appear that security and human rights cases remain viable where the company's guards or contractors are responsible for the abuses in question. Where the police are responsible for the abuses, liability will only arise if there was a high level of complicity in the abuses in question which goes significantly beyond the logistical support provided in *Kadie Kalma & Ors v. (1) African Minerals Ltd.*

[48] *Kadie Kalma & Ors v. (1) African Minerals Ltd (2) African Minerals (SL) Ltd (3) Tonkolili Iron Ore (SL) Ltd* [2018] EWHC 3506 (QB).
[49] Ibid., [103].

G. Supply and value chain cases

i. Shipbreaking

In an extension of the principles developed over the past 25 years, tort claims are also now being brought with respect to the supply and value chain of corporations. The first case concerns the value chain with regard to shipbreaking, which is the practice by which ocean-going ships that reach their end of their working life are dismantled. Around 800 vessels reach the end of their operating lives and are broken up annually, the majority of which are dismantled on beaches in India, Bangladesh, and Pakistan in rudimentary and dangerous conditions. This allows the wealthy multinational ship-owning companies to maximise their profits at the expense of impoverished workers and the environment. This practice leads to high levels of fatalities, injuries, and work-related diseases and it also causes severe damage to coastal ecosystems and local communities due to toxic spills and contamination.

In *Begum v. Maran Ltd* [2021] EWCA Civ 326, the widow of a shipbreaking worker who was killed in an accident at work in Bangladesh in 2018, sued the British shipping company who sold the ship for demolition in unsafe conditions. The High Court refused to strike out the case and held that the shipping company could have influenced where the ship was scrapped, and that it could have ensured that it was dismantled in safe conditions. The judge rejected the argument that the defendant could be not liable as it was not deviating from standard practice: 'if standard practice was inherently dangerous, it cannot be condoned as sound and rational even though almost everybody does the same'.

The Court of Appeal upheld the High Court's decision. The Court held that it was arguable that the shipping company had created the danger in circumstances where it had chosen to break up the ship in a notoriously unsafe ship-yard:

> [Maran (UK) Ltd] arguably played an active role by sending the vessel to Bangladesh, knowingly exposing workers (such as [Mr Mollah]) to the significant dangers which working on this large vessel in Chattogram entailed ... The [shipbreaking] yard's failure to provide any safety harnesses or any other proper equipment, and the tragic consequences of their not doing so, were entirely predictable. (Paragraph 64)

As a result, the case raises the prospect that liability does not automatically end once a ship or asset is sold. It potentially imposes a novel duty of care on ship owners and other companies *at the time of sale* to consider the foreseeable harm which could be caused by the disposal of assets. This has significant implications for asset disposal and decommissioning activities in high risk industries such as construction, oil and gas and mining and represents an important extension in potential tort liability for human rights and environmental abuses.

ii. Unjust enrichment and British American Tobacco

In 2019 Leigh Day filed a group action on behalf of 2,000 claimants in Malawi, who supply tobacco to British American Tobacco (BAT). The claimants allege that BAT is culpable of 'unjust enrichment'. Specifically, BAT makes vast profits from tobacco which is picked by farmers in Malawi who are effectively forced to work for very little pay under fear, duress, and false pretences and were left no option but to put their children to work on the farms. The claimants are tenant farmers who work on land owned by contract farmers. The contract farmers contract with leaf buyers for the sale of tobacco grown on their land. The tenant farmers are then brought to farm the tobacco that is then sold to the leaf buyers at a price which is effectively set by BAT.

The claimants' total earnings were, on average, no more than £100 to £200 for the work of a family of five for ten months. This is so low that the tenant farmers have no choice but to use their children to farm the land. In addition, the tenant farmers are not provided with any protective equipment for the work and many suffer injuries and illness included Green Tobacco Sickness. Many of the claimants have been threatened with physical violence and financial penalties if they try to leave the farms and they are all heavily dependent on the contract farmers for food, household products, and money throughout the season.

The claimants contend that the defendants have been enriched at the expense of the claimants by obtaining tobacco leaves and agricultural services below true and fair market value. It is claimed that the facts of this case satisfies the legal test for 'unjust enrichment' and accordingly the claim if for loss of property and loss of income. The defendants have issued a strike out application and judgment is pending at the time of writing. If successful, the case will provide a basis for potential supply chain liability in further claims.

IV. Factors relevant to the claims against multinationals

It is important to analyse the four central ingredients of such cases: jurisdiction, applicable law, and procedural rules on discovery and class actions, in order to understand how these cases are brought and the challenges faced by litigants.

A. Jurisdiction and *forum non conveniens*

Prior to Brexit the rules on jurisdiction were governed by Article 4 of the Recast Brussels I Regulation 2012[50] (previously Article 2 of the Brussels I Regulation

[50] Regulation (EU) No. 1215/2012 of the European Parliament and of the Council of 12 December 2012 on jurisdiction and the recognition and enforcement of judgments in civil and commercial matters.

(2001) as interpreted by the ECJ in *Owusu v. Jackson*)[51] which conveys mandatory jurisdiction over legal and natural persons domiciled in the jurisdiction of a Member State, irrespective of the connections of the case with a foreign State. As a result, it was not open to the court to decline jurisdiction.

Since Brexit, the rules on jurisdiction in the United Kingdom are now governed by the common law principle of *forum non conveniens*, the doctrine by which the court has general discretionary power to stay actions where there is clearly another more appropriate jurisdiction to hear the claim.[52] The English Courts deploy a two-stage inquiry as set out in *Spiliada Maritime Corp v. Cansulex Ltd* [1987] AC 460: (i) the appropriate forum and (ii) the requirements of justice. Other common law jurisdictions, including the United States, Canada, and Australia, also employ the doctrine of *forum non conveniens*. The difficulty this has caused is that forum arguments can themselves take years to litigate and defendants can deploy them as a tactical device to exhaust the resources of claimants.[53] The rules on mandatory jurisdiction meant that *forum non conveniens* arguments could not be used to delay litigation. Whether, post Brexit, Britain will remain bound by the private international rules which mirror the Brussels Regulation is unclear. In April 2020, the United Kingdom applied to accede to the 2007 Lugano Convention on jurisdiction and enforcement of judgments which applied between European Free Trade Agreement (EFTA) countries and the European Union and essentially mirrors the Brussels Regulation. If the United Kingdom does become a signatory to the Lugano Convention the mandatory jurisdiction regime will continue to apply. However, in a surprising development the EU Commission has announced that it opposes Britain's accession to Lugano, despite widespread support for accession among member states. At the time of writing, it was unclear how this will be resolved, but it appears that accession to Lugano will be some time off, if it ever takes place. In the meantime, parent company cases are once again governed by the principle of *forum non conveniens*.

In addition, provided the court is satisfied that the claim against the parent company is arguable and that the United Kingdom is the appropriate forum to hear such a case, the claimants can seek to join the foreign subsidiary as a 'necessary or proper party' through the jurisdiction 'gateway'.[54]. Hypothetically, once an English court has joined a foreign subsidiary, even if the case against the parent company ultimately fails at trial, the court will retain jurisdiction over the foreign defendant. *Vedanta* has slightly altered the traditional understanding of the jurisdiction gateway in circumstances where a UK parent company is willing to submit to the

[51] Judgment of the Court (Grand Chamber) of 1 March 2005. *Andrew Owusu v. N. B. Jackson, trading as 'Villa Holidays Bal-Inn Villas' and Others.* Reference for a preliminary ruling: Court of Appeal (England and Wales), Civil Division—United Kingdom (C-281/02); [2005] QB 801.

[52] Cheshire, North, and Fawcett, *Private International Law* (14th edn, 2008) 426.

[53] Meeran (n. 2) 11–12.

[54] Civil Procedure Rules (CPR) 1998, Practice Direction 6B section 3.1(3)(b).

jurisdiction of the foreign defendant, the risk of irreconcilable judgments will no longer be a decisive factor in determining appropriate forum. In those cases, the court would be unlikely to join the foreign subsidiary unless the claimants are able to demonstrate that there is a real risk that they will not be able to access substantial justice in the alternative forum. To that extent, even if Britain does accede to the Lugano Convention, *forum non conveniens* has seen something of a revival if there is an application to join a foreign defendant.

B. Discovery and group actions

England and Wales have onerous rules on disclosure (referred to in many jurisdictions as discovery). The general rule is that once the pleadings in a case are closed the parties must disclose all documents in their possession (pursuant to a reasonable search): (i) on which they rely and (ii) all documents which *adversely affect* or support their case.[55] Unlike many jurisdictions, the disclosure requirement kicks in automatically as part of the preparation for trial and requires no further orders from the court. This is generally an onerous requirement on corporate defendants and one which they are often anxious to avoid. In many cases internal communications emerge from the disclosure, which exposes the defendants' corporate misconduct in vivid and damaging terms. Often significant disputes arise between the parties in litigation as to the scope of any disclosure. Generally, the defendants will try to restrict the disclosure exercise they undertake on the grounds of proportionality and disputes will have to be adjudicated by the court. An important aspect of any disclosure process is electronic disclosure where the relevant custodians, search terms, and search periods are all often the subject of significant dispute. Furthermore, defendants often argue that the accounts of certain critical custodians have been deleted and no back-ups are available, which the claimants will often seek to challenge to ensure that no stone has been left unturned.[56]

Further, the English legal system benefits from a group action regime which permits large-scale claims to be brought on behalf of a large number of claimants in a cost-effective manner. This is an 'opt-in' system, not an 'opt-out' class action system which is found in other jurisdictions such as Australia and Canada. Civil Procedure Rule (CPR) 19.11 allows the court to make a group litigation order and to establish a 'group register' of claimants. The court will proceed to try a selection of 'lead claimants' and any judgment or order is binding on the other claims

[55] CPR 35.6.

[56] For examples of judgments on disclosure see *Vilca & 21 Others v. Xstrata Limited & another* [2016] EWHC 1824; *Rihan v. Ernst and Young Global Ltd* [2020] EWHC 1380 (QB).

that are on the group register. As a result, the trial of the lead cases tends to lead to the settlement of the other claims the register. Instructions must be obtained from every claimant who wishes to 'opt in' to the claim, but it is only the lead claims whose claims need to have witness statements, schedules, and expert reports to be prepared for trial. That in turn allows a large group action to be brought in a costs-effective and efficient manner, which would not be possible if each claimant had to bring a separate claim.

C. Practical challenges, security, and claimant/witness anonymity

The practical challenges of international group claims are considerable. Many of the cases concern claimants from remote and often dangerous regions where travel is difficult. Extensive risk assessments are required for any trip by the lawyers and close liaison with local and international non-governmental organisations (NGOs) who have a deep understanding of the area is critical. Furthermore, remaining in contact with clients once instructions have been obtained is essential and the widespread use of mobile phones in the Global South has rendered this possible, a transformation of the position just ten years ago.

Local governments and Bar associations are often receptive to international claims taking place, but on occasion they seek to disrupt the litigation if it is felt that it adversely affects their own interests. For example, in the *Gemfields* case, after settlement was announced, the Mozambican government prohibited the claimants' legal representatives from seeing their clients in order to distribute the damages. It was claimed that it was up to the Mozambican government to distribute the damages as they saw fit. Fortunately, Leigh Day had opened bank accounts for almost all the claimants and was able to transfer the damages directly, thus bypassing this attempt to stifle the case.

One of the more challenging and troubling issues which arises in international tort claims is the risk of harassment and the targeting of the claimants by the local government or the defendant companies. Routinely, attempts are made to harass and intimidate victims and/or to seek to settle any claims directly with the victims for a fraction of their value by bypassing their legal representatives. In particular, in security and human rights cases where claimants have been subjected to violence by guards and police, the claimants often fear reprisals and victimisation if it became known that they had brought a claim against the company. Equally, witnesses are often hesitant to come forward if their identities were publicly known for fear of victimisation. To mitigate such risks, the procedure rules in England and Wales allow for anonymity orders to ensure that claimants and witnesses' identities are withheld from the public. Such orders are granted if there is cogent evidence that the claimant or witness faces a real risk of harm. In addition, claimants can seek to limit the degree to which their identities freely circulate among the defendant companies and to agree or obtain a confidentiality club. Such an arrangement allows the claimants to disclose their names to a carefully prescribed list of individuals within the defendant companies, which will provide some level of protection from the risk of victimisation.

D. Costs and funding

International group action litigation is lengthy (the cases often run for three to five years) and costly. Disbursements alone in terms of the costs of experts, travel, disclosure costs, and court costs are invariably significant. The claimants are unable to finance any of the litigation costs and legal aid is no longer available in the United Kingdom for civil litigation. So how are these claims financed? In the United Kingdom the claims are brought on the basis of a conditional fee agreement, which allows the legal representatives to claim their costs from the defendant if the litigation succeeds. To ensure the costs are proportionate to the damages claimed such claims are generally only financially viable if they are brought as a group action. If the cohort of claimants is too small the costs of the litigation will generally be disproportionate to the value of the claims, and so unrecoverable.

In addition, the legal representatives are entitled to claim an uplift of from client damages, capped at 25 per cent of general damages. If the claim is lost the legal representatives recover none of their costs, including any disbursements which have been paid out. In addition, the claimant is, in theory, liable for any adverse costs which have been incurred by the Defendant. In the past such adverse costs risks were covered by After the Event Insurance (ATE) but since the reform of the costs regime in 2013, ATE is difficult to obtain.[57] However, the reality is that claimants in such cases have no assets to attach and so any adverse costs order is illusory and unenforceable. As a result, the risk of an adverse costs order is generally one which victims are willing to take in such litigation. A major innovation in recent years is the advent of litigation funding, which allows a third party funder to pay for the costs or a proportion of the costs of litigation in return for a proportion of client damages should the litigation succeed. Funders are showing increasing interest in international tort litigation, including human rights and environmental cases. It is expected that in the future, this will allow a greater range of cases to be brought by lawyers who previously would have had to fund all the costs of the litigation themselves and bear all the associated risk.[58]

[57] Legal Aid, Sentencing and Punishment of Offenders Act 2012 (LASPO).

[58] See Chapter 11 by Lindsay for further information in relation to litigation funding.

V. Conclusion

Transnational tort litigation is an important avenue for 'access to remedy' for human rights abuses by business and the advent of parent company litigation in the United Kingdom is novel and has seen important victories. The relative success of parent company liability and other cases in England has led some commentators to postulate that a similar approach should be adopted by lawyers in other jurisdictions.[59] However, there are significant limitations to parent company liability as highlighted by the recent parent company liability litigation. First, whether a duty of care arises depends on the nature of the corporate relationship in question in each particular case. As the recent case law from England demonstrates, the test is inevitably contextual and fact sensitive and it will depend on the degree of control or involvement by the parent company with respect to the operations of its subsidiary. The *Vedanta/Shell* principles are a long way from imposing a generalised due diligence requirement on parent companies as envisaged by the UNGPs[60] and will do little to hold corporations to account which profit from the activities of their subsidiaries but take an entirely 'hands off' approach.[61]

Second, and related, the precise nature of the relationship between the parent company and its subsidiary and whether there is sufficient control or direction to give rise to an 'assumption of responsibility' is often difficult to discern. Often there is insufficient information in the public domain for claimant lawyers to determine whether a claim has merit. By definition, only the companies themselves know the precise nature of the relationship between parent and subsidiary and yet, as in *Unilever*, claimants face the prospect of their case being dismissed at an early stage of the litigation, prior to obtaining the necessary disclosure which would reveal the reality of the situation.[62] The Supreme Court judgment in *Shell* makes it much less likely that such strike out arguments will succeed at the jurisdiction stage but this will not prevent defendant companies from attempting to do so, thus delaying the substantive litigation and the prospect of troublesome disclosure.

Third, parent company liability may have the effect of actually creating a perverse incentive on parent companies to exercise *less* control and direction over their subsidiaries rather than more, for fear that such involvement could give rise

[59] See D. Palombo, '*Chandler v Cape plc*: An Alternative to Piercing the Corporate Veil beyond *Kiobel v Royal Dutch Shell*' (2015) 4 *British Journal of American Legal Studies* 453, 460–2 and M. Goldhaber, 'Corporate Human Rights Litigation in Non-U.S. Courts: A Comparative Scorecard' (2013) 3 *University of California Irvine Law Review*, 127.

[60] See Chapter 1.V.

[61] See G. Skinner, 'Rethinking Limited Liability of Parent Corporations for Foreign Subsidiaries' Violations of International Human Rights Law' (2015) 72 *Washington and Lee Law Review* 1769, 1841–6 and C. Witting and J. Rankin, 'Tortious Liability of Corporate Groups: From Control to Coordination' (2014) 22 *Tort Law Review* 91–104.

[62] M.B. Taylor, R.C. Thompson, and A. Ramasastry, 'Overcoming obstacles to justice: Improving Access to Judicial Remedies for Business Involvement in Grave Human Rights Abuses' (Report) (2021) Fafo-report 2010, 21, 10–11.

to civil liability. Such perverse incentives run contrary to the due diligence requirements of the UNGPs. The *Vedanta* and *Shell* judgments increase the prospect that a parent company could be held liable solely on the basis of its group-wide human rights or environmental policy, particularly if it takes an active role in the implementation of that policy across its subsidiaries and incentives corporations to pull back from their human rights commitments.[63]

Overall, the parent company liability principle and other innovative tort claims which have been brought, represent an important legal innovation that goes some way to circumventing corporate structure as a barrier to access to remedy. However, as the claims which have failed illustrate, they can only apply to certain situations and cannot amount to a complete answer to the corporate impunity and the challenge presented by the UNGPs. Therefore, there is considerable debate as to what legislative reforms (such as emerging human rights due diligence laws across the globe) could further reduce the barriers to parent company liability and the corporate accountability gap.

[63] See A. Sanders, 'The Impact of the "Ruggie Framework" and the United Nations Guiding Principles on Business and Human Rights on Transnational Human Rights Litigation' in J. Martin and K. Bravo (eds), *Business and Human Rights: Moving Forward and Looking Back* (2015) 19–20.

4
Multinational Company Litigation
South Africa

Jason Brickhill and Zanele Mbuyisa

I. Introduction

Former President Thabo Mbeki famously characterised South Africa as 'two nations', one white and wealthy and the second, larger nation black and poor, living under 'conditions of a grossly underdeveloped economic, physical, educational, communication and other infrastructure.'[1] This persisting duality defines both the inner workings of the South African economy and legal system and South Africa's international trade and investment relations. It provides the context for multinational company (MNC) litigation in (and in relation to) South Africa.

Domestically, South Africa is among the world's most unequal societies with a high unemployment rate and a large proportion of the population living below the poverty line. At the same time, it has a highly developed and sophisticated economy, banking system, legal system, and legal profession, which primarily serve the economic elite located in the major cities.

Internationally, South Africa is both a major destination for foreign direct investment (FDI) and a source of investment into other countries, in particular elsewhere in Africa. This is reflected in the dichotomous set of bilateral investment treaties (BITs) concluded by South Africa, mostly in the 1990s shortly after achieving democratic rule in 1994. South Africa has concluded approximately 40 BITs, some with developed nations in Europe and others with developing countries such as Zimbabwe.[2]

The South African courts are regarded as strong and independent, having achieved major success in transforming from an all-white, illegitimate judiciary inherited in 1994 to a broadly representative bench.[3] The judiciary is increasingly

[1] T. Mbeki, 'Statement of Deputy President at the Opening of the Debate in the National Assembly on "Reconciliation and Nation Building' National Assembly, Cape Town, 29 May 1998.

[2] J. Brickhill and M. Du Plessis, 'Two's Company, Three's a Crowd: Public Interest Intervention in Investor-State Arbitration (Piero Foresti v South Africa)' (2011) 27 *South African Journal on Human Rights* 152, 154.

[3] C. Hoexter and M. Olivier, *The Judiciary in South Africa* (2014).

Jason Brickhill and Zanele Mbuyisa, *Multinational Company Litigation* In: *Human Rights Litigation against Multinationals in Practice*. Edited by: Richard Meeran, Oxford University Press. © The Several Contributors 2021.
DOI: 10.1093/oso/9780198866220.003.0004

staffed by judges familiar with the Constitution. It is among the world's most receptive jurisdictions to public interest litigation and novel legal claims, epitomised by the successful certification of the massive, complex, multi-defendant silicosis class action brought against all the major players in the gold mining industry.[4] However, as we describe below, South Africa also restricts and regulates damages, costs, contingency fees, and litigation funding in significant ways, and these constraints are also reflected to some extent in judicial attitudes to high-value, for-profit litigation.

Undoubtedly the most significant MNC litigation conducted in South Africa since the transition to democracy (and indeed before) is the litigation by former gold miners who had contracted the lung disease, silicosis. The silicosis litigation took many forms, and several different plaintiff groups and legal actors became involved. It included test case damages claims, arbitration proceedings, and class action proceedings. The actors included a public interest law centre and local and foreign law firms. The litigation both tested the potential of the existing law for complex, high-value MNC litigation, and developed the law in important respects for future cases. It was largely successful. As a result, the silicosis litigation provides an important source of precedent and illustration for this chapter. We therefore briefly describe here the genesis and unfolding course of the silicosis litigation. In the body of the chapter below, we return at various points to specific judgments and events in the litigation.

The silicosis litigation began with *Blom & Others v. Anglo American South Africa Limited* (*Blom*).[5] The *Blom* test cases were brought by 23 ex-gold mine workers who alleged that because of their occupation at an Anglo American managed and controlled mine (President Steyn), they contracted the debilitating and incurable illness, silicosis. The case was brought as a test case with the aim of establishing the liability of Anglo American South Africa Ltd, and the gold mining industry more broadly, and to lay down the general principles to govern future claims. These cases require a lot of resources as well as finances and take long periods of time to conclude. Since this type of case had never been brought before, a collaboration between a UK law firm, Leigh Day Solicitors (Leigh Day), and the Legal Resources Centre (LRC), was entered. The LRC were the attorneys of record in the matters and Leigh Day acted as consultants, given Leigh Day's specialist experience and skills and given the scale of the litigation. During the period when the *Blom* test cases were running, the parties agreed to have the matter arbitrated in order to expedite it. The matter was settled in 2012, having taken eight years to finalise from

[4] *Nkala and Others v. Harmony Gold Mining Company Limited and Others* [2016] ZAGPJHC 97; 2016 (7) BCLR 881 (GJ); 2016 (5) SA 240 (GJ) (*Silicosis Certification*). Jason Brickhill acted for the applicants.

[5] Case no. 18267/04, Witwatersrand Local Division of the High Court of South Africa.

the date of issue in court and nine years from the date of instruction. The terms of the settlement remain confidential but it may be disclosed that the settlement entailed the defendant making payments to each plaintiff. After *Blom*, the silicosis litigation took two main forms: class action proceedings and massed individual claims, both of which were successful.

Roughly coinciding with the *Blom* settlement, a series of class actions was launched against different gold mining companies by three firms: the LRC, Richard Spoor Attorneys and Abrahams Kiewitz Attorneys.[6] Ultimately, upon the LRC's proposal, these class actions were consolidated into a single, massive multi-defendant class action by all three firms. This class action was unprecedented in scale and complexity in South Africa (and arguably comparatively), being brought against all the major players in the gold mining industry in respect of almost 100 different mines for their conduct over the course of half a century.[7] The class action was certified by a full bench of the High Court[8] and, in a subsequent round of proceedings, the same bench approved a settlement.[9] The settlement scheme established a trust to which the participating defendants were required to contribute R5 billion, with the possibility of top-up contributions being required if the initial sum is exhausted by claims.

Shortly after the *Blom* settlement, in 2012, 4500 ex-mine workers brought a claim against Anglo Gold Ashanti Limited in *Qubeka & Others v. Anglo Gold Ashanti Limited* (*Qubeka*).[10] *Qubeka* was a collaboration between Mbuyisa Neale Attorneys (MN), a South African law firm, and Leigh Day. MN were the attorneys of record and Leigh Day again acted as consultants. Without these collaborations, it would have been near impossible to litigate against these MNCs. In *Qubeka*, a decision was taken not to pursue the class action route but rather to issue the claims individually. It was thought at the time that this was in the best interest of the clients who at the time were old, ill, and dying. The *Qubeka* legal representatives took the view that going through the class action route may have delayed the clients getting compensation during their lifetime. *Qubeka* was settled in 2015 for total of R500 million and the Q(h)ubeka Trust was established to distribute the compensation to the claimants.

[6] Richard Spoor Inc and Abrahams Kiewitz Attorneys were funded and supported in the litigation by international firms Motley Rice LLC and Hausfeld, respectively.

[7] See generally, J. Brickhill and J. Bleazard, 'Bill of Rights Class Actions' in M. du Plessis, J. Oxenham, I. Goodman, et al. (eds), *Class Action Litigation in South Africa* (2017) 58–78.

[8] *Gold Fields Limited and Others v. Motley Rice LLC, In re: Nkala v. Harmony Gold Mining Company Limited and Others* [2015] ZAGPJHC 62; 2015 (4) SA 299 (GJ).

[9] *Nkala and Others v. Harmony Gold Mining Company Limited and Others* [2016] ZAGPJHC 97; (GJ); 2016 (7) BCLR 881 (GJ); 2016 (5) SA 240 (GJ).

[10] Case no. 2012/44831 Witwatersrand Local Division of the High Court of South Africa.

II. Jurisdiction and applicable law

A. The hierarchy of the courts

The South African judiciary is structured as follows:

- The Constitutional Court is the highest court of the land.[11] It has jurisdiction in constitutional matters and, following an amendment to the Constitution,[12] in 'any other matter, if the Constitutional Court grants leave to appeal on the grounds that the matter raises an arguable point of law of general public importance which ought to be considered by that Court'.[13]
- The Supreme Court of Appeal (SCA) is an intermediate appellate court that hears appeals from the High Court and courts of a similar status to the High Court.[14]
- High Courts are the courts of first instance and also have jurisdiction to hear appeals from the Magistrates' Courts and from single-judge High Court decisions.[15] High courts in South Africa have inherent jurisdiction. They do not derive their powers from statute alone. The statute that governs the High Courts is the Superior Courts Act 10 of 2013.
- Magistrates' Courts are courts of first instance and are creatures of statute.[16]

In South Africa, when a claim is brought against an MNC, the claim will ordinarily be issued at the relevant High Court division in the country. The losing side can appeal to the SCA and then to the Constitutional Court.

B. Jurisdiction

Jurisdiction refers to the authority or the competence of a particular court to hear a matter which has been brought before it and to grant the relief in respect of that matter.[17] Four general principles are relevant in determining jurisdiction in civil matters, which are likely to apply to claims against MNCs: (i) *Actor sequitur*

[11] Constitution, section 167.
[12] Constitution Seventeenth Amendment Act 72 of 2012.
[13] See Chapter 2, 'Jurisdiction' in M. du Plessis, G. Penfold, and J. Brickhill, *Constitutional Litigation* (2013). For the test employed by the court to grant leave in non-constitutional matters, see *Paulsen and Another v. Slip Knot Investments 777 (Pty) Limited* [2015] ZACC 5; 2015 (3) SA 479 (CC); 2015 (5) BCLR 509 (CC).
[14] Constitution, section 168.
[15] Constitution, section 169.
[16] Magistrates' Courts Act 32 of 1944.
[17] C. Theophilopoulos, A.W.T. Rowan, C.M. van Heerden, et al., *Fundamental Principles of Civil Procedure* (2015) 37.

forum rei; (ii) the principle of effectiveness; (iii) convenience; and (iv) consent to jurisdiction.

i. *Actor sequitur forum rei*

The general principle here is that when instituting proceedings, the plaintiff must follow the defendant to the defendant's forum and institute proceedings there.

ii. The principle of effectiveness

The court will assume jurisdiction in matters where judgment can be given effect. This means that the defendant or their property must be located within the court's area of jurisdiction. The concept of effectiveness does not require that a court be fully able to enforce its judgment, it simply requires that the judgment has the potential to be enforced.[18]

This issue was raised in *Vedanta Resources Holdings Limited v. ZCCM Investment Holdings*.[19] The parties were *peregrini*, the applicant registered in England and the first respondent registered in Zambia. The parties had an existing shareholders' agreement, which included an arbitration clause providing that, in the event of a dispute between the shareholders, the dispute would be referred to arbitration and that the arbitration would be held in Johannesburg, South Africa. The first respondent argued that the matter was *lis pendens* in the Zambian High Court, in which the applicant had applied for similar relief. It argued further that the South African court should refrain from giving orders that have extra territorial effect and that cannot be given effect to the effectiveness doctrine. The court dismissed the plea of *lis pendens*. On the doctrine of effectiveness, the court held that if the disputes were arbitral disputes, then it would have jurisdiction. The court found that the arbitration clause of the shareholders agreement was sufficient connection with the court to give it jurisdiction.

In *Bid Industrial Holdings (Pty) Ltd v. Strang and Another*,[20] the court held that where effectiveness is not strictly satisfied but there is a sufficient link between the suit and South Africa, effectiveness may assume a lesser role and it will be acceptable for the plaintiff to grapple with the consequences that the judgment that they have obtained may turn out to be ineffective.

iii. Convenience

Jurisdiction will be assumed if it is convenient for the court to do so, for instance that the cause of action arose within the area of its jurisdiction. An example of this is when a cause of action arises from a contract, the court of the area in which the

[18] Ibid., 38.

[19] Unreported decision of the South Gauteng High Court, Johannesburg, case no. 2019/234462, judgment on file with authors.

[20] *Bid Industrial Holdings (Pty) Ltd v. Strang and Another* 2008 (3) SA 355 (SCA).

contract was concluded or in which performance was to have taken place will have jurisdiction.[21] It is convenient because the evidence and witnesses will mostly be physically present and/or resident in that area of jurisdiction.

iv. Consent

Even where the requirements for jurisdiction are not met, a court will have jurisdiction in a civil claim if the defendant consents to the court's jurisdiction.[22] The consent must be expressly conferred, but it may also be inferred when the defendant fails to act.[23] Consent is not sufficient to confer jurisdiction in all cases. Where the court has no basis to assume jurisdiction, that is where there is no jurisdictional link at all between the court and the matter, consent whether express or tacit will not be effective.[24]

C. Foreign *peregrini* and juristic persons

A foreign *peregrinus* is a person domiciled or resident outside South Africa and therefore a foreigner to its courts.[25] A foreign juristic person will be regarded as resident in South Africa if it has its principal place of business in South Africa, or a branch office from where it carries on its business, and the cause of action arose from the activities of that branch.[26]

This area of the law is important for MNC litigation. As we discussed in the introduction, South Africa has a dual identity in that it has South African companies operating in other countries as well as foreign multinationals who have a base in South Africa. An example of the former would be Anglo Gold Ashanti, which is headquartered in Johannesburg but has global operations. An example of the latter is Cargill Cotton Ginners Ltd, mentioned above. Cargill operates in several countries around the world and is registered as a local South African company with 100 per cent shareholding held by its ultimate holding company outside of South Africa. Other MNCs used to have a huge presence globally but have scaled down and exited some countries, and with their exit have left behind damage for which they could be found liable. Anglo American South Africa Limited (AASA), for example, used to operate in several countries in the African continent. One of the countries that they had presence in, until 2002 when they exited completely, was Zambia. A class action certification application has been issued against AASA on behalf of individuals living in the District of Kabwe, Zambia who have suffered

21 Theophilopoulos, Rowan, van Heerden, et al. (n. 17) 39.
22 Ibid.
23 Ibid.
24 Ibid.
25 Ibid., 41.
26 *Fleet Africa (Pty) Ltd v. Gargill Cotton Ginners Ltd* 2010, JDR 1253 (GSJ).

harm from elevated lead exposure in two categories: children, and women over 18 and under 50 who have fallen and can fall pregnant. They allege that AASA was responsible for the creation of an environmental disaster from the operations at the Broken Hill Development Company (Broken Hill), a lead mine which was allegedly managed and controlled by AASA for most of the period of its operations. As a result of the environmental disaster, they are suffering from lead poisoning. The class action application was issued in the South Africa where AASA is domiciled and headquartered. Anglo American no longer has a presence in Zambia. Zambian law will apply to the case. The outcome of the certification application will have wider implications for South African MNCs with foreign operations.

D. Arbitration

Arbitration is recognised in South Africa, governed broadly by the Arbitration Act 42 of 1965 and common law. The International Arbitration Act 15 of 2017 incorporates the UN Commissions on International Trade Law (UNCITRAL) Model Law into South African law. This also facilitated the enforcement of international awards in South Africa.

As prominent examples of MNC litigation being conducted by arbitration, the parties in the *Blom* test case silicosis litigation and the subsequent *Qubeka* silicosis claims opted for arbitration. One of the main reasons for this was the need to get the matters finalised. The silicosis claimants in both cases were advanced in age and very ill. It was important that they receive their compensation, if they won, during their lifetimes. Ultimately, both sets of cases were settled and the claimants did receive compensation. Court systems get clogged up and it becomes difficult for the court to assign a judge to specific cases that run for long periods of time. South Africa has several extremely qualified senior counsel and retired judges who can be appointed as arbitrators and adjudicate matters adequately and quickly.

The parties to the agreement must enter into an arbitration agreement. The agreement is likely to stipulate:

- the disagreement between the parties;
- the appointment of adjudicators or arbitrators;
- the powers and jurisdiction of the arbitrator;
- the venue;
- procedures;
- costs of the proceedings;
- recording the proceedings;
- appeal, if any, and appeal procedure;
- confidentiality, if applicable.

Arbitrations are mostly used for commercial disputes and are often confidential. However, this may be inappropriate for some MNC litigation, in which it may be important that the public and media have access to proceedings and evidence. In both silicosis arbitrations, *Blom* and *Qubeka*, the proceedings were to be public, and anyone could attend. In addition, the corporate defendants agreed to fund the arbitration process (the fees of arbitrators' and the costs of venue and transcription of hearings, etc.).

Though arbitration can be used as an alternative to court process, it may not secure access to justice for poor individuals or communities because of the costs and because confidentiality could be perceived as shielding the MNCs.

III. Causes of action

South Africa has a historically 'mixed' legal system, with its common law roots in Roman-Dutch law and English law. Under apartheid it had a system of parliamentary supremacy, replaced with constitutional supremacy governed by the Constitution of the Republic of South Africa, 1996. The Constitution preserves the common law but requires that it be developed to promote the spirit, purport, and objects of the Bill of Rights. The Bill of Rights is also directly applicable in some cases, including horizontally as between private actors. The Constitution infuses all law in South Africa and no litigation may sensibly be contemplated without considering the constitutional implications.

As a result, possible causes of action in multinational litigation in civil matters include constitutional claims, common law claims such as delict (tort), contract, or unjustified enrichment (including the development of the common law to give effect to the Constitution), and statutory claims.

A. Constitutional claims

The rights in the Bill of Rights apply horizontally—that is, against private actors—directly in at least some circumstances. In addition, the courts have recognised that it is competent to award 'constitutional damages' as a remedy for rights violations, albeit in extraordinary circumstances. Section 8(2) of the Constitution provides that '[a] provision of the Bill of Rights binds a natural or a juristic person if, and to the extent that it is applicable, taking into account the nature of the right and the nature of any duty imposed by the right'. Section 8(3) then provides that,

> When applying a provision of the Bill of Rights to a natural or juristic person in terms of subsection (2), a court

a. in order to give effect to a right in the Bill, must apply, or if necessary develop, the common law to the extent that legislation does not give effect to that right; and

b. may develop rules of the common law to limit the right, provided that the limitation is in accordance with section 36(1).

Despite the Constitution providing expressly for the direct horizontal application of the Bill of Rights, the courts have opted in almost all cases to apply the Constitution indirectly.[27] They employ section 39(2), which provides that '[w]hen interpreting any legislation, and when developing the common law or customary law, every court, tribunal or forum must promote the spirit, purport and objects of the Bill of Rights'.[28] However, the courts have applied rights directly against private persons in some recent cases, including in the context of the obligations of a private company with a monopoly over billboard advertising to respect the right to freedom of expression;[29] and, most significantly, in a recent Constitutional Court decision[30] holding that a private school's decision to remove children in terms of the school's contract with the parents implicates the right to education and the best interests of the child.[31]

The courts have also recognised the power to award *constitutional* damages in exceptional circumstances. The Constitutional Court first recognised the possibility of constitutional damages in *Fose*.[32] Since then, there have been only two successful claims for constitutional damages, in the context of a landowner's claim against the State when the scale of unlawful occupation of land made eviction impossible, and in a recent private arbitration decided by former Deputy Chief Justice Moseneke concerning right to health and right to life violations resulting from the State closing down psychiatric facilities. Despite being an arbitration award, the *Life Esidimeni* decision is likely to serve as powerful and persuasive precedent in future cases on constitutional damages given the identity of the arbitrator and the fact that the decision is carefully and fully reasoned on this point. Another high-profile claim for constitutional damages in *Komape*, arising out of the death of a primary school child who drowned in a collapsed school toilet, failed in the Supreme Court of Appeal[33] and is still on appeal to the Constitutional Court.

27 S. Woolman 'The Amazing, Vanishing Bill of Rights' (2007) 124 *South African Law Journal* 762.

28 Section 29(1)(a) of the Constitution.

29 *Boycott, Divestment and Sanctions South Africa and Another v. Continental Outdoor Media (Pty) Ltd and Others* [2014] ZAGPJHC 200; 2015 (1) SA 462 (GJ); [2014] 4 All SA 347 (GJ). Jason Brickhill appeared for the applicants in this matter.

30 *AB and Another v. Pridwin Preparatory School and Others* [2020] ZACC 12; 2020 (9) BCLR 1029 (CC); 2020 (5) SA 327 (CC).

31 Section 28(2) of the Constitution.

32 *Fose v. Minister of Safety and Security* [1997] ZACC 6; 1997 (7) BCLR 851; 1997 (3) SA 786 (CC).

33 *R K and Others v. Minister of Basic Education and Others* [2019] ZASCA 192; [2020] 1 All SA 651 (SCA); 2020 (2) SA 347 (SCA).

B. The constitutional impact on the common law

Although there have been some notable instances of the direct horizontal application of the Bill of Rights, the Constitution's most pervasive impact on the private law has been its indirect application. In the law of contract, the Constitution infuses and gives content to 'public policy'.[34] A court may invalidate a contractual clause if it is contrary to public policy or may decline to enforce it if, in the circumstances, enforcement would be contrary to public policy. In the law of delict, constitutional values similarly inform the wrongfulness inquiry.[35] Given that MNC litigation often raises novel questions of law and attempts to establish liability for the first time in particular situations, the Constitution is likely to bear significantly on such disputes.

C. Common law claims: delict, contract, and unjustified enrichment

A claim for damages in South African law is based on the law of delict. If a party brings a delictual claim against another, the following elements of a delict must be present and proven in their claim for the other party to be found liable:

- Commission or omission of an act;
- Wrongfulness;
- Fault;
- Causation;
- Damage.

The law of delict determines the circumstances in which a person is obliged to bear the damage they have caused another.[36] The law of damages then determines how the existence and extent of damage as well as the proper amount of damages or satisfaction are to be determined.[37] The law of delict and damages fall under the part of private law that is the law of obligations, alongside the law of contract and unjustified enrichment. While there will often be a contractual context underpinning MNC litigation, most claims are likely to be in delict.

[34] *Barkhuizen v. Napier* [2007] ZACC 5; 2007 (5) SA 323 (CC); 2007 (7) BCLR 691 (CC).

[35] *Carmichele v. Minister of Safety and Security* [2001] ZACC 22; 2001 (4) SA 938 (CC); 2001 (10) BCLR 995 (CC); *K v. Minister of Safety and Security* [2005] ZACC 8; 2005 (6) SA 419 (CC); 2005 (9) BCLR 835 (CC); [2005] 8 BLLR 749 (CC); *F v. Minister of Safety and Security and Another* [2011] ZACC 37; 2012 (1) SA 536 (CC); 2012 (3) BCLR 244 (CC); (2012) 33 ILJ 93 (CC); 2013 (2) SACR 20 (CC).

[36] J. Neethling, J.M. Potgieter, and P.J. Visser, *Law of Delict* (7th edn, 2016) 3.

[37] P.J. Visser and J.M. Potgieter, *Law of Damages* (3rd edn, 2012) 1.

A key question in that context is parent company liability. South African courts have yet to impose delictual liability against a parent company for harm suffered by the employees of its subsidiary company as a result of unsafe working conditions. However, such a claim is legally tenable and the courts are likely to be influenced by English law.[38] Parent company liability was recognised in the United Kingdom in *Chandler v. Cape Plc*,[39] where:

> (1) the businesses of the parent and subsidiary are in a relevant respect the same; (2) the parent has, or ought to have, superior knowledge on some relevant aspect of health and safety in the particular industry; (3) the subsidiary's system of work is unsafe as the parent company knew, or ought to have known; and (4) the parent knew or ought to have foreseen that the subsidiary or its employees would rely on its using that superior knowledge for the employees' protection… [I]t is not necessary to show that the parent is in the practice of intervening in the health and safety policies of the subsidiary.[40]

Chandler recognised that the duty of care owed by the parent company to the employee of a subsidiary is not identical to the duty owed by the subsidiary itself,[41] and that the duty does not require the parent company to have 'absolute control of the subsidiary'.[42] The duty is based on the assumption (or 'attachment')[43] of responsibility by the parent company. This is determined having regard to the relationship between the companies and their mode of operation; the parent company's knowledge of the safety risks to which the subsidiary's employees are exposed (or that the parent ought to have such knowledge); the parent company's knowledge as regards managing health and safety risks in the industry.[44]

In *Thompson v. The Renwick Group Plc*,[45] the Court confirmed that liability follows 'where it is found that the parent company assumed a duty of care to employees of its subsidiary in health and safety matters',[46] and noted that the circumstances described in *Chandler* were not exhaustive of the circumstances in which a duty may be imposed.[47] The Court further interpreted *Chandler* as an application of

[38] The English law is discussed in more detail in Chapter 3 by Leader.

[39] *Chandler v. Cape plc* [2012] EWCA Civ 525; [2012] 1 WLR 3111; [2012] 3 All ER 640 (per Arden LJ, with Moses LJ and McFarlane LJ concurring).

[40] Ibid., para. 80.

[41] Ibid., paras 65 and 69.

[42] Ibid., para. 66.

[43] The Court noted at para. 64 that '[w]hether a party has assumed responsibility is a question of law. The court does not have to find that the relevant party has voluntarily assumed responsibility… The word "assumption" is therefore something of a misnomer. The phrase "attachment" of responsibility might be more accurate.'

[44] *Chandler v. Cape plc* [2012] EWCA Civ 525; [2012] 1 WLR 3111; [2012] 3 All ER 640, paras 77–80.

[45] *Thompson v. The Renwick Group Plc* [2014] EWCA Civ 635; [2014] PIQR P18.

[46] Ibid., para. 24.

[47] Ibid., para. 33.

the general threefold test for the establishment of a new duty of care, enunciated in *Caparo Industries plc v. Dickman.*[48] Under *Caparo*, a new duty of care will be established where (i) the harm incurred is reasonably foreseeable; (ii) there is a relationship of 'proximity' between the party owing the duty and the party to whom it is owed; and (iii) the court is satisfied that, given the particular circumstances, it is fair, just, and reasonable to impose a duty.[49]

Lungowe & Others v. Vedanta Resources & Another confirmed that there is no special doctrine of 'parent company liability', but that liability arises on the same basis as liability ordinarily arises in tort for acts of a third party.[50] Liability can arise where a parent company seeks to control, supervise, or advise its subsidiary.[51] The court resisted attempts to shoehorn liability into specific categories, such as control of management or negligent advice.[52] The court also rejected the argument that a parent company is insulated from liability simply because it has set out policies for its subsidiaries to follow and that it expected them to be followed.[53]

In determining whether wrongfulness (or a legal duty) exists, South African courts have recognised a multiplicity of relevant factors,[54] including the defendant's control over a dangerous property or situation; the particular relationship between the parties; whether reasonable reliance was placed on the defendant's expertise, representations, or undertakings; the defendant's knowledge of and foreseeability of harm; the applicable constitutional and statutory duties; and whether other considerations of public policy favour imposing liability.[55]

In applying these factors, South African courts have extended liability for pure economic loss caused by negligent misstatement[56] and negligent advice.[57] There is no reason in principle why, like any other legal entity or person, a parent company which is responsible for, in control of, or has special knowledge and expertise that are relied on in respect of its subsidiary company operations and working conditions, should not be liable for harm arising from those operations and conditions.[58] Parent company liability was argued on behalf of the plaintiffs in the silicosis class action broadly on the basis of the principles outlined above, drawing in particular

48 *Caparo Industries plc v. Dickman* [1990] 2 AC 605.

49 Ibid., at 618.

50 *Lungowe & Others v. Vedanta Resources & Another* [2019] UKSC 20 paras 36–37.

51 Ibid., para. 49.

52 Ibid., para. 51.

53 Ibid., paras 52–53.

54 See, generally, J. Neethling, J.M. Potgieter, and P.J. Visser, *Law of Delict* (5th edn, 2006) 49–70.

55 For example, in *Loureiro and Others v. Imvula Quality Protection (Pty) Ltd* 2014 (3) SA 394 (CC) para. 56, the Constitutional Court found that there were 'ample public-policy reasons' in favour of imposing delictual liability on private security guards for negligence.

56 *Bayer South Africa (Pty) Ltd v. Frost* 1991 (4) SA 559 (A) 574J-575D; *Standard Chartered Bank of Canada v. Nedperm Bank Ltd* 1994 (4) SA 747 (A).

57 *Durr v. ABSA Bank Ltd and Another* 1997 (3) SA 448 (SCA).

58 See also *Silva's Fishing Corporation (Pty) Ltd v. Maweza* 1957 (2) SA 256 (A), which was cited with approval in the silicosis arbitration award in *Daniel Mosola v. Anglo American South Africa Ltd*, 20 February 2015.

from English law on the question. The certifying court broadly accepted that parent company liability constituted a common issue of law giving rise to a triable cause of action.[59]

D. Statutory claims

Legislation is likely to feature in most MNC claims, either as part of the legal context giving rise to a claim or, more directly, as the source of a legal duty underpinning a claim. For example, in the silicosis class action, the class action plaintiffs relied on the Mine Health and Safety Act 29 of 1996, alleging that mining companies had breached their legal duties under the statute and that this gave rise to a claim in delict. Legislation is likely to play a significant role in MNC litigation involving environmental law, where statutes such as the National Environmental Management Act 107 of 1998 and the Environment Conservation Act 73 of 1989 impose wide-ranging duties on private actors. Finally, South Africa's administrative law is now embodied in statute, through the Promotion of Administrative Justice Act 3 of 2000 (PAJA). PAJA defines administrative action in section 1 in terms that may bring within its ambit the decisions of some private actors if they exercise a public power or perform a public function. Section 8 of PAJA empowers courts to grant various remedies in administrative reviews, including the award of compensation 'in exceptional cases' in terms of section 8(1)(c)(ii)(bb).

IV. Access to justice and legal representation

A. Availability of legal representation

South Africa has a sophisticated and diversified legal profession. Historically, South Africa maintained a 'split bar', with attorneys and advocates admitted, regulated, and practising separately. The Legal Practice Act 28 of 2014 brought the two branches of the profession under a single statute and under a single governing structure, the Legal Practice Council, but several legal distinctions remain and, in practice, the split bar continues. As a result, it is necessary to engage attorneys and instruct them, in turn, to brief counsel.

In a high-value or complex claim, senior counsel will usually be briefed to lead the team. The crucial considerations in selecting a legal team are relevant experience, specialist expertise in the relevant areas of law, and the need for the legal team to be broadly representative. The Johannesburg Bar has a rule of professional

59 *Silicosis Certification*, para. 71.

conduct that provides that it is unprofessional conduct for a member to accept a brief involving three or more counsel where no member of the team is Black.[60]

The attorneys' profession is layered and varied, serving the legal needs of a complex market. A set of large commercial firms generally acts for major companies, while medium-size and small firms, including sole practitioners, act for smaller businesses and individuals. Foreign firms may act as consultants to local firms, though they may not institute proceedings or sign legal process.

In addition to commercial actors, the public interest law sector consisting of over ten organisations provides legal assistance to poor individuals and communities.[61] The LRC, in particular, has been involved in most of the class actions so far instituted in South Africa. While some of these organisations are generalist, the majority specialise in particular areas of law.

B. Right to civil legal aid and availability

Section 34 of the Constitution provides for the right of access to courts, which includes the right to a 'fair hearing' in civil matters. This right both protects private litigants' choice of legal representative and, where the absence of legal representation would deprive them of a fair hearing, imposes a duty on the State to provide civil legal aid.[62] The State's legal duty to provide legal aid in criminal and civil matters falls on Legal Aid South Africa (LASA). In practice, LASA heavily prioritises criminal legal aid, but it does provide some civil legal aid and, in high-impact matters, may fund other attorneys to litigate. This may be a prospect in future MNC litigation conducted on behalf of poor communities.

V. Prescription and time bars

A. Prescription

Prescription or Limitation in South Africa is governed by the Prescription Act 68 of 1969.

For the purposes of this chapter, we will concentrate on section 11(d) and section 12(3)

[60] Resolution adopted at the Annual General Meeting of the Johannesburg Society of Advocates, 29 October 2015.

[61] J. Brickhill 'Introduction: The Past, Present and Promise of Public Interest Litigation in South Africa' in J. Brickhill (ed.), *Public Interest Litigation in South Africa* (2018) 16–36.

[62] *Magidiwana v. President of the Republic of South Africa* [2014] 1 All SA 76 (GNP) para. 37; *Legal Aid South Africa v. Magidiwana* 2015 (6) SA 494 (CC) para. 22. See J. Brickhill and C. Grobler 'The Right to Civil Legal Aid in South Africa: Legal Aid South Africa v Magidiwana' 2016 (8) *Constitutional Court Review*, 256–81.

Section 11 deals with the prescription of debts and subsection (d):

> The periods of prescription of debts shall be the following ... save where an Act of Parliament provides otherwise, three years in respect of any other debt.

Through acquisitive prescription, a person may acquire rights when they have been in possession of a thing openly and as if they were the owner for an uninterrupted period of 30 years. They can also acquire extinction rights through prescription; when the creditor neglects to exercise their claim to a debt for a period, then the debt becomes extinct. Prescription becomes an issue in the enforcement of foreign judgments, where there is a conflict of laws.

B. The approach of the courts when there is a conflict of laws

According to the principles of South African private international law, matters of procedure are governed by the domestic law of the country in which the relevant proceedings are instituted (the *lex fori*). Matters of substantive law, however, are governed by the law that applies to the underlying transaction or occurrence (the *lex causae*). In South African law, prescription is regarded as substantive. Therefore, a South African court seised with the question of whether a claim to the enforcement of a foreign judgment has prescribed will apply the relevant foreign law.[63]

A distinction has traditionally been drawn, in both South African and English law, between two kinds of prescription/limitation statutes: those which extinguish a right, on the one hand, and those which merely bar a remedy by imposing a procedural bar on the institution of an action to enforce the right or to take steps in execution pursuant to a judgment, on the other.[64]

In applying the test, the court held that:

- prescription is substantive in terms of the *lex fori*;
- prescription is procedural in terms of the *lex causae*;
- considerations of policy, international harmony of decisions, justice, and convenience must be resolved by dealing with the question of prescription in terms of the *lex causae*. This was so because the contract in terms of which the defendants had been sued in the English court were governed by English law and because the English law was also the system that had the closest and most real connection with the question of prescription.

[63] *Society of Lloyds v. Price; Society of Lloyds v. Lee* (5) SA 393 (SCA).
[64] Ibid.

Section 12 of the Prescription Act deals with when prescription begins to run and subsection (3) provides:

> A debt shall not be deemed to be due until the creditor has knowledge of the identity of the debtor and of the facts from which the debt arises: Provided that a creditor shall be deemed to have such knowledge if he could have acquired it by exercising reasonable care.[65]

In *Mtokonya v. The Minister of Police*, the Constitutional Court had to decide whether section 12(3) of the Prescription Act requires a creditor to have knowledge that the conduct of the debtor giving rise to the debt is wrongful and actionable before prescription may start running against the creditor.[66] The court noted that section 12(1) makes provision for the general rule: that prescription commences to run as soon as the debt is due. However, this is subject to three exceptions which are to be found in subsections (2), (3), and (4). The first exception, in subsection (2), is that prescription does not commence to run against a creditor if the debtor wilfully prevents him or her 'from coming to know of the existence of the debt' until the creditor 'becomes aware of the existence of the debt'. So, under subsection (2), it is not every time a creditor does not know of the existence of a debt that prescription does not commence to run. It is only in those cases where the debtor is wilfully preventing or has wilfully prevented the creditor from 'coming to know of the existence of the debt'. One cannot therefore use the exception in subsection (2) to say that in all cases in which a creditor does not know of the existence of a debt prescription does not commence to run.[67]

Section 12(3) does not require the creditor to have knowledge of any right to sue the debtor nor does it require him or her to have knowledge of legal conclusions that may be drawn from 'the facts from which the debt arises'. The facts from which the debt arises are the facts which a creditor would need to prove in order to establish the liability of the debtor.[68] The appeal failed and the Court also relied on *Mdeyide*, which emphasised the importance of prescription and time limits for maintaining the quality of adjudication and securing the rule of law.[69]

VI. Class actions

Having been moribund for over a decade into the constitutional era, South Africa's class action regime has evolved significantly in the last ten years and has begun

65 Prescription Act 68 of 1969.
66 *Mtokonya v. The Minister of Police* [2017] ZACC 33; 2018 (5) SA 22 (CC).
67 Ibid., para. 32.
68 Ibid., para. 41.
69 *Road Accident Fund v. Mdeyide* [2010] ZACC 18; 2011 (2) SA 26 (CC); 2011 (1) BCLR 1 (CC).

to produce important results.[70] Civil damages litigation against MNCs in South Africa is likely increasingly to take the form of class action litigation. Initially it was largely conducted through straightforward damages claim in individual actions. Even though class action litigation brings a number of advantages for litigation against an MNC, it is not always in the best interest of the clients and may not be the best form for such litigation to take. Therefore, a decision has to be made on a case-by-case basis.

Section 38(c) of the Constitution governs standing and provides for standing to enforce the Bill of Rights 'as a member of, or in the interest of, a group or class of persons'.[71] This laid a constitutional basis for class actions. There were sustained calls for legislation to be passed to regulate class actions, including an important report by the South African Law Reform Commission.[72] However, when this did not happen, the courts took up the task of developing the law on class actions, including the substantive and procedural requirements for the certification of class actions. The first class action case in South Africa was the matter of *Permanent Secretary, Department of Welfare, Eastern Cape v. Ngxuza*, a successful class action on behalf of social grant claimants.[73]

The key development came in *Trustees for the time being of Children's Resource Centre Trust and Others v. Pioneer Food (Pty) Ltd and Others*.[74] The Supreme Court of Appeal held that any class action must be 'certified' by a court and laid down the substantive and procedural requirements that must be met. Certification is the process by which a court is approached at the outset, and before issue of summons, to authorise the action to be brought as a class action. In *Mukaddam v. Pioneer Foods (Pty) Ltd*,[75] the Constitutional Court confirmed the general approach established in *Children Resource Centre Trust* but said that the elements treated as 'requirements' by the Supreme Court of Appeal should be regarded as factors to be considered when certifying a class and stated that the interests of justice is an

70 See generally du Plessis, et al. (eds) (n. 7).

71 Section 38 provides:

Anyone listed in this section has the right to approach a competent court, alleging that a right in the Bill of Rights has been infringed or threatened, and the court may grant appropriate relief, including a declaration of rights. The persons who may approach a court are—

a. anyone acting in their own interest.
b. anyone acting on behalf of another person who cannot act in their own name.
c. anyone acting as a member of, or in the interest of, a group or class of persons.
d. anyone acting in the public interest; and
e. an association acting in the interest of its members.

72 South African Law Commission, Project 88, *The Recognition of Class Actions and Public Interest Actions in South African Law*, August 1998.

73 *Permanent Secretary, Department of Welfare, Eastern Cape v. Ngxuza* 2001 (4) SA 1184 (SCA).

74 *Trustees for the time being of Children's Resource Centre Trust and Others v. Pioneer Food (Pty) Ltd and Others* [2012] ZASCA 182; 2013 (2) SA 213 (SCA); 2013 (3) BCLR 279 (SCA); [2013] 1 All SA 648 (SCA) (*Children's Resource Centre Trust*).

75 *Mukaddam* 2013 (3) SA 89 (CC)

overriding test.[76] The relevant factors include (i) an objectively identifiable class; (ii) a triable cause of action; (iii) common issues of law or fact; (iv) that the relief sought, or damages claimed, be ascertainable and capable of determination; (v) if damages are claimed, an appropriate procedure for allocating damages to class members; (vi) that the proposed class representatives are suitable; and (vii) and the court being satisfied that a class action is the most appropriate procedure to adopt for the adjudication of the underlying claims.[77]

In *Mukaddam*, an *obiter dictum* by Jafta J left open whether certification is required in class actions based directly on a constitutional right. In the *Silicosis Certification* judgment, the High Court held that, indeed, certification is required in all class actions.[78] We support this approach, as certification enables the court to manage the litigation and ensure that potential class members receive adequate notice of the proceedings and that their interests are protected.[79] The overarching test is whether it is in the interests of justice to authorise the matter to proceed by way of class action, and the silicosis class action demonstrates that access to justice concerns lie at the heart of this inquiry.[80]

In defining the class it is not necessary to be able to identify all the members of the class. It is, however, necessary that the class be defined with sufficient precision that a particular individual's membership can be objectively determined by examining their situation in the light of the class definition. It is important to be able to do this for three reasons. First, it affects the manner in which notice is given to the members of the class. In the most common situation of an 'opt-out' class the entitlement to opt out is negated if people cannot ascertain with reasonable certainty whether they are members of the class in the first place. Second, it is necessary for people to know whether they can commence their own litigation against the defendant or defendants in the class action. Third, it is essential to the identification of those who are bound by the judgment.[81]

The need for a cause of action raising a triable issue is a low threshold inquiry to exclude legally hopeless cases. A case is legally hopeless if it could be the subject of a successful exception. It is factually hopeless if the evidence available and potentially available after discovery and other steps directed at procuring evidence will not sustain the cause of action on which the claim is based. In other words, if there is no *prima facie* case then it is factually hopeless.[82] Where

[76] Georgina Jephson, 'A False Start in the Development of Class Action Law' (2015) *VII Constitutional Court Review* 286.
[77] *Children's Resource Centre Trust*, para .23.
[78] *Silicosis Certification*, para. 38.
[79] J. Brickhill and J. Bleazard 'Bill of Rights Class Actions' in du Plessis, et al. (eds) (n. 7) 72–5.
[80] T. Broodryk, 'Individual Issues and the Class Action Mechanism: Determining Damages in Single-Accident Mass Personal Injury Class Actions' (2017) 134 *South African Law Journal* 821.
[81] *Children's Resource Centre Trust*, para. 29.
[82] Ibid., para. 36.

a novel claim has been brought before the court and no legal precedent, the court stated that, provided the novel claim is legally plausible, the standard is met and the claim survives scrutiny and must be determined in the course of the action. The court gave the example of a delictual claim based on a novel legal duty not to act negligently. The existence of such a duty depends on the facts of the case and a range of policy issues. The need for the court to be fully informed in regard to the policy elements of the enquiry militates against that decision being taken without evidence.[83] The commonality consideration does not require that every claim advanced in the class action, save possibly in relation to quantum, be identical. It requires that there be issues of fact, or law, or both fact and law, that are common to all members of the class and can appropriately be determined in one action.[84] Regarding the class representatives, the court must be satisfied with regard to two broad matters in regard to the representatives of the class. The first is that they have no interests in conflict with those whom they wish to represent. A conflict of interest arises if the purpose of the litigation is to enrich the representatives, or to serve interests other than those of the class. The second issue is whether the representative has the capacity to conduct the litigation properly on behalf of the class.[85]

After *Children's Resource Centre Trust* and *Mukaddam* clarified the requirements for class action litigation, the first class action was successfully certified and succeeded on the merits in *Linkside*.[86] This was an opt-in class action brought by the LRC on behalf of public schools that had unfilled teacher vacancies and teachers whom the State had failed to pay. Several other class action proceedings have since been launched, with the silicosis class action by some distance the largest to date. Following the certification of the class action, settlement discussions resulted in the creation of the Tshiamiso Trust, which is to pay damages to former mineworkers with silicosis or tuberculosis, according to a set of court-approved categories linking payments to degrees of illness. The liability of the mining companies to the Trust is secured in guarantees of a total of R5 billion.

The development of class actions in the South African court system has significant potential to enable poor claimants to get redress from MNCs for harm caused to them in the past or ongoing harm.[87]

[83] Ibid., para. 37.
[84] Ibid., para. 44.
[85] Ibid., para. 47.
[86] *Linkside v. Minister of Basic Education* [2015] ZAECGHC 36. Jason Brickhill acted for the applicants.
[87] See J. Brickhill 'A River of Disease: Silicosis and the Future of Class Actions in South Africa' *South African Journal on Human Rights* (2021) (forthcoming).

VII. Discovery

A. Ordinary discovery process

Both the High Court and Magistrates' Court Rules make provision for the discovery process in trial matters, the High Court Rules in exceptional cases make provision for discovery in application proceedings. The discovery procedure is a safeguard which prevents parties being surprised at trial, as well as preventing unnecessary delays, postponements, or costs.[88] The procedure is that both parties to the litigation depose to an affidavit, which is called a discovery affidavit and, in the affidavit, list all the documents in their possession. There is a description of each document listed, the source of the document and whether the document is an original or a copy. This is the same procedure in both the High Court and Magistrate Courts.

When a document is listed in the affidavit it means that the document can be produced before the court and potentially be used as evidence when it has been authenticated and admitted as evidence. One of the ways to authenticate a document for admission as evidence is to put the author of the document on the stand to authenticate it. Authentication of a document can be avoided by a party calling on the opposing party to admit to the document's authenticity, this admission will render authentication unnecessary.

Rule 35 of the Uniform Rules of Court, which cover the High Court, governs the discovery process and what should be discovered and when in High Court matters, and Rule 23 of the Magistrates' Court Rules (MCR) governs the same process in a similar manner in Magistrates' Court matters. The requirement in Rule 35 that the documents discovered must relate to any matter in question in such action does not mean that the documents must be relevant to any issue. South African courts have held that a party is obliged to discover only documents which either directly or indirectly damage the party's own case or which advance the case of the opposing party.[89]

B. E-discovery or Electronically Stored Information (ESI)

With the increasing use of technology in everyday work life, a large percentage of potential evidence or documents is stored in a digital and or electric format.

[88] *Road Accident Fund v. Mdeyide* [2010] ZACC 18; 2011 (2) SA 26 (CC); 2011 (1) BCLR 1 (CC).
[89] Theophilopoulos, Rowan, van Heerden, et al. (n. 17) 268.

Litigation is expensive and a large part of the expense is incurred during the discovery process and trial preparation where the discovered documents are largely dealt with. It then makes logical sense that reduction of these costs and more efficiency would be met through the process of e-discovery or ESI.

Other jurisdictions in the world, like the United States, have adopted this method of discovery and thereby embracing the changes in how documents are stored in the digital and electronic age.

In South Africa, Rule 23(1)(a) of MCR states: 'any party to any action may require any other party thereto, by notice in writing, to make discovery on oath within 20 days of all documents and tape, *electronic*, *digital* or other *forms of recordings* relating to any matter in question in such action'. The Rule gives the impression that this allows for electronic discovery, but the problem is that the Rule is not specific enough because there are different forms in which documents are digitally stored and electronically recorded.

Rule 35 of the Uniform Rules of Court provides, in respect of the High Court, that any party to any action may require any other party to make discovery on oath within 20 days of all documents and tape recordings relating to any matter in question in such action which are or have at any time been in the possession or control of such other party. Erasmus provides that the word 'document' is not defined in the Rules which means it must bear its ordinary meaning, namely 'a piece of written, printed or electronic matter that provides information or evidence or that serves as an official record'. When compared with foreign developments, the current wording of this subrule does not adequately provide for discovery of information created, stored, and retrieved primarily in electronic form, and it should be appropriately amended.[90]

Amending the current Rules would blow the doors wide open on the extent of evidence that can be retrieved for purposes of trial and would promote transparency. The benefits of electronically stored information are mobility, portability, searchability, volume, and ease of replication, together with the existence of hidden metadata. Access to electronically stored information in a data system that can be discovered will allow attorneys to prepare for trial thoroughly with all relevant evidence at hand. The Covid-19 pandemic compelled courts to expedite changes to permit the electronic service and filing of court documents. It is likely that similar changes will follow in relation to discovery.

[90] Rule 35, Superior Court Practice, pp. B1–251.

VIII. Damages

A. Patrimonial and non-patrimonial loss

Damage is understood in South African law as 'a diminution as a result of a damage causing event, in the utility or quality of a patrimonial or personality interest in satisfying the legally recognised needs of a person involved'.[91] Damages consist of patrimonial and non-patrimonial loss, although there is a school of thought that ascribes to a narrow approach that does not include non-patrimonial loss. Patrimonial and non-patrimonial loss have a common denominator, that is the diminution in the utility of any patrimonial or personality interest which the law deems worthy of protection; it need not be measurable in monetary terms.[92]

Patrimonial loss is the detrimental impact on any patrimonial interest deemed worthy of protection by the law.[93]

The ways in which patrimonial loss is caused:

- Loss of a patrimonial element-when property is destroyed, a patrimonial right in respect thereof is lost, and a person's patrimony diminishes in value;
- Reduction in value of the patrimonial element; when someone' earning capacity is diminished, as an example;
- The creation or increase of a debt. If a delict causes an injured person to incur reasonable medical expenses, such expenses constitute damage.[94]

B. Forms of damages

There are several forms and categories of damages recognised in South African law:

- *Damnum emergens* and *lucrum cessans*: the former refers to all forms of damage up to the date of trial and the latter refers to loss of profit and prospective loss;
- Damage to property and pure economic loss: pure economic loss is impairment of the physical object of a real right, while damage is more generic;
- Direct and consequential loss: direct loss is the immediate or direct result of the damage causing event, and consequential loss is loss that flows from direct loss;

[91] Visser and Potgieter (n. 37) 27.
[92] Neethling, Potgieter, and Visser (n. 54) 224.
[93] Ibid., 229.
[94] Ibid., 230.

- General (Intrinsic) and special (extrinsic) damage: general damages are presumed to flow from an unlawful act and need only to be pleaded generally and are sometimes used to describe non-patrimonial loss. Special damages must be specifically pleaded and proven and thus the presumption applied in general damages does not apply in special damages. In delictual claims of bodily injury, general damages may be awarded for pain and suffering (non-patrimonial damages) as well as prospective patrimonial loss, such as future medical expenses, loss of earning capacity. Monetary loss sustained up to the date of trial and medical expenses already incurred are special damages.[95]

C. Transmissibility of damages

In personal injury claims on behalf of poor claimants, general damages will often be the largest head of damages. Whether such damages are transmissible to the deceased estate of the injured party is therefore a crucial legal issue. Until recently, the law in South Africa was that general damages only become transmissible after a claim has reached close of pleadings. If the plaintiff died before that point, while special damages (such as medical expenses) would be transmissible, general damages were not. In practice, it may take several months or even years after launch to reach close of pleadings, especially in complex matters. However, in the *Silicosis Certification* judgment, the High Court developed the common law so that general damages are now transmissible after the institutions of proceedings.[96]

IX. Funding and costs

Litigation funding and the rules governing the award and recovery of costs are crucial considerations in MNC litigation. Such litigation often involves an extended period to gather evidence, prepare a case, go through the discovery process, hold hearings and/or trials, and conclude any appeal proceedings. The silicosis litigation against gold mining companies, for example, ran for over a decade in different forms. This kind of litigation therefore requires substantial up-front investment. It is also important that successful litigants are able to recover costs.

[95] Ibid., 231.
[96] *Silicosis Certification*, para. 220.

A. Litigation funding

As concerns litigation funding, there are three potential sources of the up-front financial assistance required to launch complex MNC litigation. These are private commercial funding, State funding, and private philanthropic funding. Each is regulated differently by statute and/or common law.

The first is commercial litigation funding from private sources. An agreement to fund civil litigation in South Africa is called a 'champertous agreement', which is permitted under the common law.[97] Two of the private firms involved in the silicosis class action were funded in this way by foreign law firms and recovered their funding when the class action settled.[98]

The second is State funding, in particular through LASA, the statutory body charged with the provision of criminal and civil legal aid. LASA itself conducts some limited civil litigation. In addition, it provides funding to lawyers acting for indigent litigants. For example, LASA funded the LRC's conduct of the silicosis litigation in both the *Blom* test cases and the class action on the basis that, if the LRC recovered costs, it would repay the funding, which it did.

Finally, funding from institutional donors is the main source of support that sustains public interest law centres in South Africa, such as the LRC.[99] The public interest sector in South Africa is strong and diverse, operating across most areas of the law and in all the major cities. However, in general the sector does not often conduct action proceedings for the recovery of damages, because such claims are highly costly and resource intensive. The LRC's role in the silicosis litigation and SECTION27's conduct of the Life Esidimeni arbitral claims[100] against the State on behalf of mental health patients and their families are two significant exceptions. One possibility, illustrated by the collaboration between the LRC and Leigh Day in the silicosis litigation, is for a public interest law centre and a commercial firm to act jointly.

If funding is not forthcoming, or in any event, it is permitted to conclude contingency fee agreements with plaintiffs that provide that, if the litigation succeeds, the plaintiff attorneys may recover their fees from the damages in the event of a successful claim. Contingency fees are regulated by the Contingency Fees Act 66 of 1997. A contingency fees agreement must be in writing in terms of section 3(1) of the Act, and is ordinarily concluded before litigation is instituted. The Act prescribes detailed limits on the contingency fees that may be charged and sets out detailed requirements for such arrangements.

[97] *Gold Fields Limited and Others v. Motley Rice LLC, In re: Nkala v. Harmony Gold Mining Company Limited and Others* [2015] ZAGPJHC 62; 2015 (4) SA 299 (GJ) paras 27–28.

[98] Richard Spoor Attorneys and Abrahams Kiewitz Attorneys were funded by Motley Rice and Hausfeld, respectively.

[99] J. Brickhill 'Introduction: The Past, Present and Promise of Public Interest Litigation in South Africa' in J. Brickhill (ed.) (n. 61) 18–19.

[100] The arbitral award is available on SAFLII at: <http://www.saflii.org/images/LifeEsidimeniArbitrationAward.pdf> accessed 16 April 2021.

B. Legal costs

In respect of costs, certain rules and principles govern when courts will award costs, on what scale they will do so, and the taxation of costs. The starting point is the rule that in civil litigation, costs ordinarily follow the result. In constitutional litigation, the position is different, however. In litigation seeking to vindicate constitutional rights against the State, a court will not impose costs on a losing applicant or plaintiff under the *Biowatch* rule.[101] The purpose of the rule is to avoid costs orders having a chilling effect on constitutional litigation. There are also instances in which courts in private litigation will not award costs to a successful private party as against another private party.[102]

As to scale, the default position is that costs are awarded on the 'party and party' scale. In exceptional cases, a court may grant costs on the higher 'attorney and client' scale, for example where one of the parties has misled the court or engaged in abuse of process. The successful party must then have a bill of costs prepared, ordinarily done by a specialist costs consultant. Unless the costs are agreed, they must then be referred to taxation before a taxing master. The taxing master assesses each item on the bill of costs against a set of tariffs and on the basis of common law principles, typically 'taxing off' or reducing some items.

X. Enforcement of judgments

The Enforcement of Foreign Civil Judgments Act 32 of 1998 and the common law govern the enforcement of foreign judgments in South Africa. The Act only applies to judgments handed down in countries that have been designated by the Minister of Justice. There are not many countries designated by the Minister and therefore most judgments are dealt with in accordance with the common law. South Africa is not party to any treaty regarding the reciprocal enforcement of foreign commercial judgments, as opposed to foreign arbitral awards.

South African courts will enforce a foreign judgment if certain requirements, based largely on the Roman Dutch common law, are met. A foreign judgment, therefore, is not directly enforceable in South Africa but constitutes a cause of action that will be enforced by South African courts if the following requirements laid down in *Jones v. Krok*[103] are met:

- the foreign court must have had international competence as determined by South African law;

[101] *Biowatch Trust v. Registrar, Genetic Resources* 2009 (6) SA 232 (CC) para. 22.
[102] *Bothma v. Els* [2009] ZACC 27; 2010 (2) SA 622 (CC) paras 89–98.
[103] *Jones v. Krok* 1995(1) SA 677(A).

- the judgment must be final and conclusive and must not have become superannuated;
- the enforcement of the judgment must not be contrary to South African public policy (which includes the rules of natural justice);
- the judgment must not have been obtained by fraudulent means;
- the judgment must not involve the enforcement of a penal or revenue law of the foreign State;
- enforcement must not be precluded by the Protection of Businesses Act 99 of 1978.

The courts have also developed the common law to enable the enforcement of the decisions of regional courts. *Government of the Republic of Zimbabwe v. Fick and Others* (*Fick*) concerned an attempt to enforce a decision of the Tribunal of the Southern African Development Community (SADC Tribunal) against the government of Zimbabwe in South Africa.[104] The SADC Treaty imposes an obligation on Member States to take all the necessary steps to accord the Treaty the force of national law and a commitment to 'cooperate with and assist institutions of SADC in the performance of their duties'. One of those institutions was the Tribunal.[105] Article 32 of the Tribunal Protocol requires Member States to take all steps necessary to facilitate the enforcement of judgments and orders of the Tribunal. It also makes these decisions binding and enforceable 'within the territories of the States concerned'.[106] The court held that Zimbabwe's agreement to be bound by the Tribunal Protocol, including Article 32, constituted an express waiver by Zimbabwe of its right to rely on its sovereign immunity from the jurisdiction of South African courts to register and enforce decisions of the Tribunal made against it.[107] The court accordingly held that when the farmers' rights to property, their human rights in general and the right of access to courts in particular were violated, Zimbabwe was, in terms of Article 6(6) of the Amended Treaty, obliged to cooperate with the Tribunal in the adjudication of the dispute. After the Tribunal had delivered its judgment, Zimbabwe was duty-bound to assist in the execution of that judgment and so was South Africa. The court held that the common law had been developed to extend the concept of a 'foreign court' to the Tribunal, and all common law requirements for the enforcement of foreign judgments had been met. Our domestic courts have jurisdiction and were, therefore, entitled to register the costs order of the Tribunal as the High Court did.

[104] *Government of the Republic of Zimbabwe v. Fick and Others* [2013] ZACC 22, (2013) (5) SA 235 (CC).
[105] Ibid.
[106] Ibid.
[107] Ibid.

XI. Conclusion

South Africa is a complex jurisdiction with the potential to see significant MNC litigation. Its dual identity, with which we began this chapter, means that there is the potential for claims against both companies based outside South Africa that operate within it, and companies based in South Africa operating outside, especially in other African countries.

The principles governing jurisdiction, including the rules applicable to 'foreign *peregrini*', confer jurisdiction over foreign-based MNCs in a wide range of situations. When it comes to instituting proceedings, the courts are fairly receptive to novel legal claims, especially if they are rooted in the Constitution. Where, for example, life expectancy of claimants creates urgency, arbitration is available as an effective alternative.

Anyone engaging in MNC litigation in South Africa needs to adopt the Constitution as a point of departure, even if the claim is not directly rooted in the Constitution. At the very least, the Constitution will inform the approach to key principles such as wrongfulness in delict (the existence of a legal duty) and public policy in contract. In practice, however, most claims against MNCs will be made in delict (tort). The law of delict has seen important developments, including the development of the law governing transmissibility of damages. Statute may provide the backdrop to such litigation or, in some cases, ground the legal duty in delict claims.

The legal profession in South Africa—both private and public interest—is well-equipped to conduct MNC litigation. The constitutional right to civil legal aid offers the potential for greater State provision of legal aid for MNC claims in future, but at present State civil legal aid is very limited. The most significant development in South African law over the last decade for MNC litigation is undoubtedly the consolidation of a court-crafted class action regime, with the massive multi-defendant silicosis class action the most significant to date.

Once proceedings are launched, pre-trial discovery is one of the most resource-intensive and time-consuming stages of any action. South Africa is moving towards greater use of electronic means of service and filing and it is expected that e-discovery will also become increasingly commonly used. At the end of a successful claim, the common law lays out principles that govern the award of damages. An important development in the common law, as mentioned above, now permits the transmissibility of general damages—including damages for pain and suffering, which are often the largest head of damages—if the plaintiff dies after institution of proceedings.

Finally, litigation funding and costs are crucial considerations in MNC litigation. South Africa permits third party funding of litigation, called 'champertous agreements'. In addition, contingency fee arrangements are allowed and are fairly common in practice. Generally, legal costs follow the result in South Africa, although the Constitution qualifies this rule, especially in unsuccessful constitutional claims against the State. South Africa is generally a receptive jurisdiction for the enforcement of foreign judgments, and the law has developed to facilitate the enforcement of judgments of regional tribunals.

5

Liability of Multinational Corporations in Canada for International Human Rights Violations

*Bruce W. Johnston**

I. Introduction

Is it the role of the Canadian justice system to hold Canadian corporations accountable for the harmful consequences of their operations abroad when that harm results from fault or negligence? The majority ruling in the landmark Supreme Court of Canada case of *Nevsun Resources Ltd v. Araya*[1] suggests that it is. Justice Abella, writing for the majority, referred to modern international human rights law as the 'phoenix that rose from the ashes of World War II and declared global war on human rights abuses'.[2] Recognising the Court's role in developing and defining international law, the majority stated that there was no reason for Canadian courts to be shy about implementing and advancing it.[3]

The precedent set in *Nevsun* represents a powerful signal that Canadian courts are capable of adapting to the changed realities of a globalised economy. *Nevsun* is also a significant step toward providing viable legal recourses to individuals and communities who have suffered as a result of the international operations of Canadian corporations.

The issue of domestic liability for international human rights violations is particularly relevant in the Canadian context because Canadian corporations represent a disproportionately large share of the extractive sector worldwide.[4] Such a substantial presence unavoidably impacts the human rights, ways of life,

* The author thanks Mr Louis-Alexandre Hébert-Gosselin for his invaluable assistance in researching this chapter.

[1] *Nevsun Resources Ltd v. Araya* 2020 SCC 5.

[2] Ibid., para. 1.

[3] Ibid., paras 71–72.

[4] In 2013, 1,500 companies headquartered in Canada had interests in some 8,000 properties in over 100 countries around the world representing over 50 per cent of the world's publicly listed exploration and mining companies: Global affairs Canada, 'Doing Business the Canadian Way: A Strategy to Advance Corporate Social Responsibility in Canada's Extractive Sector Abroad' <https://www.international.gc.ca/trade-agreements-accords-commerciaux/topics-domaines/other-autre/csr-strat-rse.aspx?lang=eng> accessed 20 November 2020.

Bruce W. Johnston, *Liability of Multinational Corporations in Canada for International Human Rights Violations* In: *Human Rights Litigation against Multinationals in Practice*. Edited by: Richard Meeran, Oxford University Press.
 DOI: 10.1093/oso/9780198866220.003.0005

livelihoods, and ecosystems of the people and communities in which those corporations operate. While human rights violations may occur anywhere, they are much more likely to occur in weak governance regions, especially in areas affected by armed conflicts. At the same time, in host countries with weak governance, victims seeking justice may encounter difficulties as a result of inadequate legislation, unstable judicial systems, corruption, victim intimidation, or prohibitive costs. This chapter will provide an analysis of the legal avenues open to victims of such impacts in Canadian courts, as well as of the main obstacles facing victims who wish to pursue such avenues.

II. Canadian legal context

Canada is a bijural, bilingual, federal State.[5] Canadian bijuralism is an expression of the coexistence of the civil law and common law legal traditions, a legacy of colonisation by both France and Great Britain. This coexistence found its first formal expression in the *Quebec Act, 1774*[6] by which the British Crown guaranteed continuity of their private civil law tradition to the French-speaking inhabitants of Canada after the British conquest of 1760. By contrast, public law in Canada—including constitutional, criminal, and administrative law—became British, as did private law in the colonies established in British North America after American independence.

The *Constitution Act, 1867*[7] preserved this arrangement by mandating a division of legislative authority between federal and provincial heads of power. Subsection 92(13) provides that 'property and civil rights in the province' fall within the exclusive jurisdiction of the provincial governments. This broad residuary power, which includes civil liability, is thus exercised in the French-speaking province of Quebec in a civil law environment whereas elsewhere in Canada, it is exercised in a common law environment.

In Canada, the executive branch of the federal government alone has treaty-making power. However, that power is distinct from the legislative enactment of international treaties into domestic law.[8] The result is that while the federal government has the authority to enter into international agreements that affect subject matters falling within the jurisdiction of the provinces, the provinces are only bound by the terms of such agreements if their respective legislatures enact them into law.[9] The Supreme Court nonetheless confirmed in *Nevsun* that via the

[5] See generally J.E.C. Brierley, 'Bijuridism in Canada' in *Contemporary Law: National Reports to the 1990 International Congress of Comparative Law, Montreal, 1990* (1992) 22 and ff.

[6] 14 Geo III c 83. The Quebec Act provided that 'in all Matters of Controversy, relative to Property and Civil Rights, Resort shall be had to the Laws of Canada'.

[7] *The Constitution Act, 1867* (UK), 30 & 31 Victoria, c 3.

[8] *Attorney-General for Canada v. Attorney-General for Ontario* [1937] AC 326 (PC), p. 348.

[9] *Reference re Pan-Canadian Securities Regulation* 2018 SCC 48, [2018] 3 SCR 189, para. 66.

doctrine of adoption, customary international law is automatically incorporated into the common law, in the absence of conflicting legislation.[10]

III. Jurisdictional issues

Provincial and territorial superior courts have inherent general jurisdiction, in addition to jurisdiction granted by federal and provincial statutes and oversight over all lower courts. Nominated and paid by federal authorities, superior court judges are subject to final review by the Supreme Court of Canada, which makes the court system essentially unitary.[11] The Supreme Court notably ensures the coherence and development of the common law, the development of the civil law of Quebec, a measure of convergence between the two legal traditions through a comparative approach, and the compatibility of provincial private international law with constitutional principles.

Foreign plaintiffs face no restrictions related to standing before the courts as neither Quebec nor the common law provinces distinguish between nationals and non-nationals. Standing will be recognised whenever the plaintiff has a direct personal interest in the litigation.[12]

Jurisdiction of the courts is territorial in both civil and common law provinces and, in matters of civil liability, is largely based on the establishment of a sufficient connection between the subject matter of the litigation and the forum seised.

A. Subject matter jurisdiction in common law provinces

Subject matter jurisdiction in the common law provinces can be established if the forum has a real and substantial connection to the subject matter of the dispute.[13] A real and substantial connection is established primarily on the basis of objective factors that connect the legal situation or the subject matter of the litigation with the forum,[14] thus prioritising order, stability, and predictability.[15] The connecting factors are identified in a non-exhaustive manner by the common law and in provincial legislation.[16]

[10] *Nevsun Resources Ltd v. Araya* 2020 SCC 5, para. 90. See also *R v. Hape* 2007 SCC 26, para. 39; *Civil Code of Québec*, CQLR c CCQ-1991, art. 2807(2) likewise provides that customary international law is applicable in Quebec, although it must be pleaded.

[11] *Hunt v. T&N plc* [1993] 4 SCR 289, p. 314.

[12] *Canada (Attorney General) v. Downtown Eastside Sex Workers United Against Violence Society*, 2012 SCC 45, para. 1. *Code of Civil Procedure* CQLR c C-25.01, art. 85.

[13] *Club Resorts Ltd v. Van Breda* 2012 SCC 17; *Haaretz.com v. Goldhar* 2018 SCC 28, para. 27.

[14] *Club Resorts Ltd v. Van Breda* 2012 SCC 17, para. 82.

[15] *Haaretz.com v. Goldhar* 2018 SCC 28, para. 28.

[16] *Club Resorts Ltd v. Van Breda* 2012 SCC 17, paras 75–90.

British Columbia, Saskatchewan, and Nova Scotia, as well as the territorial government of the Yukon,[17] have enacted legislation based on a model proposed by the Uniform Law Conference of Canada, the *Uniform Court Jurisdiction and Proceedings Transfer Act* (CJPTA) which sets out a list of connecting factors in section 10. In Ontario and the remaining common law provinces, the CJPTA has not been enacted and the *Rules of Civil Procedure* relevant to jurisdiction relate only to out-of-province service.[18]

The Supreme Court nonetheless drew on the CJPTA criteria in the landmark case *Club Resorts Ltd. v. Van Breda* while recasting the 'real and substantial connection' test, thus providing a measure of uniformity and coherence in the common law. Connecting factors for tort cases common to all provinces other than Quebec now include situations where the defendant is domiciled or resides in the province; the defendant carries on business in the province; the offence was committed in the province; or a contract related to the litigation was entered into in the Province.[19] The presence of the plaintiff in the forum, on its own, is not considered a sufficient connecting factor.[20] Nor is damage having been sustained in the jurisdiction.[21]

The existence of a recognised connecting factor creates a presumption of jurisdiction which can be rebutted if the defendant demonstrates that the connecting factor has little or nothing to do with the subject matter of the litigation,[22] in which case the action is stayed or dismissed, subject to the possible application of the forum of necessity doctrine.[23] If the presumption is not rebutted, the court may hear the dispute, subject to the doctrine of *forum non conveniens*.[24]

The question arose in *Airia Brands Inc v. Air Canada*[25] as to how the real and substantial connection test would apply in class action proceedings in which jurisdiction was sought over a class that included numerous foreign claimants. The Ontario Court of Appeal, applying *Van Breda*, overturned the restrictive approach adopted by the first judge. It ruled that jurisdiction over absent foreign claimants (AFCs) could be established if there was a real and substantial connection between the subject matter of the action and Ontario and jurisdiction existed over both the representative plaintiff and the defendant—provided there were common issues

[17] Ibid., paras 41–42; *Court Jurisdiction and Proceedings Transfer Act*, SBC 2003, c 28; *Court Jurisdiction and Proceedings Transfer Act*, SS 1997, c C-41.1; *Court Jurisdiction and Proceedings Transfer Act*, SNS 2003, c 2; *Court Jurisdiction and Proceedings Transfer Act*, SY 2000, c 7. See also C. Emanuelli, *Étude comparative sur le droit international privé au Canada* (2019), para. 172.

[18] *Club Resorts Ltd v. Van Breda* 2012 SCC 17, para. 43; Emanuelli (n. 17) para. 173.

[19] Ibid., para. 90; *Haaretz.com v. Goldhar* 2018 SCC 28, para. 36.

[20] *Club Resorts Ltd v. Van Breda* 2012 SCC 17, para. 86.

[21] Ibid., para. 89.

[22] Ibid., para. 96.

[23] Ibid., para. 100.

[24] Ibid., para. 100.

[25] *Airia Brands Inc v. Air Canada* 2017 ONCA 792.

between the claims of the representative plaintiff and AFCs and provided certain procedural safeguards were satisfied.[26]

None of the cases involving international human rights abuses brought against Canadian corporations in the common law provinces thus far have turned primarily on subject matter jurisdiction, as most have been directed at the parent company in the province of its domicile.[27]

B. Subject matter jurisdiction in Quebec civil law

Jurisdiction of Quebec courts over personal patrimonial actions, which include actions in civil liability, is determined in accordance with the connecting factors listed in Article 3148 of the *Civil Code of Québec* (CCQ).[28] Article 3148 appears in Book Ten of the CCQ, which regulates matters of private international law. The provision sets out a broad basis for jurisdiction which is balanced with the availability of *forum non conveniens*—as codified at Article 3135 CCQ[29]—and lists many of the same connecting factors recognised in the common law provinces. These include circumstances where the non-corporate defendant has his or her domicile or residence in Quebec;[30] the corporate defendant has its domicile[31] (head office) in Quebec; the corporate defendant has an establishment in Quebec and the dispute relates to the corporation's activities in Quebec;[32] the fault was committed in Quebec; and where one of the obligations arising from a contract is performed in Quebec. Paragraph 3148(3) CCQ also includes damage being suffered in Quebec as a connecting factor.

In the case of *Anvil Mining Ltd v. Association canadienne contre l'impunité*[33] however, the Quebec Court of Appeal adopted a restrictive interpretation of the connecting factor listed at paragraph 3148(2) CCQ. Anvil Mining, a Canadian corporation whose head office was in Perth, Western Australia, operated a copper and silver mine in the Democratic Republic of Congo (DRC). Proceedings alleging Anvil's complicity in grave human rights violations, including a massacre of dozens of civilians by the armed forces of the DRC, were served on Anvil at its only

[26] Ibid., para. 107.

[27] In *Choc v. Hudbay Minerals*, the defendant, a mining company headquartered in Toronto, was sued together with two affiliates in relation to alleged human rights abuses in Guatemala. The Guatemalan affiliate alleged lack of jurisdiction *simpliciter* in the event the case was dismissed against the other defendants. Because the case was allowed to proceed, the affiliate's motion was dismissed: *Choc v. Hudbay Minerals* 2013 ONSC 1414, paras 15, 87.

[28] *Civil Code of Québec*, CQLR c CCQ-1991, art. 3148.

[29] *Spar Aerospace Ltd v. American Mobile Satellite Corp* [2002] 4 SCR 205, paras 57–58.

[30] Emanuelli (n. 17) para. 148.

[31] CCQ, art. 307.

[32] Emanuelli (n. 17) para. 149. See *Anvil Mining Ltd v. Association canadienne contre l'impunité* 2012 QCCA 117.

[33] Ibid.

establishment in Canada, in Montreal. Anvil Mining contested the jurisdiction of the Superior Court of Quebec, arguing that its establishment in Quebec did not exist at the time of the events and that it dealt only with investor relations. The main issue with respect to jurisdiction was whether the activities of the Montreal office were related to the dispute.[34] On the basis that the defendant's sole productive asset was the mine in the DRC, the trial judge concluded that the financing and public relations activities carried out in Montreal were necessarily related to its operation and that the Superior Court therefore had jurisdiction.[35] Although Anvil argued *forum non conveniens*, the first judge concluded that Anvil had not demonstrated that either Australia or the DRC would be a clearly more appropriate jurisdiction, concluding that the evidence before him indicated that if the court were to dismiss the action on the basis of *forum non conveniens*, there would be no other possibility for the victims to be heard.[36]

The Quebec Court of Appeal reversed the finding of jurisdiction, emphasising that the activities carried out in the Montreal office did not involve the management of the mine in the DRC. The unanimous bench considered that the fact that the establishment did not exist in Quebec at the time of the October 2004 events in the DRC, while not conclusive, lent additional support for their decision to deny jurisdiction under paragraph 3148(2) CCQ. Having concluded that Quebec lacked jurisdiction, the Court of Appeal did not consider the issue of *forum non conveniens* and dismissed the plaintiffs' alternative argument of forum of necessity,[37] which will be discussed below. The Supreme Court of Canada denied leave to appeal.[38]

Accordingly, despite the Supreme Court stating that initial jurisdiction should be interpreted broadly under Quebec civil law,[39] the victims in the Anvil case were turned away from Quebec courts on a narrow reading of jurisdiction. The ruling, although criticised,[40] signalled a reluctance among the judiciary to allow Canadian courts to assume oversight over the conduct of Canadian corporations operating in weak governance countries.

[34] Superior Court judge Emery summarily dismissed Anvil's argument based on the absence of an establishment at the relevant period. See *Association Canadienne contre l'impunité (ACCI) v. Anvil Mining Ltd* 2011 QCCS 1966, para. 16, citing *Rees v. Convergia* 2005 QCCA 353, paras 48–49.

[35] *Association Canadienne contre l'impunité (ACCI) v. Anvil Mining Ltd* 2011 QCCS 1966, para. 29.

[36] Ibid., para. 39.

[37] *Anvil Mining Ltd v. Association canadienne contre l'impunité* 2012 QCCA 117, paras 95–103.

[38] *Association canadienne contre l'impunité v. Anvil Mining Limited* 2012 CanLII 66221 (SCC), no. 34733, 1 November 2012. The author's firm represented the plaintiffs in Quebec. Subsequent attempts to obtain representation for them in Australia were unsuccessful. The victims have not succeeded in obtaining access to justice.

[39] *Spar Aerospace Ltd v. American Mobile Satellite Corp* [2002] 4 SCR 205, paras 57–58.

[40] For a comment of the Court of Appeal ruling, see G. Saumier, 'Commentaire sur Anvil Mining' (2013) 9–1 *Revue de droit du développement durable de l'Université McGill* 145, 2013 CanLIIDocs 134, <http://www.canlii.org/t/2m4n> accessed 4 September 2020.

C. *Forum non conveniens*

The common law doctrine of *forum non conveniens* has been invoked with varying success by corporate defendants against plaintiffs seeking access to Canadian courts in relation to wrongs suffered abroad.[41] The doctrine is available to defendants in both civil and common law provinces.

i. *Forum non conveniens* in common law provinces

The *forum non conveniens* analysis considers not whether the court has jurisdiction but whether it should exercise it.[42] Once the jurisdiction of the court seised with a matter has been established, a defendant may then argue that another forum is more appropriate.[43] At this stage, the party invoking *forum non conveniens* has the burden to show that the court should exercise its discretion to refer the litigation to another jurisdiction. That jurisdiction must be capable of hearing the matter in accordance with its own rules and must be 'clearly a more appropriate forum' to resolve it.[44]

The analysis is contextual and the factors to be considered vary according to the facts of each case.[45] Although derived from the common law, some of the relevant factors have been codified in a non-exhaustive manner by provincial statutes inspired by section 11 of the CJPTA.[46] These factors include the comparative convenience and expense for the parties and their witnesses to litigate in the court or in any alternative forum; the law applicable to issues in the proceeding; the need to avoid a multiplicity of proceedings or conflicting decisions in different courts; the ability to enforce an eventual judgment; and the fair and efficient working of the Canadian legal system as a whole.[47]

The Supreme Court recognised the factors listed in the CJPTA as a helpful reference[48] and also listed the location of the parties and witnesses; the costs occasioned by the transfer of the case to another court or by the refusal to suspend the proceedings; the impact of the change of jurisdiction on the progress of the dispute or

[41] *Recherches internationales Québec v. Cambior inc* 1998 CanLII 9780 (QC CS); *Bil'In (Village Council) v. Green Park International Inc* 2009 QCCS 4151.

[42] *Haaretz.com v. Goldhar* 2018 SCC 28, paras 30–31; *Club Resorts Ltd v. Van Breda* 2012 SCC 17, para. 101.

[43] *Breeden v. Black* 2012 SCC 19, para. 21; *Club Resorts Ltd v. Van Breda* 2012 SCC 17, para. 102; *Lapointe Rosenstein Marchand Melançon SENCRL v. Cassels Brock & Blackwell LLP* 2016 SCC 30, para. 51; Emanuelli (n. 17) para. 197.

[44] *Breeden v. Black* 2012 SCC 19, paras 22–23, 37; *Club Resorts Ltd v. Van Breda* 2012 SCC 17, para. 103; *Lapointe Rosenstein Marchand Melançon SENCRL v. Cassels Brock & Blackwell LLP* 2016 SCC 30, para. 52; Emanuelli (n. 17) para. 197.

[45] *Breeden v. Black* 2012 SCC 19, paras 23, 28; Emanuelli (n. 17) para. 197.

[46] *Club Resorts Ltd v. Van Breda* 2012 SCC 17, para. 106, citing *Teck Cominco Metals Ltd v. Lloyds Underwriters* 2009 SCC 11, para. 22.

[47] *Breeden v. Black* 2012 SCC 19, para. 23.

[48] Ibid., para. 28.

on related or parallel proceedings; and the relative strength of the relationship with both parties.[49]

The *forum non conveniens* analysis does not require that all factors converge toward a single jurisdiction[50] but emphasises fairness and efficiency by determining on a case-by-case basis whether another jurisdiction would be 'clearly more appropriate'.[51]

Several international human rights cases initiated in common law provinces have faced *forum non conveniens* challenges.[52] In *Garcia v. Tahoe Resources Inc*,[53] plaintiffs commenced an action for damages against Tahoe in the Supreme Court of British Columbia. They alleged that the company was liable in relation to shootings of protesters by security personnel employed by its subsidiary, which operated a mine in Guatemala. The first judge granted the *forum non conveniens* application sought by Tahoe and stayed the British Columbia action, applying the principles set out in the CJPTA.[54] The Court held that if the *forum non conveniens* analysis pointed to a clearly more appropriate forum, then the plaintiff 'must take the forum as he finds it . . . unless he can establish that substantial justice cannot be done in the appropriate forum'.[55] The first judge concluded that 'that Canadian courts [should] proceed extremely cautiously in finding that a foreign court is incapable of providing justice to its own citizens'.[56]

The British Columbia Court of Appeal granted the plaintiffs' appeal.[57] Justice Garson, writing for the bench, found that the first judge had erred in placing on the plaintiffs the onus to demonstrate that her *prima facie* determination that Guatemala was the more appropriate forum was incorrect. The Court of Appeal concluded that there was a 'real risk' that the plaintiffs would not receive a fair trial in Guatemala.[58] The Court stated that, without making any general pronouncement on Guatemala's legal system, there was 'some measurable risk that the appellants will encounter difficulty in receiving a fair trial against a powerful international company whose mining interests in Guatemala align with the political interests of the Guatemalan state'.[59] *Tahoe* was the first case in which a Canadian appellate court allowed a lawsuit to advance against a Canadian-based parent company for harm suffered by victims in a developing country.

[49] *Club Resorts Ltd v. Van Breda* 2012 SCC 17, para. 110 Emanuelli (n. 17) para. 197.
[50] *Breeden v. Black* 2012 SCC 19, para. 37.
[51] *Haaretz.com v. Goldhar* 2018 SCC 28, para. 28.
[52] In *Choc v. Hudbay Minerals Inc* 2013 ONSC 1414, although the defendant had originally indicated it would raise *forum non conveniens*, it ultimately did not.
[53] *Garcia v. Tahoe Resources Inc* 2017 BCCA 39, leave to appeal refused by the Supreme Court, no. 37492, 8 June 2017.
[54] *Garcia v. Tahoe Resources Inc* 2015 BCSC 2045, para. 106.
[55] Ibid., para. 64.
[56] Ibid., para. 105.
[57] *Garcia v. Tahoe Resources Inc* 2017 BCCA 39.
[58] Ibid., paras 125–130.
[59] Ibid., para. 130.

In *Nevsun*, the case that ultimately led to the Supreme Court's landmark decision, a group of Eritrean refugees alleged that international law norms against forced labour, slavery, and torture had been violated during the construction of a gold mine owned indirectly by Nevsun, a Canadian corporation headquartered in British Columbia. At first instance, Nevsun argued that Eritrea would be the more appropriate forum. Plaintiffs submitted that a real risk existed that the Eritrean legal system would not provide a fair trial. In addition to first-hand affidavit evidence submitted by both sides, Justice Abrioux admitted certain reports prepared by governmental organisations and non-governmental organisations (NGOs) documenting human rights violations in Eritrea[60] and dismissed Nevsun's *forum non conveniens* application.[61]

The British Columbia Court of Appeal dismissed Nevsun's appeal. While recognising that a trial in British Columbia would pose substantial difficulties, the Court of Appeal considered that such difficulties were outweighed by concerns about the fairness or independence of the courts in which the plaintiffs would have to press their claims in Eritrea.[62] Nevsun did not challenge the Court of Appeal's decision on the matter of *forum non conveniens* before the Supreme Court.[63]

As one author pointed out even before the Supreme Court's ruling in *Nevsun*, the *Tahoe* and *Nevsun* appellate decisions pointed to a transition underway in which the prospect of litigation moving from foreign mining jurisdictions into Canadian courtrooms was becoming more likely.[64]

ii. *Forum non conveniens* in Quebec civil law

The doctrine of *forum non conveniens* is incorporated into Quebec civil law in Article 3135 CCQ:

> 3135. Although it has jurisdiction to hear a dispute, a Quebec authority may, exceptionally and at the request of a party, decline jurisdiction if it considers that the authorities of another State are better able to decide the dispute.

The inclusion of the common law doctrine of *forum non conveniens* in the civil law of Quebec underpins the broad basis with which jurisdiction can be assumed.[65] Exceptions to jurisdiction such as *forum non conveniens* call for a restrictive

60 *Araya v. Nevsun Resources Ltd* 2016 BCSC 1856, paras 156–172.
61 Ibid., paras 312–339.
62 *Araya v. Nevsun Resources Ltd* 2017 BCCA 401, paras 119–120.
63 *Nevsun Resources Ltd v. Araya* 2020 SCC 5, para. 26.
64 D. Newman, *Mining Law of Canada* (2018) 2–3.
65 See generally, G. Saumier, 'Le forum non conveniens au Québec, bilan d'une transplantation' in S. Guillemard (ed.), *Mélanges en l'honneur du professeur Alain Prujiner. Études de droit international privé et de droit du commerce international* (2011) 345–70.

interpretation.[66] As is the case in common law provinces, it is only where the courts have jurisdiction that the doctrine of *forum non conveniens* can be invoked.[67]

The Supreme Court discussed the Quebec civil law standard for *forum non conveniens* in *Van Breda*, mentioning that the analysis is basically identical to that of the common law courts, and that the terms 'exceptionally' found in 3135 CCQ and 'clearly more appropriate' found in common law cases both mean that 'that the normal state of affairs is that jurisdiction should be exercised once it is properly assumed'.[68]

The factors most frequently considered by Quebec courts in the exercise of their discretionary power are thus similar to those used in the common law provinces, as set out in *Oppenheim forfait GMBH v. Lexus Maritime Inc*[69] They include the place where the parties and the witnesses reside; the location of material evidence; the place where the contract giving rise to the proceedings was formed and performed; the existence and content of other proceedings instituted in another jurisdiction and the progress already made in the pursuit of those proceedings; the situation of the defendant's assets; the law applicable to the dispute; the juridical advantages enjoyed by the plaintiff in the chosen forum; the interests of justice and of both parties; and the need to have the judgment recognised in another jurisdiction.[70]

In the case of *Recherches internationales Québec v. Cambior Inc*[71] a class action lawsuit was initiated in the Quebec Superior Court against Cambior, the majority owner of a gold mine operating in Guyana whose tailings reservoir ruptured, spilling billions of litres of contaminated mine waste into nearby rivers. The *Cambior* case was the first time Canadian courts were asked to hold accountable a Canadian corporation which, acting through a subsidiary, created an environmental disaster abroad.

The plaintiffs, 23,000 Guyanese residents, argued that the resulting pollution impacted their health, food, water, livelihood, and right to a clean environment. The Superior Court judge found that the courts of both Guyana and Quebec had jurisdiction.[72] He concluded, however, that Guyana was the natural and appropriate forum to hear the case.[73] The court expressed concern that the victims should not

[66] G. Goldstein, 'De la pertinence et de la localisation du préjudice économique ou continu aux fins de la compétence internationale des tribunaux québécois' (2010) 69(169) *Revue du Barreau* 175.

[67] *Newfoundland and Labrador (Attorney General) v. Uashaunnuat (Innu of Uashat and Mani-Utenam)* 2020 SCC 4, para. 67; C. Emanuelli, *Droit international privé québécois* (3rd edn, 2011), para. 165; Emanuelli (n. 17) para. 116.

[68] *Club Resorts Ltd v. Van Breda* 2012 SCC 17, paras 107–109.

[69] *Oppenheim GMBH Package v. Lexus Maritime Inc* 1998 CanLII 13001 (CA), reiterated by the Court of Appeal of Québec in *Transax Technologies Inc v. Red Baron Corp Ltd* 2017 QCCA 626, para. 43. See also *Newfoundland and Labrador (Attorney General) v. Uashaunnuat (Innu of Uashat and Mani-Utenam)* 2020 SCC 4, para. 68; *R.S. v. P.R.* 2019 SCC 49, para. 74; *Breeden v. Black* 2012 SCC 19, para. 25; *Spar Aerospace Ltée v. American Mobile Satellite Corp* 2002 SCC 78, [2002] 4 SCR 205, para. 71.

[70] *Spar Aerospace Ltd v. American Mobile Satellite Corp* 2002 SCC 78, [2002] 4 SCR 205, para. 71.

[71] *Recherches internationales Québec v. Cambior inc* 1998 CanLII 9780 (QC CS).

[72] Ibid., para. 9.

[73] Ibid., para. 10.

be denied justice, but he was not persuaded by evidence tendered by the plaintiffs that the justice system in Guyana could not offer them a fair and impartial hearing.[74]

The *Cambior* decision, which was not appealed, was criticised by commentators as not having given due consideration to the exceptional nature of *forum non conveniens* in Quebec.[75] Subsequent suits brought in Guyana by the plaintiffs were dismissed without having been heard on the merits, leaving the victims without a remedy.[76]

In view of the similar treatment of *forum non conveniens* in civil and common law cases, and in light of the outcomes in *Tahoe* and *Nevsun*, it is unlikely a court in Quebec would reach the same result on the facts of *Cambior* today.

In *Bil'in Village Council v. Green Park*,[77] Palestinian villagers argued that by participating in the construction of settlements in occupied territories, a Canadian corporation headquartered in Quebec had committed war crimes. Unlike the situation in cases like *Tahoe* or *Cambior*, the plaintiffs had previously seised the High Court of Justice of Israel of several aspects of the dispute. Justice Cullen of the Quebec Superior Court found that they had selected a forum having little connection with the case in order to 'inappropriately gain a juridical advantage',[78] and dismissed the case of the basis of *forum non conveniens*, considering the High Court of Justice of Israel, to be the clearly more appropriate forum.[79]

D. Forum of necessity

i. Forum of necessity in the common law provinces

Forum of necessity is considered an exception to the real and substantial connection test and is interpreted as being limited to exceptional situations. In the absence of another forum in which the plaintiff may reasonably bring the action, the court seised with the matter may exercise jurisdiction over the case to avoid a denial of justice, even when it ordinarily lacks jurisdiction.

The forum of necessity doctrine has been adopted, with some minor differences, in legislation that implements the CJPTA in British Columbia and Nova Scotia.

74 Ibid., paras 11–12.

75 J. Talpis and S.L. Kath, 'The Exceptional as Commonplace in Quebec Forum Non Conveniens Law: Cambior, a Case in Point' (2000) 34 *Revue Juridique Thémis* 761, which article was cited with approval in *Spar Aerospace Ltd v. American Mobile Satellite Corp* [2002] 4 SCR 205, para. 81.

76 'Cambior Inc: Omai Lawsuit Struck and Dismissed' *CNN Money* (31 October 2006) <https://money.cnn.com/news/newsfeeds/articles/marketwire/06178759.htm> accessed 14 May 2020. See also Amnesty International, *Injustice Incorporated: Corporate Abuses and the Human Right to a Remedy* (London, Amnesty International Ltd 2014) 65–80.

77 *Bil'In (Village Council) v. Green Park International Inc* 2009 QCCS 4151.

78 Ibid., para. 335.

79 The Court of Appeal dismissed the appeal: *Yassin v. Green Park International Inc* 2010 QCCA 1455.

Similar to Article 3136 CCQ, whose language it tracks,[80] section 6 of the CJPTA can be invoked even where the court seised lacks jurisdiction. Unlike Article 3136, the CJPTA-derived provisions do not include an explicit requirement of a sufficient connection with the forum seised.

The doctrine was also recognised in Canadian common law by the Ontario Court of Appeal in *Van Breda*[81] and was further discussed by that court in *West Van Inc v. Daisley.*[82] To decide on its application, the Court of Appeal considered Quebec case law, referring to the examples offered by the Quebec Court Appeal in *Lamborghini (Canada) Inc v. Automobili Lamborghini S.P.A*,[83] which included termination of diplomatic or commercial relations, the need to protect a political refugee, and the existence of serious physical threat in the event that the dispute were to take place before a foreign court. In the *Lamborghini* case, Justice Lebel, then sitting on the Quebec Court of Appeal, referred to the standard as requiring the demonstrated impossibility of access to the foreign court, language more restrictive than that used in the CJPTA.[84] The court in *Daisley* also referred to the case of *Bouzari v. Bahremani*,[85] in which the plaintiff was tortured in Iran, as justifying the assumption of jurisdiction on the basis of forum of necessity.[86]

Though the goal of the CJPTA is uniformity of private international law across Canada, Saskatchewan's CJPTA-derived legislation does not include any provision for forum of necessity.[87] The legislative decision to exclude forum of necessity in Saskatchewan arguably denies access to the doctrine in that province, displacing its availability in the common law.[88]

ii. Forum of necessity in Quebec civil law

Inspired by Swiss private international law, the doctrine of forum of necessity was introduced into Quebec civil law in 1994 in Article 3136 CCQ:

> Even though a Québec authority has no jurisdiction to hear a dispute, it may nevertheless hear it provided the dispute has a sufficient connection with Québec, if proceedings abroad prove impossible or the institution of proceedings abroad cannot reasonably be required.

80 ULCC comment to section 6 CJPTA, reproduced in V. Black, S.G.A. Pitel, and M. Sobkin, *Statutory Jurisdiction: An Analysis of the Court Jurisdiction and Proceedings Transfer Act* (2012).

81 *Van Breda v. Village Resorts Limited* 2010 ONCA 84, para. 54. The Supreme Court left open the discussion of forum of necessity in Van Breda: see *Club Resorts Ltd v. Van Breda* 2012 SCC 17, para. 59.

82 *West Van Inc v. Daisley* (2014) 317 OAC 294.

83 *Lamborghini (Canada) Inc v. Automobili Lamborghini S.P.A.* 1996 CanLII 6047 (QC CA).

84 *West Van Inc v. Daisley* (2014) 317 OAC 294, para. 22. The Court of Appeal also referred to the Anvil Mining case, paras 24–25. See *Lamborghini (Canada) Inc v. Automobili Lamborghini S.P.A.* 1996 CanLII 6047 (QC CA), p. 21.

85 *Bouzari v. Bahremani* 2013 ONSC 6337.

86 *West Van Inc v. Daisley* (2014) 317 OAC 294, paras 26–27.

87 *Court Jurisdiction and Proceedings Transfer Act*, SS 1997, c C-41.1.

88 Black, Pitel, and Sobkin (n. 80) 174–7.

A party may invoke forum of necessity if the Quebec authorities otherwise have no jurisdiction over the subject matter of the litigation. Article 3136 is not designed to allow the parties greater convenience but rather to avoid a denial of justice, and it may only be applied in exceptional circumstances.[89]

Despite being limited to cases in which the court has no jurisdiction, unlike the CJPTA provisions and the interpretation of the Ontario Court of Appeal, there still must be a sufficient connection between the subject matter of the litigation and Quebec. The nature of the connection required will vary according to the facts of each case.[90] The International Law Association's 2012 guidelines for best practices in civil litigation involving human rights violations suggest that a sufficient connection would exist by virtue of the claimant's presence in the jurisdiction; the claimant or the defendant's nationality; or the fact that the defendant holds assets or carries out some activity in the jurisdiction.[91]

In *Anvil Mining*, the Quebec Court of Appeal interpreted Article 3136 CCQ narrowly. It referred to the *Lamborghini* case and emphasised the first branch of the test—impossibility of proceeding elsewhere—while declining to discuss the second branch, which is less demanding and available if plaintiffs cannot be reasonably expected to seise another forum.[92] The Court of Appeal also considered that despite the presence of Anvil's only Canadian establishment in Quebec, the plaintiffs had failed to demonstrate a sufficient connection with the forum.[93] The Court expressed its sympathy for the victims but, despite the discretionary nature of forum of necessity, opined that Quebec legislation could regrettably not allow Quebec courts to hear their case.[94]

The ruling in *Anvil Mining*, although it has been criticised,[95] leaves very small window for the assumption of jurisdiction based on forum of necessity in Quebec. In view of the Supreme Court's ruling in *Nevsun*, and in particular the majority's acknowledgement of the role of Canadian courts in identifying and responsively addressing breaches of international human rights,[96] it is fair to question whether a court would reach the same conclusion today.

[89] *Lamborghini (Canada) Inc v. Automobili Lamborghini S.P.A.* 1996 CanLII 6047 (QC CA) page 21.

[90] Emanuelli (n. 17) para. 119.

[91] International Law Association, *Resolution no 2 /2012: International Civil Litigation and the Interests of the Public / Sofia Guidelines on Best Practices for International Civil Litigation for Human Rights Violations*, <https://www.ila-hq.org/index.php/committees>, section 2.3, accessed 20 November 2020.

[92] *Anvil Mining Ltd v. Association canadienne contre l'impunité* 2012 QCCA 117, paras 98–100.

[93] Ibid., para. 103.

[94] Ibid., para. 104.

[95] Saumier (n. 40). See, however, *Zoungrana v. Air Algérie* 2016 QCCS 2311 (appeal dismissed *Zoungrana v. Air Algérie* 2016 QCCA 1074, leave to appeal to the Supreme Court denied, no. 37190, 16 February 2017), para. 103 in which the standard was described as placing an onus on the plaintiff to show that '[i]t must be shown that it would be impossible or nearly so to sue abroad'.

[96] *Nevsun Resources Ltd v. Araya* 2020 SCC 5, para. 2.

E. Choice of law

In both common law provinces and Quebec civil law, the substantive law applicable to the consequences of wrongful behaviour causing injury is the law of the place where the behaviour occurred.

In the common law provinces, the Supreme Court's decision in *Tolofson v. Jensen*[97] sought to ensure certainty, ease of application, and predictability by establishing *lex loci delicti*, the place where the tort occurs, as the general principle for determining applicable law.[98] While the rule is clear, the Court recognised that in an international setting, as opposed to within Canada, the strict application of *lex loci delicti* may lead to an injustice, and consequently left some discretion to apply the law of the forum instead.[99] If no proof is made of the foreign law, the court will apply its own law instead.[100]

In Quebec, *lex loci delicti* is codified in Article 3126 CCQ which provides that the applicable law is that of the State where the injurious act occurred. The article provides for two exceptions. The first stipulates that if the injury appears in a foreign State and the person who committed the injurious act should have foreseen that it would manifest itself there, the law of that State applies. The second provides that if the person who committed the injurious act and the victim have their domiciles or residences in the same State, the law of that State applies.

Article 3081 CCQ provides that even if Quebec's conflict rules render the law of a foreign State applicable, that law does not apply if its application would be manifestly inconsistent with public order as understood in international relations. The reference to public order 'as [it is] understood in international relations' sets a high bar as it is limited to situations in which the application of the foreign law would result in the violation of fundamental moral, social, or political values.[101] Quebec courts have, for example, invoked Article 3081 CCQ to refuse to apply foreign family law provisions based on strict Islamic law in which women do not have equal rights.[102]

The application of *lex loci delicti* thus makes the law of the host nation applicable in principle to cases involving human rights violations occurring abroad. To the extent that the plaintiff is invoking the direct liability of a parent corporation however, acts or omissions of the parent corporation involved in ordering, implementing, or supervising the activities alleged to have caused harm could arguably be governed by its home jurisdiction's laws. However, the Ontario Court of Appeal in *Das v. George Weston Limited*[103] held that when wrongful conduct

[97] *Tolofson v. Jensen* [1994] 3 SCR 1022.
[98] Ibid., p. 1050; see also *Haaretz.com v. Goldhar* 2018 SCC 28, para. 84
[99] *Tolofson v. Jensen* [1994] 3 SCR 1022, p. 1054.
[100] Ibid., p. 1053.
[101] Ministère de la Justice, *Commentaires du ministre de la Justice—Tome II* (1993) p. 1954.
[102] See, for example, *Droit de la famille—1535* 2015 QCCS 106.
[103] *Das v. George Weston Limited 2018 ONCA 1053*, paras 87–91.

occurs in multiple jurisdictions, the place where the injury occurs crystallises the alleged wrong and constitutes the *lex loci delicti*.

The consequences of the host nation's law applying in a Canadian court can be felt in several areas. Victims of human rights abuses often face barriers to access to justice stemming not from an absence of relevant legal norms but rather from a lack of resources, corruption, intimidation, or insufficient judicial independence. Wrongful behaviour will often be actionable under the foreign law, as most nations have norms which, on paper at least, provide that wrongful behaviour can be sanctioned if it causes injury. The host nation's substantive law must, however, be proved through expert evidence. As a result, the specifics of the applicable law may become a battleground for competing experts. As well, judges may be reluctant to hear arguments that would require any development of the foreign law.

Another obstacle potentially created by the application of host nation law is that the quantum of damages available may not be sufficient to allow a case to be viable financially, or to achieve any kind of deterrence in Canada.[104]

Limitations periods, which are considered substantive law,[105] can also vary significantly, sometimes to the advantage of the victims.[106]

IV. Justiciability issues

Extractive activities in weak governance regions frequently involve joint ventures or other types of partnerships with government agencies or State-owned corporations. Involvement of foreign governments, either directly or indirectly, has constituted an obstacle for plaintiffs.

A. Sovereign immunity

Sovereign immunity is incorporated into Canadian law through the *State Immunity Act*[107] and can be raised by a defendant State at any stage of the proceedings.[108] It extends to the subdivisions of the State and to the agencies of the foreign government, including those which have a distinct legal form.[109] The main exception provides that immunity does not apply to proceedings that relate to any commercial

104 *Tolofson v. Jensen* [1994] 3 SCR 1022, p.1058.

105 *Castillo v. Castillo* [2005] 3 SCR 870, para. 39. In Quebec, prescription (limitation periods) is governed by the law which governs the merits of the dispute: art. 3131 CCQ.

106 For example, in the *Anvil Mining* case, the limitation period applicable under the Civil Code of the Democratic Republic of Congo was 30 years.

107 RSC (1985) c S-18.

108 *Schreiber v. Canada (Attorney General)* 2002 SCC 62, para. 18. See also *Kazemi Estate v. Islamic Republic of Iran*, 2014 SCC 62.

109 *State Immunity Act*, RSC (1985) c S-18, section 3(1) and 3(2).

activity of the foreign State.[110] If an activity is commercial in its essence, the exception applies, even if the activity was performed to protect a State interest or attain a public policy objective.[111]

B. Act of State

One of the central issues before the Supreme Court in *Nevsun* was the whether the common law doctrine of act of State existed in Canada, and if so, how it should be applied. The doctrine arose in that case because Nevsun alleged that the plaintiffs' claims would require the Canadian court to assess the legality of acts committed by the government of Eritrea, which it argued would render the issue non-justiciable.[112] The majority, joined on this issue by Justices Brown and Rowe, ruled that the act of State doctrine is not part of the Canadian common law.[113] Canada has developed its own approach to such disputes, rooted in the principles of conflict of laws and judicial restraint,[114] and the act of State doctrine has been completely absorbed by this jurisprudence.[115]

V. Causes of action

A. Causes of action in common law provinces

Prior to *Nevsun*, plaintiffs seeking private law remedies for human rights violations by Canadian corporations in common law provinces relied primarily on the traditional categories of tort liability, which include negligence and the intentional torts such as assault, battery, conspiracy, conversion, or false imprisonment. Most international human rights cases invoke negligence, which requires the plaintiff to prove that the defendant owed a duty of care; that the duty of care was breached; that the breach of duty caused damage; and that such damage is not too remote. However, many commentators argued that such categories did not properly translate the seriousness of the conduct involved in war crimes, slavery, or crimes against humanity.[116]

110 Ibid., s. 5; *Kazemi Estate v. Islamic Republic of Iran* 2014 SCC 62, para. 41.
111 *Kuwait Airways Corp v. Iraq* 2010 SCC 40, [2010] 2 SCR 571, para. 30.
112 *Nevsun Resources Ltd v. Araya* 2020 SCC 5, para. 27.
113 Ibid., para. 59.
114 Ibid., para. 44.
115 Ibid., para. 57.
116 Ibid., paras 125–126.

The Supreme Court's ruling in *Nevsun* is thus perhaps most significant for its discussion of the plaintiffs' claim that breaches of customary international law are directly actionable at common law. Nevsun's motion to strike such claims was dismissed by a 5–4 majority. Justices Brown and Rowe, joined by Justices Côté and Moldaver, dissented forcefully on this issue.[117]

The split between the majority and the minority offers evidence of different views of the role of Canadian courts, with the majority acknowledging that they can and should actively implement and advance customary international law,[118] with a view to 'effectively and justly remedying breaches',[119] whereas the minority considered that the role of Canadian courts was primarily 'to adjudicate on disputes within Canada'.[120]

Although the majority left it to the trial judge to determine how claims based on breaches of customary international law should proceed,[121] it expressed opinions on several key issues which will influence how that process is implemented. It concluded that it was not plain and obvious that customary international law did not apply to corporations,[122] and that it was not plain and obvious that Canadian courts could not develop a civil remedy for such breaches.[123] In addition, in view of the majority's conclusion that violations of customary international law norms such as forced labour, slavery, crimes against humanity, and cruel, inhuman, and degrading treatment were inherently different from existing domestic torts, it opined that refusing to acknowledge such differences could 'undermine the court's ability to adequately address the heinous nature of the harm' caused by such conduct.[124] As well, as mentioned, the Court reaffirmed that customary international law is automatically adopted into domestic law[125] and ruled that courts should take judicial notice of it.[126]

While the Supreme Court's findings on these issues will not be implemented in the *Nevsun* case, as it was the object of a confidential out-of-court settlement some months after the decision,[127] the majority's ruling on these issues represents an emphatic confirmation of the paradigm shift which had begun in cases

[117] Justices Côté and Moldaver concurred with Justices Brown and Rowe on this issue and would otherwise have dismissed the case on the basis of the act of State doctrine, ibid., para. 267.

[118] Ibid., para. 72.

[119] Ibid., para. 129.

[120] Ibid., para. 259.

[121] Ibid., para. 127.

[122] Ibid., paras 113–114.

[123] Ibid., para. 122.

[124] Ibid., paras 124–125.

[125] Ibid., paras 86–96.

[126] Ibid., para. 96.

[127] Amnesty International, 'Amnesty International applauds settlement in landmark Nevsun Resources mining case' <https://amnesty.ca/news/amnesty-international-applauds-settlement-landmark-nevsun-resources-mining-case>, accessed 15 May 2021.

such as *Hudbay* and *Tahoe*, and the rulings of the lower instances in *Nevsun* and signals a willingness to allow avenues for redress which are more closely aligned with the realities of the economic relationship between multinational corporations and victims of their operations in weak governance regions.

B. Causes of action in Quebec civil law

In Quebec civil law, extra-contractual liability is founded on the general principle that wrongful conduct, whether by act or omission,[128] which causes injury, renders the wrongdoer liable for reparation of the injury.[129] There is no requirement to recognise a duty of care specific to the type of relationship although the plaintiff must show a direct causal link between the wrongful act and the harm.[130] Conduct is wrongful if it is not in conformity with the rules of conduct which apply according to the circumstances, usage, or law.[131] The objective standard is that of the reasonable person placed in similar circumstances.

The Supreme Court's discussion of the adoption of customary international law in *Hape* and *Nevsun* was founded on common law precedents. In Quebec civil law, Article 2807 CCQ states that the court takes judicial notice of the 'law in force' in Quebec. The law in force includes customary international law.[132] However, the second paragraph of Article 2807 provides that customary international law, along with other sources of law which may be less well known to a judge, must be pleaded. A judge may nonetheless take judicial notice of it if is known to him or her.[133]

Violations of customary international law constitute civil faults. In the *Bil'in* case, though he dismissed the case on the basis of *forum non conveniens*, Justice Cullen recognised that international prohibitions against war crimes contain elementary norms of prudence 'the violation of which constitutes a civil fault'.[134] Thus, a violation of customary international law will normally constitute a violation of Article 1457 CCQ, a result in close harmony with the adoption of customary international law in Canadian common law.

[128] Unlike the rule in Canadian common law, a fault of omission in civil law does not require a specific duty to act. See M. Katsivela, 'Le manquement à la norme de diligence et la faute dans le cadre du délit de négligence (Common Law) et de la responsabilité extracontractuelle du fait personnel (Droit civil) au Canada: une étude comparée' (2017) 95(2) *Canadian Bar Review* 535; J.-L. Baudouin, P. Deslauriers, and B. Moore, *La responsabilité civile, Volume 1—Principes généraux* (8th edn, 2014), para. 1-186.

[129] CCQ, art. 1457.

[130] CCQ, art. 1607.

[131] CCQ, art. 1457.

[132] C Piché, *La preuve civile* (5th edn, 2016), para. 106.

[133] CCQ, art. 2808(2).

[134] *Bil'In (Village Council) v. Green Park International Inc* 2009 QCCS 4151, para. 175.

VI. Corporate issues

The corporate veil remains one of the main obstacles facing plaintiffs seeking to hold a Canadian parent corporation liable for the activities of its subsidiaries in weak governance regions. One may question whether it is either fair or reasonable to allow a company to set up operations through subsidiaries in a developing country, to take profits from it without accounting for the true human and environmental cost of those operations, all the while enjoying the protection of limited liability. Fair or not, the legal advice routinely given to Canadian corporations in the extractive sector emphasises the need to take steps to ensure that any liability remains in the shallow pockets of the subsidiary operating in the host country.[135] Supreme Court Justice Ian Binnie expressed his doubts about this use of the corporate veil in a speech in 2013:

> This concept, deeply rooted in corporate law, is used regularly to deny liability of the head office, with its deep pockets, for the acts of its subsidiaries in the far flung regions of the world where, it is alleged, the wrongful acts occurred. In a corporate pyramid the profits flow up the chain to the top (or are taken at whatever corporate level seems most advantageous) but legal liability remains stuck at the bottom where there may be liability but shallow pockets.[136]

As in other jurisdictions, Canada has developed criteria which allow for the piercing of the corporate veil. In addition, most likely due to the onerous burden required of a plaintiff seeking to hold a parent corporation liable for the actions of its subsidiary, plaintiffs in international human rights cases are increasingly invoking the direct liability of the parent company.

A. Piercing the corporate veil in common law provinces

In all provinces, piercing the corporate veil requires that plaintiffs prove control by the parent of the subsidiary and its use for an illegitimate purpose. However, the application of the doctrine varies among the common law provinces and the terms

[135] S. Stimpson, J. Todesco, and A. Maginley, 'Strategies for Risk Management and Corporate Social Responsibility for Oil and Gas Companies in Emerging Markets' (2015) 53(2) *Alberta Law Review* 259, para. 114.

[136] The Honourable Ian Binnie, 'Judging The Judges: "May They Boldly Go Where Ivan Rand Went Before"' (2013) 26(5) *Canadian Journal of Law & Jurisprudence* 5, para. 66. On corporate liability in the extractive sector see generally: J.T. Lauzon, 'Araya v. Nevsun Resources: Remedies for Victims of Human Rights Violations Committed by Canadian Mining Companies Abroad' (2018) 31(1) *Revue québécoise de droit international* 143, para. 48; S.E.D. Fairhurst and Z. Thoms, 'Energy Law Edition Post-Kiobel v. Royal Dutch Petroleum Co.: Is Canada Poised to Become an Alternative Jurisdiction for Extraterritorial Human Rights Litigation?' (2014) 53(2) *Alberta Law Review* 389, para. 37.

employed are somewhat vague.[137] Some authors have qualified the veil piercing principles applied by the Canadian common law as a 'mishmash of indeterminate expressions' that have been 'in a state of confusion since their inception'.[138] There is also some uncertainty as to what measure of fraudulent or improper conduct is required, in addition to the element of control.[139]

The criteria used to determine that a subsidiary is under the control of the parent are those developed in the English case of *Smith, Stone & Knight, Ltd v. Birmingham Corp*,[140] and include whether the profits were treated as profits of the parent or of the subsidiary; whether the individuals involved in the day-to-day operations were appointed by the parent; whether the parent corporation was the 'brains' behind the day-to-day operations; whether the parent corporation made policy and financial decisions that were merely carried out by the subsidiary; whether the profits were directly traceable to the skill and direction of the parent; and whether control by the parent was constant, as would be the case in a typical principal–agent situation, or merely periodic and long range, as might occur in a typical corporation–shareholder situation.[141]

As regards illegitimate conduct, the Ontario Court of Appeal in *Yaiguaje v. Chevron Corporation*[142] rejected the notion that lifting the corporate veil is predicated on any type of just and equitable standard,[143] and ruled that it was restricted to situations in which either the court construes a statute or contract; the court is satisfied that a company is a 'mere façade' concealing the true facts, or it can be established that the company is 'an authorized agent of its controllers or its members, corporate or human'.[144]

In cases where the allegation is that the corporation is a 'mere façade', the court must be satisfied that there is complete control of the subsidiary such that the subsidiary is the 'mere puppet' of the parent corporation, and that the subsidiary was incorporated for a fraudulent or improper purpose or used by the parent as a shell for improper activity.[145] This high bar was not met in the *Yaiguaje* case, in which Indigenous Ecuadorian plaintiffs were seeking to enforce a multi-billion-dollar judgment obtained in Ecuador on a Canadian

137 M.F. Khimji and C.C. Nicholls, 'Piercing the Corporate Veil in the Canadian Common Law Courts: An Empirical Study' (2015) 41(1) *Queen's Law Journal* 207, paras 9, 11. See also para. 17.

138 Ibid., para. 17.

139 Avoiding liability *per se* is not an improper purpose.

140 *Smith, Stone & Knight, Ltd v. Birmingham Corp* [1939] All ER 116 (KB).

141 Reiterated in *Buanderie Centrale de Montréal v. Montréal* [1994] 3 SCR 29; *Holmes v. Jastek Master Builder 2004 Inc* 2019 SKCA 132, para. 50. See also the factors listed in M.F. Khimji and C.C. Nicholls, 'Piercing the Corporate Veil Reframed as Evasion and Concealment' (2015) 48 *University of British Columbia Law Review* 401, para. 8; Khimji and Nicholls (n. 137).

142 *Yaiguaje v. Chevron Corporation* 2018 ONCA 472 (application for leave to the Supreme Court dismissed, no. 38183, 4 April 2019).

143 Ibid., para. 67. See also Fairhurst and Thoms (n. 136) paras 38, 44.

144 *Yaiguaje v. Chevron Corporation* 2018 ONCA 472, para. 65.

145 Ibid., para. 66.

subsidiary of Chevron in relation to environmental damage caused by historical oil exploration activities.

In *Holmes v. Jastek Master Builder 2004 Inc*,[146] the Saskatchewan Court of Appeal noted that unlike the Court of Appeal of Ontario, it viewed the lifting of the corporate veil as not being limited to situations involving fraudulent or improper conduct. While it requires more than mere unfairness or a '*mere* corporate agency' it remains fact-based and requires a contextual analysis.[147]

B. Piercing the corporate veil in Quebec civil law

The Quebec legislator codified the principles applicable to lifting the corporate veil in Article 317 CCQ in an attempt to systematise the jurisprudential exceptions to the principle of limited liability of shareholders:[148]

> **317.** The juridical personality of a legal person may not be invoked against a person in good faith so as to dissemble fraud, abuse of right or contravention of a rule of public order.

This provision is intended to prevent abuses that can occur when legal personality and limited liability are diverted from their economic purpose and no longer serve to protect the shareholder against normal business risks, but rather serve an illicit purpose or produce an illicit effect.[149] The manipulation of the economic purpose can occur if the company is used to commit or legitimise fraud, an abuse of right, or a contravention of a rule of public order.[150]

Abuse of right is a flexible concept which can be used to sanction behaviour which, although not illegal per se, is not in accordance with the rules of equity and fair play.[151] A rule of public order refers to mandatory, non-derogable norms. *Charter* rights[152]—that is, constitutional or quasi-constitutional rights and civil liberties—represent public order provisions whose transgression may justify the lifting of the corporate veil.[153] It follows that *jus cogens* norms is likely to be considered rules of public order. Although violations of public order or abuses of right

[146] *Holmes v. Jastek Master Builder 2004 Inc* 2019 SKCA 132.

[147] Ibid., paras 50, 119–122. For a similar view, see *Globex Foreign Exchange Corp v. Launt* 2011 NSCA 67, paras 23–24.

[148] R. Crête and S. Rousseau, *Droit des sociétés par actions* (4th edn, 2018), para. 247.

[149] Ibid., para. 257.

[150] Ibid., paras 259–261.

[151] *Houle v. Canadian National Bank* [1990] 3 SCR 122, p. 155.

[152] *Canadian Charter of Rights and Freedoms*, Part I of the *Constitution Act, 1982*, being Schedule B to the *Canada Act 1982* (UK), 1982, c 11; *Charter of Human Rights and Freedoms*, CQLR c C-12.

[153] Crête and Rousseau (n. 148) para. 303.

are rarely invoked in the case law,[154] both could allow an equitable standard to be incorporated into the analysis of the piercing of the corporate veil.

In order for the corporate veil to be lifted a level of control must exist, which is described as the parent being the *alter ego* of its subsidiary.[155] The criteria used to determine whether a subsidiary is the *alter ego* of the parent company are the same as those developed in the English case of *Smith, Stone and Knight, Ltd v. Birmingham Corp* mentioned above, as reiterated by the Supreme Court of Canada in *Buanderie Centrale de Montréal v. Montréal*.[156]

C. The direct liability of the parent company in common law provinces

Framing the issue through the prism of the corporate veil can obscure the fact that parent companies are often actively involved in the operations carried out through subsidiaries in weak governance regions. Although corporations routinely organise their corporate structures so as to limit their potential liability, they also routinely represent to investors that such activities are in fact *their* activities, sometimes their only activities.[157] In this context, parent companies are increasingly facing claims alleging their direct liability for harm caused by such activities.

The decision of the Ontario Superior Court in *Hudbay* marked a turning point in this regard by opening the door in Canada to assessing liability of Canadian parent corporations for their own conduct.[158] In *Hudbay*, Justice Brown refused to dismiss an action against a parent company despite the fact that its corporate structure assigned operations to a Guatemalan-based subsidiary, concluding that it was not clear that a novel duty of care could not be established against the parent.[159]

In that case, the Court reviewed the *Anns* test for establishing a new duty of care[160]—as applied in Canada by the Supreme Court in *Cooper v. Hobart*[161]—and found that the plaintiffs had satisfactorily pleaded that the harm they suffered was

154 Ibid., para. 307.

155 *3458296 Canada inc v. SIRR Desjardins Inc* 2005 QCCA 826, para. 27.

156 *Buanderie Centrale de Montréal v. Montréal* [1994] 3 SCR 29, pp. 46–7. See generally, Crête and Rousseau (n. 148) para. 272 and following.

157 For example, in an SEC filing of Nevsun Resources Inc. for 2011, its sole productive asset was listed as the Bisha mine in Eritrea which was held by an Eritrean subsidiary through a chain of three other companies. It also informed investors that it had eight employees in Canada and 550 in Eritrea. See 'Annual Information Form for the fiscal year ending December 31, 2010', filed with the Securities and Exchange Commission <https://www.sec.gov/Archives/edgar/data/0000919991/000113717111000176/ex991.htm>, accessed 27 September 2020.

158 D. Newman, *Mining Law of Canada* (2018) Chapter 14-4; I. Tchotourian, V. Deshaye, and R. MacFarlane Drouin, 'Entreprises et responsabilité sociale: évolution ou révolution du droit canadien des affaires' (2016) 57 *Cahiers de droit* 635, para. 41.

159 *Choc v. Hudbay Minerals Inc* 2013 ONSC 1414, paras 54–75.

160 *Anns v. Merton London Borough Council* [1977] AC 728 (HL).

161 *Cooper v. Hobart* [2001] 3 SCR 537, para. 30 and following.

the foreseeable consequence of Hudbay's own negligence, that there was sufficient proximity between the parties, that it would not be unjust to impose a duty of care upon the parent company, and that there was no policy reason to negate that duty.[162]

In its analysis, the Court referred to the fact that Hudbay had publicly stated that it had done everything in its power to prevent some of the alleged abuses, which suggested a relationship of proximity with the plaintiffs.[163]

Although there has not yet been a decision on the merits that recognises a new duty of care of a parent company in relation to activities conducted abroad through its subsidiaries,[164] it is noteworthy that the plaintiffs in *Nevsun* have also invoked the direct liability of the Canadian parent corporation[165] and that the Supreme Court's majority ruling mentions the finding of the first judge that the parent company had operational control over the Eritrean operations.[166] In view of the Supreme Court's findings regarding the potential liability of corporations for violations of customary international law,[167] and its recognition of the need for adequate remedies,[168] it seems likely such a duty will be recognised.

Nonetheless, it remains that this avenue is not likely to be available with respect to a parent company that is not directly involved in its subsidiary's activities. Paradoxically, this situation incentivises parent companies to turn a blind eye to the activities of their subsidiaries, even though they financially benefit from such activities carried out in high-risk environments.[169]

D. The direct liability of the parent company in Quebec civil law

Article 309 CCQ codifies the corporate veil in Quebec civil law, mandating that corporations are distinct from their shareholders and that 'their acts bind none but themselves'. The obvious corollary is that a corporation's acts bind the corporation.

If a corporation participates in wrongful behaviour, regardless of whether a subsidiary also participated, it can be held liable. In such cases, there is no necessity

162 *Choc v. Hudbay Minerals Inc* 2013 ONSC 1414, para. 75.

163 Ibid., para. 68; M. Conway, 'A New Duty of Care? Tort Liability from Voluntary Human Rights Due Diligence in Global Supply Chains' (2015) 40(2) *Queen's Law Journal* 741, para. 45.

164 See also *United Canadian Malt Ltd v. Outboard Marine Corp*, 2000 CanLII 22365 (ON SC) in which the Ontario Superior Court refused to strike allegations as they could form the basis of a claim directly against the parent independent of any issue as to whether the corporate veil should be pierced.

165 *Araya v. Nevsun Resources Ltd* 2016 BCSC 1856, para. 43. At para. 52, Justice Abrioux quotes a Nevsun corporate document stating that '[t]hrough its majority representation on the board of BMSC, [Nevsun] is involved in all aspects of Bisha operations'.

166 *Nevsun Resources Ltd v. Araya* 2020 SCC 5, para. 17.

167 Ibid., para. 116.

168 Ibid., paras 117–122.

169 A. Michoud, 'Mind the (Liability) Gap: The Relevance of the Duty of Care to Hold Transnational Corporations Accountable' (2019) 40(141) 40 *Windsor Review of Legal & Social Issues* 159.

to pierce the corporate veil,[170] as the mere fact that one of the persons involved in the relationship is a corporation does not create any veil over its relationships with other persons.[171]

Many cases which appear to pierce the corporate veil merely recognise that a sufficient direct juridical link exists between shareholders or directors and third parties. For example, it is well established that directors of a corporation can incur liability if they have committed a personal fault, or participated in an extra-contractual fault of the corporation, without any need to lift the corporate veil.[172] In a similar way, in *Houle v. Canadian National Bank*,[173] a landmark decision in extra-contractual liability in Quebec, the Supreme Court reaffirmed that shareholders could not sue for the wrongful acts of a third party defendant against a corporation because the right to do so belongs to the corporation itself.[174] However, the Court recognised that if the defendant breached a separate obligation to the shareholders and that breach caused them direct harm, they would have a personal right of action.[175]

The possibility of direct liability of a parent company which participated, either by act or omission, in wrongful behaviour causing injury is a straightforward application of recognised principles of Quebec civil law. However, as in Canadian common law, to the extent that the parent company is only involved as a shareholder of a subsidiary, the corporate veil remains an obstacle.

VII. Financial issues

A. Costs regimes and security for costs

i. Costs regimes

In all Canadian provinces, the power to award costs is discretionary,[176] but unsuccessful litigants must typically pay costs to the successful party. In most common law provinces, costs are awarded on a partial indemnity basis which usually represents a significant portion of the actual legal fees and disbursements of the winning party.[177] As a result, the loser-pays regime in the common law provinces is a significant deterrent for impecunious foreign victims.

In Quebec, costs are established on the basis of a tariff which does not include legal fees per se. Consequently, legal costs represent a smaller fraction of the legal

[170] P. Martel, *La société par actions au Québec: Les aspects juridiques* (2020), para. 1-218.
[171] Ibid., para. 1-211.
[172] *Transax Technologies inc* v. *Red Baron Corp Ltd* 2017 QCCA 626, para. 25.
[173] *Houle v. Canadian National Bank* [1990] 3 SCR 122.
[174] Ibid., pp. 177–80; *Brunette v. Legault Joly Thiffault, s.e.n.c.r.l.* 2018 SCC 55, para. 29.
[175] Ibid., para. 29.
[176] *British Columbia (Minister of Forests) v. Okanagan Indian Band* 2003 SCC 71, para. 19.
[177] M.M. Orkin, *Orkin on the Law of Costs* (2nd edn, 1987) 2-9 to 2-11.

fees actually incurred. Costs can be awarded on a solicitor–client basis, which can represent full indemnity, but only if the party ordered to pay them conducted the litigation in a reprehensible manner.[178]

ii. Security for costs

In every province, a defendant is entitled to request security for its costs against a foreign plaintiff.[179] Payment of the security is a condition which must be met before proceeding with the action. The amount of security may be updated at the defendant's request as the litigation progresses. Security for costs can represent a substantial obstacle for foreign plaintiffs.

B. Legal fees

Though they are regulated, contingency fee agreements, in which lawyers are only paid in if they are successful, are permitted in civil cases in all Canadian provinces.[180] With victims most often not being able to contribute to fees or costs except as a share of the outcome, the possibility for the lawyers to share in an eventual damages award is of vital importance as cases involving international human rights violations by multinational corporations are typically complex, costly to fund, defended by deep pocketed determined adversaries, and of unknown duration.

C. Litigation funding

In cases where the expected out of pocket expenses or the potential adverse costs are too high, or the lawyers are not capable or willing to assume the risks, litigation funding is also available in all provinces, though its parameters are still evolving.[181]

D. Availability of damages

In cases where the application of *lex loci delicti* results in the host country's law applying, the damages available under that law may be insufficient for the case to be financially viable.

[178] *Viel v. Entreprises immobilières du terroir Ltée* 2002 CanLII 41120 (QC CA), paras 72–82. Solicitor-client costs are also reserved for cases exhibiting reprehensible conduct in the common law provinces. See *Mackin v. New Brunswick (Minister of Finance)* 2002 SCC 13, para. 86.

[179] *Code of civil procedure* CQLR c C-25.01, art 492; see also, for an example of the common law provisions, Ontario Rules of Civil Procedure, RRO 1990, Reg 194, art. 56.01.

[180] For example, see *Solicitors Act*, RSO 1990, c S.15, art. 28.1.

[181] *9354-9186 Québec inc v. Callidus Capital Corp* 2020 SCC 10, paras 93–96.

VIII. Procedural issues

A. Discovery

Documentary and oral discovery is a central component of civil litigation in Canada in all provinces. Although it is less extensive than what is typically allowed in the United States, it allows parties to prepare for trial by knowing the case of their opponents, or to resolve their disputes in an informed manner.

B. Availability of class proceedings

All Canadian provinces except Prince Edward Island have enacted class action legislation. Class actions allow one plaintiff to bring an action on behalf of many who have a common interest. Among the fundamental objectives of class action legislation are to provide access to justice for victims and to achieve behaviour modification. By sharing costs among many plaintiffs and deferring them with a contingency agreement, claims can become economically viable which would not otherwise have been. This fact may encourage corporations to internalise the true cost of their activities.[182]

IX. Conclusion

One of the primary roles of civil liability is to allocate the true cost of economic activities to the beneficiary of the goods and services those activities produce. One of the primary challenges of globalisation has been the failure of national courts to hold domestic corporations accountable for the true human and environmental cost of their activities abroad. Former Supreme Court Justice Ian Binnie has argued that Canadian courts should take a more innovative approach to corporate accountability, bridging the gap between the laws that protect human rights across national boundaries and the laws and conventions designed to facilitate corporate activities on a global scale.[183] In his 2013 article, Justice Binnie suggested three avenues which could facilitate access to justice for victims of international harms before Canadian courts: an explicit recognition of the forum of necessity doctrine; the domestic application of *jus cogens* norms; and reform to the doctrine of piercing the corporate veil.

In the spirit of Justice Binnie's exhortation, the Supreme Court's ruling in *Nevsun* demonstrates a willingness to progress beyond a black letter approach and shape

[182] *Western Canadian Shopping Centres Inc v. Dutton* 2001 SCC 46, paras 27–29.
[183] The Honourable Ian Binnie (n. 136) para. 66

the law in order to protect human rights more effectively. With respect to the crucial second item on Justice Binnie's list, the ruling confirms that compulsory norms of international law are part of Canadian common law, and that their violation may give rise to domestic remedies. On the issue of the corporate veil, the Court noted that Nevsun controlled the operations of the mine in Eritrea, suggesting the possibility that the Canadian parent could ultimately be held liable, as was argued in *Hudbay*. On these issues and others, a comparative approach favours the development of both legal traditions of Canada in a manner that is consistent with our shared values and international commitments.

Although many obstacles remain, and no case has yet been argued on the merits, the Supreme Court's openness in *Nevsun* stands in stark contrast to the reluctance which characterised earlier attempts to seise courts of human rights violations committed abroad by Canadian corporations and confirms a trend that began in Ontario and British Columbia with cases such as *Hudbay* and *Tahoe*. This suggests that the Canadian courts increasingly recognise their role in holding Canadian corporations accountable to victims of their international activities and are willing to innovate in order to provide redress for their claims.

6

Civil Liability in Australia for International Human Rights Violations

Peter Cashman

I. Introduction

> The involvement of corporations in human rights violations has a long history but it is only fairly recently that business came onto the human rights agenda and, subsequently, human rights onto the business agenda.[1]

This chapter examines a number of issues concerning the civil liability of corporations in Australia for international conduct which violates human rights.

The topic of business and human rights gives rise to a wide range of legal and policy issues. This includes consideration of whether there should be a treaty to address compliance and enforcement problems.[2] This gives rise to problematic questions concerning the effectiveness of various forms of regulation. Although important, these issues are outside the scope of the present chapter.

The present focus is more modest. This chapter examines a number of complex questions concerning whether civil legal proceedings may be brought in Australia against (i) Australian companies and (ii) related corporations, for conduct resulting in loss or damage outside Australia.

It also touches on remedies that may be available under Australian law where Australian corporations may be dealing commercially with otherwise unrelated entities in the chain of supply of products or services where such other entities may have violated human rights in the course of their commercial conduct.[3]

[1] The research assistance of Amelia Simpson is gratefully acknowledged. Professor David Kinley provided helpful advice in respect of an early draft of this chapter.

C. van Dam, 'Tort Law and Human Rights: Brothers in Arms. On the Role of Tort Law in the Area of Business and Human Rights' (2011) 2(3) *Journal of Education, Teaching and Learning* 221, 225. As the author notes, international human rights law currently only plays a modest role in holding corporations to account.

[2] See, for example, C. Methven O'Brien and J. Ford, 'Empty Rituals or Workable Models? Towards a Business and Human Rights Treaty' (2017) 40(3) *University of New South Wales Law Journal* 1223.

[3] This issue is considered in more detail by various authors. See, for example, J. Nolan, 'Human Rights and Global Supply Chains: Is Effective Supply Chain Accountability Possible?' in S. Deva and D.

Peter Cashman, *Civil Liability in Australia for International Human Rights Violations* In: *Human Rights Litigation against Multinationals in Practice.* Edited by: Richard Meeran, Oxford University Press. © The Several Contributors 2021.
DOI: 10.1093/oso/9780198866220.003.0006

Of interest is the fact that Australia has recently adopted a 'modern slavery' law to address forced labour in the supply chains of Australian companies.[4] The legislation requires large Australian companies and organisations (those with consolidated revenue of A$100 million) to report annually on steps they are taking to address forced labour. However, there are no penalties for companies that fail to comply and limited independent scrutiny. Moreover, smaller companies are under no obligation to report but may do so voluntarily. The first statements were originally due on 30 June 2020 but the deadlines were extended due to the Covid 19 crisis. Reporting entities are required to provide statements to the Australian Border Force for publication on an online public register.[5]

The State of New South Wales has also passed its own legislation[6] which imposes a lower revenue reporting threshold of A$50 million and provides for penalties for businesses that do not comply. It also creates the position of Independent NSW Anti-Slavery Commissioner.

In recent times there has also been an increasing focus on the role of banks and financial institutions in financing mining and infrastructure projects which result in adverse human rights impacts on local communities.[7]

Bilchitz (eds), *Building a Treaty on Business and Human Rights: Context and Contours* (2017); J. Nolan, 'Regulating Human Rights and Responsibilities in Global Supply Chains' in J. Murray, A. Malik, and A. Geschke (eds), *The Social Effects of Global Trade* (2017). See also Law Council of Australia, Submission to the Department of Foreign Affairs and Trade, *Consultation Paper on International Strategy on Human Trafficking and Modern Slavery* (11 May 2020). The Law Council has advocated, *inter alia*, strengthening sanctions and improving remediation processes. For an international perspective, see M. Scheltema, 'The Mismatch between Human Rights Policies and Contract Law: Improving Contractual Mechanisms to Advance Human Rights Compliance in Supply Chains' in L. Enneking, I. Gieson, A.J. Schaap, et al. (eds), *Accountability, International Business Operations and the Law: Providing Justice for Corporate Human Rights Violations in Global Value Chains* (2019).

4 *Modern Slavery Act 2018* (Cth) which took effect on 1 January 2019.

5 The online register may be accessed at <https://modernslaveryregister.gov.au/>. Recent Australian developments are referred to in the submission by the Law Council of Australia to the Department of Foreign Affairs and Trade: Law Council of Australia, *International Strategy on Human Trafficking and Modern Slavery* (11 May 2020). See also A. Mc Gregor, 'Modern Slavery Act: What Businesses in Australia need to know', <https://www.nortonrosefulbright.com/en/knowledge/publications/06a565ee/modern-slavery-act-what-businesses-in-australia-need-to-know>, August 2020, accessed 21 May 2021.

6 *Modern Slavery Act 2018* (NSW). As a result of concerns over inconsistencies between the Commonwealth and NSW statutes, the NSW legislation was reviewed by the NSW Legislative Council's Standing Committee on Social Issues. In March 2020, the Committee tabled its report, expressing support for the NSW Act, proposing amendments to allow for harmonisation with the federal law, and recommending its commencement on or before 1 January 2021. On 24 September 2020 the NSW Government tabled its response to the report. Although committed to implementing the legislation it was accepted that there should be greater harmonisation with the Commonwealth legislation.See generally, A. Sinclair and J. Nolan, 'Modern Slavery Laws in Australia: Steps in the Right Direction?' (2020) 5 *Business and Human Rights Journal* 164.

7 See, for example, C. Hutto and A. Jenkins, 'Report on Corporate Complicity Litigation in the Americas: Leading Doctrines, Relevant Cases, and Analysis of Trends' (*Human Rights Clinic, University of Texas*, February 2010) <https://law.utexas.edu/wp-content/uploads/sites/11/2015/04/2010-HRC-Report-CorporateComplicity.pdf> accessed 18 November 2020; B. Thompson, 'The Dutch Banking Sector Agreement on Human Rights: An Exercise in Regulation, Experimentation or Advocacy?' (2018) 14(2) *Utrecht Law Review* 84.

More recently there has been an increasing focus on human rights in the context of environmental degradation[8] and in respect of privacy concerns arising out of increasingly sophisticated forms of technology. The latter is presently the subject of inquiry by the Australian Human Rights Commission.[9]

The violation of human rights may of course give rise to criminal proceedings against the individuals and/or corporate entities responsible. This is the subject of a considerable body of jurisprudence[10] but a detailed consideration of this is outside the scope of this chapter. It would appear that Australia's criminal laws have seldom if ever been used in connection with extraterritorial violation of human rights by Australian corporations.[11] Moreover, corporations are not within the jurisdiction of the International Criminal Court.[12] By way of contrast, Australian legislation imposes criminal liability on corporations and the previous introduction of 'international offences' in the *Criminal Code Act 2005* (Cth)[13] encompasses the crimes of genocide, crimes against humanity, and war crimes.[14]

[8] See, for example, L.E. Bartlett, 'Human Rights Guidance for Environmental Justice Attorneys' (2020) Saint Louis University School of Law Legal Studies Research Paper No. 2020-20, published in 97 *University of Detroit Mercy Law Review* 373–427(2019–2020); J. Bell-James and B. Collins, 'Queensland's Human Rights Act: A New Frontier for Australian Climate Change Litigation?' (March 2020) 43(1) *University of New South Wales Law Journal* 3–38.

[9] Further information is available at: Australian Human Rights Commission website <https://tech.humanrights.gov.au>. In July 2018 the Commission published an Issues Paper. A Discussion Paper was published in December 2019. A response to the issues paper by academics and students at the law school at the University of NSW has been published as a research paper: A. Yu, A. Lo, R. Clarke, et al., 'Response to Issues Paper on Human Rights and New Technology' [2019] *University of New South Wales Law Research Series* 12 <http://ssrn.com/link/UNSW-LEG.html> accessed on 18 November 2020. Due to Covid 19 the Commission extended its deadline for submissions and at the time of writing had not published its final report.

[10] See, for example, R. Ivory and A. John, 'Holding Companies Responsible? The Criminal Liability of Australian Corporations for Extraterritorial Human Rights Violations' (Sept 2017) 40(3) *University of New South Wales Law Journal 1175-1199*; several chapters dealing with criminal prosecutions in Enneking, Gieson, Schaap, et al.,. (eds), (n. 3). See also the recent comparative analysis by J. Hill, 'Legal Personhood and Liability for Flawed Corporate Cultures' (2020) *European Corporate Governance Institute Working Paper Series in Law Working Paper No. 431/2018* <http://ssrn.com/abstract=3309697> accessed on 18 November 2020; and N. Friedman 'Corporations as Moral Agents: Trade-Offs in Criminal Liability and Human Rights for Corporations' (2020) 83(2) *The Modern Law Review* 255–84 <http://ssrn.com/abstract=3309697> accessed 18 November 2020.

[11] Human Rights Law Centre, *Nowhere to Turn: Addressing Australian corporate abuse overseas* (December 2018), 4. As noted by Bronitt and Brereton, an important shortcoming of the *Criminal Code Act* is that there are no provisions which expressly extend liability to agents or subsidiaries of the corporation: S. Bronitt and Z. Brereton, Submission to the Attorney General's Department, *Proposed amendments to the foreign bribery offence in the Criminal Code Act 1995 (Cth)* (10 May 2017) [4.1]. <https://www.ag.gov.au/Consultations/Documents/Proposed-amendments-to-the-foreign-bribery-offence-criminal-code-act-1995/Foreign-bribery-submission-Bronitt-Brereton.pdf>.

[12] As noted by Grear and Weston, the International Criminal Court only has jurisdiction over natural persons: A. Grear and B. Weston, 'The Betrayal of Human Rights and the Urgency of Universal Corporate Accountability: Reflections on the Post-Kiobel Lawscape' (2015) 15 *Human Rights Law Review* 21, 41.

[13] Previously Division 268, *Criminal Code Act 1995* (Cth). As Kyriakakis notes, the provisions were introduced by the *International Criminal Court (Consequential Amendments) Act 2002* (Cth) as part of the ratification of the *Rome Statute of the International Criminal Court.* J. Kyriakakis, 'Freeport in West Papua: Bringing Corporations to Account for International Human Rights Abuses under Australian Criminal and Tort Law' (2005) 31 *Monash University Law Review* 95, 104. Commonwealth criminal legislation has subsequently been substantially amended, the details of which are outside the scope of the present chapter.

[14] In the *Anvil Mining* matter in 2005 representations were made by solicitors acting for those seeking compensation resulting in the referral of issues to the Australian Federal Police for investigation of

Human rights violations occurring outside Australia may also give rise to civil liability for breach of applicable civil laws in the jurisdictions in which such conduct occurred. However, many countries lack meaningful civil remedies, or effective enforcement mechanisms, for conduct that may violate domestic or international law. As Gear and Weston note: 'Highly problematic is the plain fact that the states in which [transnational corporations] operate are frequently developing states which, for lack of effective administrative, judicial and policing mechanisms or because of a widespread culture of corruption (frequently encouraged by TNC management), are commonly unable to regulate TNC conduct effectively or are unwilling to do so.'[15]

This chapter examines a number of cases in which tort law has been invoked for the purpose of seeking redress on behalf of persons suffering loss or damage as a result of human rights abuses or other corporate conduct. As noted by one author, many recent cases comprise civil liability claims pursued on the basis of the tort of negligence rather than the corporate law doctrine of piercing the corporate veil or customary international law on human rights.[16] The objective in some such cases is to establish direct liability of the parent company, including through the breach of the duty of care it is alleged that it owed to the claimants, who are often employees of foreign subsidiaries or members of the local community who have suffered loss and damage.[17] Whether or not the parent owes a duty of care to those making a claim is often a vexed and highly disputed legal question. As noted below, this will often turn on complex issues of fact relating to its management and supervision of the activities of subsidiaries.[18]

It is of course the case, that not all 'tort rights' are also 'human rights' and not all 'human rights are also 'tort rights' but there is considerable overlap and human rights and tort law may be considered as 'brothers in arms'.[19]

The mechanisms for effective legal redress for human rights abuses by domestic or transnational corporations, through tort law or otherwise, are limited.[20]

whether the company was responsible for aiding and abetting crimes against humanity under the *Criminal Code*. It was alleged that the company helped government troops quell an uprising in the Democratic Republic of Congo. See A. McBeth, 'Crushed by an Anvil: A Case Study on Responsibility for Human Rights in the Extractive Sector' (2008) 11(1) *Yale Human Rights and Development Law Journal* 127.

15 Grear and Weston (n. 12) 27.

16 E. Aristova, 'Tort Litigation against Transnational Corporations in the English Courts: The Challenge of Jurisdiction' (2018) 14(2) *Utrecht Law Review* 6.

17 See, for example, *Connelly v. RTZ* [1998] AC 854 (HL) and *Guerrero v. Monterrico Metals Plc* [2009] EWHC 2475 (QB).

18 In the European context, see generally M. Petrin and B. Choudhury, 'Group Company Liability' (2018) 20 *European Business Organisation Law Review* 1. The authors examine a number of reform proposals including a UN sanctioned business and human rights treaty. In the Australian context, see, for example, H. Anderson, 'Piercing the Veil on Corporate Groups in Australia: The Case for Reform' (2009) 33(2) *Melbourne University Law Review* 333.

19 van Dam (n. 1) 243.

20 Proposals for reform include a binding treaty outlined by the Human Rights Council, *Legally Binding Instrument to Regulate, in International Human Rights Law, the Activities of Transnational*

Moreover, there are considerable procedural, economic, and legal constraints and hurdles to be overcome in seeking to counter what others have referred to as the 'rights evading mutations of corporate power'.[21]

One obvious difficulty arises out of the 'fundamental discrepancy between the transnational nature of ... powerful entities and the territorially limited assumptions of the traditional state-centric international human rights system [which] ... presents a profound impediment to effective human rights accountability in the corporate sector'.[22]

As Grear and Weston note, the problem is exacerbated by the 'complicated interlocking layers of corporate entities that present a structural density that makes accountability extremely difficult'.[23]

Before turning to the Australian context, we examine a number of developments in the United States, the United Kingdom, and Canada where various strategies have been adopted to hold corporate entities responsible for human rights abuses in which they have been implicated. Although this emerging international jurisprudence is of relevance to Australia the analysis is brief because other authors of chapters in the present book deal with these jurisdictions in detail.

II. Developments in English law

English jurisprudence is particularly instructive for its consideration of traditional tort law remedies, including those arising out of the law of negligence. As Meeran notes, tort litigation has the advantage of less complexity.[24]

English consideration of the liability of parent companies for human rights abuses informs debate and legal developments across the globe.[25] However, most

Corporations and other Business Enterprises-Zero Draft (16 July 2018). The UN Human Rights Council's Intergovernmental Working Group on Transnational Corporations and Other Business Enterprises with respect to Human Rights (the Working Group) released a report on 6 February 2019, summarizing the fourth session of negotiations on the Zero Draft.

[21] Grear and Weston (n. 12) 24.

[22] Ibid., 26.

[23] Ibid., 28.

[24] R. Meeran, 'Tort Litigation Against Multinational Corporations for Violation of Human Rights: An Overview of the Position Outside the United States' (2011) 3 *City University of Hong Kong Law Review* 1. Notwithstanding this 'lack of complexity' as Meeran notes, many cases in the UK and Australian courts have resulted in protracted delay and procedural warfare.

[25] Amnesty International, 'Submission to the Supreme Court of the United Kingdom, Okpabi and others vs Royal Dutch Shell plc and another UKSC 2018/0068' (*Amnesty International*, 26 April 2018) <https://www.amnesty.org/download/Documents/AFR4483212018ENGLISH.PDF> accessed 17 April 2021. See also Amnesty International, 'Injustice Incorporated: Corporate Abuses and the Human Right to Remedy' (2014), <https://www.amnesty.org/en/documents/POL30/001/2014/en/>, accessed 17 April 2021.

English cases involving attempts to sue parent companies in England arising out of the conduct of foreign subsidiaries have been resolved at an early procedural stage following applications to strike out or stay the proceedings on the basis of lack of jurisdiction, summary judgment, or *forum non conveniens* grounds.[26] Very few cases have gone to trial,[27] and where jurisdictional barriers are overcome, there may still be vexed choice of law complications as to the applicable substantive law.

English civil procedural rules allow a foreign subsidiary to be sued in England where there is a legitimate claim between the claimant and the UK-domiciled parent and where the subsidiary is a necessary and proper party.[28]

In *Vedanta*, proceedings were brought against a Zambian company and its UK parent arising out of pollution from a copper mine alleging negligence and, in respect of the subsidiary, contraventions of Zambian environmental laws. In 2016, the Technology and Construction Court held that there was *good arguable case* that the parent company owed a duty of care to the Zambian villagers. This decision was upheld by a majority of the Court of Appeal.[29]

The appeal from the decision of the Court of Appeal was heard in January 2019.[30] The Supreme Court dismissed the appeal, allowing the suit to proceed to trial on the substantive issues.[31]

[26] As noted by Aristova, following the decision in *Owusu v. Jackson* [2005] ECR 1-1383 there are constraints on English courts staying proceedings on the basis of *forum non conveniens*: Aristova (n. 16) 11.

[27] Two notable exceptions are *Chandler v. Cape Plc* [2012] EWCA Civ 525 and *Thompson v. Renwick Group Plc* [2014] EWCA Civ 365, which went to trial in relation to the duty of care alleged to be owed by the parent to *employees* of a subsidiary.

[28] A. Sanger, 'Transnational Corporate Responsibility in Domestic Courts: Still out of Reach?' (2019) University of Cambridge Faculty of Law, Legal Studies Research Paper 4/2019, 5, citing UK *Practice Direction* 6B, 3.1(3) at note 14. As noted by Aristova, establishment of jurisdiction on this basis could be exceptionally wide as it does not require the existence of any territorial connection between England and the joined defendant. Thus Aristova notes that English courts have approached claims brought under the '*necessary or proper party*' gateway carefully to ensure that a specious claim against an 'anchor' defendant is not used as a device to bring a foreign defendant within the jurisdiction: Aristova (n. 16) citing: *Witted v. Galbraith* [1893] 1 QB 577, 579; *Multinational Gas & Petrochemical Co v. Multinational Gas & Petrochemical Services Ltd* [1983] Ch. 258, 274; *Golden Ocean Assurance Ltd v. Martin (The Goldean Mariner)* [1990] 2 Lloyd's Rep 215, 222; *AK Investment CJSC v. Kyrgyz Mobil Tel Ltd*, [2011] UK PC 7 [76]–[87].

[29] *Lungowe v. Vedanta* [2017] EWCA Civ 1528 (UK). The Court reviewed decisions applying the three-part test articulated in *Caparo Industries Plc v. Dickman* [1990] 2 AC 605 (HL). The three elements comprise: (i) a sufficient degree of proximity between the parties, (ii) foreseeability of harm, and (iii) whether it is fair, just, and reasonable to impose liability.

[30] In oral argument and written submissions, the appellant referred to Australian authorities on the duty of parent companies to ensure that subsidiary operations are not harmful. In *CSR v. Wren* (1997) 44 NSWLR 463 (CA NSW) it was held that CSR owed a duty to ensure that the operations of the subsidiary were not harmful to subsidiary employees. There has been considerable litigation against the James Hardie group by claimants suffering injury from exposure to asbestos. The legal history is summarised in a Research Note prepared by the Australian Parliamentary Library, 'In the shadow of the corporate veil: James Hardie and asbestos compensation' (10 August 2004), <https://www.aph.gov.au/binaries/library/pubs/rn/2004-05/05rn12.pdf>, accessed 17 April 2021.

[31] *Vedanta Resources PLC and Anor v. Lungowe and Ors* [2019] UKSC 20 (10 April 2019).

The Court rejected the contention that finding a duty of care would involve a novel and controversial extension of the boundaries of negligence. As Lord Briggs observed:

> Everything depends on the extent to which, and the way in which, the parent availed itself of the opportunity to take over, intervene in or control, supervise or advise the management of the relevant operations (including land use) of the subsidiary.[32]

By way of contrast to the outcome in *Vedanta*, in *Shell* both the High Court[33] and the Court of Appeal[34] rejected the claim that the English parent company, Royal Dutch Shell, owed a duty of care in respect of oil spills emanating from the pipelines and infrastructure operated by its Nigerian subsidiary.[35] The Court of Appeal distinguished between the conduct of a parent company which takes steps to ensure that there are proper controls in place by establishing an overall system of policies, processes, and practices from those situations where a parent company actually seeks to exercise control.[36] It was held that only in the latter situation a duty of care may arise. At the time of writing this case is on appeal before the Supreme Court.[37]

In *Unilever* both the High Court and the Court of Appeal[38] held that Unilever did not owe a duty of care to the claimants to take effective steps to protect them from 'serious inter-tribal violence' at the time of the 2007 Kenyan presidential election. The court found that the foreign subsidiary did not receive relevant advice from the parent company and regarded itself as being responsible for risk management and the handling of the crisis. In what appears to be the most recent decision, the Court of Appeal confirmed that a UK mining company was not liable in relation to human rights abuses in Sierra Leone arising out of the use of excessive force by police when local unrest broke out.[39]

[32] Ibid., [49]. The Court went on to approve at [50] the 'correct summary' by Sales LJ in *AAA v. Unilever plc* [2018] EWCA Civ 1352 [36]. The judgment is also of interest for the discussion of whether the English forum was the 'proper place to bring the claim' and the real risk that substantial justice could not be obtained in Zambia, at [66], [86], and [101]–[102].

[33] *Okpabi v. Royal Dutch Shell* [2017] EWHC 90.

[34] *Okpabi v. Royal Dutch Shell* [2018] EWCA Civ 191.

[35] See also *Thompson v. Renwick Group Plc* [2014] EWCA Civ 365 where no duty of care was found to exist between the parent company and the employees of its subsidiary given the absence of evidence of any relevant involvement in the activities of the subsidiary other than the holding of shares.

[36] In an earlier decision, the House of Lords held in *Lubbe v. Cape Plc* [2000] 1 WLR 1545 (HL) 1555 that the question of parental corporate liability 'will be likely to involve and inquiry into what part the defendant played in controlling the operations of the group'.

[37] The Supreme Court recently granted permission for two written interventions by Corner House Research, and the International Commission of Jurists and CORE Coalition.

[38] *AAA v. Unilever* [2018] EWCA Civ 1532 (UK).

[39] *Kadie Kalma & Ors v. African Minerals Ltd* [2020] EWCA Civ 144.

As the English cases demonstrate, questions of jurisdiction, duty of care, and liability may turn on very specific factual questions in each case as to the nature of the relationship between the parent and the subsidiary.

III. Developments in Australian law

Under Australian law the question of whether there may be direct liability of an Australian corporate parent or related entity for tortious or other unlawful conduct by related entities has been considered in a number of cases.

In *CSR Ltd v. Wren*[40] the NSW Court of Appeal upheld a judgment in favour of an injured worker who succeeded in a tort claim against the defendant, CSR Ltd, following an injury suffered on the premises of its wholly owned subsidiary, Asbestos Products Pty Ltd. In their joint judgment Beazley JA and Stein JA noted that in the normal course of events the management staff are responsible for the day-to-day operational aspects of a business operation and in that case the management staff were all CSR staff. That, in their opinion, was sufficient to establish a relationship between the plaintiff and CSR so as to give rise to a duty of care owed by CSR to the plaintiff.[41]

As to whether there is a breach of any such duty of care, the well-known passage from *Wyong Shire Council v. Shirt*[42] is frequently invoked, where Mason J stated:

> In deciding whether there has been a breach of a duty of care the tribunal of fact must first ask itself whether a reasonable man [sic] in the defendant's position would have foreseen that his conduct involved a risk of injury to the plaintiff or to a class of persons including the plaintiff. If the answer be in the affirmative, it is then for the tribunal of fact to determine what a reasonable man [sic] would do by way of response to the risk. The perception of the reasonable man's [sic] response calls for a consideration of the magnitude of the risk and the degree of probability of its occurrence, along with the expense, difficulty and inconvenience of taking alleviating action and any other conflicting responsibilities which the defendant may have. It is only when these matters are balanced out that the tribunal of fact can confidently assert what is the standard of response to be ascribed to the reasonable man [sic] placed in the defendant's position.[43]

40 (1997) 44 NSWLR 463; (1998) *Aust Torts Reports* 81–461.
41 Ibid., [7].
42 (1980) 146 CLR 40.
43 Ibid., 47–48.

The circumstances in which there may be direct liability of corporate parent or related entities for tortious or other unlawful conduct by associated corporate entities or persons may be a vexed question depending upon the facts in issue. In many instances, the limited liability of companies, based on the *Salomon*[44] principle, may become an 'unyielding rock' on which 'complicated arguments' become 'shipwrecked'.[45] As the former Chief Justice of the Victorian Supreme Court has noted: 'issues of corporate morality and fairness are constrained by established legal principles'.[46]

However, established legal principles in Australia have adapted to and accommodated the direct liability of parent companies for the tortious conduct of subsidiaries through a series of cases determined in the 1980s and 1990s, particularly in the context of personal injury claims arising out of exposure to asbestos.[47]

Notwithstanding these developments, it has not always been plain sailing for plaintiffs. In *James Hardie*[48] a New Zealand plaintiff exposed to asbestos in New Zealand sought to recover against both the employer New Zealand entity and also two NSW companies which the plaintiff alleged controlled and managed the factory in New Zealand where he worked. Although successful at first instance the NSW Court of Appeal found that the two NSW companies did not have a duty of care to the plaintiff. The decision in *CSR Ltd v. Wren* was distinguished and narrowly interpreted.

As noted by former Victorian Chief Justice Warren,[49] the Australian cases up to and including *James Hardie* were decided at a time when the '*proximity*' test was determinative of whether there was a duty of care, whereas this was subsequently rejected by the High Court.[50] However, as she proceeds to note: 'the analysis in those cases was not wedded to the proximity analysis such that they would not be relevant under the modern "salient features" approach'.[51] In her view, the main difference between then then applicable English law and the Australian approaches

> is not so much the different test applicable for duty of care, but rather a difference in attitude towards imposing direct liability on parent companies. The approach

[44] *Salomon v. A Salomon & Co Ltd* [1897] AC 22.

[45] Adopting the language of Lord Templeman, 'Company Law Lecture-Forty Years on' (199) 11 *Company Lawyer* 10, 10 quoted by the former Chief Justice of the Victorian Supreme Court, Marilyn Warren AC, 'Corporate Structures, the Veil and the Role of the Courts' (2016) 40 *Melbourne University Law Review* 657, 670.

[46] Ibid.

[47] In addition to *CSR Ltd v. Wren* (ibid.) see, for example, *Barrow v. CSR Ltd* (unreported, Supreme Court of Western Australia, Rowland J, 4 August 1988); *CSR v. Young* (1998) Aust Torts Reports 81–468.

[48] *James Hardie & Co Pty Ltd v. Hall* (1998) 43 NSWLR 554.

[49] Warren (n. 45) 684.

[50] *Sullivan v. Moody* (2001) 207 CLR 562, 578–9 [48].

[51] Warren (n. 45) 684.

in the Australian cases is rooted in a reluctance in corporations law to lift the corporate veil, and thus sets the bar high for the parent-subsidiary relationship that would give rise to a duty of care on the part of the parent.[52]

However, more recently, in *Strategic Framework Pty Ltd v. Hitchen*[53] both the company that employed the plaintiff and another related company that exercised *control* over the employer were found liable for breaches of the duty of care that both owed to the plaintiff.

At this 'hazy intersection of company and tort law' established principles sometimes coalesce but frequently collide.[54] Problems in establishing liability are exacerbated where it is sought to hold parent companies directly liable for the conduct of foreign subsidiaries which impacts on persons who are not employees.

Moreover, apart from doctrinal and jurisprudential issues, problems of proof loom large. As noted by Warren: 'this kind of litigation against a parent requires the plaintiff to provide a considerable amount of evidence about the parent subsidiary relationship and the control the parent exercises over the subsidiary. This is no easy task in many cases.'[55]

At least in proceedings brought or anticipated in Australia, procedures for discovery of documents and preliminary discovery of documents are available.

IV. Discovery and preliminary discovery of documents

There are established and frequently utilised procedures for discovery of documents in civil cases in all Australian State and federal jurisdictions. For example, in the federal sphere the *Federal Court Rules 2011* (Cth) make provision for orders for discovery of documents.[56]

Most if not all jurisdictions also now have relatively liberal, but seldom utilised, rules for obtaining orders for preliminary discovery, before substantive proceedings are commenced. Some permit such discovery not only to ascertain the identity of the appropriate defendant but also to ascertain whether there may be a good cause of action. In many jurisdictions, historically restrictive rules against 'fishing' expeditions have been superseded. In large and

52 Ibid.

53 [2018] NSWCA 54 (Basten JA, Simpson JA, and Sackville AJA).

54 Adapting an extract from M. Petrin, 'Assumption of Responsibility in Corporate Groups: Chandler v Cape plc' (2013) 76 *Modern Law Review* 603, referred to by Warren (n. 45) 685.

55 Warren (n. 45) 686.

56 See, for example, the discussion by the Full Federal Court in *Clifton (Liquidator) v. Kerry Investment Pty Ltd* [2020] FCAFC 5; 379 ALR 593 (Besanko, Markovic, and Banks-Smith JJ).

complex litigation orders are not infrequently made for the use of technology assisted review of documents.[57]

Foreign defendants sued in Australian courts are subject to orders being made for discovery of documents in their possession or control.

Relevant documents that are the subject of valid claims of privilege need not be produced but are usually required to be identified.

V. The involvement of Australian companies in human rights abuses and environmental damage in other jurisdictions

A report by the Human Rights Law Centre (HRLC) in Australia refers to the alleged involvement of various Australian companies in various parts of the world where human rights violations and major environmental damage have occurred. According to that report, some of Australia's most prominent companies, from ANZ Bank to BHP (BHP Group Limited), have been implicated in serious human rights violations overseas.[58]

A recent report by Friends of the Earth Australia alleges that Australia's big four banks are providing financial assistance to companies accused of land grabs, deforestation, and labour abuses in developing countries. It is also alleged that there have been widespread human rights abuses in the supply chain of companies and subsidiaries in the palm oil trade, financed by Australian banks.[59]

The HLRC report identifies a number of case studies and incorporates various recommendations for action by the Australian government. The case studies encompass:

- BHP's responsibility for the Samarco Dam disaster in Brazil
- The involvement of ANZ Bank in providing financial backing to a Cambodian company allegedly responsible for forced evictions and other human rights violations
- The alleged involvement of an Australian security firm in criminal conduct against asylum seekers in in offshore detention centres

[57] See the discussion in P. Cashman and E. Ginnivan, 'Digital Justice: Online Resolution of Minor Civil Disputes and the Use of Technology in Complex Litigation and Class Actions' (2019) 19 *Macquarie Law Journal* 39–79.

[58] Human Rights Law Centre, 'Nowhere to Turn: Addressing Australian corporate abuse overseas' (*Human Rights Law Centre*, December 2018), <https://www.hrlc.org.au/reports/nowhere-to-turn>, accessed 18 November 2020.

[59] Friends of the Earth Australia, 'Draw the line: A black book about the shady investments of Australian banks in palm oil' (*Business & Human Rights Centre*, 28 June 2019), <https://www.business-humanrights.org/en/australia-report-accuses-big-four-banks-of-financing-palm-oil-companies-linked-to-land-grabbing-human-rights-violations#c190598>, accessed 18 November 2020.

- The alleged involvement of an Australian-Canadian mining company in the torture, rape, and murder of residents in a small town in the Congo where an uprising was brutally suppressed by the Congolese military
- The alleged involvement of an Australian-managed development company and an Australian-based building and construction company in the forcible eviction of residents of Port Moresby from their homes
- The alleged involvement of Rio Tinto in human rights abuses and environmental damage on the island of Bougainville[60]
- The alleged involvement of a security firm in sexual assaults alleged to have occurred at an offshore immigration detention centre
- The responsibility of an Australian petroleum company for major environmental damage from a major oil spill in the Timor sea and significant financial loss alleged to have been suffered in Indonesia, including by seaweed farmers
- The responsibility of an Australian manufacturer of medical safety equipment for allegedly exploitive and unsafe working conditions in Sri Lanka
- The role of a private technology company in supplying technology allegedly used to locate, identify, and target peaceful protesters in Bahrain.

A number of these matters have resulted in major civil litigation before Australian courts.

- A class action on behalf of Indonesian seaweed farmers arising out of damage allegedly caused by the Montara oil spill progressed (slowly) to a trial in the Federal Court in Sydney in 2019. Judgment in the case of the lead applicant, Mr Sanda, was handed down on 19 March 2021.[61] The respondent to the proceeding, the Australian company that operated the offshore oil drilling operation, denied that it owed a duty of care to the Indonesian class members, and denied that oil or dispersant reached the parts of Indonesia in question.[62] The trial judge, Justice Yates, found that: a duty of care existed; the respondent was in breach of that duty; oil from the Montara well reached certain area in Indonesia and caused or materially contributed to the damage to the applicant's seaweed crops. Damages were awarded to the applicant, albeit discounted due to evidentiary difficulties in establishing the quantum of loss.

60 This was the subject of a further detailed report by the Human Rights Law Centre, 'We are calling on mining giant Rio Tinto to take responsibility for multiple human rights violations caused by pollution from its former mine in Bougainville' (March 2020), <https://www.hrlc.org.au/rio-tinto-deadly-legacy>, accessed 18 November 2020.

61 *Sanda v PTTEP Australasia (Ashmore Cartier) Pty Ltd (No 7)* [2021] FCA 237.

62 As one member of the Federal Court of Australia has commented extrajudicially: 'Such litigation is costly, time- and resource-consuming, and its outcome is ever uncertain until settled or judgment is given.' Justice Steven Rares, 'Charting a new course—Promoting the development of an international convention on liability and compensation relating to transboundary damage from offshore oil and gas activities' [2019] 11 Federal Judicial Scholarship 11 .

- At the time of writing, several investor class actions had been commenced in Australia (and elsewhere) against BHP arising out of the environmental and other damage following the failure of a dam holding back wastewater from a mine operated by joint venture partners in Brazil. The disaster resulted in the death of 19 people. Recently, the company had been unsuccessful in its application to stay the consolidated Australian class actions in light of pending criminal proceedings elsewhere. Three competing and overlapping shareholder class actions in the Federal Court of Australia have given rise to a number of interlocutory applications seeking to challenge the proceedings and the inclusion of non-Australian group members[63] and an appeal[64] as to which of the claims should be allowed to proceed.
- A class action against the security company, the Australian government and various contractors arising out of events at the Manus Island detention centre was settled before trial in 2017 for $70 million.[65]
- Proceedings arising out of events in the Congo were brought in both Australia and Canada but failed at early procedural stages.
- The legal proceeding brought in New Guinea by displaced residents of Port Moresby was dismissed on procedural grounds.
- Proceedings brought by Bougainville residents in the United States were ultimately dismissed on jurisdictional grounds after 13 years and a number of appeals.
- A number of women who allege that they were raped at the offshore detention centre in Nauru have brought proceedings in Australia. In November 2019, Wilson Security settled out of court with a woman who alleged that she was raped in 2014.
- Striking workers in Sri Lanka who were dismissed were eventually reinstated after a complaint made to Australia's Organisation of Economic Co-operation and Development (OECD) National Contact Point for alleged breaches of human rights and following years of negotiations and an international campaign.
- In 2014, 681 Cambodian families brought a complaint against ANZ Bank through the OECD National Contact Point, seeking to have ANZ divest its profits from the loan in question and to compensate the affected families. In

[63] See *Impiombato v. BHP Group Limited (No 2)* [2020] FCA 1720.

[64] *Klemweb Nominees Pty Ltd v. BHP Group Limited* [2019] FCAFC 107.

[65] *Kamasaee v. Commonwealth of Australia and Ors* [2017] VSC 537. Detailed information on the proceedings may be found at A. and R. Kaldor Centre for International Refugee Law, 'Kamasaee v The Commonwealth of Australia' (*Andrew & Renata Kaldor Centre for International Refugee Law*, 12 September 2018), <https://www.kaldorcentre.unsw.edu.au/publication/kamasee-v-commonwealth-australia-ors-2017-vsc-537>, accessed 18 November 2020. In a later decision Justice Cameron Macauley declined to allow 64 persons to belatedly be included in the settlement: *Kamasaee v. The Commonwealth of Australia* [2018] VSC 138.

February 2020, ANZ agreed to pay compensation of the gross profits of the loan to the families and admitted its failure to conduct adequate due diligence.

At the time of writing, in addition to investor class actions against BHP arising out of the mine disaster in Brazil (referred to above) claims for damages by victims against BHP in England had been instituted. Efforts to stay the lawsuit were initially deferred after the British and Brazilian governments imposed lockdowns hindering the company's lawyers and experts from travelling to review the evidence. The company filed a motion to halt the proceeding on jurisdictional grounds over concerns it overlaps with litigation in Brazil, where BHP faces massive claims for damages and reparation. Proceedings were originally filed in Liverpool ostensibly on behalf of 235,000 Brazilian individuals and organisations, including municipal governments, utility companies, indigenous tribes, and the Catholic Church. Originally the action was just against BHP's UK-listed company, but it subsequently included the Australian-listed company. The English High Court dismissed the case in November 2020[66] and permission to appeal was granted by the Court of Appeal in July 2021.

Historically, there have been other cases against Australian companies arising out of their conduct in other countries. Notably, in 1994 proceedings were brought by Papua New Guinean (PNG) villagers in the Victorian Supreme Court against BHP arising out of major environmental damage at the Ok Tedi mine.[67] This eventually resulted in a substantial settlement in 1996 and agreement to remediation works.

This became the subject of ongoing controversy.[68] In 2000 and 2001 further proceedings were commenced in the Victorian Supreme Court against BHP Billiton and Ok Tedi Mining Company seeking injunctive, declaratory, and other relief, including specific performance, arising out of alleged failures to comply with a settlement agreement entered into in June 1996. Interlocutory proceedings were also instituted for alleged contempt of court. The proceedings resulted in a number of judgments.[69]

[66] *Municipio de Mariana v. BHP Group plc and BHP Group Ltd* [2020] EWHC 2930 (TCC) (Turner J) Judgment granting permission to appeal on 27 July [2021] EWCA Civ 1156.

[67] See *Dagi v. The Broken Hill Propriety Company Ltd (No. 2)* [1997] 1 VR 428. The plaintiff's claims included causes of action in trespass, nuisance, and negligence arising out of the discharge of by-products of copper mining into the local river(s) in PNG. An issue arose as to the jurisdiction of the Victorian Supreme Court to entertain actions in respect of foreign land (the so-called *Moçambique* rule, derived from the case *British South Africa Company v. Companhia de Moçambique* (1893) AC 602).

[68] For a brief history by John Gordon, one of the lawyers involved in the case, see: J. Gordon, 'Ok Tedi—Reflecting on the case today' (*Slater and Gordon*, 10 August 2018), <https://www.slatergordon.com.au/blog/ok-tedi-reflecting-on-the-case-today>, accessed 18 November 2020.

[69] See, for example, *Dagi v. Broken Hill Proprietary Company; Gagarimabu v. Broken Hill Proprietary Company* [2000] VSC 486 (Hedigan J); *Gagarimabu v. BHP & Ok Tedi* [2001] VSC 304 (Hedigan J); *Gagarimabu v. BHP* [2001] VSC 517 (Bongiorno J); *Gargarimabu v. BHP* [2002] VSC 525 (Bongiorno J); *Gargarimabu v. BHP* [2003] VSC 416 (Bongiorno J).

In 2002 BHP completed its withdrawal from the Ok Tedi copper mine by transferring its 52 per cent equity to PNG Sustainable Program Limited following a failure to secure agreement for closure of the mine. The arrangement sought to protect BHP Billiton from any further liabilities, including legal claims, arising from the operation of the mine subsequent to its exit.

At the time, further proceedings, including class action proceedings under Order 18A of the Victorian *Supreme Court Rules*, were still pending in the Victorian Supreme Court in respect of alleged breaches of 1996 agreement to compensate local communities for the damage resulting from the dumping of tailings and to carry out remediation work.[70] These proceedings were eventually resolved by a settlement in December 2003 and the subsequent dismissal of the class action proceedings in January 2004, notwithstanding a substantial number of objections by Papua New Guineans concerned at the ongoing failure to remediate the environmental damage.

Whether or not Australian courts have jurisdiction in respect of claims against Australian corporations and their foreign subsidiaries arising out of conduct outside Australia may be a vexed question, depending on the facts in issue and the nature of the conduct in question.

Even where personal or subject matter jurisdiction is established, there may be controversy over which is the most appropriate or convenient forum.

In a number of respects, the Australian legal system and jurisprudence incorporate a number of attractive features which may permit local courts to accept jurisdiction over claims arising out of extraterritorial human rights violations where civil suits are brought against corporations. As Holly notes:[71]

- Foreign corporations are amenable to the exercise of personal jurisdiction where they conduct business in Australia.
- Australian courts may deal with cases where damage has been suffered partly within the jurisdiction in claims arising out of torts, wherever occurring.
- Assuming jurisdiction, cases will only be dismissed or stayed on *forum non conveniens* grounds where Australia is a clearly inappropriate forum.[72]

[70] See generally J. Marychurch and N. Stoianoff, 'Blurring the lines of environmental responsibility: how corporate and public governance was circumvented by the OK Tedi Mining Limited disaster', paper presented at the 61st Annual ALTA Conference, Victoria University, Melbourne, 4–7 July (2006).

[71] G. Holly, 'Australia as a jurisdiction for transnational human rights litigation: Kamassee v Commonwealth' (*Cambridge Core Blog*, 30 April 2019), <https://blog.journals.cambridge.org/2019/04/30/australia-as-a-jurisdiction-for-transnational-human-rights-litigation-kamasaee-v-commonwealth/>. See also G. Holly, 'Transnational Tort and Access to Remedy under the UN Guiding Principles on Business and Human Rights: Kamasaee v Commonwealth' (2018) 19(1) *Melbourne Journal of International Law* 52.

[72] See generally *Oceanic Sun Line v. Fay* (1988) 165 CLR 197 and *Voth v. Manildra Flour Mills* (199) 171 CLR 538.

- Under Australian choice of law rules a *lex loci delicti* rule prevails in respect of both domestic and international torts[73] and this may provide for the application of foreign law.

More recently, the same author notes that 'Australian courts have shown themselves to be receptive to tort claims with an extraterritorial dimension, making it an underexplored but potentially attractive jurisdiction in which to bring such claims'.[74] She suggests that, while the application of the *lex loci delicti* rule is strict (and the harm may not be recognised in the place where the wrongdoing occurred), flexibility around the test for where the wrongdoing occurred provides scope 'to advantageously frame a claim through the characterization process to advance a credible case for Australian law to apply'.[75]

Although Australian choice of law rules provide for the application of the law in the jurisdiction in which the relevant conduct occurred (*the lex loci delicti*), in the absence of evidence to the contrary the Australian court will proceed on the assumption that this is the same as Australian law.[76] However, an obvious problem arises where the choice of law rules of that jurisdiction provide for the application of the law in which the proceedings are brought (the *lex loci fori*). As Prosser has suggested:

> The realm of the conflicts of laws is a dismal swamp, filled by quaking quagmires, and inhabited by learned but eccentric professors who theorise about mysterious matters in a strange and incomprehensible jargon. The ordinary court, or lawyer is quite lost when engulfed and entangled in it.[77]

In particular, Australian courts have had difficulty in dealing with this problem of *renvoi*.[78] In the decision of the Australian High Court in *Neilson*, the majority were divided on various issues.[79] In his analysis of the case Davies commented that:

> the Court did not speak with one voice, or even two or three. The seven Justices produced six judgments and majorities of different composition on different

[73] See *Regie Nationale de Usines Renault SA v. Zhang* (2002) 210 CLR 491.
[74] G. Holly, 'Challenges to Australia's Offshore Detention Regime and the Limits of Strategic Tort Litigation' (2020) 21 *German Law Journal* 549, 550.
[75] Ibid., 556.
[76] *Neilson v. Overseas Projects Corporation of Victoria Ltd* [2005] HCA 54; 223 CLR 331 at 372 [125], 416–17 [267], and 411 [249].
[77] W. Prosser, 'Interstate Publication' (1953) 51 *Michigan Law Review* 959, 971, cited by Chief Justice Spigelman AC (Speech at the launch of the 8th edition of *Nygh's Conflicts of Laws in Australia*, Sydney, 16 April 2010).
[78] For example, in *Neilson v. Projects Overseas Corporation of Victoria* [2005] HCA 54; 223 CLR 331.
[79] A convenient summary is to be found in M. Davies, A. Bell, and P. Le Gay Brereton., *Nygh's Conflicts of Laws in Australia* (8th edn, 2010) p. 320.

> issues. Between them, the six judgments contained support for each of the three 'wrong' answers to the renvoi question. A narrow majority chose the answer of double renvoi, which has the most profound and apparently insoluble defect, that of infinite regression. The majority managed to dodge the problem of infinite regression on the facts of the case, without giving any indication of how the problem should be solved when it does arise, or indeed, whether they would give the same answer in a case involving infinite regression. As a result, the decision virtually invites further litigation.

This led him to the conclusion that '[r]envoi is a question without an answer—or, rather, it is a question with three possible answers, all of which are wrong for some reason or another'.[80]

A problem may also arise in determining *where* the relevant culpable conduct in fact occurred.[81] Whilst this may be a vexed question in product liability cases (involving foreign designed, manufactured, or tested products), it will normally be a relatively straightforward issue in cases of human rights abuse.

Whilst choice of law and conflicts of law questions may loom large as potential problems in a number of instances, in practice they do not normally give rise to insuperable difficulties.

In the Australian context, McGrath outlines the case for litigation against an Australian polluter in the forum of PNG, with subsequent enforcement of that foreign judgment in Australia. He argues that customary landowners seeking to vindicate their human rights 'who have established an enforcing a causal link between a company polluting their environment situated in Australia and the damage they are suffering would have a strong case *in favour of* their award of damages not being defeated on public policy grounds'.[82]

Leaving aside considerations of private international law, as is the case with many other forms of civil litigation, claimants may face additional formidable economic and procedural barriers in seeking redress. A number of these barriers, including the issue of costs, are considered below.

[80] M. Davies, 'Case Note: Neilson v Projects Overseas Corporation of Victoria, Renvoi and Presumptions about Foreign Law' (2006) 30 (1) *Melbourne University Law Review* 8.

[81] See, for example, the discussion by A. Gray, 'Before the High Court: Getting it Right: Where is the Place of the Wrong in a Multinational Torts Case (2008) 30(3) *Sydney Law Review* 537.

[82] C. McGrath, 'Identifying Opportunities for Climate Litigation: A Transnational Claim by Customary Landowners in PNG' (2020) 37 *Environmental and Planning Law Journal* 42, 64–5. There has recently been a number of instances in Australia where claims arising out of climate change have been pursued on human rights grounds. In May 2019, a formal complaint was lodged to the United Nations Human Rights Committee against the Australian Government by of a group of Torres Strait Islanders affected by climate change with the support of ClientEarth. There is also a challenge to the Galilee Coal Project in the Land Court in Queensland by a youth organisation, Youth Verdict, represented by the Environmental Defenders Office.

VI. Procedural mechanisms for obtaining redress in Australia

Where multiple parties are seeking redress representative action procedures in court rules or statutory class action mechanisms may be utilised. Australia has a very effective statutory class action regime available in the Federal Court and in the Supreme Courts of various States.

At a federal level, class actions were introduced when Part IVA of the *Federal Court of Australia Act 1976* (Cth) came into force in 1992. In subsequent years similar legislation has been enacted in Victoria, New South Wales, and Tasmania, and is under consideration in Western Australia.

The statutory regimes in each Australian jurisdiction are similar. The threshold criteria for the commencement of a class action are minimal. A class action may be commenced by one or more persons where there are (i) seven or more persons (ii) with claims against the same person (iii) arising out of the same similar or related facts (iv) giving rise to a substantial common question of law or fact.

Unlike in the United States and Canada, there is no 'certification' requirement: a class action can be commenced if these minimal criteria are satisfied, without judicial approval being required. However, a defendant who objects to the matter proceeding on a class basis may contest the claim that the proceeding satisfies the class requirements. Also, the various statutes provide that the court may order that the case not proceed as a class action in a number of circumstances, including where the court considers that (i) the costs to the defendant of distributing money to class members would be excessive having regard to the amounts in issue, or (ii) the class action will not provide an efficient and effective means of dealing with the claims of class members, or (iii) it is otherwise inappropriate to proceed by way of a class action.[83]

The class action regime is available irrespective of the causes of action (within the jurisdiction of the court) relied upon. However, in proceedings in the Federal Court at least one of the causes of action must arise under federal law.

It is an 'opt-out regime' whereby any person that fits the definition of the class is automatically a class member unless they formally exclude themselves by 'opting out'.

In Australia there have been a number of class actions brought, against Australian-based parties, arising out of alleged 'human rights' violations and other allegedly unlawful conduct by such bodies in Australia. These include actions arising out of unlawful detention of young people;[84] systemic physical and sexual abuse perpetrated on children at a children's home;[85] allegations of physical mistreatment, psychological abuse, unjustified retention of pension

[83] See, for example, sections 33M and 33N of the *Federal Court of Australia Act 1976* (Cth).
[84] *Konneh v. State of NSW (No. 3)* [2013] NSWSC 1424.
[85] *Giles v. Commonwealth of Australia* [2014] NSWSC 83.

payments, misappropriation of pension monies, failures to maintain and secure the premises so as to avoid the residents injuring themselves, and failures to adequately supervise and look after residents, especially those who were older or high-care residents and those at risk of self-harm;[86] the rights of asylum seekers;[87] claims by Aboriginal and Torres Strait Islander people on Palm Island against the State of Queensland and the Commissioner of the Police Service of Queensland, alleging various breaches of section 9(1) of the *Racial Discrimination Act 1975* (Cth) arising out of the conduct of members of the Queensland Police Service in November 2004;[88] offshore detention;[89] wages 'stolen' from Aboriginal and Torres Strait Islanders;[90] and the treatment of juveniles in detention centres in the Northern Territory.[91]

The question of whether or not class action proceedings can be brought in Australia on behalf on non-resident class members is presently the subject of controversy. Although turning on its idiosyncratic facts, the respondent (BHP Group Limited (BHP)) in a shareholder class action in the Federal Court of Australia[92] has contended that the Australian federal class action regime does not apply to claims on behalf of persons who are not residents of Australia and who are not either a named party or have otherwise overtly invoked or submitted to the jurisdiction of the Court for the purpose of the proceedings.[93] It argued that as a matter of statutory construction the class action legislation does not operate extraterritorially. It has also contended that the alleged contraventions of Australian law by the Australian corporate entity cannot have caused loss to persons outside Australia (who purchased shares in a different, albeit related company, on a foreign stock exchange).[94] BHP accepts that the Commonwealth Parliament has power to legislate extraterritorially with respect to the subject matter of class action proceedings but contends that it has not done so.[95] The joint applicants in the proceeding opposed BHP's application, including on the basis that the class action legislation applies to bind both resident and non-resident group members in circumstances where the Court has jurisdiction

86 *McAlister v. New South Wales (No. 2)* [2017] FCA 93; *McAlister v. New South Wales (No. 3)* [2018] FCA 636.

87 *Kamasaee v. Commonwealth* [2017] VSC 537; *Kamasaee v. Commonwealth* [2018] VSC 138.

88 *Wotton v. State of Queensland (No. 10)* [2018] FCA 915.

89 *AUB19 v. Commonwealth of Australia* [2019] FCA 1722.

90 *Pearson v. State of Queensland (No. 2)* [2020] FCA 619.

91 *Sister Marie Brigid Arthur (Litigation Representative) v. Northern Territory of Australia (No. 2)* [2020] FCA 215; *Jenkings v. Northern Territory of Australia (No. 2)* [2018] FCA 1706 (9 November 2018) (White J).

92 *Impiombato v. BHP Group Limited* (Federal Court of Australia, VID 649/2018, commenced 31 May 2018).

93 BHP's submissions in support of its interlocutory application dated 12 May 2020 and 10 July 2020 [5]. The contentions are amplified in BHP's submissions in reply, dated 4 September 2020.

94 Ibid., [11].

95 Ibid., [16].

over the proceeding derived from other statutory sources of jurisdiction.[96] The Federal Court has rejected the arguments advanced by BHP.[97]

VII. Legal costs

Although lawyers are permitted to act on a 'no win, no pay' basis in Australia, to date percentage contingent fees have been prohibited notwithstanding the recommendations for reform arising out of various law reform commission reports and inquiries.[98]

At the time of writing percentage contingent fees were being introduced in the State of Victoria, over the objection of parts of the business community and the legal profession.

In most cases Australian lawyers in private practice enter into costs agreements with clients whereby charges are calculated on the basis of specified hourly rates. If a civil case is conducted on a 'no win, no fee' basis it is permissible to provide in the costs agreement that the hourly rates may be increased by up to 25 per cent of the base hourly rate in the event of 'success' (as defined in the costs agreement).

Although there are a number of legal aid and non-government not-for-profit organisations providing legal services in human rights cases in Australia, such as the Public Interest Advocacy Centre and the Human Rights law Centre, complex, expensive, and protracted civil cases, including class actions, are normally conducted by private law firms. As in the United Kingdom, such firms will usually also engage barristers from the private bar to handle most of the advocacy in court.

In an increasing number of complex civil cases and class actions, financial assistance is being provided by commercial litigation funders.

VIII. Adverse costs, security for costs, and litigation funding

Although various law reform bodies have recommended that a publicly funded class actions fund should be established in Australia, modelled on the provincial Canadian class actions funds, to date this has not occurred.

In Australian civil litigation, although courts have an unfettered discretion as to whether to order costs in favour of the prevailing party at the conclusion of the

[96] Joint applicants' outline of submissions in opposition to BHP's interlocutory application dated 12 May 2020, [2].

[97] *Impiombato v. BHP Group Limited (No 2)* [2020] FCA 1720 (Moshinsky J).

[98] Australian Law Reform Commission (ALRC), 'Integrity, Fairness and Efficiency-An inquiry into Class Action Proceedings and Third-Party Litigation Funders' Final Report 134 (Commonwealth of Australia 2018); Victorian Law Reform Commission (VLRC), Access to Justice—Litigation Funding and Group Proceedings (Victorian Government Printer 2018).

litigation, in practice the losing party is usually ordered to pay most of the legal costs incurred by the winning party. In class actions, class members are statutorily immune from being ordered to pay such costs and thus the representative applicant is liable to be ordered to pay such costs.

This creates obvious problems and disincentives. Thus, in most cases a commercial litigation funder will agree to meet any such 'adverse' order for costs or any order to provide security for costs during the conduct of the litigation. In many cases an insurance policy may be taken out with a commercial insurer in order to obtain an indemnity in respect of such costs (at a substantial premium).

Commercial funding of litigation has become common place in class actions in Australia in recent years, particularly in shareholder or investor class actions. Unlike lawyers, commercial funders are entitled to seek payment of a commission, calculated as a percentage of the amount recovered by way of settlement or judgment. This has become widespread following the imprimatur of the High Court of Australia.[99] Initially this was often done through entering into litigation funding agreements with individual class members. In many cases this resulted in 'opt-in' class actions, limited to those who had entered into funding agreements, whereas the statutory regimes were designed to facilitate 'opt-out' class actions. A solution to this problems occurred when the Full Court of the Federal Court of Australia determined that the Court had power to make a 'common fund' order, whereby the funder became entitled to a commission (approved by the court) from all class members, not just those who had entered into contractual arrangements.[100] However, in two recent cases, heard concurrently, orders by the NSW Court to Appeal and the Full Court of the Federal Court upholding judicial power to make common fund orders at an early stage in the litigation were overturned (by majority) by the High Court of Australia.[101]At the time of writing there is controversy, and uncertainty, as to whether similar orders may be made at the conclusion of the case (under different statutory powers).[102] In order ostensibly to improve the regulation of commercial litigation funding in Australia, and somewhat controversially, the Commonwealth government has recently changed the law so as to bring commercial litigation funding arrangements in class actions within the *managed investment scheme* regulatory requirements and to require funders to obtain an Australian Financial Services License.

The present class action in the Federal Court[103] brought against an Australian oil company on behalf of 15,000 Indonesian seaweed farmers who allegedly

[99] *Campbells Cash and Carry Pty Ltd v. Fostif* (2006) 229 CLR 336.

[100] *Money Max Int Pty Ltd v. QBE Insurance Group Ltd* [2016] FCAFC 148.

[101] *BMW Australia Ltd v. Brewster; Westpac Banking Corporation v. Lendthall* [2019] HCA 45.

[102] There are divergences of view amongst Federal Court judges on this issue.

[103] See, for example, the decision concerning objections to evidence at trial: *Sanda v. PTTEP Australasia (Ashmore Cartier) Pty Ltd (No. 6)* [2019] FCA 1853 and the decision following the trial of the lead applicant's case *Sanda v. PTTEP Australasia (Ashmore Cartier) Pty Ltd (No 7)* [2021] FCA 237.

suffered losses arising out of the Montara oil spill off the north coast of Australia is being funded by a UK-based commercial litigation funder (Harbour).

Apart from commercial funders, in human rights and public interest cases some financial assistance, including by way of indemnity in respect of adverse costs, may be provided by not-for-profit bodies such as the Public Interest Advocacy Center and the Grata Fund. In most instances, legal aid through established legal aid organisations is not available for major civil litigation.

Although the 'loser pays' rule applies in most civil cases, in cases which are considered to be of public interest the court may in the exercise of its discretion determine that the losing (public interest) litigant should not be ordered to pay the costs of the successful defendant.[104] Moreover, many if not most courts may, in the exercise of their discretion, make orders at an early stage of the litigation capping the costs that may be recovered in order to ensure that access to justice is not frustrated by the impecuniosity of the plaintiff or an unwillingness to proceed with the matter in light of the prospect of an adverse costs order.[105]

IX. Confidentiality constraints

Difficulties obtaining information present a further barrier to the successful conduct of human rights litigation in Australia. Employees can present an invaluable source of evidence of proximity of multinational corporations to conduct amounting to human rights abuses. However, in the class action context, the Australian courts have supported the enforcement of express or implied confidentiality obligations in employment contracts to prevent lawyers from conferring with employees and former employees.

In *AG Australia Holdings Ltd v. Burton and Another*,[106] lawyers acting for a plaintiff in class action proceedings against AG Australia prepared a draft witness statement for a former employee of that company. Campbell J granted injunctive relief to AG Australia and held that enforcement of the contract did not contravene public policy.[107]

In a 2016 Victorian Supreme Court case, Forrest J concluded that confidentiality obligations would not be enforced by a Court where it has an adverse effect on the administration of justice, outweighing the public interest in the protecting the confidence.[108] In that case, lawyers for an infant seeking asylum in offshore detention sought to interview a former Serco employee before trial.

[104] See *Oshlack v. Richmond River Council* (1998) 193 CLR 72.

[105] Various earlier cases are referred to in the decision of the Victorian Court of Appeal in a human rights case: *Sophie Aitken & Ors v. State of Victoria, Department of Education and Early Childhood Development* [2013] VSCA 28.

[106] (2002) 58 NSWLR 464.

[107] (2002) 58 NSWLR 464, at [170]–[172], [177].

[108] *AS v. Minister for Immigration and Border Protection and Others* (2016) 53 VR 631, at [26]–[27].

Murphy J followed this approach in the Federal Court in *Zantran Pty Ltd v. Crown Resorts Ltd.*[109] This interlocutory decision formed part of a pending class action alleging misleading and deceptive conduct in relation to Crown's risks of conducting its business in China. Murphy J granted orders that various former employees of Crown Resorts Ltd (Crown) be relieved of obligations of confidence owed to Crown for the limited purpose of conferring with lawyers for Zantran and providing statements. However, this decision was unanimously reversed on appeal to the Full Court of the Federal Court, disapproving of the approach of Forrest J.[110]

A further problem, not unique to Australia, arises where corporate documents are produced on discovery in litigation in circumstances which preclude their disclosure or use in connection with other claims, whether by virtue of the implied *Harman*[111] undertaking, express terms of agreement,[112] or court-imposed confidentiality/protective orders.

In appropriate circumstances, a court may grant leave for use of a document or information for a purpose other than that for which it was initially obtained.

X. Non-litigious strategies

Even if there is a viable cause of action and an available Australian forum, there may still be a problematic lack of legal accountability for various forms of extraterritorial conduct which amount to human rights violations in which Australian or related companies may be directly or indirectly implicated. This has led some authors to focus on the need for a wide range of non-litigation strategies.[113] The Non-Judicial Human Rights Redress Mechanisms Project, an academic research collaboration, conducted almost 600 interviews over 5 years with 1,100 persons with a view to analysing the effectiveness of these mechanisms in responding to alleged human rights violations associated with transnational business activity. The authors conducted empirical research into communities and workers pursuing a remedy for grievances in the garment and footwear manufacturing, mining, industrial, and agribusiness sectors in India and Indonesia. This encompassed multinational corporations with links to Australian business, including agriculture (tea and palm oil), industrial projects (steel, mining, stone quarries), and garment manufacturing (homebased workers and factory workers). The links to Australia included loans and investments from Australian financial institutions, and the

[109] (2019) 370 ALR 516, at [7], [114].

[110] *Crown Resorts Ltd v. Zantran Pty Ltd* (2020) 374 ALR 739, at [2], [64], [135].

[111] *Harman v. Secretary of State for the Home Department* [1983] 1 AC 280. See also *Hearne v. Street* [2008] HCA 36; (2008) 235 CLR 125 and *Haswell v. Commonwealth of Australia* [2020] FCA 915.

[112] For an interesting analysis see S.K. Endo, 'Contracting for Confidential Discovery, University of Florida Levin College of Law' (2020) *Legal Studies Research Paper No. 20-15*, <http://ssrn.com/abstract=3620434>, accessed on 18 November 2020.

[113] A number of proposals by various authors are outlined in Grear and Weston (n. 12) 37–9.

sourcing of products by Australian companies and retailers. Not all of this activity has been beneath the radar. For example, as the authors note,[114] the operations of Australian mining companies have had negative impacts on Indigenous peoples' rights to land, health, living environments, and livelihoods and this has been documented by a UN Committee.[115]

The study led to a number of recommendations concerning ways that *non-judicial mechanisms* can provide redress and justice to vulnerable communities and workers; how non-government organisations and worker representatives can more effectively utilise the mechanisms to provide support for and represent vulnerable communities and workers; and how redress mechanisms can contribute to long-term and sustainable respect and remedy of human rights by businesses throughout their operations, supply chains, and other business relationships.[116] A detailed consideration of these issues is outside the scope of the present chapter.

XI. Conclusion

The globalisation of capital, markets, and sources of (cheaper) goods and services has served as a catalyst for corporate expansion and increased profit, on the positive side, but also an opportunity for exploitation and wrongdoing on an increasing scale. Not only have corporations continued to expand in terms of their geographical reach they also continue to penetrate hitherto unknown and public sectors resulting in the privatisation of formerly public functions. As two authors have noted: 'corporations today have assumed central and controlling roles in the delivery of nearly all tele-communication services, vast portions of health care, municipal waste disposal and urban development and planning, infrastructure financing and even military warfare through extensive sub-contracting arrangements'.[117] In their view, the increasing transnational human rights litigation against multinational corporations 'emphasizes the need to closely scrutinize the relations between corporations and local communities'.[118]

[114] K. Macdonald, S. Marshall, M. Miller-Dawkins, et al., 'Redress for Transnational Business-Related Human Rights Abuses in Australia' (2016) *Non-Judicial Redress Mechanisms Report 3*, note 3, published under a Creative Commons Attribution Non-commercial Share Alike (CC-BY-NC-SA) licence, details of which can be found at <https://creativecommons.org/licenses/by-nc-sa/3.0>, accessed 17 April 2021.

[115] UN Committee on the Elimination of Racial Discrimination, Concluding Observations of the Committee on the Elimination of Racial Discrimination, Australia (13 September 2010) UN Doc CERD/C/AUS/CO/15-17 [13].

[116] Macdonald, Marshall, Miller-Dawkins, et al. (n. 114).

[117] D. Katelouzou and P. Zumbasen, 'The New Geographies of Corporate Law Production' (2020) Transnational Law Institute Think! Paper 12/2020, <https://ssrn.com/abstract=3575009> 4 (2020) 42(1) *University of Pennsylvania Journal of International Law*.

[118] Referring to P. Parma, *Indigeneity and Legal Pluralism in India: Claims, Histories, Meanings* (2015); C. Ochoa, 'Generating Conflict: Gold, Water and Vulnerable Communities in the Colombian Highlands' in C. Tan and J. Faundez (eds), *Natural Resources and Sustainable Development: International*

As MacDonald, Marshall, Miller-Dawkins, and others observe:

> In addition to positive impacts on livelihoods, ideas or technologies, business activities are also sometimes associated with significant human rights abuses—for example through land dispossession and forced resettlement, exploitation of workers, environmental damage or harm to peoples' health. Access to a remedy for these abuses is frequently impeded by failures of domestic legal systems, limited options in terms of redress mechanisms, significant structural imbalances of power between corporations and local communities, and distance of various types including—geographic, cultural, bureaucratic, political and economic—from decision-makers and established redress mechanisms.[119]

Failures of corporate governance, flawed corporate cultures,[120] and the limitations of governmental and regulatory oversight mean that in many instances the only effective remedy available for persons in 'local communities' who suffer and sustain loss from unlawful corporate conduct is through private litigation in a jurisdiction other than where the events occurred. The developing jurisprudence in other jurisdictions, and domestic Australian law and procedure, provide some encouragement for those seeking a remedy in Australia for human rights violations outside Australia which implicate Australian companies or their associated entities.

However, there continue to be a range of barriers to accessing judicial remedies in Australia. These include those which have been categorised as follows:

- financial: prohibitive costs and lack of funding or other forms of support for legal action;
- procedural: jurisdiction of the courts, statutes of limitations, disclosure requirements and rules governing applicable law;
- practical: public awareness and access to information, claimant security and difficulties associated with evidence gathering; and
- legal: limitations on parent company legal liability due to doctrines of limited liability, separate legal personality of companies and operation of the corporate veil.[121]

Economic Law Perspectives (2017); L. Coyle, 'Tender Is the Mine: Law, Shadow Rule, and the Public Gaze in Ghana' in C. Walker-Said and J. Kelly (eds), *Corporate Social Responsibility? Human Rights in The New Global Economy* (. 2015).

[119] MacDonald, Marshall, Miller-Dawkins, et al. (n. 114) 5.

[120] See Hill (n. 10). In her analysis, Hill focuses on two specific types of liability for misconduct arising from flawed corporate cultures: (i) criminal liability of the corporation as a legal person and (ii) personal liability of directors and officers for breach of duty to their company.

[121] Australian Human Rights Commission, 'Joint Civil Society Statement: Implementing the UN Guiding Principles on Business and Human Rights in Australia' (August 2016) [7.4(a)] referred to (at note 14, p. 26) by MacDonald, Marshall, Miller-Dawkins, et al. (n. 114).

As Bradshaw notes, parent companies 'reap the financial rewards of risky activity but are, generally, insulated from the subsidiary's liability', often leaving victims without an effective remedy.[122] Application of the principles such as those enunciated in *Vedanta* may improve the chances of victims being successful, at least at the threshold jurisdictional stage.[123] But Bradshaw emphasises that the 'court placed limits on jurisdiction, and its focus on a voluntary assumption of responsibility may be the undoing of post-Vedanta optimism'.[124] In future, multinational corporations may be less willing to set up and implement policies centrally, for fear of assuming responsibility.[125] It is clear that the 'emphasis on control and assumption of responsibility underscores the fact parent duty of care to third parties is an exceptional form of liability and that in many transnational tort cases, separate legal personality will continue to obstruct access to justice'.[126]

Even where conduct outside Australia is susceptible to legal avenues for redress before Australian courts, whether through a class action or otherwise, mere access to the courts does not usually facilitate a quick or inexpensive resolution. Problematic corporate conduct is often exacerbated by a corporate culture which all too often steadfastly refuses to accept either responsibility or liability and a legal culture which not infrequently results in the aggressive defence of claims.

The current class action litigation in the Federal Court of Australia on behalf of Indonesian seaweed farmers against an Australian company, and the litigation on behalf of Australian consumers against the German Volkswagen (VW) company arising out of the diesel emissions scandal, are illustrative of the forensic difficulties that those seeking a remedy may experience.[127]

The oil spill giving rise to the Montara class action occurred in August 2009. In 2010 the Commonwealth government appointed a Commission of Inquiry. The Commission described the most likely causes of the blowout arose from 'systematic' errors of a 'more deep-seated kind'. The Commission concluded that the oil company's actions did not come within a 'bull's roar' of sensible oilfield practice.

[122] C. Bradshaw, 'Corporate Liability for Toxic Torts Abroad: Vedanta v Lungowe in the Supreme Court' (2020) 32 *Journal of Environmental Law* 139, 140.

[123] D. Palombo, 'The Duty of Care of the Parent Company: A Comparison between French Law, UK Precedents and the Swiss Proposals' (2019) 4 *Business and Human Rights Journal* 265.

[124] Bradshaw (n. 122) 141.

[125] M. Croser, M. Day, M. van Huijstee, et al., 'Vedanta v Lungowe and Kiobel v Shell: The Implications for Parent Company Accountability' (2020) 5 *Business and Human Rights Journal* 130, citing: G. Holly, 'Zambian Farmers can Take Vedanta to Court over Water Pollution. What are the Legal Implications?' (*Business and Human Rights*, 10 April 2019), <https://www.business-humanrights.org/en/blog/zambian-farmers-can-take-vedanta-to-court-over-water-pollution-what-are-the-legal-implications/>, accessed 18 November 2020; and R. McCorquodale, 'Vedanta v Lungowe Symposium: Duty of Care of Parent Companies' (*Opinio Juris*, 18 April 2019), <http://opiniojuris.org/2019/04/18/symposium-duty-of-care-of-parent-companies/>, accessed 18 November 2020.

[126] A. Sanger, 'Parent Company Duty of Care to Third Parties Harmed by Overseas Subsidiaries' (2019) *Company Law Journal* 486, 489.

[127] The author acted as lead counsel for the applicants in two of the five class actions in the Federal Court of Australia against VW and from its inception until 2019 was one of the counsel acting for the applicant in the Montara oil spill class action in the Federal Court.

The Commission said further, '[t]he Blowout was not a reflection of one unfortunate incident, or of bad luck', instead '[the company's] systems and processes were so deficient and its key personnel so lacking in basic competence, that the Blowout can properly be said to have been an event waiting to occur'. It further noted that the company 'did not seek to properly inform itself as to the circumstances and the causes of the Blowout. The information that it provided to the regulators was consequently incomplete and apt to mislead.'[128]

The Commission recommended that the then-Minister for Resources and Energy review the company's operating licence at the Montara Oilfield. The Minister declined to issue a 'show cause' notice. The company subsequently pleaded guilty to four breaches of the *Offshore Petroleum and Greenhouse Gas Storage Act 2006* (Cth) and was fined A$510,000.

Class action proceedings were commenced in the Federal Court of Australia in July 2017 and are being pursued on behalf of 15,000 Indonesian seaweed farmers whose income and livelihood is alleged to have suffered substantially due to the loss of seaweed they were cultivating. The case proceeded to trial in late 2019. Judgment on the common issues and the lead applicant's case was delivered on 19 March 2021. At the time of writing (May 2021) final orders had not been made, pending further submissions from the parties. Moreover, each of the group members requires an extension of the limitation period. If there is an appeal, the outcome of the appeal may not be known until 2022, or years later if the matter proceeds on appeal to the High Court. Throughout the proceeding the oil company has contended, *inter alia*, that it did not owe a duty of care to the Indonesian seaweed farmers because it was not reasonably foreseeable that the oil would reach the parts of Indonesia in question; the oil did not reach the areas in question; and the loss of seaweed was not caused by the Montara oil spill.

The events giving rise to the Australian class actions against the German VW company, and related companies, arose out of the admission by VW in September 2015 that 'dual function' software had been installed in various models of diesel vehicles in numerous countries, including Australia, whereby the vehicles were able to meet emissions limits during laboratory testing but operated considerably in excess of such emission limits during on road use. Five class actions seeking damages on behalf of 100,000 Australian consumers were commenced in Australia in late 2015. Two regulatory proceedings seeking civil penalties were commenced at later dates by the Australian Competition and Consumer Commission (ACCC).

[128] In June 2010 the Montara Commission of Inquiry reported on an oil and gas leak in the Montara oil field. The leak took place in the Timor Sea, off the northern coast of Western Australia, between 21 August and 3 November 2009. The incident resulted from a wellhead accident on an offshore drilling platform owned by PTT Exploration and Production (PTTEP) Australasia. The inquiry was established under Part 9.10A of *the Offshore Petroleum and Greenhouse Gas Storage Act 2006* (Cth). It examined the likely cause of the incident and the effectiveness of regulations.

Throughout the Australian proceedings, and in litigation in other jurisdictions, the defendants steadfastly denied, on a multiplicity of highly problematic grounds, that the vehicles were fitted with illegal 'defeat devices'. The dual mode software was said at one point to have been implemented by a small number of 'rogue' engineers.[129] The forensic position maintained throughout the Australian litigation was that the VW Board and senior management were not aware of the use of the 'cheat' software and that the European companies did not carry on business within Australia and thus were not amenable to being sued under certain Australian statutory laws.

The class action proceedings were recently resolved whereby VW has agreed to pay compensation of around A$120 million to around 40,000 class members who filed claims within the required time.[130] This was after almost five years of forensic warfare. The legal costs incurred in the class action litigation are in excess of $A100 million. The civil penalty proceedings were concluded recently after VW agreed to pay an amount of A$75 million. The presiding Federal Court Judge, Justice Foster, increased this to $A125 million[131] . This resulted in an unsuccessful appeal to the Full Federal Court[132] and is now the subject of an application for leave to appeal to the High Court.

These cases are illustrative of the excessive costs and delays endemic in much Australian class action litigation against large multinational companies. The litigation defence strategies exemplify what an American author has recently referred to as 'industrial strength denial'.[133]

Those seeking redress in Australian courts against multinational corporations implicated in human rights abuses outside Australia need to be mindful of these potential problems and devise creative forensic strategies to circumvent or overcome them.

129 Comments by Michael Horn, Head of VW's US operations, in response to questioning by the US House of Representatives Oversight and Investigations Panel: 'Top US VW Exec Blames "A Couple of Software Engineers" for Scandal', *Reuters Associated Press* (8 October 2015) cited by Hill (n. 10) 7, note 48.

130 *Cantor v. Audi Australia Pty Limited (No. 5)* [2020] FCA 637.

131 *Australian Competition and Consumer Commission v. Volkswagen Aktiengesellschaft* [2019] FCA 2166 (20 December 2019) (Foster J).

132 *Volkswagen Aktiengesellschaft v. Australian Competition and Consumer Commission* [2021] FCAFC 49 (9 April 2021)

133 Albeit with reference to other large corporations 'defending the indefensible' from the slave trade to climate change: B. Freese, *Industrial-Strength Denial* (2020).

7
International Human Rights Litigation in the United States

Paul Hoffman

I. Introduction

In recent years, human rights victims have used US courts to seek accountability for corporate participation and complicity in such violations. This chapter considers the main litigation tools used in these efforts and the prospects for such litigation for the future.[1]

The last 25 years of US corporate human rights litigation focused largely on the Alien Tort Statute (ATS), a statute dating back to the First Judiciary Act of 1789.[2] After initial success, the utility of the ATS as a vehicle for corporate accountability has been limited by a series of obstacles created by Supreme Court decisions. Further limiting options for human rights litigation, the Court also held that the Torture Victim Protection Act (TVPA), another significant human rights statute, is inapplicable to corporations.[3]

In response to these developments, litigators have turned to other strategies to hold corporations accountable. For example, common law tort actions can be filed either in State or federal courts.[4] For certain claims, there are specific statutes such as the Trafficking Victim Protection Act (TVPRA)[5] which provides for suits against corporations for participation or complicity, *inter alia*, in trafficking or forced labour, including knowingly receiving the benefit of such abuses.[6] There may also be State statutes (e.g. consumer protection laws) which provide alternative mechanisms for accountability.

[1] This chapter will also address extraterritorial environmental and other public interest cases seeking corporate accountability.

[2] 28 USC section 1350 (1948) ('The district courts shall have original jurisdiction of any civil action by an alien for a tort only, committed in violation of the law of nations or a treaty of the United States.') A.M. Burley, 'The Alien Tort Statute and the Judiciary Act of 1789: A Badge of Honor' (1989) 83 *American Journal of International Law* 461 (discussing the history of the ATS).

[3] *See Mohamad v. Palestinian Authority*, 566 US 449 (2012).

[4] 28 USC section 1332. The statute requires complete diversity of citizenship thus suits by foreign citizens against US corporations may qualify under the statute. State or federal claims can be included in cases filed under federal statutes based on supplemental jurisdiction. 28 USC section 1367.

[5] 18 USCA sections 1581–1595.

[6] 18 USCA section 1595.

Paul Hoffman, *International Human Rights Litigation in the United States* In: *Human Rights Litigation against Multinationals in Practice*. Edited by: Richard Meeran, Oxford University Press.
DOI: 10.1093/oso/9780198866220.003.0007

This chapter focuses on the viability of cases involving allegations of corporate complicity in extraterritorial human rights violations in State or federal US courts. Abuses occurring on US soil can be addressed under an extensive domestic statutory and common law regime.[7] The last section considers some of the advantages of litigation in US courts to foreign plaintiffs seeking justice against defendants in the United States.

II. Alien Tort Statute (ATS)

The ATS has been the main vehicle for litigating extraterritorial human rights violations against corporate defendants in US courts. The ATS allows non-citizens to bring tort actions for violations of the law of nations in federal court. Although the ATS was enacted as part of the 1789 Judiciary Act, its modern use in human rights cases derives from *Filartiga v. Pena-Irala*,[8] a case alleging torture committed in Paraguay. While the human rights violation occurred in Paraguay, the Filartiga family filed their lawsuit in the United States when they found the perpetrator living in New York.[9] The *Filartiga* decision recognised that the 'law of nations' (i.e. customary international law) included at least some modern human rights norms, including the prohibition of torture, and that the ATS provided a federal court forum for human rights victims. Using *Filartiga*, human rights victims from around the world brought cases seeking to enforce the modern customary international law of human rights.

It was not until the mid-1990s that cases were brought seeking corporate accountability for complicity in extraterritorial human rights violations. The first case was *Doe v. Unocal*,[10] a case seeking to hold Unocal, a California-based oil company (since purchased by Chevron), Total, a major French oil company, and Myanmar's State-owned oil company accountable for human rights violations committed by the Myanmar military in connection with a natural gas pipeline project.[11] After a decade of litigation, the case was settled in 2005 for an undisclosed amount.[12] Since

[7] This domestic legal regime and its criminal sanctions are beyond the scope of this chapter.

[8] 630 F. 2d 876 (2d Cir. 1980). See, for example, *Abebe-Jira v. Negewo*, 72 F. 3d 844 (11th Cir. 1996) (Ethiopia); *In re Estate of Ferdinand Marcos*, 25 F. 3d 1467 (9th Cir. 1994) (Philippines). For a comprehensive discussion of the ATS and other human rights litigation as of 2008 in the United States see B. Stephens, et al., *International Human Rights Litigation in U.S. Courts* (2nd edn, 2008).

[9] *See* W.J. Aceves, *The Anatomy of Torture: A Documentary History of Filartiga v. Pena Irala* (2007).

[10] *Doe v. Unocal Corp.*, 963 F. Supp. 880 (CD Cal. 1997). In the early 1990s a Holocaust Justice movement led to dozens of lawsuits and multibillion-dollar settlements on behalf of victims of the Holocaust. See M.J. Bazyler, *Holocaust Justice: The Battle for Restitution in America's Courts* (2003).

[11] Total was dismissed for lack of personal jurisdiction. *Doe v. Unocal Corp.*, 248 F. 3d 915, 930–31 (9th Cir. 2001).. The Myanmar State oil company was dismissed on sovereign immunity grounds (discussed below). *Doe v. Unocal. Corp.*, 395 F. 3d 932, 958 (9th Cir. 2002).

[12] K.H. Wa, 'Opinion, when big business and human rights collide' (*Los Angeles Times*, 26 February 2012), <https://www.latimes.com/opinion/la-xpm-2012-feb-26-la-oe-ka-nigerians-20120226-story.html>, accessed 18 November 2020.

the Unocal case dozens of other corporate accountability ATS cases have been filed with mixed results. Recent Supreme Court decisions have created doubt about the future of ATS corporate accountability litigation. This section discusses the most important current issues.

A. Possible ATS claims

In *Sosa v. Alvarez-Machain*,[13] the Supreme Court found that the ATS authorised federal courts to recognise human rights claims for relief using their federal common law authority.[14] The Court held, though, that any new ATS claims had to be supported by a showing that the new norm had the same degree of international consensus as supported by 18th century 'historical paradigms'.[15] While allowing such claims to proceed, the Court admonished lower courts to exercise judicial restraint and consider the 'practical consequences' of recognising any new causes of action before doing so.[16] Since *Sosa*, federal courts have recognised claims, *inter alia*, for genocide, crimes against humanity, forced labour, torture, and summary execution.[17]

Over the years, litigators have tried to expand the universe of ATS claims to include environmental claims without success.[18] For example in *Flores v. Southern Peru Copper Co.*, the Court rejected an argument by Peruvian plaintiffs based on customary international law prohibiting intra-national pollution and environmental degradation. The Second Circuit rejected the argument that such norms were specific, universal, and obligatory and thus found that they could not be enforced under the ATS.[19]

Indian plaintiffs sought to obtain accountability from Union Carbide in US courts for the Bhopal disaster without success.[20] Plaintiffs in *Okpabi v. Royal Dutch*

[13] 542 US 692 (2004). Prior to *Sosa*, courts had found that the ATS itself provided the cause of action in ATS cases. See, for example, *Hilao v. Marcos (In re Estate of Marcos)*, 25 F. 3d 1467, 1475 (9th Cir. 1994) (ATS creates a cause of action for violations of specific, universal, and obligatory international human rights standards which confer fundamental rights).

[14] 542 US at 715.

[15] The 'historical paradigms' were attacks on Ambassadors, breaches of neutrality, and piracy. Ibid. W. Blackstone, *Commentaries on the Law of England* (1979). The Court found that the arbitrary arrest and detention claim in the case did not meet its standard. 542 US at 734–7.

[16] Ibid., at 732–3.

[17] *Velez v. Sanchez*, 693 F 3d 308, 321 (2d Cir. 2012) (forced labour); *Al Shimari v. CACI Premier Tech., Inc.*, 758 F 3d 516, 530 (4th Cir. 2014) (torture); *Wiwa v. Royal Dutch Petroleum Co.*, 626 F. Supp. 2d 377, 385 (SDNY 2009) (crimes against humanity).

[18] For more optimistic views see M. Delinger, 'Post-Jesner Climate Change Lawsuits Under the Alien Tort Statute' 44 *Columbia Journal of Environmental Law* 241; R.M. Bratspies, Reasoning Up to Human Rights: Environmental Rights as Customary International Law, in J. Knox and R. Pejan (eds), *The Human Right to a Healthy Environment* (2018).

[19] *Flores v. Southern Peru Copper Co.*, 414 F. 3d 233, 265–66 (2d Cir. 2003).

[20] Following over a decade of litigation the Second Circuit found that plaintiffs had not proved that Union Carbide was sufficiently involved in the Bhopal plant. *Sahu v. Union Carbide Corp.*, 650 Fed. Appx 53 (2d Cir. 2016).

Shell sought to hold Royal Dutch Shell and its Nigerian subsidiary for environmental degradation in the Niger Delta. Due to increasing barriers to ATS litigation in the US the American case was dismissed by the plaintiffs in favour of seeking relief in the UK courts under common law theories.[21]

As US remedies contract, litigants will increasingly consider filing cases in foreign courts.

Plaintiffs were more successful in challenging Pfizer's non-consensual medical experimentation in Nigeria.[22] The Second Circuit found that plaintiffs' claims were based on specific, universal, and obligatory customary norms enforceable under the ATS. Ultimately, the cases were settled.[23]

B. Theories of liability

The ATS applies to both direct and indirect perpetrators of law of nations' violations. To date, few ATS cases have claimed that the corporate defendants directly committed extraterritorial human rights violations. Instead, the ATS corporate cases typically allege secondary theories of liability such as aiding and abetting the human rights violations committed by State actors or under the colour of State authority.[24] To date, every Circuit to have considered the issue has found that aiding and abetting liability is a viable theory of liability under the ATS; however, there has been a lack of uniformity in defining the *mens rea* and *actus reus* elements for aiding and abetting liability.

Initially, some courts adopted the definition of aiding and abetting set forth in section 876b of the Restatement (Second) of Torts.[25] Most Circuits now look to

[21] Reuters, 'UK Supreme Court to hear Nigerians' case for pursuing Shell spill claim in England' *Engineering News* (24 July 2019). *See Okpabi & Ors v. Royal Dutch Shell PLC & Anor* (Rev. 1)[2018] EWCA Civ. 191 (14 February 2018).

[22] *See Abdullahi v. Pfizer, Inc.*, 562 F. 3d 163 (2d Cir. 2009); *Adamu v. Pfizer, Inc.*, 399 F. Supp. 2d 495 (SDNY 2005).

[23] S. Resinger, 'Pfizer Settles Lawsuits Over Drug Trials on Children in Nigeria' (*Law.com*, 23 February 2011), <https://www.law.com/almID/1202482854504/>, accessed 14 July 2020. It is unclear whether cases like this would surmount the presumption against extraterritoriality discussed below.

[24] Conspiracy and agency claims have also been made in ATS cases. See, for example, *Cabello v. Fernandez-Larios*, 402 F. 3d 1148, 1159 (11th Cir. 2005) (conspiracy); *In re Chiquita Brands Int'l, Inc. Alien Tort Statute & S'holder Derivative Litig.* (*Chiquita*), 190 F. Supp. 3d at 1119–20 (SD Fla. 2016) (conspiracy, aiding and abetting); *Presbyterian Church of Sudan v. Talisman Energy, Inc.*, 582 F 3d 244, 254 (2d Cir. 2009) (agency); *Bowoto v. Chevron Texaco Corp.*, 312 F. Supp. 2d 1229, 1239 (ND Cal. 2004) (conspiracy, aiding and abetting, agency). Agency theories may be important where a corporate parent attempts to shield itself from the complicity of its subsidiaries in human rights violations. See, for example, *Balintulo v. Ford Motor Co.*, 796 F. 3d 160, 169 (2d Cir. 2015).

[25] Section 876(b) provides for liability if the defendant 'knows that the other's conduct constitutes a breach of duty and gives substantial assistance or encouragement to the other so to conduct himself'. Restatement (Second) of Torts, section 876(b) (American Law Institute 1979). See, for example, *Abebe-Jira v. Negewo*, 72 F. 3d 844, 845–6 (11th Cir. 1996); *Doe v. Drummond Co.*, 782 F. 3d 576, 608 (11th Cir. 2015). See also *Khulumani v. Barclay's Nat'l Bank Ltd.* (*Apartheid Cases*) 504 F. 3d 254, 290–1 (2d Cir. 2007) (Hall J, Concurring) (finding the knowledge standard applicable).

international law for the elements of aiding and abetting liability.[26] Although the international law standard, similar to section 876(b), is knowledge,[27] many courts have held that a showing of 'purpose' is required.[28] The Second Circuit's interpretation of 'purpose' was akin to a showing of specific intent (which generally only attaches, under international law, to specific intent crimes, such as genocide).[29] The Ninth Circuit in *Doe v. Nestle* found that allegations that the corporate defendants supported child slave labour as a means of reducing production costs were sufficient to meet either a purpose or knowledge standard. But the court did not decide which was the appropriate standard. The Court defined 'purpose' as being met where a corporate defendant knew about the likelihood that its actions would lead to human rights violations and continued to aid and abet those violations intentionally or with reckless disregard.[30]

US courts have also wrestled with the *actus reus* for aiding and abetting liability in corporate cases. In particular, corporate defendants argue that 'ordinary' business activity, including the normal means that corporations employ to supervise the activities of their subsidiaries, cannot serve as the predicate act for aiding and abetting liability. International law does not recognise such a categorical 'ordinary business' exception to aiding and abetting liability. It is unclear whether US courts will accept this argument.[31] The Fourth and Eleventh Circuits require a showing that the defendant provided substantial assistance to the person that committed the wrongful act.[32] This standard is met by allegations that corporate officials provided funding to individuals or organisations despite knowing that this funding would support human rights violations.[33] Although conflicts over the meaning and application of aiding and abetting liability remain unresolved, these issues have been overshadowed by the Supreme Court's recent decisions in *Kiobel* and *Jesner*, discussed below.

[26] See, for example, *Khulumani*, 504 F. 3d at 269–77 (Katzmann, J., concurring). The *Apartheid Cases* were ultimately dismissed based on the Kiobel presumption against extraterritoriality discussed below.

[27] See, for example, *Prosecutor v. Blagojevic*, No IT-02-60-A, para. 127 (ICTY 9 May 2007); *Prosecutor v. Taylor*, SCSL-03-01-A, para. 483 (SCSL Appeals Chamber, 26 Sept. 2013). *See generally* J. Green and M. Bazyler, 'Nuremberg-Era Jurisprudence Redux: The Supreme Court in *Kiobel v. Royal Dutch Shell Petroleum Co.* and the Legacy of Nuremberg', (2012) 7 *Charleston Law Review* 23.

[28] For a discussion of the cases addressing the *mens* requirements for aiding and abetting liability see Note, The Circuit Split on Mens Rea for Aiding and Abetting Liability Under the Alien Tort Statute' (2018) 59 *Boston College Law Review* 2953.

[29] See, for example, *Talisman*, 582 F. 3d at 259. The Fourth Circuit adopted the same standard in *Aziz v. Alcolac, Inc.*, 658 F. 3d 388, 401 (4th Cir. 2011). These decisions relied on their view that the Rome Statute required a *mens rea* of purpose to satisfy aiding and abetting liability and should set the standard in ATS cases.

[30] *Doe v. Nestle*, 766 F. 3d 1013, 1024 (9th Cir. 2014).

[31] See, for example, *Talisman*, 582 F. 3d at 261–4 (rejecting use of ordinary business activities such as air strips or maintaining roads as satisfying *actus reus* for aiding and abetting).

[32] Talisman, 582 F. 3d at 280–1; *Doe v. Drummond Co.*, 782 F. 3d at 608.

[33] *Chiquita*, 190 F. Supp. 3d at 1119.

C. Presumption against extraterritoriality

In *Kiobel v. Royal Dutch Petroleum, Co.*, the Supreme Court created the most significant obstacle to ATS corporate cases involving extraterritorial human rights violations. The Court held that the presumption against extraterritorial application of US statutes applied to federal common law claims recognised under the ATS.[34] This effectively barred the litigation of ATS cases where all the relevant conduct occurred abroad.[35] The *Kiobel* decision recognised that some ATS claims might 'touch and concern' the United States substantially enough to overcome this presumption.[36] The Court did not elaborate on or define the scope of the new 'touch and concern' standard.

The Circuit courts have been divided over the meaning and application of the 'touch and concern' standard. At one end of the spectrum, the Fourth Circuit found that the standard was met in a case against a US contractor for the torture and ill-treatment at Abu Ghraib during the Iraq war.[37] The US connections in the case were found to be sufficient to satisfy the 'touch and concern' test. At the other end of the spectrum are courts that apply the presumption as a complete bar if the injuries caused by the human rights violations occur outside US territory[38] Other Circuits have applied a multi-factor analysis that almost always results in the application of the presumption and a bar to litigation.[39]

34 *Kiobel v. Royal Dutch Petroleum, Co.*, 569 US108, 117 (2013). The *Kiobel* decision was part of an expanded use of the presumption to limit access to US courts for extraterritorial claims. See *Morrison v. National Aust. Bank, Ltd.*, 561 US 247 (2010) (requiring clear statement of Congressional intent for statutes to apply extraterritorially). Interestingly, after the dismissal of this case the plaintiffs initiated litigation in the Netherlands based on the same allegations against Shell Nigeria and its parent corporations. L. Roorda, 'Kiobel v Royal Dutch Shell—het vervolg?' (*Utrecht Centre for Accountability and Liability Law Blog*, 3 November 2016), <http://blog.ucall.nl/index.php/2016/11/kiobel-v-royal-dutch-shell-het-vervolg>, accessed 27 April 2021.

35 *Balintulo v. Daimler AG*, 727 F. 3d 174, 188 (2d Cir. 2013); *Balintulo v. Ford Motor Co.*, 796 F. 3d 160, 166–70 (2d Cir. 2015).

36 *Kiobel*, 569 US at 124–5. *Kiobel*, of course, involved foreign plaintiffs and defendants and events occurring entirely outside the United States. Brief of the Governments of the United Kingdom of Great Britain and Northern Ireland and the Kingdom of the Netherlands as Amicus Curiae Supporting Respondents, *Kiobel v. Royal Dutch Petroleum Co.*, 2012 WL 2312825.

37 *Al Shimari v. CACI Premier Technology, Inc.*, 758 F. 3d 516, 527–8 (2014) (finding sufficient US contacts to meet the 'touch and concern' test) (torture committed by US citizens hired in the United States by a US corporation, CACI, and CACI managers were aware of misconduct, attempted to cover it up, and encouraged the conduct).

38 *Daimler AG*, 727 F. 3d at 188.

39 See, for example, *Cardona v. Chiquita Brands Int'l, Inc.*, 760 F. 3d 1185, 1189–91 (11th Cir. 2014) (payments to right wing paramilitaries in Colombia insufficient to overcome the Kiobel presumption); *Doe v. Drummond*, 782 F. 3d 576, 601 (11th Cir. 2015). *See also Adhikari v. Kellogg Brown & Root*, Inc., 845 F. 3d 184, 199 (5th Cir. 2017) (trafficking of Nepalese men to US military base insufficient to overcome presumption). However, more specific allegations of US based aiding and abetting liability by the same contractor sufficient to overcome presumption at the pleadings stage. *Adhikari v. KBR, Inc*, No. 4:16-CV-2478, 2017 WL 4237923, at *6 (SD Tex. 25 September 2017).

In 2016, the Supreme Court applied the presumption against extraterritoriality again in *RJR Nabisco v. European Community*.[40] Relying in part on *Kiobel*, the Court held that the private cause of action provided for in the Racketeer Influenced and Corrupt Organizations Act was limited by the presumption because the 'focus' of the provisions in question were extraterritorial. The courts have yet to elaborate on how the 'focus' test relates to *Kiobel*'s 'touch and concern' test.

While many cases have been dismissed after *Kiobel*, there is a line of cases in which some courts have found that if a corporation aids and abets extraterritorial human rights violations from US territory, the corporation commits a violation on US soil and the presumption against extraterritoriality does not apply. *Mastafa v. Chevron Corp* is the most prominent of these cases.[41] In *Mastafa*, the plaintiffs alleged that Chevron's aiding and abetting occurred while committing an international law violation, *inter alia*, by engaging in domestic purchases and financing transactions conducted through a New York bank account and that these allegations satisfied *Kiobel's* 'touch and concern' test.[42]

D. Corporate liability

In 2010, a hotly divided Second Circuit panel in the *Kiobel* case decided *sua sponte* (without being asked) that the ATS did not apply to corporate defendants. The majority opinion determined that the issue of corporate liability should be determined by customary international law and plaintiffs' claims failed because there was no customary norm of corporate liability.[43] No other Court had come to this conclusion previously.[44] Every other Circuit to have considered the issue has found that corporate liability exists under the ATS.[45]

The Supreme Court granted certiorari (i.e. ordered the review of the decision of the lower court) in *Kiobel* to decide whether corporate liability exists under the ATS. After the case was argued in February 2012, the Court asked for re-argument on the issue of whether the ATS applied to human rights violations committed on

40 136 S. Ct 2090 (2016). The Court reaffirmed the application the *Morrison* 'focus' test. This test is designed to determine whether a case brought under a statute which is not extraterritorial is a domestic application of the statute by looking at the statute's 'focus'. *RJR Nabisco*, 136 S. Ct at 2101.

41 770 F. 3d 170, 181 (2d Cir. 2014).

42 Ibid., at 189–91. The claims in *Mastafa* were dismissed because the plaintiffs' allegations were insufficient to meet the 'purpose' standard for aiding and abetting liability. Ibid., at 191–4.

43 *Kiobel v. Royal Dutch Petroleum Co.*, 621 F. 3d 111 (2d Cir. 2010). Compare the majority opinion of Judge Cabranes, 621 F. 3d at 115, with the concurrence of Judge Leval, 621 F. 3d at 149. The Second Circuit denied a petition for hearing en banc (i.e. by the whole court) by a 5–5 vote. *Kiobel v. Royal Dutch Petroleum Co.*, 642 F. 3d 379 (2d Cir. 2011).

44 The first hint of the argument that corporations could not be sued under the ATS came in Judge Korman's separate opinion in *Khulumani*, 504 F. 3d at 321.

45 See, for example, *Flomo v. Nat. Rubber Co.*, 643 F. 3d 1013, 1021 (7th Cir. 2011); *Doe v. Exxon*, 654 F. 3d 11, 47–9 (DC 2011). In *Sarei v. Rio Tinto, PLC*, 671 F. 3d 736, 759 (9th Cir. 2011), the Ninth Circuit found corporate liability but determined that the issue should be decided on a norm-by-norm basis.

the territory of a foreign sovereign.[46] After re-argument the Court did not address the corporate liability issue in its decision, but instead, dismissed the case based on plaintiffs' failure to meet the Court's new 'touch and concern' standard.

The Court returned to the corporate liability issue in *Jesner v. Arab Bank PLC*,[47] a case alleging claims that the Arab Bank had aided and abetted suicide bombers by making payments to their families. Justice Kennedy's plurality opinion (i.e. where no opinion was supported by the majority) held that the ATS could not be used to sue foreign corporations. This categorical exclusion of ATS claims against foreign corporations was based on the Court's assessment that such cases inherently raised foreign affairs concerns.[48] This was an aggressive application of the judicial gate-keeping principle under the second step in *Sosa*, which the *Jesner* court grounded in a 'general reluctance to extend judicially created causes of action'.[49] The *Jesner* analysis will be asserted by corporate defendants to seek further limitations on ATS claims. However, the *Jesner* court did not resolve the issue of whether domestic corporations could be sued under the ATS.

E. *Doe v. Nestle* and the Trump Administration position

The *Doe v. Nestle* case challenges the alleged complicity of Cargill and Nestle USA in child slavery and forced labour on cocoa plantations in the Ivory Coast. The Ninth Circuit had previously found that plaintiffs' aiding and abetting allegations were sufficient to survive dismissal.[50] On remand, the district court dismissed the case based on the *Kiobel* presumption against extraterritoriality.[51] On appeal, the Ninth Circuit held that plaintiffs could amend their complaint to state a claim for aiding and abetting based on defendants' actions on US territory.[52] Defendants sought Supreme Court review on both the corporate liability and presumption against extraterritoriality issues.[53]

In January 2020, the Court asked the Solicitor General to give its views on defendants' petitions. The Solicitor General's brief suggested that the Court grant review and changes the Justice Department's position on corporate liability.[54] In both

[46] *Kiobel*, 565 US 1244 (2012) ('Whether and under what circumstances the Alien Tort Statute, 28 USC section 1350, allows courts to recognize a cause of action for violations of the law of nations occurring within the territory of a sovereign other than the United States.').

[47] 138 S. Ct 1386 (2018)

[48] 138 S. Ct at 1407.

[49] 138 S. Ct at 1402.

[50] *Doe v. Nestle*, 766 F. 3d 1013, 1024–7 (9th Cir. 2014).

[51] *Doe v. Nestle S.A.*, 2017 WL 6059134, at *1 (CD Cal. 2 March 2017).

[52] *Doe I v. Nestle USA, Inc.*, 929 F.3d 623, 642–3 (9th Cir. 2019).

[53] Petitions for Writ of Certiorari, *Doe v. Nestle*, No. 19-416 (2019 WL 4747982), and *Doe v. Cargill*, No. 19-453 (2019 WL 4933067).

[54] Brief for United States as *Amici Curiae*, *Nestle USA, Inc. v. Joe Doe I, et al.* (2019 No. 19-416), 2020 WL 129527.

Kiobel and *Jesner*, the Justice Department submitted *amicus* briefs arguing in favour of corporate liability under the ATS.[55] In stark contrast to previous briefs, the new brief asks the Court to eviscerate the ATS as a vehicle for redress against corporate complicity not only in extraterritorial cases but in all cases, arguing that extending ATS liability to corporations of any kind would be inappropriate without further action from Congress.[56]

On 2 July 2020, the Court granted the petitions. The cases were argued on 1 December 2020, with a decision expected by June 2021.

III. Torture Victims Protection Act (TVPA)

The TVPA was passed in 1991 as a companion statute to the ATS. It provides a cause of action to victims of torture and extrajudicial execution regardless of where such acts occur.[57] In *Mohammed v. Palestinian Auth.*,[58] the Court limited the TVPA to 'individual' defendants and excluded corporations from liability.[59]

However, the Court noted that the TVPA 'contemplates liability against officers who do not personally execute the torture or extrajudicial killing'.[60] Therefore, although TVPA cases against corporate entities are precluded, this raises the possibility of TVPA actions against corporate officers and managers for complicity in extraterritorial human rights violations remains. For example, in *Doe v. Chiquita*, a district court allowed TVPA claims to proceed against Chiquita's corporate officers, managers, and board members for aiding and abetting extrajudicial killings committed by right-wing paramilitaries in the banana-growing regions of Colombia.[61]

To be liable under the TVPA, an individual who subjects another to torture or extrajudicial killing must be 'acting under the actual or apparent authority, or color of law, of any foreign nation'.[62] To determine whether someone has acted under actual or apparent authority or colour of law, courts may look to principles of

[55] Brief for United States as *Amici Curiae* Supporting Petitioners, *Kiobel v. Royal Dutch Petroleum Co.*, 569 US 108 (2010), 2011 WL 6425363; Brief for United States as *Amici Curiae* Supporting Neither Party, *Jesner v. Arab Bank*, PLC, 138 S. Ct 1386 (2018), 2017 WL 2792284.

[56] Brief for United States as *Amici Curiae*, *Nestle USA, Inc. v. Joe Doe I, et al.* at 10 (2019 No. 19-416), 2020 WL 129527.

[57] 28 USC section 1350. The TVPA was, in part, a response to Judge Bork's concurring opinion in *Tel-Oren v. Libyan Arab Republic*, 726 F. 2d 774, 816 (DC Cir. 1984) (Bork J. concurring), in which he suggested that the ATS was limited to the claims, if any, existing at the time the ATS was enacted in 1789. The TVPA was intended as a supplement, not a replacement for the ATS.

[58] 566 US 449, 453–4 (2012).

[59] Ibid., at 456.

[60] Ibid., at 458.

[61] *Chiquita*, 190 F. Supp. 3d at 1116. *See also Romero v. Drummond Co.*, 552 F. 3d 1303, 1315 (11th Cir. 2008). *Wiwa v. Royal Petroleum, Co.*, 226 F. 3d 88, 106–8 (2d Cir. 2000).

[62] 28 USC section 1350. The TVPA is explicitly extraterritorial. *See Chowdhury v. Worldtel Bangladesh Holding, Ltd.*, 746 F. 3d 42, 51 (2d Cir. 2014).

agency law and domestic civil rights jurisprudence.[63] The TVPA's legislative history expressly notes that responsibility under the statute for torture and extrajudicial killings extends beyond those who actually commit these crimes.[64] Aiding and abetting, agency,[65] command responsibility,[66] and conspiracy[67] claims are all available against TVPA defendants. Courts have employed federal common law standards when applying these principles.[68] One practical obstacle to using the TVPA in corporate accountability cases is the difficulty of identifying the appropriate individual corporate officials or managers with a sufficient factual basis to meet federal pleading requirements.[69] Notwithstanding this obstacle, it seems likely that the TVPA will be used to address corporate responsibility for extraterritorial human rights violations as obstacles to ATS claims increase.

A. Exhaustion of remedies

The TVPA requires potential claimants to exhaust all adequate and available remedies in the place where the violation occurred.[70] The exhaustion defence is an affirmative one, and the defendant has the burden of proving that a plaintiff has not exhausted their local remedies.[71] A plaintiff may be excused from showing

[63] *Kadic v. Karadzic*, 70 F. 3d 232, 245 (2d Cir. 1995).

[64] S. Rep. No. 102-249, at 9 (1991).

[65] To establish actual agency a party must demonstrate the following elements: '(1) there must be a manifestation by the principal that the agent shall act for him; (2) the agent must accept the undertaking; and (3) there must be an understanding between the parties that the principal is to be in control of the undertaking.' *Bowoto v. Chevron Texaco Corp.*, 312 F. Supp. 2d 1229, 1239 (ND Cal. 2004)

[66] 'The elements of the command responsibility doctrine are: "(1) the existence of a superior-subordinate relationship between the commander and the perpetrator of the crime; (2) that the commander knew or should have known, owing to the circumstances at the time, that his subordinates had committed, were committing, or planned to commit acts violative of the law of war; and (3) that the commander failed to prevent the commission of the crimes, or failed to punish the subordinates after the commission of the crimes ... [A] civilian superior—including a civilian corporate officer—could feasibly be held liable under the doctrine provided the plaintiffs demonstrated a superior-subordinate relationship between the civilian and the perpetrator, averring that the civilian was in the requisite position of authority and control.' *Doe v. Drummond Co.*, 782 F. 3d at 609–10..

[67] Plaintiffs must allege and prove (i) two or more persons agreed to commit a wrongful act; (ii) the defendant joined the conspiracy knowing of at least one of the goals of the conspiracy and with the intent to help accomplish it; and (iii) one or more of the violations was committed by someone who was a member of the conspiracy and acted in furtherance of the conspiracy. *Chiquita*, 190 F. Supp. 3d at 1119–20.

[68] See, for example, *Chowdhury*, 746 F. 3d at 53; *In re. Chiquita Brands Int'l, Inc. Alien Tort Statute & S'holder Derivative Litig.*, 190 F. Supp. 3d at 1117.

[69] *Bell Atlantic Corp. v. Twombly*, 550 US 544, 570 (2007); *Ashcroft v. Iqbal*, 556 US 662, 678–80 (2009).

[70] 28 USC section 1350.

[71] *Mamani v. Berzain*, 21 F. Supp. 3d 1353, 1369 (SD Fla. 2014), *aff'd in part, appeal denied in part*, 825 F. 3d 1304 (11th Cir. 2016). In March 2018 a Florida jury rendered a $10 million verdict in the case. The District Judge granted the defendants' post-trial motion for Judgment as a Matter of Law. In August 2020 the Eleventh Circuit reversed that decision and sent the case back for further proceedings. *Mamani v. Sanchez Bustamante*, 968 F. 3d 1216 (11th Cir. 2020).

exhaustion if they demonstrate that the local remedies are ineffective, inadequate, or obviously futile.[72]

B. Statute of limitations

TVPA claims are subject to a ten-year statute of limitations.[73] However, this period can be extended under the equitable tolling doctrine.[74] Equitable tolling is based on a factor specific analysis to determine whether the defendant's wrongful conduct or extraordinary circumstances prevented a plaintiff from timely asserting a claim.[75]

IV. Trafficking Victims Protection Act (TVPRA)

In addition to the statutory provisions outlined above, there are some specialised statutes available for certain categories of human rights claims. The TVPRA is one of these specialised statutes.[76]

The TVPRA provides civil remedies for a range of trafficking-related offences[77] including forced labour, involuntary servitude, peonage, and sex trafficking.[78] Although some offences such as involuntary servitude required a showing of physical restraint or harm under past precedent,[79] the TVPRA was amended to recognise more subtle forms of coercion including actual or threatened psychological, financial, or reputational harm used to compel a person's labour.[80]

There is no question about the TVPRA's application to corporations. In addition to remedies available against direct perpetrators, remedies are also available against entities who knowingly benefit from participation in a venture they know or should have known engaged in TVPRA violations.[81] The TVPRA is explicitly

[72] *Doe v. Qi*, 349 F. Supp. 2d 1258, 1319 (ND Cal., 2004). Any doubt about whether a plaintiff has exhausted local remedies is resolved in favour of the plaintiff. *Jean v. Dorelian*, 431 F. 3d 776, 782 (11th Cir. 2005).

[73] 28 USC section 1350. Courts have adopted the TVPA's limitations period in ATS cases. See, for example, *Papa v. United States*, 281 F. 3d 1004, 1012 (9th Cir. 2002).

[74] *Chavez v. Carranza*, 559 F. 3d 486, 494 (6th Cir. 2009); *Cabello v. Fernandez-Larios*, 402 F. 3d 1148, 1154 (11th Cir. 2005); *Hilao v. Estate of Marcos*, 103 F. 3d 767, 773 (9th Cir. 1996).

[75] *Cabello*, 402 F. 3d at 1154–6; *Marcos*, 103 F. 3d at 773.

[76] A comprehensive analysis of the TVPRA is beyond the scope of this chapter. For further information, see L. Ezell, 'Human Trafficking in Multinational Supply Chains: A Corporate Director's Fiduciary Duty to Monitor and Eliminate Human Trafficking Violations' (2016) 69 *Vanderbilt Law Review* 499; R.L. Lampley, 'Mitigating Risk, Eradicating Slavery' (2019) 68 *American University Law Review* 1707.

[77] The TVPRA also provides for criminal penalties. See, for example, 22 USC section 7109.

[78] 18 USC section 1590 (2008).

[79] *United States v. Kozminski*, 487 US 931 (1988).

[80] 18 USC section 1589(c).

[81] 18 USC section 1595 (2018).

extraterritorial. It can reach trafficking offences committed outside the United States if the offences are committed by a US national or an offender present in the United States.[82] The TVPRA may be a useful tool for challenging such violations that occur in international supply chains.[83]

One significant issue for supply chain claims is what constitutes the 'knowing benefit'[84] from the participation in a venture engaged in trafficking. Some courts have suggested that the defendant must directly participate in the trafficking.[85] However, appellate courts have found TVPRA liability based on 'knowing benefit' without evidence that the defendant benefitting was a participant in the underlying trafficking offences.[86]

Another important issue is when foreign corporations are 'present in' the United States for TVPRA purposes. At least one court has found that this element is satisfied when a corporation is physically present in the United States, is registered to do business or has an address in the United States, or has a relationship of agency, joint venture, or is the alter ego an offending corporation present in the United States.[87] The broadest view is that a foreign corporation is 'present in' the United States whenever there is personal jurisdiction over it.

There are several pending cases in which the key provisions in the TVPRA relating to human rights violations in the supply chain are at issue. For example, *Ratha v. Phattana Seafood Co.* alleges that Thai companies involved in processing shrimp and US importers violated the TVPRA by supplying seafood processed with forced and trafficked labour. The US companies were alleged to have knowingly benefitted from the importation of the seafood processed with trafficked labour as part of this ongoing venture to distribute it. The defendants won summary judgment in the district court.[88] The appeal was argued on 13 September 2019 and is awaiting a decision as of this writing. *Ratha* involves the full range of issues typical of supply chain cases including the definition of what constitutes knowing benefit, ventures, and presence in the United States.

[82] 18 USC section 1596(a) (2008). This provision was added in 2008 and found not to be retroactive in *Adhikari v. Kellogg Brown & Root, Inc.*, 845 F. 3d 184, 204–5 (5th Cir. 2017). A similar case against KBR for labour trafficking during the Iraq war has been allowed to proceed under the ATS and State and Iraqi law claims. *Adhikari v. KBR Inc.*, WL 4237923, at *5 (SD Tex. 25 September 2017).

[83] Ezell (n. 76), at 522.

[84] The term 'benefit' has been given a broad reading. See, for example, *Ricchio v. Bijal, Inc.*, 386 F. Supp. 2d (D. Mass. 2019) (holding the benefit need not 'reach a particular threshold of value').

[85] See, for example, *Ratha v. Phattana Seafood Co.*, 2017 WL 8293174 (CD Cal. 21 December 2017); *Bistline v. Jeffs*, 2017 WL 108039 (D. Utah 11 January 2017), *rev'd sub nom, Bistline v. Parker*, 918 F. 3d 849 (10th Cir. 2019).

[86] See, for example, *Ricchio v. McClean*, 853 F. 3d 553 (1st Cir. 2017); *Bistline*, 918 F. 3d at 849; *Gilbert v. United States Olympic Comm.*, 2019 WL 1058194, at *12 (D. Colo. 6 March 2019) (outlining the differences between the two interpretations of participation).

[87] *Ratha v. Phattana Seafood Co.*, 2016 WL 11020222, at *5 (CD Cal. 9 November 2016).

[88] *Ratha v. Phatthana Seafood Co.*, 2017 WL 8293174 (CD Cal. 21 December 2017). The district court found that the Thai defendants were not 'present in' the United States. The court found that the US companies had not participated in the trafficking component of the venture and that there was insufficient evidence that they knew or should have known about the trafficking.

It can be expected that litigators will sue corporations involved in international supply chains implicated in trafficking offences with US connections under the TVPRA.

In addition to the TVPRA's substantive advantages and its extraterritorial reach, the TVPRA has a ten-year statute of limitations[89] and provides for attorneys' fees for prevailing plaintiffs, making it more likely that such cases will be filed.[90] It seems likely that many additional cases will be brought under the statute for this category of claims especially as scope of available ATS claims shrinks.

V. Foreign Sovereign Immunities Act (FSIA)

In some circumstances, it may be possible to sue corporations deemed to be 'instrumentalities'[91] of foreign sovereigns for extraterritorial human rights violations.[92] Foreign sovereigns and their instrumentalities are presumptively immune from suit in US courts.[93] The FSIA was enacted to codify the doctrine of restrictive immunity and respect the sovereign power of foreign governments, so in order to police the behaviour of instrumentalities outside of the United States, there must be an applicable statutory exception.[94]

The FSIA provides for the circumstances in which foreign sovereigns or their instrumentalities can be sued in US courts. If foreign sovereigns or their instrumentalities commit human rights violations on US territory, then there is no sovereign immunity.[95] There have been several successful cases against foreign sovereigns for

[89] 18 USC section 1595(c) (2018)

[90] 18 USC section 1595(a) (2018)

[91] Foreign corporations may deemed a State 'instrumentality; if a majority of their shares or other ownership interests are owned by a foreign State and it is not a 'citizen' of any State in the United States. 28 USCA section 1603(b) (2005) Corporate defendants that wish to be classified as government instrumentalities under the FSIA have the burden of overcoming the presumption that they have legal status separate from that of their sovereign. *Simon v. Republic of Hungary*, WL 1170485, at *17 (DDC 11 March 2020).

[92] 28 USCA section 1603(a) (2005).

[93] Corporate defendants may be found to be instrumentalities of a foreign State if the corporation is so extensively controlled by its owner that a relationship of principal and agent is created, or if recognition of the instrumentality as an entity apart from the State would work fraud or injustice. See, for example, *McKesson Corp. v. Islamic Republic of Iran*, 52 F. 3d 346, 352 (DC Cir. 1995) (principal–agent relationship existed between Iran and instrumentalities partly owned by an American corporation). See also *Arch Trading Corp. v. Republic of Ecuador*, 839 F. 3d 193, 202 (2nd Cir. 2016) (touchstone inquiry used to determine whether the sovereign State or its instrumentality exercises significant and repeated control over the instrumentality's day-to-day operations).

[94] E.M. Lopes, 'Seeking Accountability and Justice for Torture Victims: The Hurdle of the Foreign Sovereign Immunities Act in Suing Foreign Officials Under the Torture Victims Protection Act' (2010) 6 *Seton Hall Circuit Review* 389, 401.

[95] 28 USC section 1605(a)(5) (2005). This section precludes immunity for torts committed on US territory. It does not include torts committed outside the United States causing damage (e.g. emotional distress) within the United States. *Denegri v. Republic of Chile*, WL 91914, at *2 (DDC 6 April 1992).

human rights violations on US soil;[96] however, the FSIA's 'tort' exception does not apply to extraterritorial torts.

The FSIA also includes a 'commercial activity' exception to foreign sovereign immunity. The exception is based on the view that once a foreign sovereign acts like a private party in commercial transactions, it should lose its immunity and be subject to suit based on these activities. If the foreign State's actions are based upon (i) a commercial activity carried out in the United States; (ii) an act performed in the United States in connection with a commercial activity elsewhere; or (iii) an act related to a commercial activity that occurs outside the United States but causes a direct effect in the United States, its actions are subject to suit in U. S. courts.[97] Courts determine the commercial character of a foreign State's activity by its nature rather than by a profit motivation or purpose.[98] In assessing the nature of the activity, courts consider whether the foreign State's particular actions are the type of actions that a private party engaged in trade, traffic, or commerce would take.[99]

A prominent Supreme Court case concerning the commercial activity exception in the human rights context is *Nelson v. Saudi Arabia*.[100] In *Nelson*, the US Supreme Court rejected a claim that the 'commercial activities' exception of the FSIA applied where a contract employee was detained and tortured in Saudi Arabia by Saudi security agents for making public statements about safety issues he uncovered at the hospital where he was employed after having been recruited in the United States for this position.[101] Even though Saudi Arabia's hiring of the contractor was a commercial activity, the Court held, tracking the language of the commercial activities exception, that the lawsuit must be 'based upon' the commercial activity. In *Nelson*, the Court found that the plaintiff's torture was based upon sovereign police acts and not the commercial activity, thus Saudi Arabia was entitled to sovereign immunity.[102]

Similarly, the Ninth Circuit granted immunity to Myanmar and its State-owned oil company for claims by human rights victims of torture and other human rights violations committed on a pipeline project in Myanmar. Although contract negotiations occurred in part in Los Angeles, the court found that the plaintiffs' claims were not 'based upon' that US-based commercial activity.[103]

A country may also waive its sovereign immunity, thereby exposing itself and its instrumentalities to liability for human rights claims. *Siderman v. Republic of Argentina*

[96] *Letelier v. Republic of Chile*, 488 F. Supp. 665 (DDC 1980); *Liu v. Republic of China*, 892 F. 2d 1419, 1425 (9th Cir. 1989); *Domingo v. Republic of the Philippines*, WL 3140 (WD Wash. 18 July 1984).

[97] 28 USC section 1605(a)(2) (2005).

[98] 28 USC section 1603(d) (2005); *In re Estate of Ferdinand Marcos Human Rights Litig.*, 94 F. 3d 539, 546 (9th Cir. 1996).

[99] *Republic of Argentina v. Weltover, Inc.*, 504 US 607, 614 (1992).

[100] 507 US 349 (1993).

[101] Ibid., at 353.

[102] Ibid., at 363.

[103] *Doe I v. Unocal Corp.*, 395 F. 3d 932, 958 (9th Cir. 2002), *on reh'g en banc sub nom. John Doe I v. Unocal Corp.*, 403 F. 3d 708 (9th Cir. 2005).

is an example of this kind of waiver.[104] In *Siderman*, the Ninth Circuit reluctantly decided that sovereign immunity applied even to *jus cogens* norms but nonetheless, found that Argentina had waived its sovereign immunity by invoking US courts to prosecute the plaintiff by pursuing false criminal charges against him in his US exile.[105] The waiver exception is narrowly construed[106] and does not seem to have been successful in subsequent cases.[107] The Ninth Circuit also found the commercial activities exception applied because Argentina unlawfully expropriated the plaintiff's hotel which was found to have sufficient US connections to fit within this exception.[108]

There is a broader exception from sovereign immunity for governments designated as State sponsors of terrorism.[109] This exception only applies to foreign sovereigns so designated by the State Department.[110] Additionally, in February 2019, the Supreme Court held that foreign organisations such as the International Finance Corporation and the World Bank enjoy the same limited immunities applied to foreign governments under the FSIA, rather than absolute immunity under an outdated statute.[111]

VI. Anti-Terrorism Act (ATA)

The ATA provides a cause of action for any US national or their estate who is injured in their person, property, or business by reason of an act of international terrorism.[112] International terrorism is defined as violent or dangerous acts that would violate US criminal law and are intended to intimidate or coerce a civilian population, influence government policy by intimidation or coercion, or affect government conduct by mass destruction, assassination, or kidnapping.[113] The statute is explicitly extraterritorial, as the definition of international terrorism applies to conduct occurring primarily outside of the US.[114]

104 28 USC section 1605(a)(1). *Siderman v. Republic of Argentina*, 965 F. 2d 699 (9th Cir. 1992).
105 Ibid., at 722.
106 *In re Estate of Ferdinand Marcos Human Rights Litig.*, 94 F. 3d at 546.
107 *Cabiri v. Gov't of Republic of Ghana*, 165 F. 3d 193, 202 (2d Cir. 1999); Working Group of the American Bar Association, 'Reforming the Foreign Sovereign Immunities Act' (2002) 40 *Columbia Journal of Transnational Law* 489, 546.
108 *Siderman*, 965 F. 2d at 709–11. The *Siderman* case settled on the eve of trial in 1996. P.J. McDonnell, 'A lone battle for vindication pays off', *Los Angeles Times* (16 September 1996).
109 28 USC section 1605(A)(a)(2)(A)(i)(I)(2005). US courts have jurisdiction over a foreign State that was designated as a State sponsor of terrorism at the time the qualifying act occurred, or was designated as a result of the Act, and remains designated within the statutory period. See *Opati v. Republic of Sudan*, 140 S. Ct 1601, 1608–10 (2020)(2020 WL 2515447) (availability of punitive damages under exception).
110 See US Dep't of State, Bureau of Counter Terrorism, State Sponsors of Terrorism (2020), <https://www.state.gov/state-sponsors-of-terrorism/>, accessed 19 April 2021.
111 *Jam v. Int'l Fin. Corp.*, 139 S. Ct 759 (2019).
112 18 USCA section 2333 (2018).
113 18 USC section 2331 (2012).
114 18 USCA section 2331(c) (2018). The ATA has a ten-year statute of limitations, 18 USC section 2335 (2013), and does not extend to acts of war. 18 USC section 2336 (2013).

Corporations are liable under the ATA as they qualify as 'persons' capable of committing an act of international terrorism under the statute.[115] Corporations can also be held secondarily liable for aiding and abetting, knowingly providing substantial assistance, or conspiring with the primary perpetrator of terrorism.[116] The ATA also criminalises providing material support to terrorists or providing funds to terrorists knowing or intending for those funds to be used in preparing or carrying out specific, terror-related crimes.[117]

To prove an ATA claim, a plaintiff must establish an unlawful act, the requisite *mens rea*—held by some courts to be knowledge or deliberate indifference[118]—and causation.[119] In ATA human rights litigation, corporate liability is usually based upon funding the groups that directly commit the ATA violation.[120] Recent cases indicate that plaintiffs must prove proximate cause in order to establish ATA liability.[121] Under this proximate cause standard, plaintiffs must prove that the actions of the defendant(s) were the natural and direct cause of the plaintiffs' injury, rather than a more removed causal element.

The *mens rea* is whether the corporation knew the aims and activities of the organisation and that the funds given would enable the organisation to carry out acts of international terrorism.[122] This element is easier to prove when a corporation funds a known terrorist group like Hamas, which has been analogised to giving a loaded gun to a child.[123] However, merely providing routine financial services to members and associates of terrorist organisation would not trigger liability.[124] Some courts use a relaxed substantial factor test to determine causation,[125] while others use but-for causation that demands a direct link between the defendant's crimes and plaintiff's injuries.[126]

[115] 18 USCA section 2333(d) (2018). See *Jesner*, 138 S. Ct at 1386; *Mohammed*, 566 US at 453–4.

[116] Ibid. See Justice Against Sponsors of Terrorism Act, PL 114-222 (28 September 2016)(providing for secondary liability). Some cases have found that the statute does not provide for secondary liability. See, for example, *Chiquita*, 690 F. Supp. 2d 1296, 1310 (SD Fla. 2010). It seems clear that the ATA provides for secondary liability at least for events since the 2016 Amendments.

[117] 18 USC section 2339(A) (2009); 18 USC section 2339(C) (2006). In *Miller v. Arab Bank*, 372 F. Supp. 3d 33, 47 (EDNY 2019) PLC found that the defendant did not need to be aware of the specific attacks at issue when it provided financial support for terrorist organisations to be secondarily liable. The fact that the defendant was generally aware of the violent activities committed by the terrorist group it funded was sufficient to find it secondarily liable. Ibid.

[118] *Boim v. Holy Land Found. for Relief & Dev.*, 549 F.3d 685, 693 (7th Cir. 2008).

[119] *Waldman v. Palestine Liberation Org.*, 835 F. 3d 317, 335 (2d Cir. 2016).

[120] *In re Chiquita Brands Int'l, Inc.*, 284 F. Supp. 3d 1284, 1293 (SD Fla. 2018).

[121] See, for example, *Kemper v. Deutsche Bank AG*, 911 F. 3d 383, 391 (7th Cir. 2018) (making it clear that proximate cause is the standard notwithstanding any suggestion in *Boim* to the contrary); *Fields v. Twitter, Inc.*, 881 F. 3d 739, 744–5 (9th Cir. 2018); *Rothstein v. UBS AG*, 708 F. 3d 82, 95–6 (2d Cir. 2013).

[122] *Boim*, 549 F. 3d at 694.

[123] Ibid. at 690.

[124] *Linde v. Arab Bank, PLC*, 882 F. 3d 314, 327 (2d Cir. 2018).

[125] *Boim*, 945 F. 3d at 685.

[126] *Rothstein v. UBS AG*, 708 F. 3d 82, 95 (2d Cir. 2013)

VII. RICO

RICO is one of the US federal government's most powerful tools to combat long-running criminal organisations. While typically used in criminal prosecution, the statute provides a civil cause of action for any person injured in his business or property by reason of a RICO violation.[127] To state a civil claim under RICO, a plaintiff must show that the defendant violated the Act and the plaintiff was injured as a result of the violation.[128]

A RICO violation occurs through the commission of certain predicate offences in relation to an enterprise.[129] The racketeering activity must affect or be engaged in interstate or foreign commerce,[130] and the 'enterprise' must comprised a group of persons who, over a period of time, have a common purpose of engaging in a course of conduct to commit an act.[131] There must also be a pattern to the acts committed by the enterprise which amounts to or poses a threat of continued criminal activity.[132] This can be satisfied by showing that the predicate offences were part of the enterprise's regular way of doing business[133] and that the events were either an interrelated series of predicate acts over a substantial period of time,[134] or that there is a threat of continuing criminal activity beyond the period in which the predicate offences were performed.[135] RICO claims have a four-year statute of limitations but are subject to equitable tolling if factors outside of a diligent plaintiff's control prevent them from filing a timely claim.[136]

RICO's extraterritorial reach was limited in *RJR Nabisco, Inc. v. European Community*.[137] There, relying on the reasoning in *Morrison* and *Kiobel*, the Supreme Court held that at least some applications of RICO's private cause of action were barred by the presumption against extraterritoriality.[138] The Court did note that some predicate acts for RICO liability (e.g. a pattern of killing Americans abroad, section 2332(a)) were explicitly extraterritorial and thus actionable in US courts. Thus, the availability of a RICO claim will depend on whether particular predicate acts are explicitly extraterritorial.

[127] 18 USC section 1964(c) (2016).
[128] Ibid.
[129] *RJR Nabisco, Inc. v. European Cmty.*, 136 S. Ct 2090, 2093 (2016).
[130] *Wiwa*, 2002 WL 319887 at *25.
[131] Ibid. See also *Sedima S.P.R.L. v. Imrex Co., Inc.*, 473 US 479, 496 (1985).
[132] *Adhikari*, 697 F. Supp. 2d at 693.
[133] Ibid. *H.J., Inc. v. Nw. Bell Tel. Co.*, 492 US 229, 239–43 (1989).
[134] Ibid. 492 US at 242 (1989); *Lopez v. Council on American-Islamic Rels. Action Network Inc.*, 657 F. Supp. 2d 104, 111 (DC Cir. 2009).
[135] *H.J., Inc.*, 492 US at 242.
[136] See, for example, *Koch v. Christie's Int'l PLC*, 785 F. Supp. 2d 105, 116 (SDNY 2011). In some cases, plaintiffs have had difficulty effecting service in extraterritorial cases. See, for example, *Doe v. Unocal*, 27 F. Supp. 2d 1174, 1184 (CD Cal. 1998).
[137] 136 S. Ct at 2090
[138] Ibid., at 2095

VIII. Environmental statutes

Some foreign plaintiffs have attempted to use US environmental statutes to obtain relief. For example, in *ARC Ecology v. U. Dept. of Air Force*, two environmental non-governmental organisations (NGOs) and Philippine residents brought a claim based on the Comprehensive Environmental Response, Compensation and Liability Act (CERCLA) to remedy environmental degradation on former US military bases. The case was dismissed based on the presumption against extraterritoriality.[139] In *Pakootas v. Teck Cominco Metals, Ltd*, the Court rejected an argument from the Canadian defendant that the fact that decisions made in Canada which had impacts in the United States were extraterritorial and sustained the application of CERCLA to the Canadian company.[140]

IX. Common law claims

In addition to statutory claims, human rights litigators have also brought common law claims based on US State laws or foreign law in both State and federal courts.[141] Indeed, as the scope of the ATS is limited, litigators may increasingly turn to common law claims to achieve corporate accountability. State courts may now be more strategic venues to provide remedies for human rights violations.

Unlike federal courts, which have uniform procedural rules, each State has its own procedural rules for personal jurisdiction, *forum non conveniens*, and other relevant doctrines when suing a corporation for out-of-State human rights abuses.[142] A benefit of State litigation is that it may offer a more human rights-friendly court system. State litigation for human rights violations will be based primarily on traditional torts, such as assault and battery, wrongful death, intentional infliction of emotional distress, negligent infliction of emotional distress, negligence, negligent hiring, negligence per se, and loss of consortium.[143] State courts will be able to assert jurisdiction over such claims, assuming there is personal jurisdiction over the defendant, based on the transitory tort doctrine, which allows a tortfeasor to be sued where he is found.[144] The statute of limitations and tolling doctrines (doctrines that allow for a pause in the time set by a statute of

[139] 411 F. 3d 1092, 1097–8 (9th Cir. 2005).

[140] 452 F. 3d 1066 (9th Cir 2006).

[141] G.L. Skinner, 'Beyond Kiobel: Providing Access to Judicial Remedies for Violations of International Human Rights Norms by Transnational Business in a New (Post-Kiobel) World' (2014) 46 *Columbia Human Rights Law Review* 158, 200. See generally S. Davis and C.A. Whytock, 'State Remedies for Human Rights' (2018) 98 *Boston University Law Review* 397, 412.

[142] P. Hoffman and B. Stephens, 'International Human Rights Cases Under State Law and in State Courts' (2013) 3 *University of California at Irvine Law Review* 9, 17–18.

[143] *In re Chiquita Brands Int'l, Inc. Alien Tort Statute & S'holder Derivative Litig.*, 792 F. Supp. 2d 1301, 1355 (SD Fla. 2011)

[144] See Restatement (Third) of Foreign Relations Law of the United States, sections 402, 404 (1987).

limitations due to external intervening factors) in State and foreign law cases will vary depending on the State.[145]

International human rights claims based on foreign law have often been raised in human rights cases alongside statutory claims. State and foreign law claims have frequently been brought in the same case. Courts have applied conflict of law principles[146] to determine which law applies.[147] Foreign law will often be applied to extraterritorial common law human rights claims.[148]

Doe v. Exxon[149] and *Doe v. Chiquita*[150] are typical of cases asserting foreign law claims. In *Doe v. Exxon* villagers from the Indonesian province of Aceh sued Exxon and its Indonesian subsidiary for torture, arbitrary detention, and ill-treatment under the ATS and Indonesian law. Ultimately, the ATS claims were dismissed based on *Kiobel*, but the case was permitted to continue based on the Indonesia law claims.[151]

In *Doe v. Chiquita*,[152] the heirs of thousands of victims of a mass murder campaign by the Autodefensas Unidas de Colombia (AUC)[153] in the banana-growing regions of Colombia sued Chiquita for its complicity in these human rights crimes. Their ATS claims were dismissed based on *Kiobel*,[154] but the district court denied Chiquita's *forum non conveniens* arguments[155] and allowed plaintiffs Colombia law claims to proceed.[156]

Cases bases on environmental degradation or medical experimentation may fare better in US or State courts based on common law theories. These cases are likely to face *forum non conveniens* arguments (see below) but the infamous Chevron/Texaco Ecuador litigation is a cautionary tale for companies seeking to litigate in other countries. Texaco successfully won such a motion to have an environmental case sent back to Ecuador[157] only to be found liable in Ecuador court system for a

[145] *Deutsch v. Turner Corp.*, 324 F. 3d 692, 717 (9th Cir. 2003)

[146] See Restatement (Second) of Conflicts of Law, sections 6, 145 (. 1969) (the law of the State or nation that has the most significant relationship to the occurrence of the injury and the parties is controlling).

[147] Skinner (n. 141), 227.

[148] Ibid.

[149] *Doe v. Exxon Mobil Corp.*, 654 F. 3d 11, 70 (DC Cir. 2011), *vacated*, 527 F. App'x 7 (DC Cir. 2013).

[150] *In re Chiquita Brands Int'l, Inc.*, 792 F. Supp. 2d at 1359 (State law dismissal reaffirmed by *Chiquita*, 190 F. Supp. 3d at 1112).

[151] *Doe v. Exxon Mobil Corp.*, 393 F. Supp. 2d 20, 29 (DDC 2005) (genuine and serious risk of reprisal and to personal safety precluded *forum non conveniens* claim).

[152] *Chiquita*, 190 F. Supp. 3d at 1107.

[153] The AUC is a Colombian paramilitary group believed to have massacred over 100,000 persons in Colombia between 1995 and 2006. Chiquita pled guilty to criminal charges and paid a $25 million fine for funding the AUC during this period.

[154] *Cardona v. Chiquita Brands Int'l, Inc.*, 760 F. 3d 1185, 1189 (11th Cir. 2014)

[155] *Chiquita*, 190 F. Supp. 3d at 1123.

[156] Ibid., at 1123.

[157] *Aguinda v. Texaco*, 945 F. Supp. 625 (SDNY 2002). Texaco agreed to jurisdiction in Ecuador. 303 F. 3d 470, 480 (2d Cir. 2002).

$18 billion judgment.[158] Chevron obtained an injunction against the enforcement of the judgment in US courts on the ground that the judgment in Ecuador was obtained by fraud.[159]

Although these cases were brought in federal court based on diversity and supplemental jurisdiction, they could have been brought in State courts instead.[160] Diversity jurisdiction (28 USC section 1332) allows US federal courts to hear cases where the amount in controversy exceeds $75,000 and the parties are either citizens of different US States or one is a citizen of another nation. Supplemental jurisdiction (28 USC section 1367) allows federal courts to assert jurisdiction over claims (e.g. State claims) over which they would not otherwise have jurisdiction if the claims arise out of the same facts as the federal claims. The transitory tort doctrine is well established in US jurisprudence allowing U.S. courts to assert jurisdiction over torts arising outside US territory so long as the tortfeasor is found in the United States.[161]

The Supreme Court has on several occasions employed the foreign affairs pre-emption doctrine to invalidate State legislative efforts because they conflict with federal supremacy in foreign affairs.[162] Some defendants have argued that the same pre-emption analysis should apply to State tort actions. While the Supreme Court has not yet decided this issue, it can be expected that the issue will be raised if litigators bring more cases in State courts to sue corporations for human rights violations. Historically, State tort actions have been deemed within the province of State governments within the US federal structure.[163] Whether the increasingly conservative federal courts would respect State sovereignty in this context or preclude such cases based on the federal interests involved is an open question.[164]

[158] BBC News, 'Chevron Wins Ecuador Rainforest "Oil Dumping" Case' (*BBC News*, 7 September 2018), <https://www.bbc.com/news/world-latin-america-45455984>, accessed 18 November 2020.

[159] *Chevron Corp. v. Donziger*, 768 F. Supp. 2d 581 (S.D.N.Y. 2011), *vacated sub nom. Chevron v. Naranjo*, No. 11-1150-CV-L, 2011 WL 4375022 (2d Cir. Sept. 19. 2011), and *rev'd and remanded sub nom. Chevron Corp. v. Naranjo*, 667 F. 3d 232 (2d Cir. 2012). Courts in Canada, Brazil, and Argentina also refused to enforce the judgment. See, for example, *Yaiguaje v. Chevron Corp.*, (2018) ONCA 472.

[160] In *Doe v. Unocal*, 110 F. Supp. 2d 1294 (CD Cal. 2000), after the ATS claims were initially dismissed by the district court, plaintiffs filed a case in Los Angeles Superior Court which was scheduled to go to trial in 2005 on Unocal's liability on plaintiffs' agency theory of liability at the time the case was settled. At the time of the settlement the federal case was scheduled for rehearing en banc in the Ninth Circuit. *See Doe I v. Unocal Corp.*, 403 F. 3d 708 (9th Cir. 2005).

[161] *Kiobel*, 569 US at 119. *Slater v. Mexican Nat. R. Co.*, 194 US 120 (1904) (recognising transitory tort doctrine); *See generally* C.I. Keitner, 'State Courts and Transitory Torts in Transnational Human Rights Cases' (2013) 3 *University of California at Irvine Law Review* 81.

[162] *Crosby v. Nat'l Foreign Trade Council*, 530 US 363 (2000); *Am. Ins. Ass'n v. Garamendi*, 539 US 396 (2003).

[163] J.C. Toro, 'Why Principles of Federalism and Communitarianism Demand that Tort Law be Left op to the States' (2009) 7 *Georgetown Journal of Law and Public Policy* 655.

[164] S. Singh, 'Brandeis's Happy Incident Revisited: U.S. Cities as the New Laboratories of International Law' (2005) 37 *George Washington International Law Review* 537.

X. State statutory claims

Other possible avenues for corporate accountability litigation include consumer protection laws.[165] One example of an attempted claim under these laws concerns the alleged involvement of corporations in perpetuating forced and child slave labour in West Africa. Cases seeking to impose an affirmative duty to disclose such practices in their supply chains have not been successful to date.[166]

However, more recent cases have sought to hold chocolate companies accountable for making affirmative misstatements on their labels. For example, in *Walker v. Nestle* and *Myers v. Starbucks*, plaintiffs have alleged that chocolate companies have misled consumers with claims on their labels that their products are 'sustainably sourced', 'traced from farm to factory', or that they are certified by the Rainforest Alliance.[167] Plaintiffs claim that the companies know that forced or child slave labour and environmental degradation are endemic in their supply chains, yet they deceptively trumpet alleged commitments to human rights and environmental protection on their labels. These cases are in the early stages and it remains to be seen whether this theory will be successful. If successful, this theory of liability might be a potent tool to accompany grass-roots activism and media scrutiny of corporate practices of this kind.[168]

There have been similar innovative attempts to hold corporations accountable for misrepresentations using federal securities laws and related theories to address climate change.[169]

XI. Defences to corporate accountability claims

This section discusses the most frequent defences to corporate accountability litigation. These defences should be considered when bringing corporate accountability

[165] There may be other State statutes relevant to corporate accountability, but it is likely that such statutes are limited to corporate actions within the particular jurisdiction.

[166] See, for example, *Tomasella v. Nestle*, 1:18-cv-10269 (D. Mass. 2018) (appeal pending). There are several similar cases working their way through the courts.

[167] See *Walker v. Nestle*, 3:19-cv-00723 (SD Cal. 2019); *Myers v. Starbucks et al.*, 5:20-cv-00335 (CD Cal. 2020).

[168] Corporations attempt to profiteer from their 'sustainability story' because fair trade and sustainability (both social and environmental) sells. See CPG, FMCG & RETAIL, 'Unpacking the Sustainability Landscape' (*Nielson Report*, 11 September 2018), <https://www.nielson.com/us/en/insights/report/2018/unpacking-the-sustainability-landscape>, accessed 18 November 2020 (The majority (73 per cent) of consumers say they would definitely or probably change their consumption habits to reduce their impact on the environment).

[169] *See Ramirez v. Exxon*, 334 F. Supp. 3d 832 (ND Tex. 2018); *City of Birmingham Retirement and Relief System v. Tillerson*, 3:19-cv-20949 (DNJ 2019); *People v. Exxon Mobil Corp.*, WL 6795771 (Sup. Ct NY 10 December 2019); *In re Exxon Mobil Corporation Derivative Litigation*, 3:19-cv-01067 (ND Tex. 2019).

cases in US courts. The way these defences will be addressed may differ depending on the particular claims asserted in the case.

A. Personal jurisdiction

Plaintiffs seeking to hold foreign corporations accountable, including the foreign subsidiaries of US corporations, may face an increasingly restricted view of personal jurisdiction. There are two forms of personal jurisdiction: general jurisdiction over a defendant for all claims, and specific jurisdiction relating to particular claims. Typically, obtaining general jurisdiction over US corporations poses little difficulty. Obtaining either form of personal jurisdiction over foreign corporations or the foreign subsidiaries of US corporations is more difficult.

Recent Supreme Court cases have made it increasingly difficult to establish personal jurisdiction over corporations, which reflects the broader efforts of conservative jurists to restrict access to US courts in transnational cases.[170] The Supreme Court's decision in *Daimler AC v. Bauman*[171] illustrates these new obstacles to jurisdiction. In *Daimler*, human rights plaintiffs sought to hold Daimler liable for the complicity of its Argentine subsidiary in widespread torture and summary execution during the 'Dirty War' in Argentina. They relied on the ubiquitous presence of Daimler and its products in the US market as the basis for jurisdiction over Daimler in US courts. The Supreme Court held that because the claims did not relate to Daimler's activities in the United States there was no basis for personal jurisdiction over Daimler for these claims. In the wake of *Daimler*, more human rights claims are being dismissed for lack of personal jurisdiction.[172]

B. *Forum non conveniens*

Transnational human rights cases will often be met with a motion to dismiss based on the *forum non conveniens* doctrine. Defendants may argue that it is more convenient to litigate the case in the country where the human rights violations occurred, even though jurisdiction and venue in the United States are proper.[173]

170 *Helicopteros Nacionales de Columbia v. Hall*, 466 US 408, 415 (1984); *Goodyear v. Dunlop Tires Operations, S.A. v. Brown*, 564 US 915, 920 (2011); *Daimler AG v. Bauman*, 134 S. Ct 746 (2014). See J.T. Knoblett, 'Mind the Gap: Ensuring That Quasi-State Actors Are Held Liable for Human Rights Abuses' (2019) 87 *George Washington Law Review* 740, 756. See, for example, Waldman, 835 F.3d at 332; C. Nucha, '"Piercing the Jurisdictional Veil": Holding Corporations Accountable for Human Rights Violations after Kiobel and Daimler' (2017) 4 *St Thomas Journal of Complex Litigation* 1, 9.

171 134 S. Ct 746 (2014).

172 *Krishanti v. Rajaratnam*, 2014 WL 1669873, at *7 (DNJ 2014); Skinner (n. 141) , at note 192.

173 *Gulf Oil Corp. v. Gilbert*, 330 US 501, 507 (1947).

To assess whether a dismissal on *forum non conveniens* grounds is proper, courts must first to determine if an alternative forum exists.[174] The alternative forum must be both available and adequate, meaning that defendants are amenable to process in a forum that can provide an adequate remedy for plaintiff's injuries.[175] If an alternative forum does exist, courts must then balance private interests of the parties and any public interests at stake.[176] A district court's decision to dismiss on *forum non conveniens* grounds is subject only to abuse of discretion review.[177]

In considering a *forum non conveniens* defence, courts will ordinarily defer to a US citizen plaintiff's choice of a US forum.[178] Foreign plaintiffs seeking to litigate extraterritorial human rights violations will receive less deference.[179] Furthermore, private and public interests factors may weigh against jurisdiction in US courts because, *inter alia*, most of the relevant evidence and witnesses are likely to be in the country where the violations occurred.[180] Of course, evidence of corporate complicity may be located in the United States and foreign fora may not be safe or effective for human rights plaintiffs. Such considerations led to the rejection of the *forum non conveniens* argument in *Doe v. Chiquita*.[181] Even if a case is sent to a foreign jurisdiction the US court can impose conditions on the transfer, including acceptance of service, waiver of statutes of limitation, and agreement to pay a foreign judgment.[182]

The plaintiffs in *Wiwa v. Royal Dutch Petroleum Co.* successfully survived a motion to dismiss based on *forum non conveniens* by claiming that the US had a national interest in furnishing a forum to litigate international human rights claims.[183] Subsequent cases have limited *Wiwa* to its facts, pointing out the several plaintiffs were US citizens and the alternative forum was not the country where the

[174] *Piper Aircraft Co. v. Reyno*, 454 US 235, 254, 102 S. Ct 252, 265, 70 L. Ed. 2d 419 (1981).

[175] *In re Chiquita Brands Int'l, Inc. Alien Tort Statute & S'holder Derivative Litig.*, Case No. 08-MD-01916-MARRA, *4–5 (SD Fla. 29 November 2016).

[176] The private interests of the parties include (i) the accessibility of evidence, (ii) the availability of compulsory process for attendance of unwilling witnesses, (iii) the cost of obtaining the attendance of willing witnesses, (iv) the ease of viewing evidence if appropriate to the action, (v) whether the judgment will be enforceable in the alternative forum, and (vi) any other considerations affecting the ease, cost, and fairness of the trial. The public interest factors include (i) docket congestion, (ii) whether the burden of jury duty should be imposed on the community, (iii) whether the court will face difficult problems dealing with conflict of law or foreign law, and (iv) the local interest in having the controversy decided at home. *Gulf Oil Corp.*, 330 US at 508–9.

[177] *Wiwa*, 226 F. 3d at 100. It seems unlikely that *Wiwa* would have survived recent decisions restricting access to US courts. *Wiwa* was settled in 2009 for $15.5 million. J. Mouawad, 'Shell to Pay $15.5 Million to Settle Nigerian Case' (*New York Times*, 8 June 2009), <http://www.nytimes.com/2009/06/09/business/global/09shell.html>, accessed 18 November 2020.

[178] *Piper Aircraft Co.* 454 US at 255–6.

[179] J.E. Baldwin, 'International Human Rights Plaintiffs and the Doctrine of Forum Non Conveniens' (2007) 40 *Cornell International Law Journal* 749, 757.

[180] Ibid.

[181] See n. 174 above.

[182] *Aguinda*, 303 F. 3d at 478; *Delgado v. Shell Oil Co.*, 890 F. Supp. 1324, 1356 (SD Tex. 1995), aff'd, 231 F. 3d 165 (5th Cir. 2000).

[183] *Wiwa v. Royal Dutch Petroleum Co.*, 226 F. 3d 88, 101 (2d Cir. 2000).

events occurred.[184] The court in *Turedi v. Coca Cola Co.* also applied the *forum non conveniens* doctrine in a TVPA case.[185]

Plaintiffs have also avoided transfer by arguing that it was too dangerous for them to litigate in their home countries and that the foreign forum would be unfair to human rights plaintiffs.[186] These claims can be substantiated by evidence that plaintiffs would be likely to be in grave danger or unlikely to obtain basic justice if they were to litigate their case where the human rights violation occurred.[187] In *Doe v. Chiquita*, the court considered the threats faced by human rights defenders when determining that Colombia was not an adequate forum.[188] The court also found that the public and private interest factors did not meet the defendant's burden of establishing its *forum non conveniens* defence, paying particular attention to the US interest in monitoring and deterring unethical and illegal conduct of American corporations in supporting foreign terrorist organisations.[189]

Sometimes defendants regret the decision to seek transfer to a foreign forum. For example, in the infamous Chevron environmental degradation cases, Chevron (then Texaco) successfully had the case sent back to Ecuador[190] and then suffered a $18 billion judgment in Ecuadorian courts.[191]

C. Political question doctrine

Since *Filartiga*, defendants have often argued that enforcing customary international law in human rights cases is a political question better left to the political branches of the US government and beyond the capacity of the judiciary.[192] In general, this argument has been rejected by courts finding that there were judicially manageable standards enabling courts to resolve such claims.[193] The test

184 *Turedi v. Coca Cola Co.*, 460 F. Supp. 2d 507, 523 (SDNY 2006).

185 Ibid.

186 *Cabiri v. Assasie-Gyimah*, 921 F. Supp. 1189, 1199 (SDNY 1996); *Presbyterian Church of Sudan v. Talisman Energy, Inc.*, 244 F. Supp. 2d 289, 336 (SDNY 2003); *Mujica v. Occidental Petroleum Corp.*, 381 F. Supp. 2d 1134, 1142 (CD Cal. 2005); but see *Aldana v. Del Monte Fresh Produce N.A., Inc.*, 578 F. 3d 1283, 1291 (11th Cir. 2009). In many cases plaintiffs have been permitted to proceed under pseudonyms to protect them and their families from retaliation. See, for example, *Doe v. Saravia*, 348 F. Supp. 2d 1112, 1147–8 (ED Cal. 2004); *Doe v. Drummond*, 782 F. 3d at 581.

187 Ibid.

188 *Chiquita*, 190 F. Supp. 2d at 1116.

189 Ibid.at 16.

190 *Aguinda v. Texaco, Inc.*, 303 F. 3d 470 (2002).

191 N.V. Binder, 'Making Foreign Judgment Law Great Again: The Aftermath of Chevron v. Donziger' (2018) 51 *Suffolk University Law Review* 33, 44; Business and Human Rights Resource Centre, 'Texaco/ Chevron Lawsuits (re Ecuador)' (*Business and Human Rights Resource Centre*, 1 January 2008), <https:// business-humanrights.org/en/texacochevron-lawsuits-re-ecuador>, accessed 18 November 2020.

192 *Tel-Oren v. Libyan Arab Republic*, 726 F. 2d 774, 825 (DC Cir. 1984) (Robb, concurring).

193 See, for example, *Al Shimari v. CACI Premier Technology, Inc.*, 758 F. 3d 516, 532 (2014). Prominent on the surface of any case held to involve a political question is found: '[1] a "textually demonstrable constitutional commitment of the issue to a coordinate political department;" [2] "a lack of judicially discoverable and manageable standards for resolving it;" [3] "the impossibility of deciding without

for determining whether a case presents a non-justiciable political question is not whether the proceeding might touch upon any foreign policy concerns but rather whether the proceeding would require a federal court to undermine the constitutional authority of the political branches.[194] Occasionally, human rights cases have been found to present a 'political question',[195] but this doctrine should not pose a significant obstacle to corporate accountability litigation in US courts. It is even less likely to pose an obstacle in cases based on statutory claims.

This may occur if the US government suggests that a case should be dismissed on political question grounds. The Supreme Court has indicated that federal courts should give serious weight to the executive branch's view of the case's impact on foreign policy, even though the ultimate decision is made by the court.[196] In *Hwang Geum Joo*,[197] the court relied heavily on the State Department's policy of achieving peace with Japan by treaty in the aftermath of the Second World War in holding that the claims of former comfort women against Japan presented a non-justiciable political question.[198]

D. International comity

The international comity doctrine requires federal courts to defer to the legislative, executive, or judicial acts of another country in certain circumstances.[199] Similar to the doctrines of *forum non conveniens* and political question, it seeks to respect a sovereign's authority over claims within its jurisdiction to maintain amicable relations between nations.[200] The doctrine also allows for deference to the policy decisions of the political branches.[201]

Traditionally, the international comity doctrine applied only if it would be impossible for a defendant to comply with the decisions or legislative acts in both

an initial policy determination of a kind clearly for nonjudicial discretion;"' [4] "the impossibility of a court's undertaking independent resolution without expressing lack of the respect due coordinate branches of government;" [5] "an unusual need for unquestioning adherence to a political decision already made;" or [6] "the potentiality of embarrassment from multifarious pronouncements by various departments on one question."' Ibid. (citing *Baker v. Carr*, 369 US 186, 217 (1962)).

194 S. Buchanan, 'Questioning the Political Question Doctrine: Inconsistent Applications in Reparations and Alien Tort Claims Act Litigation' (2009) 17 *Cardozo Journal of International and Comparative Law* 345, 355.

195 *Al Shimari v. CACI Premier Tech., Inc.*, 840 F. 3d 147, 157 (4th Cir. 2016); *Corrie v. Caterpillar, Inc.*, 503 F. 3d 974, 984 (9th Cir. 2007).

196 *Sosa*, 542 US at note 21.

197 *Hwang Geum Joo v. Japan*, 413 F. 3d 45, 52 (DC Cir. 2005).

198 Ibid., at 53.

199 See generally W.S. Dodge, 'International Comity in American Law' (2018) 115 *Columbia Law Review* 2071.

200 *Khulumani*, 504 F. 3d at 298.

201 See, for example, *Usoyan v. Republic of Turkey*, 2020 WL 588134, at *16 (DDC Feb. 6, 2020).

countries.[202] However, in *Mujica v. AirScan*,[203] the Ninth Circuit applied the doctrine, at the behest of the State Department, to a case where there was no true conflict between domestic and foreign law under existing precedent.[204] The *Mujica* plaintiffs, who had fled Colombia, sought to hold Occidental Petroleum and Air Scan responsible for the deaths of their family members. Even though the corporations were not part of the Colombian proceedings and arguably could not have been sued there, the Ninth Circuit held that the case could not proceed because of the international comity doctrine, based in part on the US government's submission that US courts should defer to Colombian proceedings in these circumstances.[205]

E. Act of State doctrine

The principle that US courts will not sit in judgment over the sovereign acts of foreign governments on their own territory is likely to be raised in any human rights litigation against corporations.[206] The Act of State doctrine directs US courts to treat the official acts of foreign sovereign as conclusive.[207] The Supreme Court's seminal decision in *Banco Nacional de Cuba v. Sabbatino* articulated the factors to be considered in determining if the doctrine applies. These factors include the degree of codification or consensus regarding the norms in question, the implications of the issue on US foreign relations, and whether the government which perpetrated the act is no longer in existence.[208]

Federal courts have been reluctant to find that violations of fundamental human rights are the kinds of sovereign acts justifying this immunity from judicial scrutiny, especially when the acts have not been ratified or authorised by government officials.[209] To date, the Act of State doctrine has not presented a significant obstacle to most human rights cases.[210] It is unclear whether the doctrine will pose a more significant obstacle in other contexts (e.g. environmental degradation claims).

[202] *Hartford Fire Ins. Co. v. California*, 509 US 764, 765 (1993).

[203] *Mujica v. AirScan Inc.*, 771 F. 3d 580, 597 (9th Cir. 2014).

[204] Ibid., at 603

[205] Corporate access to the US government in order to obtain assistance in limiting human rights litigation is another practical obstacle to human rights plaintiffs who seldom have such access and lack the political power of major corporations.

[206] *Banco Nacional de Cuba v. Sabbatino*, 376 US 398, 423 (1964).

[207] Restatement (Fourth) of Foreign Relations Law section 441 cmt. A (Am. Law Inst. 2018).

[208] Ibid., at 427–8. *See W.S. Kirkpatrick & Co. v. Envt. Tectonics Corp. Intern.*, 493 US 400, 408–10 (1990).

[209] Initially, the ATS litigation against Ferdinand Marcos was dismissed on Act of State grounds supported by the Reagan Administration. *Trajano v. Marcos*, 878 F. 2d 1439 (9th Cir. 1989). See also *Kadic*, 70 F. 3d at 250 (act of State official violating national law, without government ratification, not an act of State).

[210] See, for example, *Mujica v. Occidental Oil Corp.*, 381 F. Supp. 2d 1164, 1190–1 (CD Cal. 2005).

XII. Access to justice in US courts

There are many reasons why foreign litigants have initiated litigation in US courts rather than seek redress in the countries where the violations occur. It is possible that as US opportunities contract following the recent trend of more conservative courts there will be a shift toward litigating these issues in other countries. Some of the specific issues bearing on the effectiveness of US litigation are discussed below. Before considering those specific issues there are some general observations.

There is a vibrant plaintiffs' bar throughout the United States with ample resources to litigate complex social justice cases. Most plaintiffs' firms take cases on a contingency basis, where the plaintiff's attorney takes a percentage of the damages award as payment if the case is successful.[211] Therefore, the willingness of large plaintiffs' firms to litigate these cases may depend on the financial viability of the cases, factoring in the size of the potential damage award, costs to the firm, and the chances of success, so the conservative trend in the case law described above may have an adverse impact on the availability of litigation resources.[212]

A small number of public interest lawyers and organisations have been willing to take on these cases, including many of the cases cited in this chapter, despite the uncertain possibilities of success and the reality that these cases often take many years to resolve. Non-governmental organisations like the New York-based Center for Constitutional Rights and Washington, DC-based EarthRights International are supported by contributions from individuals and foundations.[213] There are funding sources like the Impact Fund that have made grants to lawyers handling these cases.[214] There is also a private litigation funding industry that has developed in recent years and has been used to help finance some of these cases. Thus, there are resources in the United States to pursue at least some of these large, complex social justice cases.

One factor supporting litigation in the United States is the American rule relating to attorneys' fees. The standard rule is that each side bears its own fees and most of its costs no matter the outcome.[215] Thus, plaintiffs and their lawyers do not usually bear the risk of paying the other side's legal fees if they do not prevail in the case.[216] Corporate defendants often spend tens of millions of dollars in legal fees in

[211] Though this fee can vary by State, firm, or the specific case, per the agreement between the client and attorneys, a typical contingency fee is roughly one-third of the final monetary award.

[212] This trend can be seen in the withdrawal of many class action law firms from ATS litigation after the Supreme Court decisions in *Sosa* and *Kiobel*.

[213] <https://ccrjustice.org/donate; https://earthrights.org/get-involved/donate>.

[214] S. Ahmed, 'Access to Justice: Litigation Financing and the New Developments' (2017) 4(1) *International Academic Journal of Accounting and Financial Management* 89–99.

[215] *Alyeska Pipeline Svc. Co. v. Wilderness Soc'y*, 421 US 240, 245 (1975).

[216] In a couple of cases defendants have initiated defamation and other litigation against plaintiffs' lawyers. Perhaps the most prominent example has been the actions taken by Chevron against the plaintiffs' lawyer, Steven Donziger, leading to his house arrest as a result of contempt proceedings. C. Krauss, 'Lawyer who beat Chevron in Ecuador faces trial of his own' *New York Times* (30 July 2013). Defendants can be expected to attack plaintiffs' lawyers with Rule 11 sanctions motions and other means to raise

defending these cases so a different fee-shifting rule would make it nearly impossible to bring these cases. On the other hand, there are few areas where plaintiffs can obtain statutory fees from defendants when they prevail.[217]

Access to US media is relevant to the impact of social justice cases. Even given the uncertainty of success in court, these cases perform the very important function of bringing the injustices and violations underlying these cases to the public's attention in the United States and around the world. The First Amendment of the US Constitution provides a protective shield for public statements relating to these cases and allow the facts about corporate violations to get broader public attention. This public scrutiny itself may lead to changes in corporate practices and supports the work of activists working on these issues.

The jury system in the United States is also typically welcoming to plaintiffs. Although there are some constitutional limits on the award of punitive damages in US litigation,[218] jury awards in the United States can be substantial and compare favourably with the size of damages awards in other legal systems. There is, of course, no guarantee of success with juries in these cases but on balance plaintiffs' lawyers believe that jurors will be open to making awards on behalf of foreign plaintiffs when presented with the kinds of factual contexts presented by these cases.

A. Class actions

The availability of class actions and the class action bar provides a major basis for the litigation of these cases. Although class actions are available in federal and State courts, few classes have been certified in human rights cases. One of the major bars to class certification is the issue of international preclusion in classes including foreign plaintiffs. Issues of preclusion arise when the foreign plaintiffs reside in a nation that is unlikely to enforce a US judgment,[219] meaning that another trial against the same defendants in that nation's courts is not precluded. Many US judges are wary of subjecting defendants to this risk and will therefore only certify classes including foreign plaintiffs if those plaintiffs are citizens of a nation that will enforce the US judgment.

The major exception to the lack of class certifications in human rights cases is the litigation against the Estate of Ferdinand Marcos. A class of approximately 10,000

the cost of bringing these actions. Plaintiffs' lawyers have had to take extra care in gathering evidence in these cases to avoid these problems.

[217] The TVPRA is a significant exception where statutory fees are available. 18 USC section 1595.

[218] See *BMW of North America, Inc v. Gore*, 517 US 559 (1996); *State Farm Mutual Automobile Insurance Co. v. Campbell*, 538 US 408 (2003).

[219] There is no binding international law requiring such enforcement; see the Enforcement of Judgments section for elaboration.

victims of torture, disappearances, and summary execution was certified and a class judgment entered after trial. This judgment was affirmed on appeal.[220] In subsequent cases, class certification has been denied. For example, in *Doe v. Chiquita* the district court denied class certification and required the cases to proceed on behalf of more than 8,000 individual plaintiffs.[221]

Despite these setbacks in human rights cases, the prospects for class certification in other areas are likely to be more promising. For example, the State consumer actions discussed above will almost always be pursued on behalf of a class of consumers. The same is likely to be true in environmental litigation. The class mechanism can also be used as a way of efficiently settling cases on behalf of large groups of victims.[222]

It should be noted that even where class certification is denied or unavailable, U.S courts have devised mechanisms to handle mass tort cases. For example, in *Doe v. Chiquita*, a case involving thousands of Colombian plaintiffs, the Court has created a process of trying the cases of small groups of 'bellwether' plaintiffs as a means of resolving the claims of the broader group of plaintiffs. The result of the first set of plaintiffs was summary judgment entered for the defendants and an interlocutory appeal of this judgment on issues likely to advance the resolution of the entire case after an appellate ruling.[223]

B. Discovery

One of the advantages for plaintiffs in US litigation is the availability of broad-ranging discovery. This is especially vital where the content and timing of internal corporate knowledge, communications, and decisions which are central to establishing the facts would otherwise be inaccessible to plaintiffs. Plaintiffs may obtain discovery under the Federal Rules of Civil Procedure and similar State rules.[224] Beyond the Federal Rules, litigants can obtain discovery through several supplementary means including (i) The Hague Convention on the Taking of Evidence Abroad in Civil or Commercial Matters;[225] (ii) letters rogatory to foreign courts; (iii) subpoenas under the Walsh Act;[226] and (iv) other available procedures in foreign countries. These methods are not exclusive and will vary depending on the foreign country in question. For a comprehensive review of relevant discovery

[220] *Hilao v. Estate of Marcos*, 103 F. 3d 767, 774 (9th Cir. 1996).

[221] *In re Chiquita Brands Int'l Inc*, 331 FRD 675, 685 (SD Fla. 2019).

[222] There are some other collateral benefits of class actions as well. For example, the existence of a pending class action will toll the statute of limitations for victims who have yet to file their cases.

[223] *Cardona v. Chiquita Brands International, Inc.*, 760 F. 3d 1185, 1187-90 (11th Cir. 2014).

[224] See *Societe Nationale Industrielle Aerospatiale v. U.S. District Court*, 482 US 522 (1987) (litigants can proceed under the Federal Rules to obtain discovery abroad).

[225] 28 USC section 1781.

[226] 28 USC section 1783.

procedures litigators should consult 'Discovery in International Civil Litigation: A Guide for Judges' prepared by the Federal Judicial Center.[227]

In general, the combination of these methods provides effective means for obtaining the evidence necessary to prove plaintiffs' claims in these cases. There are frequently protective orders limiting public access to at least some of the information generated in discovery, including anonymising names or redacting certain identifying information of victims. Nonetheless, some discovery does become publicly available during the course of litigation and even materials covered by protective orders will ordinarily become public during trial.[228] Thus, these cases can become vehicles for the exposure of long-standing wrongdoing. The information in these cases may also form the basis for Congressional hearings or executive action.

Under 28 USC section 1782, discovery in US courts is available in support of foreign judicial proceedings. This option enhances the effectiveness of cases brought outside the United States whether the defendant is a US or foreign corporation.[229]

C. Enforcement of US judgments

Enforcement of domestic human rights judgments against defendants found in the US follows the same procedures as other US judgments, subject to applicable federal or State laws. If the US court has personal jurisdiction over the defendant to issue a valid judgment against them, enforcement of that judgment should be proper. However, the US is not a signatory to any bilateral or multilateral treaties that would require US courts to recognise or enforce any foreign judgments.[230] Individuals seeking to have foreign human rights judgments recognised in the US must file suit in a competent US court[231] and follow the specific enforcement procedures in that court.[232]

[227] Federal Judicial Center, 'Discovery in International Civil Litigation: A Guide for Judges' (*International Litigation Guide*, 2015), <https://www.fjc.gov/sites/default/files/2015/Discovery%20in%20International%20Civil%20Litigation.pdf>, accessed 18 November 2020.

[228] Of course, there are risks to clients in the public disclosure of facts in litigation so plaintiffs' lawyers have had to be very sensitive to the security issues in human rights cases. There have been several possible cases that have not been able to proceed because of undue risks to clients or their families. These cases require constant vigilance in limiting such risks.

[229] EarthRights International, 'Foreign Legal Assistance Guide' (*EarthRights International*), <https://earthrights.org/publication/foreign-legal-assistance-guide/>, accessed 18 November 2020.

[230] See S.A. Edelman, 'United States' in P. Doris, *Enforcement of Foreign Judgments: in 28 Jurisdictions Worldwide* (Law Business Research Ltd 2014), <https://www.gibsondunn.com/wp-content/uploads/documents/publications/Edelman-Jura-Enforcement-of-Foreign-Judgments-US.pdf>, accessed 18 April 2021. Certain specific treaties or conventions ratified by the United States apply to enforcement of international arbitration awards or investment disputes, but none apply general to enforcement of court judgments.

[231] See US Department of State Guidance on Enforcement of Judgments, available at <https://travel.state.gov/content/travel/en/legal/travel-legal-considerations/internl-judicial-asst/Enforcement-of-Judges.html>, accessed 21 April 2021.

[232] There are no federal statutory rules governing enforcement of foreign judgments and each State handles them differently. See n. 230.

Reciprocally, no other nations are required by treaty or convention to recognise or enforce US judgments. Other nations are able to choose whether to enforce US judgments, a decision that is dependent on their local judicial rules and broader policy considerations.[233] With that in mind, plaintiffs seeking to pursue US litigation should consult the local rules of any nation(s) in which they may later seek to have a judgment enforced prior to bringing the action in the United States.

While each other nation will have unique rules and policy concerns when deciding whether to recognise or enforce a US judgment, there are recurring themes that are helpful to consider. As a general rule, foreign courts will only enforce final judgments that meet their standards for proper service and due process.[234] These rules are based on policy concerns of fairness, adequate notice, and a chance to defend. Additionally, on a nation-by-nation basis, considerations of sovereignty and geopolitical influence also come into play. Certain norms within US litigation are also ill favoured in other nations, including damage awards that are perceived as being too high[235] and invasive US discovery procedures.[236] Discussions of encouraging reciprocity have accompanied recent US trends toward a uniform domestic regime for recognition of foreign judgments, but at this time no such regime has been implemented.

D. Settlement

Another aspect of US litigation to note is the recent general trend toward mediation. Several of the cases discussed in this chapter have been resolved using the services of private mediators, including *Doe v. Unocal*.[237] There are mandatory settlement processes required in almost all federal and State courts.[238] In *Wiwa v. Royal Dutch Petroleum* a settlement was reached with the assistance of the federal trial judge.[239] There has also been a number of confidential settlements of social justice cases. The insistence on confidentiality in mediation is at odds with the ability of public interest litigation to expose corporate wrongdoing but this trend toward mediation will continue to be a significant feature of the US legal system.

233 US Department of State Guidance on Enforcement of Judgments (n. 231).

234 S.P. Baumgartner, 'Understanding the Obstacles to the Recognition and Enforcement of U.S. Judgments Abroad' (2013) 31 *Akron Law Publications* 6.

235 Ibid., at 12, citing *Castanho v. Brown & Root (U.K.) Ltd.*, (1980) 1 WLR 833, 859 (Shaw, J.) (estimating that 'in the United States the scale of damages for injuries of the magnitude sustained by the plaintiff is something in the region of ten times what is regarded as appropriate by ... the courts of [England]').

236 See, for example, G.B. Born and P.B. Rutledge, *International Civil Litigation in United States Courts* (4th edn, 2007) 910–12.

237 C. Kahn, 'Unocal Settles Myanmar Suit' *National Public Radio* (14 December 2004).

238 See, for example, Cal. Ct Rule 3, 1380; W.P. Lynch, 'Why Settle For Less Improving Settlement Conferences in Federal Court' (2019) 94 *Washington Law Review* 1233.

239 E. Pilkington, 'Shell Pays Out $15.5 Million Over Saro-Wiwa Killing' *The Guardian* (8 June 2009).

XIII. Conclusion

As the federal judiciary is increasingly antagonistic to transnational human rights claims, human rights litigators are likely to turn to State courts or the assertion of common law and other foreign law claims in achieving corporate accountability. Such cases are bound to generate new issues and new applications of old doctrines. The Supreme Court's general disinclination to open US courts to transnational cases, reflected most starkly in its decisions expanding the presumption against extraterritoriality, and precluding foreign corporations from certain theories of liability, seems likely to continue in the Roberts Court.

However, it is also likely that corporate accountability litigation will continue and even expand despite these challenges. The political support for corporate accountability efforts will hopefully lead to additional legislative reforms and a judiciary in State and federal courts willing to hold corporations accountable for their complicity in extraterritorial human rights, environmental, or other violations.

On 17 June 2021, the Supreme Court issued its decision in *Nestle USA, Inc. v. Doe*.[240] Justice Thomas wrote the main opinion in the case. Sections I and II of Justice Thomas' opinion were joined by all of the other Justices except Justice Alito. These sections found that the allegations in the plaintiffs' operative complaint were insufficient to overcome the presumption against extraterritoriality the Court had applied to the ATS in the *Kiobel* case.

In Section III of his opinion, joined only by Justices Gorsuch and Kavanaugh, Justice Thomas argued that the ATS should only apply to the torts recognized by Blackstone in the 18th century (e.g. piracy, and violating the rights of ambassadors or the right to safe conduct). Significantly, this view did not command a majority and it appears that the Court continued to adhere to the *Sosa* framework. Justice Sotomayor's concurring opinion, joined by Justices Breyer and Kagan, rejected this narrow view of the ATS and reaffirmed the *Sosa* framework. Chief Justice Roberts and Justices Barrett and Alito did not weigh in on these issues.

The Court did not resolve many of the issues presented in the briefs concerning, *inter alia*, the 'focus' of the ATS (e.g. where the injury, or the underlying substantive violation occurred. Eight Justices found that the alleged aiding and abetting conduct plaintiffs complained of (e.g. providing training and other assistance to farmers) occurred in the Ivory Coast. The Court characterized the plaintiffs' claims as being too general because they alleged 'major operational decisions' were made in the United States. The Court held that 'allegations of general corporate activity—like decision-making—cannot alone establish a domestic application of the ATS' under the analysis established by the *Morrison* line of cases, because they were too 'generic' and not specific enough. The Court held that '[t]o plead facts sufficient to

[240] Nestlé USA, Inc. v. Doe, 141 S.Ct.1931 (2021).

support a domestic application of the ATS, plaintiffs must allege more domestic conduct than general corporate activity'.

The Court did not indicate what additional domestic conduct was sufficient to overcome the presumption and this issue is likely to be the subject of continuing litigation. In fact, even the plaintiffs in the *Nestle* case intend to amend their complaint to comply with the Court's insistence on additional domestic conduct. There will be additional motion practice on this issue in several pending cases. The issue of what the 'focus' (or focii) of the ATS is will be hotly contested in pending litigation now that the Court appears to use this framework for the analysis of the presumption against extraterritoriality in ATS cases.

Significantly, the Court did not accept the defendants' invitation to bar all ATS cases where the plaintiffs' injuries or the principal's violations occurred outside US territory. Nor did the Court take up the Trump Administration's suggestion that it should not recognize aiding and abetting liability at all under the ATS. The Court's opinion was based on the availability of aiding and abetting liability under the ATS.

One of the issues before the Court was whether corporations could be sued under the ATS. The Court had previously granted review in the *Kiobel* and *Jesner* cases to decide this issue but failed to do so. The *Nestle* majority once again avoided reaching a final decision on corporate ATS liability. Indeed, Justice Alito dissented mainly on the grounds that he thought the Court should answer this question and hold that corporations can be sued under the ATS. As he put it, '[c]orporate status does not justify special immunity.' This was also the view expressed by Justice Gorsuch in his concurring opinion. Thus, five Justices are now on record as believing that corporations can be sued under the ATS. Technically, this is not a holding of the Court but it seems that the debate about corporate liability under the ATS is over as a practical matter.

The bottom line is that the Court decided the case in the narrowest way possible and left other issues relating to the circumstances in which allegations of domestic aiding and abetting conduct will overcome the presumption against extraterritoriality to another day. The Court's previous decisions in *Kiobel* and *Jesner* have already limited the scope of the ATS. The *Nestle* decision appears to narrow ATS liability a little bit more but declines to accept a range of other draconian arguments designed to eviscerate the statute. ATS plaintiffs live to fight another day.

8

Foreign Direct Liability of Multinational Corporations in the Dutch Legal Order

*Channa Samkalden**

I. Introduction

As in other European States, liability of multinational corporations is a rapidly developing field of law in the Netherlands. As the home State of a number of larger multinational corporations such as Shell, Heineken, and Unilever, the question of the extent to which these corporations can be held to account within the Netherlands is one with potentially important implications.

With the legal framework being mainly determined by the European regulations, the applicable substantive law in such cases will more often than not be foreign law. This section will discuss the relevant provisions of Dutch law when litigating cases on foreign direct liability. Before doing so, it may be helpful to take note of some aspects of Dutch legal culture that can play an implicit but important role when looking at these particular cases and the receptiveness of the Dutch judiciary towards them.

First, Dutch civil law is characterised by many open-ended concepts found in the statutory provisions of the Dutch civil code (DCC), these include the principles of good faith, reasonableness, fairness, proper social conduct, and reasonable attribution. The Dutch legislature has granted the courts a relatively large degree of discretion to develop the law further while taking into account the specific circumstances of a case. The courts, when applying these concepts, are also able to derogate from specific statutory or contractual provisions to avoid unjust results. In addition, the Netherlands has a monist system which allows for the direct application of human rights treaties in private disputes; and sees international treaties supersede national legislation and the constitution within the Dutch legal hierarchy. The *Urgenda* case (although not a *foreign* liability case) provides a good illustration of this: in 2019 the Supreme Court confirmed the order of the District Court (upheld on appeal) which directed the State to reduce greenhouse gases by

* The author thanks Barbara van Straaten and Thomas van der Sommen for their contribution to the chapter.

Channa Samkalden, *Foreign Direct Liability of Multinational Corporations in the Dutch Legal Order* In: *Human Rights Litigation against Multinationals in Practice*. Edited by: Richard Meeran, Oxford University Press.
 DOI: 10.1093/oso/9780198866220.003.0008

at least 25 per cent compared to 1990 by the end of 2020, while directly applying Articles 2 and 8 of the European Convention on Protection of Human Rights and Fundamental Freedoms (ECHR).[1] It may well be a consequence of these two features—the power to develop the law and the monist system—that the Dutch judiciary has traditionally shown an open attitude towards international cases as well as to the application of unclearly defined standards, which in principle provide a good basis to pursue cases dealing with foreign direct liability in the Netherlands.

While the judiciary may be relatively receptive to these types of cases, there remain nonetheless important legal hurdles. The cases concerning liability for human rights violations by multinational corporations have all hit procedural obstacles. That said, the Dutch judiciary has generally shown a willingness to accommodate these cases. In *Milieudefensie v. Shell*, the Court of Appeal of The Hague ordered both the Dutch parent company and its Nigerian subsidiary SPDC to install a leak detection system in one of its Nigerian pipelines, while holding SPDC liable for the damages that had occurred as a consequence of two different oil spills.[2] In an earlier interim-judgment, it had confirmed its jurisdiction, confirmed that the claimants had standing and ordered the disclosure of evidence.[3] In *Kiobel v. Shell* the District Court also established jurisdiction, dismissed Shell's defence that the claim was time barred and allowed the plaintiffs to provide evidence for their substantive claims.[4] Moreover, in two cases against Trafigura, the courts confirmed their jurisdiction as well as the standing of the representative organisation and allowed the cases to proceed.[5]

In the Netherlands, foreign direct liability is still very much a matter of case law rather than specific statutory obligations; indeed it is only in the field of child labour that specific statutory duties for companies have been developed. The relevant cases and statutory provisions governing human rights violations by multinational corporations committed abroad will be discussed in this chapter. The focus in this chapter will be largely on civil litigation as this is where the injured parties have most direct influence on the procedure and outcome of the case.

[1] Supreme Court 20 December 2019, ECLI:NL:HR:2019:2007 (*Urgenda v. The Netherlands*).

[2] Court of Appeal The Hague 29 January 2021, ECLI:NL:GHDHA:2021:132 (*Oguru, Efanga & Milieudefensie v. Shell*), available at <http://deeplink.rechtspraak.nl/uitspraak?id=ECLI:NL:GHDHA:2021:132>, accessed 13 July 2020 (English translation expected). It should be noted that where the text refers to the *Milieudefensie* case, this actually concerns three different cases regarding three different spills in Nigeria. The other cases concern the case of *Dooh & Milieudefensie v. Shell*, ECLI:NL:GHDHA:2021:133 and that of *Akpan & Milieudefesie v. Shell*, ECLI:NL:GHDHA:2021:134. Akpan won his case against Nigerian Shell subsidiary SPDC in first instance (ECLI:NL:RBDHA:2013:BY9854, in Dutch), the appeal is still pending at the time of publication.

[3] Court of Appeal The Hague 18 December 2015, ECLI:NL:GHDHA:2015:3586 (*Dooh & Milieudefensie v. Shell*), ECLI:NL:GHDHA:2015:3588 (*Oguru, Efanga & Milieudefensie v. Shell*), and ECLI:NL:GHDHA:2015:3587 (*Akpan & Milieudefesie v. Shell*).

[4] District Court The Hague 1 May 2019, ECLI:NL:RBDHA:2019:4233 (*Kiobel v. Shell*).

[5] Supreme Court 3 April 2020, ECLI:NL:HR:2020:587 (*UVDTAB v. Trafigura or Trafigura I*); Court of Appeal Amsterdam 14 April 2020, ECLI:NL:GHAMS:2020:1157 (*VTDCI v. Trafigura* or *Trafigura II*).

II. Corporate criminal liability

Under Article 51 of the Dutch Criminal Code (*Wetboek van Strafrecht*), corporations can be prosecuted for (international) crimes. Civil parties can initiate prosecution by filing a criminal complaint with the Office of the Public Prosecutor (*Openbaar Ministerie*). It remains, however, the public prosecutor's decision whether or not to prosecute a (corporate) person. If the prosecutor declines , the party that filed the complaint can appeal the decision to a Court of Appeal following a procedure based on Article 12 of the Dutch Code of Criminal Procedure (*Wetboek van Strafvordering*). If that appeal is upheld, the public prosecutor is forced to prosecute. In these circumstances , the role of the injured parties remains limited; the public prosecutor is entirely responsible for conduct of the criminal proceedings and the injured party is not a formal party to the case (*procespartij*). However, when the case goes to trial, an injured party (*benadeelde partij*) can obtain victim status, which confers certain rights and privileges in the criminal proceedings. These include the right: to review the case file and evidence; to request that the prosecutor put forward new evidence (submitted by the injured party); to speak in court; and to claim compensation as an injured party.

Prosecutions are initiated and conducted, by the public prosecutor. The plaintiff/civil party therefore plays a significantly less important role in the conduct of proceedings in a criminal case than in a civil case. That said, there are some advantages to criminal proceedings that should not be overlooked. Notably, criminal litigation is significantly cheaper . Although it is certainly preferable in complicated international cases, criminal complaints need not necessarily be filed or prepared by lawyers. Moreover, the preparation work of a lawyer in criminal proceedings is less intensive, due to the fact that the public prosecutor takes a leading role. The burden of proving the case , after all, lies with the prosecutor, not the party filing the complaint. In addition, the public prosecutor has powers allowing for wider means of evidence gathering than that which can normally be obtained in civil litigation. This can be particularly helpful in factually complicated cases. Criminal cases are also usually concluded faster than civil cases. Finally, for some crimes (such as inflicting grievous bodily harm) the payment of damages awarded through criminal procedure is guaranteed as it is initially made by the State.

Only human rights violations that have been defined as a criminal act can be prosecuted under Dutch criminal law. Prosecution of corporations most typically relates to economic or environmental crimes. There is an ongoing criminal investigation into Shell and ENI which concerns allegations of bribery of more than US$1 billion to get the concessions of a major oil field (OPL 245) off Nigeria's coasts. In the case of SBM Offshore, the Dutch public prosecutor reached an out-of-court settlement in relation to corruption charges and did not proceed with criminal prosecution of the company or its directors. In 2018 it also concluded an agreement with the ING in relation to money laundering violations; in return the public prosecutor agreed not to prosecute any individuals for these criminal acts. In the criminal case against Trafigura, the Court of Appeal issued a €1 million fine for the dumping of toxic waste in Ivory Coast.[6]

In addition to economic and environmental crimes, relevant areas concerning foreign criminal liability include the criminalisation of exploitation (which falls under the crime of human trafficking), or profiting from exploitation, and (complicity in) human trafficking, as well as the Child Labour Due Diligence Act which will be discussed later in this chapter. Finally, the Dutch International Crimes Act codifies as crimes the international crimes that have been recognised under the Rome Statute of the International Criminal Court, including the crime of genocide, crimes against humanity, war crimes, and torture. It has been established that a person or company can be held liable for complicity in war crimes if it delivers materials for chemical weapons to be created and used abroad.[7]

A. Jurisdiction

As a rule, Dutch criminal courts are competent to hear cases about crimes committed in the Netherlands ('territoriality principle', Article 2 Dutch Criminal Code). This rule is broadened at times , for example when a criminal act is committed partly abroad and partly in the Netherlands, or when specific crimes are concerned, such as membership of a criminal organisation of which some members are based in the Netherlands.

Article 4 of the Dutch criminal code establishes universal jurisdiction of the Dutch criminal courts as regards some very serious crimes such as genocide. Moreover, following Article 5 of the Dutch Criminal Code, certain crimes committed abroad against persons with Dutch nationality or citizenship, including legal persons registered in the Netherlands, may be prosecuted in the Netherlands ('passive nationality principle'), provided that the relevant act is punishable in both jurisdictions and the crime is punishable with a minimum of eight years imprisonment under Dutch law.

In addition, Article 7 of the Dutch Criminal Code incorporates the 'active nationality principle', granting Dutch courts jurisdiction as regards (legal) persons with Dutch nationality or citizenship who have committed crimes abroad that are punishable in both the Dutch and foreign jurisdiction, as well as with regard to some specific crimes. This article is of particular interest in relation to crimes of Dutch (parent) companies committed abroad.

[6] Court of Appeal 23 December 2011, ECLI:NL:GHAMS:2011:BU9237.
[7] Supreme Court 30 June 2009, ECLI:NL:HR:2009:BG4822 (*Van Anraat*).

B. Boundaries of criminal liability of corporations

Both natural persons and legal entities can incur criminal liability under Article 51 of the DCC. The classic modes of liability under Dutch law include (co-) perpetratorship, complicity (aiding and abetting), and incitement. Pursuant to Article 51, a legal entity can be criminally liable for any criminal act that can be attributed (*toegerekend*) to it, or for 'factually directing' a criminal act (*feitelijk leidinggeven*) committed by its employees or subsidiaries.

i. Direct liability on the basis of attribution

In order to establish the criminal liability of a legal entity for certain acts, these acts must be attributable to the legal entity.[8] Following the case law of the Supreme Court, this may be the case when the following circumstances apply:

- where the behaviour concerns an act or an omission of someone who works for the corporation, whether or not under a formal contract of employment;
- the behaviour occurred during the course of the legal person's normal course of business or performance of duties;
- the behaviour served the legal person in its business or performance of duties;
- the behaviour was at the 'disposal' of the corporation, and the corporation has 'accepted' or tended to accept such or similar behaviour—including the failure to take reasonable care to prevent the behaviour from occurring.[9]

The threshold applied in court is reasonableness: it must be established that the offence can *reasonably* be attributed to the legal entity based on these criteria. For that purpose, all the facts and circumstances of the case must be taken into account. In order to attribute an offence to a legal entity, it should, as a minimum,

(1) be established that that the legal entity had knowledge of the considerable chance that an offence could occur; and
(2) the legal entity should therefore have taken all measures within its powers to prevent the offence from occurring and has reasonably failed to do so.

ii. Factually directing

In addition, under Article 51 of the DCC a legal entity or natural person can commit a criminal offence on the basis of what is referred to as 'factually directing'.

[8] Referred to in Dutch as '*de leer van de redelijke toerekening*'.

[9] HR 21 October 2003, NJ 2006, 328 (*Drijfmest*). See also B.F. Keulen and E. Gritter, 'Corporate Criminal Liability in the Netherlands' (December 2010) 14(3) *Electronic Journal of Comparative Law* 1–12, <http://www.ejcl.org>, accessed 18 November 2020; see also V. van den Berg, 'Corporate liability in the Netherlands' (*Baker McKenzie, Global Compliance News*), <https://globalcompliancenews.com/white-collar-crime/corporate-liability-in-the-netherlands/>, accessed 13 July 2020.

In order to establish that a (legal) person has been factually directing an offence, it is not sufficient nor a prerequisite that the (legal) person is, for example, the legal director.[10] Factually directing can often be logically established through the legal entity's active behaviour or policies. But factually directing may also be established when the role of the company has been more passive in nature. Following the case law of the Supreme Court, a parent company can be held liable for factually directing a criminal offence committed by its subsidiary when it:

(1) failed to take measures to prevent the offence from being committed, even though it had the authority and reasonable duty to do so; and
(2) it consciously accepted the reasonable chance that the offence would be committed.

iii. Other grounds for liability

In addition to the options described above, a company may be liable as the functional perpetrator, or the author in an organised context. This mode of liability emanates from the capacity of a (legal) person to influence the occurrence of certain events and is regularly used in environmental crimes such as pollution cases: the legal entity will then be liable because of its capacity as polluter (i.e. as producer of toxic materials). The focus in this type of liability is therefore on the element of *actus reus* (the actual act), rather than *mens rea* (intention). The required *mens rea* is often fault (*schuld*).

As stated above, companies may also be held liable under one of the classic modes of liability under Dutch law. These are (i) (co-)perpetration (*medeplegen*); (ii) complicity/aiding and abetting (*medeplichtigheid*); and (iii) incitement (*uitlokking*). In the event of co-perpetration, the perpetrators must play a more or less equal part in the commission of the crime and there must be a conscious and close cooperation between the co-perpetrators. Complicity requires a 'double' *mens rea* under Dutch law: the accomplice must have intended (directly or conditionally) to facilitate or promote the crime to take place, and the accomplice must have intended (directly or conditionally) that the actual perpetrator would commit the offence. Incitement under Dutch law means to intentionally have another person commit a criminal offence by (i) offering gifts; (ii) promises; (iii) abuse of power; (iv) violence; (v) threats; (vi) misleading; or by providing the (vii) opportunity, (viii) means, or (ix) information, to commit the crime.

Finally, a corporation may incur criminal liability through membership of a criminal organisation: clause 140 of the DCC criminalises membership of an organisation which has the aim (*oogmerk*) of committing criminal acts. Pursuant to case law, it is not required that the defendant actively participated in the

[10] HR 26 April 2016, ECLI:NL:HR:2016:733, NJ 2016/375.

commission of crimes. Nor is there any *mens rea* (i.e. intent) required on the part of the defendant that any *specific* crimes would be committed. It is sufficient that the suspect knew that the organisation committed crimes, and that the defendant was a member of the organisation and that it had materially contributed to fulfilling the organisation's purposes.

III. Civil liability

When looking at civil liability for corporate human rights violations abroad, a number of procedural issues and possible complications arise. First, international private law will normally appoint the foreign law as the applicable law to the case. Secondly, if the case involves a foreign company—for example a subsidiary or chain partner—the rules on jurisdiction may point towards a foreign forum. These procedural issues are briefly discussed below , before the substantive grounds for liability under Dutch law are further explored.

It should be kept in mind that—like most jurisdictions—Dutch corporate law acknowledges the separate entity doctrine. This means that in principle, a parent company cannot be held liable for the actions or omissions of its subsidiary. Options for piercing the corporate veil are extremely limited and not usually available in cases concerning human rights. As a consequence, cases pertaining to parent company responsibility have focused on direct liability through the actions and omissions of the parent company itself. This will also be the focus of the legal framework discussed in this chapter.

A. Applicable law

As a rule, civil cases concerning foreign liability against Netherlands-based companies will not be governed by Dutch law, but by the law of the country where the damage occurs. This general rule is expounded in the Rome II convention. On the basis of Article 10:159 of the DCC, the same rule applies to cases not governed by the Rome II regulation. There is no specific Dutch law dealing with the responsibility of Netherlands-based (parent) companies.

There are some exemptions to this basic rule. Parties may, also on the basis of (Article 14 of) the Rome II regulation, agree on the application of a different system of law. It can be expected that each party in litigation will first explore which legal system he considers more opportune for the case.

On the basis of Article 4 (section 3) of the Rome II regulation, which is also incorporated in Article 10:8 of the DCC for cases to which the Rome regulation does not apply, the law of another jurisdiction is applicable when based on all the circumstances of the case it is clear that the unlawful act is manifestly more closely connected to that jurisdiction as opposed to the jurisdiction of the country where the damage occurred or where both parties have their habitual residence.

Finally, pursuant to Article 7 of the Rome II regulations, claimants in a case involving environmental damage may also choose to base their claim on the law of the State where the events occurred that gave rise to the damage.

Following Article 10:6 of the DCC and Article 26 of the Rome II Regulation, foreign law will not be applied if this application leads to a situation that is contrary to Dutch public order ('public order exception'). One may think of legislation that embodies a form of discrimination or child abuse. The provision, however, is only applied in exceptional circumstances. As will be discussed in section VI, this includes the question as to what types of damages can be awarded.

B. Jurisdiction

Dutch courts have international jurisdiction if this follows from legislation or if the parties have selected a Dutch court as the forum for their disputes. The most important set of rules in this regard is included in the Regulation (EU) No. 1215/2012 of the European Parliament and of the Council of 12 December 2012 on jurisdiction and the recognition and enforcement of judgments in civil and commercial matters (Brussels I-bis regulation). If this regulation (or any other international rule on jurisdiction) is not applicable, then Articles 1–14 of the Dutch Code of Civil Procedure (DCCP) apply. This will be the case for example as regards a foreign subsidiary based outside the European Union.

Pursuant to both the Brussels I-bis regulation and the DCCP, a Dutch court has jurisdiction with regard to claims against Netherlands-based companies. The principle of *forum non conveniens* is not accepted as a principle of Dutch law (except for certain matters in family law that are irrelevant in this context).

Article 7 DCCP states that a Dutch judge also has jurisdiction in cases against foreign defendants if these cases are so closely connected that for reasons of efficiency they should be dealt with together. Unlike Article 8 of the Brussels I-bis regulation, Article 7 DCCP does not explicitly require that 'it is expedient to hear and determine [the cases] together to avoid the risk of irreconcilable judgments resulting from separate proceedings'. In practice, Dutch courts may take this factor into account, in addition to other relevant indications such as whether the cases against the different defendants are based on the same facts and/or legal grounds.

In the *Milieudefensie* case Shell argued that (i) the cases against the Dutch parent company and the Nigerian subsidiary SPDC were not sufficiently connected to allow the Dutch court to assume jurisdiction on the basis of Article 7 DCCP, and that (ii) claimants abused procedural law by suing the Dutch parent company with the alleged purpose of establishing jurisdiction as regards its Nigerian subsidiary (SPDC), while the case against the parent company—according to Shell—was evidently ill founded. As a consequence, Shell argued, the claim against the parent company could not serve as an 'anchor claim' for the purpose of applying Article 7 DCCP. Both arguments were dismissed by the District Court and subsequently by the Court of Appeal when they assumed jurisdiction over both defendants.[11] Similarly, in *Kiobel v. Shell* the court asserted that it had jurisdiction over RDS and SPNV both based in the Netherlands and also over STTC (an English company) and SPDC based on the connectedness between the claims since they referred to the same factual situation.[12]

Article 9 DCCP adds as a ground for jurisdiction either a tacit choice of forum (Article 9a) or the principle of *forum necessitates*. The latter applies when no jurisdiction can be established based on the Articles 2–8 DCCP and it is shown that a procedure outside the Netherlands is impossible (Article 9b) or when a case is sufficiently linked to the Dutch legal sphere and it is unacceptable to require the claimant to submit its case to a judge of a foreign State (Article 9c).

C. Article 6:162 DCC

There is no procedural distinction under Dutch law between claims arising out of human rights violations and those founded in tort or delict. The basic provision of relevance for civil liability for an unlawful act is Article 6:162 DCC, which states in its first paragraph that "a person who commits a tortious (unlawful) act against another person that can be attributed to him must repair the damage that this other person has suffered as a result thereof". Pursuant to the second paragraph of article 6:162 DCC, a tortious act in this regard can be a violation of (i) someone else's right (entitlement), or an act or omission in violation of (ii) a duty imposed by law or of (iii) what according to unwritten law has to be regarded as proper social conduct, insofar as there was no justification for this behaviour. The third paragraph clarifies that a tortious act can be attributed to the tortfeasor (the person committing the unlawful act) if it results from his fault or from a cause for which he is accountable by virtue of law or generally accepted principles.

In addition, Article 6:163 DCC incorporates the Schutznorm theory: the standard breached must serve to protect against damage such as that suffered by the claimant.

In order to bring a claim based on a tort/wrongful act successfully, a claimant must thus prove that he has suffered damage as a consequence of the wrongful act

[11] *Dooh & Milieudefensie v. Shell*, Court of Appeal The Hague 18 December 2015, ECLI:NL:GHDHA:2015:3586, see footnote 2 above. See more elaborately in this issue: Roorda, *Jurisdiction over foreign direct liability claims against transnational corporations in EU Member States, Increasing access to remedy for victims of corporate human rights violations* (diss. Utrecht University, 2019) pp. 150–2.

[12] District Court The Hague 1 May 2019, ECLI:NL:RBDHA:2019:4233 (*Kiobel v. Shell*).

committed by a person or company, and it must be established that the tortious act is attributable to the perpetrator. The wrongful act can be rooted either in a violation of a right, a duty or of 'proper social conduct'. Each of these categories can be relevant in a transnational case concerning human rights violations and therefore each will be briefly discussed. It should be noted that in practice, no strict distinction can be drawn between these categories and case law often does not clarify under which of these categories an unlawful act should be categorised exactly.

i. The violation of someone else's right

The first category includes most importantly the specific rights and entitlements that are provided by the law, such as employment, consumer, or property rights. In addition, fundamental rights as safeguarded in the constitution or international treaties may also be brought under this category to the extent that their horizontal application has been recognised by the Dutch courts. As has been pointed out earlier, as a consequence of the Dutch monistic approach, international treaties are directly applicable in the Dutch legal order and even trump national legislation in hierarchy. These international norms can be directly relied upon legally to the extent that they create specific rights for individuals. Case law shows that this is the case particularly in relation to the right to private life and equal treatment.

ii. An act or omission in violation of a duty imposed by law

An act or omission in violation of a statutory duty also amounts to tort on the basis of Article 6:162 DCC if that act or omission results in harm. Most duties relevant in this respect will mainly regard the domestic activities of a company, such as its duties as an employer, duties arising from environmental licenses, etc.

The Netherlands has recently seen the establishment of a new category of statutory duty that is relevant to a company's activities abroad: in 2019, the Child Labour Due Diligence Law was adopted by the Senate. This law is elaborated below; at this stage it suffices to point out that whereas the law adopts a specific legal complaint regime granting the Dutch regulatory authorities the power to investigate and fine companies, the duties encompassed in the regulation can also give rise to a civil claim on the basis of Article 6:162 DCC.

Besides statutory duties incorporated in Dutch legislation, it has been established that the violation of statutory norms of foreign origin may also constitute an unlawful act for the purpose of Article 6:162 DCC.[13]

iii. Proper social conduct

Finally, a corporation in the Netherlands may be liable for acting contrary to 'proper social conduct'. What is considered proper social conduct can be influenced

[13] *Interlas*, HR 24 November 1989, NJ 1992, 404.

by fundamental rights and soft law instruments, for example. It has been established that under certain circumstances, a party may have an obligation to prevent another party from suffering harm and/or to remedy such harm.[14] The basis for this obligation was laid down in the Dutch *Kelderluik* (cellar hatch) judgment, wherein the Supreme Court held that an employee of the Coca-Cola Corporation (and through him the corporation itself) was liable for the harm inflicted on the visitor of an Amsterdam-based café who fell into a cellar hatch that was left open and unattended by the Coca-Cola employee.[15] The Supreme Court found that the employee had acted negligently and in doing so took into account (i) the likelihood of inattentive or careless behaviour of visitors; (ii) the likelihood that this may lead to accidents; (iii) the severity of the consequences of such accidents; and (iv) the burden of adequate precautions. In brief, the higher the likelihood of accidents or harm and the lower the burden of precautionary measures, the more likely it is that a duty of care can be established. The same principles are still applied nowadays including in cases related to corporate responsibility.

An example of the application of these principles in the context of imposing a duty of care on corporations is the Dutch *Eternit* case, which dealt with liability for exposure to asbestos. The Supreme Court considered that 'from the moment when companies such as Eternit can be deemed to have known that working with asbestos posed health dangers, they had an increased duty of care to protect the interests of those in the immediate vicinity of a place where asbestos was being used'. The measures they could have been expected to take depended on the circumstances of the case and the knowledge that existed at the time. The court found it 'highly reproachable' that Eternit had not warned the public of the risks associated with asbestos. Interestingly, this also led the Supreme Court to conclude that Eternit could not rely on the statute of limitations (which would leave the claim time barred) as this would be contrary to the principle of reasonableness and fairness.

Generally speaking, the question asked under this provision is what may, in the specific circumstances, be expected of a (natural or legal) person acting reasonably. For this assessment, the specific expertise or industry of that person must be taken into account. These principles can also be applied to cases where the harm was not inflicted directly (such as in the case of a parent company or supply chain) if, for example, the (legal) person was instrumental to that harm occurring or in a unique position to prevent it.[16]

In order to establish what must be regarded as proper social conduct, reference may be made to industry norms or to soft law provisions such as the Organisation for Economic Co-operation and Development (OECD) Guidelines

[14] See also I. Giesen, E. de Jong, and M. Overheul, 'How Dutch Tort Law Responds to Risks', pp. 165–93 in M. Dyson (ed.), *Regulating Risk through Private Law* (2018).

[15] *Kerlderluik*, HR 5 November 1965, NJ 1966, 136.

[16] See A.G. Huydecooper for the Supreme Court, 25 November 2005, ECLI:NL:HR:2005:AU4019, NJ 2009/550, m.nt. P.B. Hugenholtz *(Lycos/Pessers)*, para. 46.

for Multinational Enterprises and the UN Guiding Principles on Business and Human Rights, although in existing case law the latter instruments appear to have been of limited value. An early example however can be found in the *Batco* judgment, wherein the court of appeal referred to the OECD Guidelines, among other sources, to conclude that a corporation had acted unlawfully.[17]

D. (Child Labour) Due Diligence Law

The Netherlands has recently seen the establishment of a new category of (not strictly civil) statutory duty which is relevant to a company's activities abroad: in 2019, a new law introducing a duty of care to prevent child labour was adopted by the Dutch Senate. The *Wet Zorgplicht Kinderarbeid* (Child Labour Due Diligence Law) requires companies to investigate whether there is a 'reasonable suspicion' that child labour occurs in their operations or in their supply chain and to set out a plan of action to prevent or combat it. Companies are obliged to submit a statement to the appointed Dutch regulatory authority twice a year describing the steps they have taken. This applies not only to companies registered in the Netherlands but also to foreign companies that deliver their products or services to the Dutch market twice or more often a year. The regulator publishes the corporate due diligence statements in an online public register. If there is evidence that goods or services have been produced with child labour, a third party complaint can be filed with the Dutch regulatory authorities on the basis of this law. The authorities may impose a fine of up to €4,350 for failure to produce the required declaration on applying due care to avoid child labour or a fine of up to €870,000 or 10 per cent of annual revenue for a failure to comply with the due diligence duties. In addition, violation of the duties encompassed in the law could give rise to a civil claim on the basis of Article 6:162 DCC. The law is yet to enter into force (expected in 2022) but may be confidently anticipated by companies and even courts.

In 2021, members of parliament proposed a new law encompassing a general duty of care as well as specific due diligence obligations for multinational corporations.[18] The draft law is currently pending in parliament, while initiatives have also been taken on an EU-level[19] and the Dutch minister for Foreign Trade and

[17] See however the *Batco* case, wherein reference was made to the OECD Guidelines, Ondernemingskamer Amsterdam, 21 June 1979, NJ 1980, 71. See for an extensive examination of the UN Guiding Principles under Dutch law L. Enneking, F. Kristen, T. Pijl, et al., *Zorgplichten Van Nederlandse Ondernemingen Inzake Internationaal Maatschappelijk Verantwoord Ondernemen* (2015).

[18] *Wetsvoorstel verantwoord en duurzaam internationaal ondernemen*: <https://www.tweedekamer.nl/kamerstukken/wetsvoorstellen/detail?cfg=wetsvoorsteldetails&qry=wetsvoorstel%3A35761> (in Dutch) accessed 13 July 2020.

[19] European Parliament resolution of 10 March 2021 with recommendations to the Commission on corporate due diligence and corporate accountability (2020/2129(INL)), <https://www.europarl.europa.eu/doceo/document/TA-9-2021-0073_EN.html>, accessed 13 July 2020.

Development Cooperation has announced possible national legislation depending on the pace of EU-developments.[20]

E. Alternative legal grounds

In addition to liability for an unlawful act on the basis of 6:162 DCC, the provisions in the DCC deal with several specific grounds for liability, such as vicarious liability for an employee (Article 170 DCC), liability of the possessor of dangerous substances (Article 6:175 DCC), liability for the operator of mining activities (Article 6:177 DCC), and product liability (Article 6:186 DCC).

An alternative road to hold Netherlands-based companies accountable for human rights violations abroad can also be found in the EU Unfair Commercial Practices Directive,[21] as transposed in Article 6:193a to Article 6:193t DCC. The law provides that traders (i.e. companies) act unlawfully against a consumer when they engage in unfair commercial practices. A practice is considered unfair when 'it is contrary to the requirements of professional diligence' and noticeably limits or may limit the ability of an average consumer to make an informed decision, which results or may result in a decision that the consumer would otherwise not have made. Of particular relevance to this topic is Article 6:193g DCC, which determines that under all circumstances a commercial practice is misleading (and, by virtue of Article 6:193b DCC, unfair) when a corporation claims to be bound by a code of conduct and claims to act accordingly while this is not the case.

In a context where a regulatory framework for business and human rights is largely absent and soft law and voluntary codes of conduct prevail, this law potentially provides an unconventional way to hold human rights violators accountable. This path has been discussed by Vytopil and Verburg in the Dutch context and is being put to the test in a recent collective action of Stichting Diesel Emissions Justice against Daimler (the manufacturer of Mercedes-Benz).[22] A claim on this

[20] Minister for Foreign Trade and Development Cooperation, letter to parliament, 11 February 2021, <https://www.rijksoverheid.nl/binaries/rijksoverheid/documenten/kamerstukken/2021/02/11/kamerbrief-inzake-voortgang-uitvoering-beleidsnota-van-voorlichten-tot-verplichten/kamerbrief-inzake-voortgang-uitvoering-beleidsnota-van-voorlichten-tot-verplichten.pdf>, (in Dutch) accessed 13 July 2020.

[21] Directive 2005/29/EC of the European Parliament and of the Council of 11 May 2005 concerning unfair business-to-consumer commercial practices in the internal market and amending Council Directive 84/450/EEC, Directives 97/7/EC, 98/27/EC, and 2002/65/EC of the European Parliament and of the Council and Regulation (EC) No. 2006/2004 of the European Parliament and of the Council (Unfair Commercial Practices Directive).

[22] A.L. Vytopil and F.M. Verburg, 'Aansprakelijkheid in verband met "greenwashing" Over oneerlijke handelspraktijken en wettelijk (on)verplichte MVO-verklaringen' (2017) 2 Tijdschrift voor Vennootschapsrecht, Rechtspersonenrecht en Ondernemingsbestuur (*TvOB)* 46; Writ of summons Stichting Diesel Emissions Justice against Daimler A.G., registered in the central register for collective actions, available at <https://www.rechtspraak.nl/SiteCollectionDocuments/dagvaarding-collectieve-vordering-Daimler-AG-c.pdf>, accessed 20 April 2021.

basis can only be made on behalf of consumers and not the victims of the human rights violations abroad. A major opportunity in this regard – particularly in view of the limited disclosure in Dutch legal procedure, which will be described later in this chapter – is provided for by Article 6:193j DCC. This article entails a reversal of the burden of proof, meaning that the trader has the burden of proof for the material correctness and completeness of the information he has provided. This reversal is allowed when deemed appropriate considering the circumstances of the case and taking into account the legitimate interest of all parties to the proceedings. If this article is applied, the corporation must substantiate its claims that it acts in accordance with its own code of conduct.[23]

F. Direct reliance on the ECHR

The ECHR is of great importance in the Dutch legal order . The Supreme Court has ruled that 'pursuant to articles 93 and 94 of the Dutch Constitution, Dutch courts must apply every provision of the ECHR that is binding on all persons'.[24] Since the ECHR is directly applicable in the Dutch legal order this means that Dutch courts have the obligation to apply the ECHR in accordance with the case law of the European Court of Human Rights (ECtHR). This stands in contrast to Article 120 Dutch Constitution that prohibits courts from testing the constitutionality of laws. Thus, whereas a legal party in the Netherlands cannot rely on the constitution to set aside legislation that infringes on fundamental (constitutionally protected) rights, it may ask the court to do so on the basis of the ECHR. In the *Urgenda* case the Supreme Court directly applied the rights and obligations pursuant to the ECHR.[25] In proceedings between private parties the ECHR only has an indirect horizontal effect, although it is nonetheless an important one. Many scholars suggest that ECHR rights can have effect via unwritten law in establishing what proper social conduct is. In case law the distinction between direct application or via unwritten law is often not explicitly made.

IV. Collective action

Cases concerning human rights violations usually affect a large number of people. Under Dutch law, these cases can be brought as grouped individual cases or through a collective action. In the first circumstance, practical complications can be overcome either through the instruction of a joint lawyer or through the

23 Ibid., 51.
24 Supreme Court 20 December 2019, ECLI:NL:HR:2019:2007, para. 5.6.1.
25 Supreme Court 20 December 2019, ECLI:NL:HR:2019:2007, para. 5.8.

assignment of the individual claims to a specific (legal) person. However, since formally it remains a group of individual claims and thus cases, each claim, with its particular circumstances, must still be proved individually. Alternatively, a foundation or association can bring a collective action based on Article 3:305a DCC. This law has recently seen some important changes.

The Collective Action Act (*Wet Collectieve Aansprakelijkheid*, Dutch acronym WCA), established in 1994, introduced Article 3:305a DCC and therewith created the possibility for organisations to bring claims on behalf of the interests of other people. Its successor, the Collective Settlement of Mass Damage Act (Dutch acronym: WCAM), came into force in 2005 and allowed for amicable collective settlements to be declared binding on all persons that suffered damage.[26] As of 1 January 2020, the Collective Redress of Mass Damages Act (Dutch acronym WAMCA) took effect. This act amends Article 3:305a DCC and introduces additional substantive and procedural rules. With the WAMCA the legislator aimed to fill a lacuna in the existing collective action framework and to solve several issues that emerged in legal practice in relation to the WCAM. As the WAMCA has only recently taken effect, it has not been the subject of much case law and the focus hereafter will therefore be mainly on the text of the new law. That said, the previous provision and the cases based on it will provide a valuable basis for the interpretation of the new legislation.

Under both the old and the new law, Article 3:305a DCC allows for a representative (collective) action by a foundation or association either on behalf of a group of people and/or on behalf of a public interest, such as the environment. Under the old law, organisations acting in a representative capacity could not claim damages; they would instead claim a declaration of law, which would form the basis of either a settlement or a separate procedure on damages for the people directly affected. Under the new law this has changed, and damages may now be claimed on behalf of those people by the foundation or association acting in a representative capacity. It is likely that as a consequence, the popularity of collective actions, as opposed to grouped claims, will increase.

A. Admissibility in the *Milieudefensie* and *Trafigura* cases

In the cases of *Milieudefensie v. Shell*, Milieudefensie, on behalf of the locally affected people and in the interest of a clean environment, applied for an injunction and a declaration of law on the basis of Article 3:305 DCC. In addition, several Nigerians who had been affected by the oil spills brought their claims on

[26] W.H. Van Boom and C.M.D.S. Pavillon, 'The Netherlands Takes Collective Redress to a Next Level—An Introduction to the Collective Redress of Mass Damages Act 2019' (2019/04) *Verbraucherrecht (VbR)* 133–7.

an individual basis. In its 2015 interim judgment, the Court of Appeal confirmed that Milieudefensie could pursue the case in a representative capacity.[27] The Court of Appeal rejected Shell's position that the question as to who can commence a collective action on behalf of others is an issue of substantive (applicable) law. It held that the question of whether, and if so to what extent and in which manner, a claim can be brought as a collective action in the Netherlands is to be determined by Dutch law. The same reasoning on the admissibility of a representative organisation based on Article 3:305a DCC was applied in the *Trafigura* case.[28]

Article 3:305a DCC as it was then required that an organisation acting in a representative capacity had to be a foundation or an association with full legal capacity. Moreover, the articles of association had to make it clear that the organisation advocates the specific interests of those it represents in the collective action. Furthermore, it had to be established that the organisation protects the similar interests of other persons. In assessing these requirements in the *Milieudefensie* case, the Court of Appeal held that the condition to protect similar interests of other persons is met

> if the interests that the action seeks to protect are suitable to be joined, so that an efficient and effective safeguarding of legal rights can be promoted for the benefit of the interested parties. In this manner the matters in dispute and claims advanced in the proceedings can be reviewed in one action, without having to take into consideration the special circumstances of the interested parties individually.[29]

In the *Trafigura* case the Court of Appeal added that if the representative organisation does not only represent the similar interests of a defined group of individuals but also a general public interest in protection of the rights of a much larger group of undefined people, it can meet the requirement of similar interest.[30] The Supreme Court has held that for environmental interests the bundling of interest in an action by a representative organisation is particularly efficient and effective.[31]

The Court of Appeal in the *Milieudefensie* case also dismissed Shell's argument that the interests of the persons represented were allegedly not 'sufficiently safeguarded', considering that this condition 'is meant to serve as a handle for the critical assessment of admissibility in those cases where the motives for instituting a class action are in doubt. This prevents claims that organizations could abuse the right to start a class action for their own commercial motives.'[32] Remarkably, in the

[27] Court of Appeal The Hague 18 December 2015, ECLI:NL:GHDHA:2015:3586, para. 4.2. See also footnote 3.
[28] Court of Appeal Amsterdam 14 April 2020, ECLI:NL:GHAMS:2020:1157, para. 3.17.
[29] Court of Appeal The Hague 18 December 2015, ECLI:NL:GHDHA:2015:3586, para. 4.4.
[30] Court of Appeal Amsterdam 14 April 2020, ECLI:NL:GHAMS:2020:1157, para. 3.19.
[31] Supreme Court 20 December 2019, ECLI:NL:HR:2019:2007.
[32] Court of Appeal The Hague 18 December 2015, ECLI:NL:GHDHA:2015:3586, para. 4.4.

Trafigura case the Court of Appeal considered it not an unacceptable commercial motive that third party funders would receive up to three times their initial investment upon a successful resolution of the case.[33] Finally, the Court of Appeal also held that it was not required for Milieudefensie under Article 3:305a DCC to work or to be established in the respective area and that Milieudefensie's campaigning activities did not stand in the way of its admissibility.[34]

B. The new Act on collective damages in class actions

The purpose of the new provision is to facilitate the efficient and effective collective redress of mass damage.[35] Its aim is not to alter the substantive law of torts and damages.[36] For now, both the WCAM and WCA remain in effect: the new Article 3:305a DCC is applicable to cases where the unlawful act occurred on or after 15 November 2016, whereas the old Article 3:305a DCC still applies to unlawful acts preceding this date.

As under the old law, the first section of Article 3:305a DCC (new) requires (i) an association or foundation, (ii) which—following its articles of association, advocates for the specific interests of those it represents in the collective action, thereby (iii) protecting the similar interests of other persons. In addition, the new law embodies stricter conditions as regards governance, financing, and representativeness. The government has indicated that these additional requirements should provide the judge the opportunity to examine the suitability of the collective interest organisation thoroughly.[37] Contrary to the previous law, Article 3:305a DCC now explicitly requires that the organisation be 'sufficiently representative' and the interests they represent 'sufficiently guaranteed'.[38]

Following the second section of Article 3:305a DCC, interests are 'sufficiently guaranteed' when the legal person is 'sufficiently representative of the potential beneficiaries and the proportion of represented claims' and when, in addition, several additional criteria are met. These criteria are listed in (a) to (e) of that section and demand that the representative organisation has a supervisory board; a mechanism for the represented individuals to participate in the decision-making process; sufficient means to commence proceedings; an accessible website where among others the articles of association, the management structure, the board minutes, and year reports are available; and sufficient experience and expertise to

33 Court of Appeal Amsterdam 14 April 2020, ECLI:NL:GHAMS:2020:1157, para. 3.28.
34 Court of Appeal The Hague 18 December 2015, ECLI:NL:GHDHA:2015:3586, para. 4.4.
35 *Kamerstukken II* 2016-17, 34608, nr. 3 (MvT), p. 1.
36 Ibid.
37 Ibid., p. 7.
38 Article 3:305a sub 1 DDC.

carry out the proceedings.[39] Section 5 moreover requires the publication of minutes and financial statements.

On the basis of section 6, a judge can exempt an organisation from these additional admissibility requirements if the purpose of the claim is idealistic (e.g. an injunction) and the financial interest is limited, or 'if the nature of the claim gives rise to such exemption', provided that the claim does not entail compensation in the form of damages. This is again an undefined norm that leaves its application largely to the judiciary; it has yet to be determined what kind of claims may give rise to this exemption.[40]

The third section of 3:305a DCC lists additional admissibility requirements that remain applicable regardless of the nature of the claim. First, it is stated that directors and founders of the organisation acting in a representative capacity cannot have a direct or an indirect financial motive. More complications could arise from the second, newly worded requirement, which says that there needs to be a sufficiently close link with the Dutch legal sphere. This condition, section 3b states, is met when the majority of represented persons live in the Netherlands, or the defendant has its seat in the Netherlands *and* there are additional circumstances which indicate a sufficiently close link with the Netherlands, or the unlawful act occurred in the Netherlands. It follows that, contrary to the general rules on jurisdiction including the Brussels I-bis regulation, the defendant having its statutory seat in the Netherlands does not in itself indicate a sufficiently close link with the Dutch legal sphere for the purpose of filing a collective action. In fact, it has been suggested during the parliamentary debates that the requirement entails an illicit limitation of the Brussel 1-bis regulation.[41] The new condition can be of particular relevance in cases dealing with international human rights violations. For now, it remains to be seen how the courts will deal with this largely undefined criterion. However, from the wording alone, Article 3:305a DCC (new) appears to create additional complications for collective actions concerning international human rights violations that are not aimed at obtaining financial compensation, rather than alleviating them.[42]

Following section 7 of the provision, a public, central register has been created where representative organisations have to register new collective actions. This is connected to a range of new procedural requirements introduced with WAMCA

[39] In the *Trafigura* case, based on the old provision, the Court of Appeal clarified that the requirement of expertise can be met by acquiring knowledge on the subject or by reliance on experts. Whether this holds under the new provision is uncertain, but it seems reasonable.

[40] The case of two foundations (Stop Online Shaming and Expertise Agency Online Child Abuse) against the operator of a pornographic website provides one of the first examples of the application of section 6. District Court of Amsterdam 28 October 2020, ECLI:NL:RBAMS:2020:5271, 5.1–5.10.

[41] *Kamerstukken II* 2016-17, 34608, nr.3 (MvT).

[42] See for example: District Court of Rotterdam, 18 September 2020, ECLI:NL:RBROT:2020:8228 *(Both ENDS v. Royal Boskalis).* The strict interpretation of the Rotterdam court was not followed by other courts to date.

in the DCCP. For a period of three months after the registration, other organisations can bring collective actions based on the same wrongful act (1018c sub 2 and 3 DCCP).[43] When multiple representative organisations commence collective actions based on the same wrongful act, a judge appoints the most suitable among them as the Exclusive Representative (1018c sub 1 DCCP). In doing so the judge considers the size of the represented group of people, their financial interests, other work the representative organisations have done for the represented people, and previous work or collective actions of the representative organisation (1018e DCCP). Representative organisations may thus have to compete to bring a collective action.

Another hurdle that could arise is that the representative organisation needs to show that on balance the collective action is more efficient and effective than individual claims because (i) the factual and legal questions are sufficiently common between the individuals whose interests are being sought to be protected, (ii) there is a sufficiently high number of people whose interests are protected by the claim, and (iii) the value of the claim is sufficiently high if financial compensation is sought (1018c sub 5 DCCP). If the court cannot establish that these requirements are fulfilled, the case will be dismissed. This not only means that the case will not be dealt with on its merits but it also encompasses a big financial risk for the organisation that has brought the collective claim: if on the face of it a claim appears unsound, the judge can award the defendant up to five times his legal costs, unless this would be not equitable (1018l sub 1 DCCP). Looking at Shell's litigation strategy in the *Milieudefensie* case, which sought to get the case dismissed on a numerous procedural grounds, the possibility that corporations will try to use this provision to get cases struck out and deter organisations from bringing collective claims cannot be excluded.[44] That said, the new law may also present an opportunity for these organisations since it allows for compensation claims and it enables the judge to award the real legal costs to the winning side, instead of the fraction thereof that would be awarded under the standardised norms usually applied (1018l sub 2 DCCP).[45]

In conclusion, for non-financial ('idealistic') claims, the new regime provides some opportunities but also quite a few potential hurdles, both from a financial (risk) and a procedural perspective. Since the aim of the legislator has clearly been to facilitate 'idealistic' claims, it will be up to the courts to ensure that the new law cannot be used as another tool by corporations to block access to justice for the victims of human rights violations abroad.

[43] The central register is available online at <https://www.rechtspraak.nl/Registers/centraal-register-voor-collectieve-vorderingen> accessed 20 April 2021.
[44] See subsections III.B and IV.A.
[45] See also subsection VIII.A.

V. Limitation

The Rome II regulation determines that the applicable law to a claim is also the law that determines the question of limitation of that claim.[46] This is also a fundamental principle of Dutch private international law.[47] As discussed in subsection III.A, this often results in the law where the unlawful acts were committed being the applicable law in the case of human rights violations of a MNC with victims abroad.[48]

When Dutch law is applicable Article 3:310 DCC contains the relevant provisions on limitation. A plea by the defendant that a claim is time-barred is considered an absolute defence in the Netherlands. The principal limitation period is five years. This period starts the day after the injured person is aware of the damage and the identity of the perpetrator. A claim expires regardless of the 5-year period 20 years after the damage has occurred. For claims concerning damage caused by air, water, or soil pollution, dangerous substances, or by ground movements this period is extended to 30 years.[49]

Notwithstanding this provision, the Supreme Court has held that a party cannot successfully rely on the defence of statutory limitation if that would be unacceptable by standards of reasonableness and fairness. In the renowned case *Van Hese/De Schelde* the Supreme Court set out seven guiding principles in determining whether this is the case.[50] It stated that all circumstances of the case need to be considered and in particular:

(1) Whether the damages claimed are pecuniary or non-pecuniary, and in relation to this whether the damages would be to the benefit of the victims themselves, their heirs or a third party;
(2) The extent to which the victims or their heirs have a title to compensation of the damages on other grounds;
(3) The degree to which the defendant is culpable for the events;
(4) The extent to which the defendant, prior to the expiration of the limitation period, took account or should have taken account of the possibility of being liable for the damage;
(5) Whether the defendant reasonably still has the possibility to defend itself against the claim;
(6) Whether the liability is (still) covered by insurance;

[46] Asser/Vonken 10-I 2018/198.

[47] Conclusion Strikwerda for Supreme Court 19 November 1993, NJ 1994/622, ECLI:NL:HR:1993:ZC1148, para. 46.

[48] For example, in the case of *Milieudefensie v. Shell*, Nigerian law was held to be the applicable law and thus the Nigerian rules on limitation were applicable (District Court The Hague 1 July 2019, ECLI:NL:RBDHA:2019:6670, para. 4.47).

[49] Article 3:301 DCC section 2.

[50] Supreme Court 28 April 2000, ECLI:NL:HR:2000:AA5635, NJ 2000/430.

(7) Whether after the manifestation of the damage within a reasonable period a letter of liability was sent and a claim for damages was initiated.

In practice, this exception has been applied mainly in cases against the Dutch State. For example, in the case on behalf of the widows and children of men that had been executed in 1946 by the Dutch State in its former colony the Dutch East Indies, the Hague Court of Appeal concluded that the State's defence that the claim was statute barred was unacceptable based on standards of reasonableness and fairness.[51] Instead, the Court found, the limitation period started once the claimants were contacted by a non-governmental organization (NGO) about the matter in 2012. It reached its conclusion considering the extremely serious character of the unlawful act; the high degree of culpability of the State; the severe violations of human rights in the colonial war; the fact that under criminal law these types of severe war crimes and crimes against humanity do not have a limitation period; the fact that the State bears responsibility for not properly documenting the violations; and that the plaintiffs did not have practical access to justice due to their legal, economic, cultural, social and political position.[52]

The limitation period of Article 3:310 DCC can be halted through the institution of a legal action (Article 3:316 DCC) or through a letter or formal notice in which the claimant unambiguously reserves his right to institute such legal action (Article 3:317 DCC). The institution of a collective action on the basis of Article 3:305a DCC also interrupts the limitation period. An interesting correlation can occur in cases wherein a collective action is brought while foreign law applies. As we have seen in the previous section, under the old regime of Article 3:305a DCC damages could not be claimed. In the *Milieudefensie* case, Shell argued that the collective action of Milieudefensie could not halt the limitation for individual claimants, who would separately and individually have to apply for compensation of damages (governed by Nigerian law) after a declaration of law to Milieudefensie was granted. The Court in its final judgment put the relevance of this defence into perspective, while granting the declaration of law.[53]

VI. Damages

Under Dutch law, determining damage is part of establishing a tort. This can be dealt with in two phases. In phase one it must be established that damage has occurred as a consequence of the act or omission. For this purpose, the court assesses

[51] The Hague Court of Appeal 1 October 2019, ECLI:NL:GHDHA:2019:2524 (Children of executed men in Zuid-Sulawesi).
[52] Ibid.
[53] Court of Appeal The Hague 29 January 2021, ECLI:NL:GHDHA:2021:132 (*Oguru, Efanga & Milieudefensie v. Shell*), at 3.8, 5.28. See also footnote 2.

the plausibility of the damage. This plausibility is sufficient to grant a declaration of law or a (mandatory or prohibitory) injunction. In phase two, the concrete amount of damage is determined. This second phase can follow in a separate procedure. In more complex cases such as those concerning business and human rights, often a declaration of law concerning the unlawfulness of the act or omission is sought first, possibly with an injunction; if the case is successful, damages are then decided separately in either settlement negotiations or a damage assessment procedure.

(Full) damages and a declaration of law can only be granted in full, substantive procedures; in summary (preliminary relief) proceedings, plaintiffs can obtain an injunction as well as a so-called advance on damages. In practice, summary proceedings need not necessarily be followed by a full procedure.

The type of damages that can be recovered is a matter of substantive and therefore the applicable law. For international human rights violations that occurred abroad this means that more often than not foreign law applies.[54] However, as explained in subsection III.A, the application of a provision of foreign law may be precluded by the public order exception. Specifically, in view of the fact that Dutch tort law is considered to have a compensatory and not a punitive function, punitive damages have been found to be in contradiction with fundamental principles of the Dutch public order.

As a rule, damage under Dutch law is compensated in money. Pursuant to Article 6:103 DCC, the court may grant another kind of compensation than a sum of money at the request of the injured party. If expressed in terms of money, the principle in Dutch law is that damage should be determined concretely. If this cannot be done accurately, the damage may be estimated, which is also referred to as abstract calculation.

The DCC identifies as damage that has to be compensated 'material loss and other disadvantages, the latter as far as the law implies that there is an additional entitlement to a compensation for such damage'.[55] Material loss, following Article 6:96 DCC, includes losses suffered and lost profits. In addition, reasonable costs to prevent the damage, costs for determining the nature and scope of the damage and reasonable costs made in attempting to reach an out-of-court settlement also qualify for compensation as material loss.[56]

Non-pecuniary damages can be awarded (i) if damage was intentionally inflicted; (ii) if physical injury was incurred; (iii) if honour and reputation is injured; or (iv) if someone is 'harmed otherwise in person'; and finally (v) if the damage consists of harming the memory of a deceased person and that the deceased would have been entitled to damages if still alive.[57]

[54] See, for example, the *Milieudefensie* and *Trafigura* cases described above.

[55] Article 6:95 DCC.

[56] Article. 6:96 section 2 DCC.

[57] 6:106 DCC. Article translations by <http:www.dutchcivillaw.com>, accessed 20 April 2021. Prior to the introduction of the last category in 2019, the only available compensation for persons with a close affectionate relationship to the victim was so-called shock damage. This meant that the tort is also

The category of non-pecuniary damages for 'harm otherwise in person' relates to the impairment of quality of life. First of all, this covers mental injury. In order to claim damages on this basis, the psychological damage and its relation to the circumstances at hand must be objectively established.[58] In addition, the nature and seriousness of the norm violation and the consequences for the victim may also give rise to non-pecuniary damages on this basis. The violation of a fundamental right in itself is not considered 'harm otherwise in person'.[59]

Generally, non-pecuniary damages remain relatively low. The highest amounts of non-pecuniary damages concerning personality rights have been around €30,000 for graphic sexual content that was made publicly available to a large online audience or concerned public figures.[60] In cases of discrimination, the amounts often stay below €1,000.[61] In cases of damage resulting from shock the highest amounts awarded have been around €40,000 and concern the witnessing of murder.[62]

VII. Evidence

The basic rule under Dutch law is that the party who asserts a fact must prove it. This can be complicated in cases concerning foreign corporate liability, wherein relevant documentation is often in the hands of the corporation. In contrast to the extensive options concerning disclosure or discovery that exist in common law jurisdictions, Dutch law does not enable litigants to gain access to a wide range of possibly relevant documents preceding or during trial. While a party under Dutch law has a general obligation 'fully and truthfully' to disclose facts that are relevant to the case (Article 21 DCCP), this obligation is not clearly defined and there are often no consequences for failing to meet the obligation.[63] Instruments available to the Dutch litigant include a (preliminary) request for the disclosure of documents and (preliminary) witness hearings, which will be discussed below.

considered wrongful to the person with a close relationship to the victim who witnessed the tort and who is severely emotionally shocked by the tort or its direct consequences and as a result incurred psychological injury.

[58] Supreme Court 15 March 2019, ECLI:NL:HR:2019:376, para. 4.2.1.

[59] Ibid., para. 4.2.2.

[60] A.J. Verheij, 'De hoogte van smartengeld: een vergelijking tussen Nederland en Duitsland' (2019) *Smartengeldgids*.

[61] Ibid.

[62] Ibid.

[63] In the *Milieudefensie* case, the Court of Appeal concluded that Shell had acted in breach of its obligation to disclose fully and truthfully the relevant facts and to cooperate with the court-appointed experts investigating the cause of the leaks. As a consequence, the Court considered that any doubt as regards that cause came at the risk and expense of Shell. Court of Appeal The Hague, 29 January 2021, ECLI:NL:GHDHA:2021:133, at 5.28. See also footnote 2.

Dutch courts are not allowed to take into account facts or rights that have not been presented and adequately substantiated by one of the parties; only undisputed facts need not be further substantiated and must be treated as proved (Article 149 DCCP). There are no restrictions as to the types of evidence that can be used (including, for example, tape recordings, *de auditu* (or in common law terminology, hearsay) witness statements, expert statements, evidence acquired in a different jurisdiction). The courts are free in their assessment of such evidence, unless the law provides otherwise. In addition to expert reports submitted by a party, a court may also—at the request of a party or on its own motion—appoint an expert to provide an expert report on a specific matter.

A draft bill to modernise and simplify the law of evidence in civil procedure is currently pending.[64] This new law seeks to enhance the role of courts in the investigation of facts and introduces a broader obligation for both parties to disclose relevant information pre-trial. The law is expected to be beneficial for victims of corporate human rights violations, as it is a known and still too often successful strategy of corporations not to disclose any information in these cases. Since the draft law has not been adopted yet, the following paragraphs will discuss the situation as it currently is.

A. Rules on disclosure

A party can apply for the disclosure of specific documents if it has a legitimate interest to do so. A petition to this end can be filed either in summons or in a request to the court and either during or preceding the main case.[65] The legal basis is found in Article 843a DCCP, which states that the following cumulative conditions must be satisfied in order for such application to be granted:

(1) The requesting party must have a legitimate interest in obtaining the requested documents;
(2) The documents and their existence must be sufficiently determined;
(3) The documents must be in the possession of the other party or at his disposal; and
(4) The documents must concern a legal relationship to which the requesting party is a party.

[64] Wet Vereenvoudiging en modernisering bewijsrecht, available at <https://www.rijksoverheid.nl/documenten/rapporten/2020/06/08/tk-wet-vereenvoudiging-en-modernisering-bewijsrecht>, accessed 20 April 2021.

[65] Supreme Court 26 October 2018, ECLI:NL:HR:2018:1985, para. 3.3.2.

A petition on the basis of Article 843a DCCP may also be made on behalf of a party involved in or potentially pursuing litigation in a foreign jurisdiction.

The company does not have to comply with the demand when it has 'weighty' reasons not to or when it can reasonably be assumed that the administration of justice is guaranteed without disclosing the documents.

Milieudefensie v. Shell provides an example of how these criteria are brought into practice and what results the disclosure procedure can yield.[66] In this case the application to disclose documents was filed together with the main case and dealt with in an interlocutory judgment. Milieudefensie et al. petitioned the disclosure of a number of documents that would help substantiate their claims that the leakage of oil was not due to sabotage and that Shell had been negligent in maintenance and oversight. The District Court rejected the petition, stating that it was not convinced that the documents contained the evidence sought by the claimants. As a consequence the claimants were barred from such evidence, needed to substantiate their claim, even if it did exist. The Court of Appeal, however, later ordered the disclosure of the documents, albeit under strict conditions. Considering that expert investigation could provide a way to establish the cause of the leaks, it concluded that there was no reason to order the disclosure of documents relating to that matter.[67] It did order the disclosure of documents relating to the parent company control mechanisms and incident records. In view of Shell's argument that some documents contained confidential company information, the Court of Appeal ordered that a public notary's office should be selected where the documents would be deposed for inspection by the lawyers only. The use of information was limited to the current proceedings and no copies or pictures were allowed to be made.[68]

In addition to the Article 843a DCCP procedure, judges have the discretionary power to in all circumstances and at any moment in the procedure order a party to provide specific documentation concerning the case (Article 22 DCCP). This power can also be used in discovery proceedings based on Article 843a DCCP where, for example, the requirements of the latter provision are not met but the court considers it important to examine specific documents nonetheless.[69]

B. Witnesses and witness protection mechanisms

Besides an application for disclosure, evidence may stem from witness statements or witness hearings. Witness statements may be submitted in writing by a party (to

[66] Court of Appeal The Hague 18 December 2015, ECLI:NL:GHDHA:2015:3586, para. 6.1. e.v.
[67] Court of Appeal The Hague 18 December 2015, ECLI:NL:GHDHA:2015:3586, para. 6.4.
[68] Court of Appeal The Hague 18 December 2015, ECLI:NL:GHDHA:2015:3586, para. 6.11.
[69] Court of Appeal Amsterdam 16 July 2019, ECLI:NL:GHAMS:2019:2602, para. 2.4.

be assessed by the court as any other type of evidence) or be given during a witness hearing in court, either pre-trial or during the main trial.

Witnesses have a duty to appear in court and render a truthful testimony. If a witness does not appear, the court may issue a warrant for his or her arrest. In international cases, parties in practice depend on the voluntary cooperation of foreign witnesses as any such court order cannot be simply enforced internationally. Witnesses heard in court will have to take an oath or promise to tell the truth. They will usually be asked questions by the court and can be cross-examined by the other party. The assessment of the evidence they provide remains a matter of discretion for the court.

No explicit witness protection mechanisms are in place in the Netherlands in civil procedures. A court has several tools to protect the privacy of witnesses. In principle, court proceedings in the Netherlands are public and so are witness hearings. At the request of a party, the court may decide that a certain matter is heard 'behind closed doors' (Article 27 DCCP). This means that no members of the public are allowed and it is usually connected to a court order not to disclose the information that has been shared (Article 28 DCCP). Article 27 DCCP lists the exceptional circumstances that must apply to do so, including the interest of public order, State security, the privacy of minors or parties, or if a public hearing would seriously harm the proper instruction of justice.

As a hearing behind closed doors is considered a very far-reaching, highly exceptional measure, courts will often seek more pragmatic methods to protect the interests at stake. In the case of *Kiobel et al. v. Shell*, witnesses were heard about alleged bribery by Shell. These witnesses feared repercussions if it became public that they testified; some of them already having had to flee Nigeria during the events in 1995. The claimants thus submitted a request to the court to have these witnesses heard behind closed doors in order to protect their identity.[70] The court considered that the fear of repercussions was not sufficiently objective and concrete and that it could therefore not justify an exception to the fundamental rule of public access. The court did, however, issue an order prohibiting all those present during the testimony hearing from disclosing the names of the witnesses as well as the names mentioned by them in their testimonies. Other methods courts have used to protect the identity of witnesses have included placing them behind screens in court rooms—thus making them invisible—and using voice modulators.

[70] District Court The Hague 7 October 2019, ECLI:NL:RBDHA:2019:10511 (Witness hearing *Kiobel v. Shell*).

VIII. Legal costs and funding

Civil litigation is costly and complicated cases on foreign direct liability are not an exception to that rule. While court fees and legal costs in case of loss in the Netherlands are relatively low, lawyers' fees and other expenses such as travel and translation costs, and expert fees make such cases nonetheless expensive. This is further illustrated by the fact that the *Milieudefensie*-case has been pending for over 12 years. Funding, therefore, will always be an important issue when prospecting a case in the Netherlands or elsewhere.

A. Legal costs

Legal costs include court fees, bailiff costs, and lawyers' fees. The losing party is usually—at the request of the plaintiff—ordered to pay the legal costs of the opposing party.[71] For this purpose, the salary of the attorney is calculated on the basis of a fixed rate per procedural act performed in the case (such as a hearing, written arguments, etc.) and may be subject to a maximum cap depending on the size of the financial claim.[72] The bigger the financial interest at stake, the higher rate attorney's fee rate. The total amount awarded is usually substantially lower than the party's actual lawyers' fees. For instance, following the schedule that applies in 2021, the total amount granted for a case demanding a declaration of law (a matter of 'undetermined value') cannot exceed €3,378 for a case at the District Court and a similar amount for the Court of Appeal.

Court fees too are dependent on the size of the claim in question. For a case of 'undetermined value' at the District Court, the court fee in 2021 amounts to €6,67 for a legal person and €3,09 for a natural person. To natural persons with an income below a defined threshold an adjusted fee applies of €85 for claims for damages. The maximum court fee at a District Court in 2020 amounts to €4,200 for a 'non-natural (legal) person' and a claim exceeding €100,000.[73]

In so far as not already covered as legal costs, a party can also be ordered to pay reasonable costs made for the calculation of damages and reasonable costs made for extrajudicial settlement.[74] Depending on the proceedings, additional costs such as for producing evidence following Article 843a DCCP or (actual) costs related to experts or witness hearings, will also be part of the litigation costs.

[71] If a judgment rules partially against both parties, costs may also be awarded .

[72] de Rechtspraak, 'Liquidatietarief rechtbanken en gerechtshoven' (*de Rechtspraak*, 1 February 2021), <https://www.rechtspraak.nl/Voor-advocaten-en-juristen/Reglementen-procedures-en-formulieren/Civiel/paginas/liquidatietarief.aspx>, accessed 18 May 2021.

[73] For a full overview see <https://www.rechtspraak.nl/Naar-de-rechter/Kosten-rechtszaak/Griffierecht/Paginas/Griffierecht-civiel.aspx>, accessed 18 May 2021.

[74] Article 6:96 DCC.

As has been discussed in section IV, under the new procedural rules on collective damages in class actions the court has the power to award up to five times the defendant's attorneys fee if the court concludes that the claim appears unsound on the face of it. The law also enables the judge to award the real litigation costs to the winning side in a class action (1018l sub 2 DCCP). A similar option already existed in intellectual property cases.

B. Funding

Under the ethical rules applying to attorneys, law firms are not allowed to work on a 'no win, no fee' basis. The ban on doing so has been lifted temporarily for personal injury cases only. Alternative fee arrangements, such as a basic fee in combination with a bonus or uplift, are permitted.

Collective or individual claims in the sphere of business and human rights must thus be financed through an external party, which can be either the client/litigation party or a third party. An example of third party funding of a collective action was seen in the *Trafigura* case in which the Court of Appeal considered it not an unacceptable commercial motive that third party funders would receive up to three times their initial investment upon a successful result of the case.[75] Third party litigation funds have become increasingly common in the Netherlands, but less so in the sphere of (business and) human rights cases. This is probably related to the Dutch tradition of awarding only modest damages that has been discussed in section VI. As an alternative, funding may also be acquired through crowdfunding or charities.

Individuals with low income and property may apply for State-supported legal aid. It is not necessary for legal aid applicants to have Dutch nationality or live in the Netherlands. Hence, foreign victims of corporate human rights violations may also apply for legal aid, provided that their claim is sufficiently sound and connected to the Dutch legal sphere.[76] If legal aid is granted, they must pay a personal contribution (between €208 and €875 in 2021) towards legal costs as well as an adjusted court fee. They can choose any lawyer who is registered with the Legal Aid Board and willing to work on a legal aid (*pro bono*) basis. The Legal Aid Board normally awards a flat fee for each type of case based on an estimated average number of hours (expressed in points) that is notoriously low.[77] When the case is won and

[75] Court of Appeal Amsterdam 14 April 2020, ECLI:NL:GHAMS:2020:1157, para. 3.28.

[76] Obtaining legal aid for foreign applicants, however, has proven increasingly difficult in recent years.

[77] For a summons procedure regarding a tort claim the Legal Aid Board awards 11 points, which is equivalent to a total sum of €1,252 for up to 33 hours of legal work (€1,13.85 per point as of 1 January 2021). Only if cases are exceptionally complicated either from a factual or a legal perspective, a new application can then be made for the coverage of a limited number of extra hours.

more than roughly €15,000 for damages is granted, the legal aid will be withdrawn retroactively and must be repaid.

While the legal aid system clearly does not offer a commercially attractive incentive for lawyers to take up these kinds of cases, it has nonetheless shown to be of great importance in (international) human rights cases wherein funding is often lacking. It should be noted that legal aid does not cover additional costs that are often incurred in foreign corporate liability cases, such as costs for travel, translation, (legal) experts, etc., which makes it practically impossible to rely solely on legal aid in such cases.

IX. Conclusion

The Dutch legal order seems to provide a willing platform to hold multinational corporations to account, although a large part of the territory remains still to be explored. In terms of jurisdiction, claimants can be quite confident of having the opportunity to challenge the actions and omissions of Dutch corporations as well as, in their wake, foreign subsidiaries or possibly chain partners. Whether or not these companies will also be held liable may—depending on the case and the parties involved—be determined on the basis of Dutch or the applicable foreign law, which are all still being developed as far this issue is concerned. Generally speaking, the DCC offers sufficient possibilities to hold a corporation to account for negligence if it can be shown that it knew or should have known about a substantially dangerous situation abroad which it could but nevertheless failed to prevent, resulting in a violation of human (including environmental) rights or (other) damages. These actions may be brought by individuals or collectively and can also be brought by an NGO with the purpose of obtaining relief in the form of an injunction and/or damages.

In practice, there are still many hurdles to overcome however, including the gathering of evidence—in the absence of a regime comparable to discovery as in Anglo-Saxon countries—and funding, which remains a big challenge for these cases that are typically lengthy and complicated. Some of these complications will hopefully be more easily overcome with time when the boundaries of legal liability will be more firmly anchored and fewer legal uncertainties remain.

9

Human Rights Litigation against Multinational Companies in France

*Sandra Cossart and Lucie Chatelain**

I. Introduction

The last two decades have seen the advent of a new generation of human rights and environmental cases against multinational companies in France, on a variety of legal bases.

To a large extent, these legal actions are the result of the creativity of practitioners and human rights non-governmental organisations (NGOs), helped by some academics, who have developed new legal strategies and arguments to expose the current impunity of multinational companies under existing legal concepts. The development of strategic human rights and environmental litigation (understood here as 'litigation that pursues goals—or which concerns interests—that are broader than those of the immediate parties')[1] is relatively recent in France.

So far, many of these legal actions have encountered systemic and recurring obstacles throughout the litigation process—illustrating in particular, the difficulty of establishing the jurisdiction of French courts. Although none of these cases have yet led to a final, favourable judicial decision on the merits, some historic decisions have recently been reached, such as the indictment of the defendant company in the *Lafarge* case.[2]

Most importantly, these pioneering cases have exposed existing human rights and environmental violations committed by multinational companies and have shed light on the structural incapacity of existing legal mechanisms to tackle corporate impunity. These cases have been decisive in the adoption in 2017 of the French Law on the Duty of Vigilance, which requires large companies to take adequate measures to mitigate risks and prevent abuses within their value chains, failing which they may be held liable.[3] This law undeniably offers new avenues to

* The authors thank Léa Karila-Cohen for her help in preparing this chapter.

[1] H. Duffy, *Strategic Human Rights Litigation—Understanding and Maximising Impact* (2018).

[2] Sherpa, 'Lafarge indicted for complicity of crimes against humanity' (*Sherpa*, 28 June 2018) <https://www.asso-sherpa.org/landmark-decision-company-lafarge-indicted-complicity-in-crimes-against-humanity-included> accessed 18 November 2020

[3] Loi n°2017-399 du 27 mars 2017 relative au devoir de vigilance des sociétés mères et des entreprises donneuses d'ordre (Law on the Duty of Vigilance or LDV). accessed 22 April 2021.

Sandra Cossart and Lucie Chatelain, *Human Rights Litigation against Multinational Companies in France* In: *Human Rights Litigation against Multinationals in Practice*. Edited by: Richard Meeran, Oxford University Press.
 DOI: 10.1093/oso/9780198866220.003.0009

seek remedies for victims of corporate abuses, although it also raises a number of legal issues.

This chapter aims to provide an overview of some of the legal mechanisms that may be used to hold multinational companies liable in France for human rights and environmental violations committed by their subsidiaries or within their supply chains in other countries. It does not pretend to be a comprehensive exposition of the law in this area, rather it presents several important and distinctive legal features and their practical limitations in cases of transnational corporate abuses, and in so doing, it illustrates the need for legislative reform. The majority of the cases cited throughout have been initiated by Sherpa, a French non-profit organisation that seeks to fight corporate impunity and defend victims of economic crimes through legal innovation, strategic litigation, and advocacy.[4] This specific mandate probably explains why the organisation has been one of the few actors to initiate cases and to explore new legal grounds on these matters.

Section II describes some of the existing legal avenues under French law that have been or are being used in human rights and environmental litigation against companies. Section III details how the Law on the Duty of Vigilance may address some of the obstacles faced in these cases, creating new legal avenues and potentially improving access to justice. While this legal evolution is welcomed, it is insufficient, and section IV outlines some of the legal hurdles that still obstruct access to justice in such cases.

II. Overview of some existing legal avenues under French law

Different legal bases have been put forward to hold multinational companies accountable before French courts. This section focuses on the applicable legal regime and emblematic cases in criminal law (subsection II.A), consumer law (subsection II.B), tort law (subsection II.C), and labour law (subsection II.D).

A. Criminal law

Victims of corporate abuses and NGOs have relied on a number of offences provided in French criminal law, including complicity in torture, crimes against humanity, forced labour, endangerment, or concealment, filing criminal complaints against major corporate actors with French prosecuting authorities.[5]

[4] https://www.asso-sherpa.org/home accessed 22 April 2021.

[5] For an overview of these cases, see Directorate General for External Policies of the EU, 'Access to legal remedies for victims of corporate human rights abuses in third countries' (2019) European Parliament.

In addition to the difficulties in establishing the constitutive elements of these specific offences, the application of French criminal law to corporate abuses committed outside France raises some general legal issues, including the right of victims or NGOs to trigger criminal proceedings, the legal bases for extraterritorial jurisdiction of French criminal courts, and the criminal liability of corporations.

i. Rights of victims in criminal trials

First, an interesting feature of French criminal law relates to the recognition of the rights of victims and, to a certain extent, NGOs, in criminal proceedings.

In France, prosecutions are initiated and conducted by the prosecutor, on its own motion or following a complaint filed by a victim. Criminal procedural law however enables victims to play an important role in criminal proceedings, as 'civil parties'. This mechanism, called in French *plainte avec constitution de partie civile* (complaint with 'civil party' constitution, also known as 'criminal indemnification proceedings'), enables victims to trigger the appointment of an independent investigating judge in the event that the prosecutor decides not to proceed. Those victims may therefore access the investigation files and claim compensation during the criminal trial. This mechanism can often be crucial in sensitive cases, given the lack of independence of the prosecutor in the French legal system.

Notably, Sherpa's use of this mechanism has permitted the opening of formal investigations in the *Vinci* and *Samsung* cases[6]—amongst others—after the prosecutor had decided not to proceed.[7]

It has indeed been recognised by case law that NGOs may file such complaints on their own behalf[8] and, in parallel, the French legislature has enacted a number of specific provisions explicitly recognising the legal standing of NGOs to file complaints for certain offences, providing they meet certain conditions.[9] Granting NGOs legal standing seems particularly relevant when the direct victims may not be identified, may fear reprisals, or may not have the resources or the legal knowledge to file a complaint in France.

[6] See, on Sherpa's website, the chronology of the *Vinci*, Sherpa, 'FIFA World cup 2022: modern slavery in Qatar' (*Sherpa*) <https://www.asso-sherpa.org/modern-slavery-2> accessed 18 November 2020 and Sherpa, 'Samsung in China: an attack on the fundamental rights of workers' (*Sherpa*) <https://www.asso-sherpa.org/samsung-in-china-an-attack-on-the-fundamental-rights-of-workers> accessed 18 November 2020.

[7] P. Bienvault, 'Vinci dans le collimateur de la justice pour ses chantiers au Qatar' (*La Croix*, 26 February 2020) <www.la-croix.com/France/Vinci-collimateur-justice-chantiers-Qatar-2020-02-26-1201080619> accessed 1 June 2020; Le Monde avec AFP, 'Samsung Electronics France mis en examen pour "pratiques commerciales trompeuses"' (*Le Monde*, 3 July 2019) <www.lemonde.fr/police-justice/article/2019/07/03/la-filiale-francaise-de-samsung-mis-en-examen-pour-pratiques-commerciales-trompeuses_5484820_1653578.html> accessed 1 June 2020.

[8] Cass Crim 9 November 2010 09-88.272; Cass Crim 12 September 2006 05-86.958; Cass Civ 1 18 September 2008 06-22.038.

[9] Criminal Procedure Code, arts 2-1 to 2-24.

As explained below, this feature of French criminal law is, however, strictly limited in certain cases where extraterritorial jurisdiction is at issue. In addition, it has been challenged in recent cases, affecting the legal predictability of NGOs' legal actions in criminal matters.[10]

ii. Jurisdiction over offences committed overseas

Provisions on the criminal jurisdiction of French courts are decisive in cases of abuses committed by French companies in other countries. In those cases, it may indeed be crucial that the French courts accept jurisdiction over the French parent company, as the entity holding the decision-making power and having the resources to compensate the victims.

In criminal matters, French courts have jurisdiction over an offence if 'one of the constitutive facts' has been committed on French national territory.[11] Importantly, territorial jurisdiction is also deemed established for acts of complicity in France where an offence or crime has been committed abroad, subject to the following very strict conditions: French courts will only have jurisdiction if the offence or crime is also punishable in the foreign country (double criminality) and the foreign jurisdiction must have issued a final ruling condemning the principal perpetrator.[12] This latter condition appears particularly problematic in cases of corporate abuses in jurisdictions with weak governance where the failure of local authorities to investigate and prosecute violations—owing to a lack of resources, political pressure, or corruption—is the main cause of impunity.

The *Rougier* case is a clear example. It was alleged that a Cameroonian subsidiary of French company Rougier had unlawfully broken into local plantations and cut down rare tree species, causing serious harm to small farmers. In 2002, Sherpa assisted the victims to file a complaint against Rougier and its directors as accomplices. The courts however dismissed the complaint against the company, ruling that French courts did not have jurisdiction in the absence of a final decision against the subsidiary from a Cameroonian judge.[13] After several years of judicial proceedings, the victims were left with no remedy.

In addition, French courts can also exercise extraterritorial jurisdiction on the basis of the active nationality principle; that is, jurisdiction over offences committed by a French national abroad. This jurisdictional basis is particularly relevant to the prosecution of parent companies incorporated in France as well as to French managers of foreign subsidiaries. Depending on the severity of the offence, this principle may however be limited. In particular, for some offences considered *délits* under French law (i.e. offences less severe than crimes, or 'misdemeanours'),

[10] See section IV below.
[11] Criminal Code, art. 113-2.
[12] Criminal Code, art. 113-5.
[13] CA Paris 13 February 2004; Cass Crim 12 April 2005 04-82.318.

the jurisdiction of French courts is subject to several conditions, including that of double criminality, the requirement that the prosecution be initiated by the prosecutor alone (not by the victims) (the prosecutor's exclusive power), and that the prosecution follows a complaint from a victim or an official complaint from a government authority in the country where the act occurred.[14]

This prosecutor's exclusive power led a case relating to Perenco's activities in Ecuador to be dismissed. Assisted by Sherpa, Ecuadorian victims filed a complaint in 2008 alleging that Perenco's gas oil extraction had involved land grabbing, pollution, serious harm, and threats to the health and life of communities, as well as destruction of property and means of livelihood in Ecuador.[15] Ruling on jurisdiction, both the first instance tribunal, the Court of Appeal, and the *Cour de Cassation* considered that the allegations could not be qualified as crimes—as Sherpa had argued in order to establish French courts' jurisdiction and obtain remedy for the victims—but at best as *délits*. They concluded that the prosecutor had full discretion not to prosecute the offence.[16] Once again, after years of judicial battle, victims were left with no remedy.

Finally, universal jurisdiction has been recognised for some of the most serious crimes, including torture,[17] some acts of terrorism,[18] or forced disappearance,[19] provided that the suspect is a permanent resident of France.

For the crimes contemplated in the Rome Statute, that is, genocide, crimes against humanity, and war crimes, universal jurisdiction is further limited.[20] Criminal proceedings can only be initiated by the prosecutor (and not the victims or NGOs), and only on the condition that neither the International Criminal Court (ICC) nor another State have requested the extradition of the suspect. Furthermore, jurisdiction can only be exercised for crimes against humanity and war crimes if that crime is punishable in the State where it was committed, the State is a Party to the Rome Statute, or if the suspect is a national of a State Party.

It is on the basis of this provision that Lafarge SA was indicted (*mise en examen*)[21] for complicity in crimes against humanity in June 2018. In 2010, while other companies in the region withdrew all activities because of the conflict, Lafarge decided to remain active in north-east Syria. Allegations against Lafarge include transactions with armed groups, including the purchase of raw materials through intermediaries and payments made in order to cross checkpoints, as well as violations

[14] Criminal Code, arts 113-6 and 113-8.
[15] CA Paris 14 January 2010 2009/06377; Cass Crim 26 October 2010 10-81.342.
[16] Ibid.
[17] Criminal Procedure Code, art. 689-2.
[18] Criminal Procedure Code, art. 689-9.
[19] Criminal Procedure Code, art. 689-13.
[20] Criminal Procedure Code, art. 689-11.
[21] A '*mise en examen*' is a decision taken by an investigating judge against a suspect when sufficiently serious elements (*indices graves et concordants*) have been found against them in the investigation.

of Syrian employees' rights.[22] In 2016, Sherpa and its partner filed a criminal complaint for various offences, including complicity in crimes against humanity, financing of terrorism, and endangerment.

The Paris Court of Appeal relied on Article 689-11 of the Code of Criminal Procedure to rule that French courts had jurisdiction over Lafarge SA's alleged complicity in crimes against humanity. It found that this provision applies to the principal perpetrator as well as to their accomplice and that, because the ICC is not competent over corporations, there was no need to verify whether it had declined to proceed.[23] It however found that there were not sufficient grounds to justify the indictment of the company for complicity in crimes against humanity and so annulled the indictment with respect to those charges. The NGOs have appealed against this decision and at the time of writing the appeal is still pending.

iii. Corporate criminal liability

Unlike in some other jurisdictions, corporations may be held criminally liable under French law. Article 121-2 of the Criminal Code provides that legal persons, with the exception of the State, are criminally liable for the 'offences committed on their behalf by their organs and representatives'. Since 2004, corporate criminal liability is general and no longer limited to specific offences.

Corporate organs include executive officers and the board of directors, while corporate representatives also include physical persons able to represent the company, including certain employees—depending on their position and attributions. It has been recognised that a person is acting on behalf of the company if it is acting in its interest or if this act falls within the activities, organisation, operations, strategy, or commercial policy of the company.

Nevertheless, under the Criminal Code the corporate veil is not pierced in relation to the different corporate entities of a multinational company: each entity may only be criminally liable for the actions of their own representatives. However, critical decisions and actions are very often taken at the parent company or group level, with respect to the operations of subsidiaries. If certain offences can be attributed to representatives of the parent company—even if they relate to activities that took place abroad—it can be argued that the parent company is criminally liable. It may, however, be very difficult to prove the exact origin of a decision or lack of decision.

It is noteworthy that, in the *Lafarge* case, the Court of Appeal confirmed the indictment of Lafarge SA for endangerment of the Syrian employees.[24] It found—at this stage of the investigation—sufficient elements suggesting that decisions

[22] D. Keohane, 'LafargeHolcim's French arm faces inquiry over Syria claims' (*Financial Times*, 28 June 2018) <https://www.ft.com/content/79d6e5da-7acb-11e8-8e67-1e1a0846c475> accessed 4 June 2020.

[23] CA Paris 7 November 2019 2018/07495.

[24] CA Paris, ibid.

relating to the safety of employees of the Syrian subsidiary were in fact taken at the level of the parent company and that the employees were therefore under the 'effective authority' of that company.

B. Consumer law

Some of the difficulties noted above—in particular those relating to the limits on the courts' jurisdiction and to the difficulty of piercing the corporate veil to establish the parent company's liability for human rights and environmental violations committed by their subsidiaries and in their supply chain abroad—have prompted Sherpa and the victims it represents, to rely on novel grounds, including consumer law.

Multinational companies have developed purportedly ambitious, yet often vague, ethical commitments to improve their environmental and social practices. By many accounts, these ethical commitments are the result of the development of corporate social responsibility at the crossroads between of self-regulation, corporate communication, and advertising.

Different attempts have been made to expose the lack of effectiveness of corporate social responsibility. Human rights and consumer organisations have taken issue with these ethical declarations, including on the basis of false advertising. These declarations partly target consumers, who are increasingly paying attention to the principle of respect for fundamental rights in supply chains.[25] However, when Sherpa filed a complaint against Disney in 2010, the French Professional Advertising Regulatory Authority nevertheless considered that a 'Code of Conduct... [did] not constitute advertising'.[26]

Since 2013, Sherpa has also brought cases on the basis of a criminal offence provided under consumer law: misleading or unfair commercial practices.[27] This offence is characterised by a commercial practice which 'materially alters, or is likely to materially alter, the economic behaviour of a reasonably well-informed, observant and circumspect consumer in respect of a good or service'.[28]

One of these cases was brought further to the Rana Plaza collapse in Bangladesh that killed 1,138 people in 2013. Brand tags belonging to the French supermarket Auchan were found among the debris—exposing the disasters arising from

[25] Business and Human Rights Resource Center, 'The use of consumer protection laws as a strategic tool for corporate due diligence and transparency in global supply chain' (*Business and Human Rights Resource Center*, June 2018) <https://us3.campaign-archive.com/?e=%5bUNIQID%5d&u=bdd1a6a40fffad39c8719632f&id=4793e04c7a> accessed 4 June 2020.

[26] Sherpa, 'Disney en Chine—la RSE instrumentalisée à des fins commerciales' (*Sherpa*, 3 December 2010) <https://www.asso-sherpa.org/disney-en-chine-la-rse-instrumentalisee-des-fins-commerciales> accessed 18 November 2020.

[27] Consumer's Code, arts L. 121-1, L. 121-1-1, L. 121-3, L. 121-4, L. 121-5, L. 121-6, L. 121-7, L. 213-6.

[28] Consumer's Code, art. L. 121-1.

complex supply chains in the garment industry. Auchan had published several declarations highlighting the corporation's commitments to respect human rights, including within its business relations, displayed on the company's website and within its stores.[29]

To expose the gap between the company's declarations and the reality of its supply chain, Sherpa and its partners lodged a first complaint against the company for misleading advertising, which was dismissed by the prosecutor without further action.[30] The submission of a *plainte avec constitution de partie civile* (see subsection II.A above) enabled the appointment of an investigating judge,[31] who opened an investigation and sent a request for cooperation through diplomatic channels to the Bangladeshi authorities.[32] Despite this initial success, this request remains pending at the time of writing, and the investigation appears to be at a standstill. These difficulties are also a clear illustration of the need for specific international cooperation principles in matters of business and human rights, necessary to conduct meaningful international investigations.

Sherpa's second complaint for misleading commercial practices concerned Korean company Samsung, which claimed on its website that it 'aim[ed] to become one of the most ethical companies in the world' and include[d] detailed commitments on workers' rights.[33] These declarations appeared to stand in stark contrast with inhumane working conditions documented in its supply chain. From August to December 2012, the Chinese investigating NGO China Labour Watch reported employment of children under the age of 16, abusive working hours, and working and living conditions incompatible with human dignity in the premises of Samsung's suppliers.[34]

Sherpa and its partners lodged a complaint for misleading commercial practices in 2013, which, as in the *Auchan* case, was dismissed by the prosecutor after a preliminary investigation, demonstrating prosecutors' reluctance to acknowledge that ethical commitments can be considered commercial practices.

The organisations filed three more complaints on different procedural bases, and Samsung was finally indicted in April 2019 for misleading commercial

[29] Auchan Group, 'Ethical Charter' (2017).

[30] Sherpa, 'Auchan et le Rana Plaza: plainte pour pratiques commerciales trompeuses' (*Sherpa*) <https://www.asso-sherpa.org/auchan-le-rana-plaza-des-pratiques-commerciales-trompeuses> accessed 4 June 2020.

[31] Subsection II.A above.

[32] Sherpa, 'Rana Plaza / Auchan: 5 ans après, le silence règne' (*Sherpa*, April 2018) <https://www.asso-sherpa.org/rana-plaza-auchan-5-ans-apres-silence-regne> accessed 18 November 2020.

[33] Samsung, 'Business Principles' (*Samsung*) <http://www.samsung.com/levant/aboutsamsung/vision/philosophy/business-principles/> accessed 29 May 2020.

[34] China Labor Watch, 'Samsung's Supplier Factory Exploiting Child Labor' (*China Labor Watch*, 8 August 2012) <http://www.chinalaborwatch.org/newscast/172> accessed 24 November 2020; 'China Labor Watch, 'An Investigation of Eight Samsung Factories in China' (*China Labor Watch*, 4 September 2012) <http://www.chinalaborwatch.org/report/64> accessed 24 November 2020; China Labor Watch, 'Follow-up Investigations of Five Samsung Factories' (*China Labor Watch*, 26 November 2012) <http://www.chinalaborwatch.org/report/65> accessed 24 November 2020.

practices. This indictment has however been annulled: the court found that the NGOs had no legal standing to file a criminal complaint in the field of consumer law without a specific approval to do so.[35] The NGOs have referred to case to the *Cour de cassation*.

It is worth noting that this criminal offence may help to prevent green or social washing, but a successful prosecution in relation to misleading or unfair trading practice only leads to compensation for misled customers not for direct victims of human rights violations (affected workers).

C. Tort law

Tort law actions against French multinationals for human rights and environmental violations committed abroad have so far been extremely limited.

Among the reasons such cases are scarce are the material and financial constraints of collecting evidence. In contrast to the criminal complaints described above—where the investigating judge may conduct investigations, seize documents, interrogate witnesses, and where the prosecutor bears the burden of proof—the burden of collecting and presenting sufficient evidence falls on the claimant in civil proceedings. Although a judge may order the defendant to produce some specific documents that are within its possession, this possibility is extremely limited compared to other jurisdictions.[36] In many cases, claimants need to possess all the crucial evidence to prove their case.

The other main hurdle in civil liability cases came, until recently, from the combination of the applicable jurisdictional rules and the corporate veil doctrine.

For French courts to have jurisdiction over a corporate abuse that occurred abroad, the defendant company must be domiciled in France, as per Article 4 of the Brussels I Regulation. Connected claims against multiple defendants may be brought before the tribunal of the domicile of any of these defendants, provided that there is a serious *prima facie* case against that defendant, sufficient to 'anchor' the claim in France.[37]

However, the civil liability law precept that one can only be liable for one's own action, combined with the corporate veil doctrine (*autonomie de la personne morale* in French law), make any such legal action contingent on the proof that the wrongful act that caused the harm can be attributed to a French company. As Olivera Boskovic summarised:

[35] S. Jung-a, 'Samsung faces charges in France over alleged labour violations' (*Financial Times*, 4 July 2019) <https://www.ft.com/content/8a7adbe0-9e19-11e9-9c06-a4640c9feebb> accessed 4 June 2020; Sherpa, 'Violation of workers' rights at Samsung: NGOs barred from court' (*Sherpa*, 8 April 2021) <https://www.asso-sherpa.org/violation-of-workers-rights-at-samsung-ngos-barred-from-court>.

[36] Subsection IV.A below.

[37] Civil Procedure Code, art. 42.

> [P]rior to [the Law on the Duty of Vigilance], French courts could not hear actions brought against subsidiary companies in this type of case because, to simplify matters, neither the place of the harm nor the domicile of the defendant provided a basis for jurisdiction. On the contrary, they had, of course, jurisdiction for actions brought against French parent companies on the basis of domicile, but such actions were, because of the screen of legal personality, a priori doomed to failure.[38]

The *Jerusalem Tramway* case, brought in 2007 by the NGO France-Palestine Solidarité against French companies Alstom and Veolia with respect to their involvement in the consortium selected to build and operate a tramway in Jerusalem, illustrates this issue.

The first instance tribunal's decision, upheld by the Versailles Court of Appeal, confirmed the jurisdiction of French courts on the basis of the domicile of both defendant companies.[39] However, the difficulty in attributing wrongful acts to these companies caused the claims on the merits to be rejected.[40] The Court of Appeal held that the humanitarian law provisions relied on by the claimants were not self-executing—so that they could not be invoked as such before French courts—and that they did not directly apply to the defendant companies. The court also refused to give any legal effect to the content of the United Nations Global Compact,[41] ratified by both companies, noting its purely voluntary nature, and concluded that the companies' commitments to respect human rights in their different codes of conduct and corporate social responsibility (CSR) documentation could not be regarded as legal commitments that could be invoked by third parties.[42]

This does not, however, mean that no civil liability action may be brought against a French company for human rights or environmental violations committed abroad. First, it may be possible to attribute wrongful acts to the French company itself, irrespective of any attempt to attribute a subsidiary's conduct to its parent company. Whether a company is implicated in a concrete way in the causing of damage—including, for example, through its decision-making powers, its global human rights and environmental policies, or the involvement of its own personnel in the project at stake—is fact-dependent and the facts should be decisive. In practice, however, evidence of operational involvement often rests within the company itself, making access to evidence a significant barrier in French civil proceedings.[43]

[38] O. Boskovic, 'La compétence des juridictions des pays source pour connaître des actions intentées à l'encontre des entreprises multinationales' (2018) 14 *Recueil Dalloz* 732 (our translation); see also P. Abadie, 'Le juge et la RSE' (2018) 6 *Recueil Dalloz* 302.

[39] TGI Nanterre 15 April 2009 07/02902; CA Versailles 17 December 2009 09/04772.

[40] TGI Nanterre 30 May 2011 10/02629; CA Versailles 22 March 2013 11/05331.

[41] The United Nations Global Compact is a non-binding United Nations pact to encourage businesses worldwide to adopt sustainable and socially responsible policies, and to report on their implementation.

[42] CA Versailles 22 March 2013 11/05331.

[43] See subsection IV below.

Most importantly, as detailed in section III below, the Law on the Duty of Vigilance adopted in 2017 is bound to have a significant impact on the viability of such civil liability actions in cases where the company concerned is subject to that law.

D. Labour law

To circumvent jurisdictional and legal obstacles to civil liability, attempts have been made to use certain doctrines that create direct obligations upon French entities (such as the rules on co-employment under French labour law), or to have French courts' jurisdiction recognised under the *forum necessitatis* doctrine, even in the absence of a French defendant.

The seminal *Comilog* saga illustrates the practical limitations of these doctrines in enabling foreign human rights victims—here, former employees of a foreign entity— access to justice in France. It is also emblematic of the significant delays foreign claimants are subjected to merely to obtain a decision on jurisdiction, not to mention on the merits of their claims. Judicial timeline is often insensitive to the victims' timeline.

The case originated in a major accident in the freight line connecting a manganese mine in Gabon to the Congolese port of Pointe Noire in 1991. The accident led the company operating the line, Comilog, to suspend the line and dismiss all its employees. Some of those employees sought remedy before the Congolese courts, in vain: while the lower instance courts rejected the defendant's jurisdictional objections, no decision on the appeal had since been rendered, and the case was still pending some 15 years later.

In 2008, Sherpa helped 867 former employees to initiate litigation before the Paris *Prud'hommes* Tribunal against Comilog and three French companies of the Comilog group, claiming that their contract had been unlawfully terminated by the companies and requesting compensation.[44] Sherpa argued that the French courts had jurisdiction to hear the case on two different bases. First, the claimants submitted that the French Comilog companies were to be considered former co-employers, so that Comilog could be judged before French courts as a co-defendant. In the alternative, French courts had jurisdiction under the *forum necessitatis* doctrine, as the claimants could not have access to justice in Congo and the case presented sufficient links with France.

On 10 September 2015, the Paris Court of Appeal ruled that the French Comilog companies could not be regarded as co-employers,[45] applying a very restrictive definition of co-employment.

[44] The Prud'hommes tribunals are special, tripartite jurisdictions competent in first instance for matters of employment and labour law.

[45] CA Paris 10 September 2015 11/05953, 11/05955, 11/05956, 11/05957, 11/05959, 11/05960.

However, it found it had jurisdiction over Comilog on the basis of the *forum necessitatis* principle: the absence of judgment by the Congolese courts constituted a denial of justice contrary to the right to have access to justice in a reasonable period of time under Article 6 of the European Convention on Human Rights (ECHR) and Article 4 of the French Civil Code, and the case presented a sufficient connection with France.[46]

This decision was unfortunately overruled by the *Cour de Cassation*. Although the Court formally enshrined the *forum necessitatis* principle for the first time, it spelt out extremely stringent requirements to its application.[47] On the first criterion (denial of justice), the Court adopted a formalistic approach, finding that the impossibility for the employees to access to the competent judge was not established, their case still being pending before the Congolese courts. Similarly, regarding the second criterion (a sufficient connection with France) it held that the fact that the French company Eramet had acquired a majority in Comilog's shareholding was not sufficient to warrant the application of the *forum necessitatis* rule, failing to take into account the economic reality of multinational companies. Almost 30 years after the dramatic event and after 10 years of long, complex, and costly judicial proceedings, some of the victims had passed away and the others were, once again, left with no remedy.

E. Section II conclusion

The above-mentioned human rights and environmental cases introduced under criminal, consumer, civil, and labour law provisions are emblematic. They reveal how existing legal provisions are either ill-equipped to govern transnational business or applied in a restrictive manner that is blind to the reality of corporate abuses. Concrete obstacles faced in these cases have shown the need for legislative reform and have contributed to its development.

III. The duty of vigilance: a new legal basis in civil liability cases

The Law on the Duty of Vigilance of Parent and Instructing Companies (hereinafter LDV) creates a new legal obligation for companies applying to their value chain, including their activities abroad (subsection III.A), and which may be

[46] CA Paris 10 September 2015 11/05959 and 11/05960.

[47] Cass Soc 14 September 2017 15-26.737 and 15–26.738. On this decision, see S. Cossart and O. Oesterlé, 'Pour la consécration d'un forum necessitatis en cas de violations de droits humains par les entreprises transnationales' (2018) 1808 *Semaine sociale Lamy* 5.

judicially enforced (subsection III.B). It creates a potentially viable cause of action for cases of human rights and environmental violations committed by multinational companies, although some important legal questions still remain to be decided (subsection III.B).

A. The creation of a corporate duty of vigilance

The LDV was adopted in 2017 after protracted debates in both chambers of the French Parliament, and a partial annulment by the *Conseil Constitutionnel*.[48]

The initial legislative proposal, submitted in 2013, provided for the creation of a statutory duty of vigilance, defined as an obligation for companies to prevent risks and harm to health, human rights, and the environment in the context of their activities, as well as the activities of their subsidiaries and subcontractors.[49] Failure to respect this duty of vigilance would give rise to civil liability under the Civil Code, where fault would be presumed in the absence of evidence to the contrary (that is, reversing the burden of proof), as well as criminal liability, through an amended definition of negligence in the Criminal Code.[50]

This proposal resulted from the unprecedented mobilisation of a coalition of NGOs, trade unions and members of parliament that sought to prevent disasters like the Rana Plaza collapse.[51] The *Auchan*, *Lafarge*, or *Vinci* cases initiated by Sherpa contributed to shape the ensuing debates.[52] Clear references were also made to the limitations of existing soft law principles such as the UN Guiding Principles on Business and Human Rights and to the Organisation for Economic Co-operation and Development (OECD) Guidelines on multinational companies.[53] The proposal's purpose was to transform soft law principles into binding obligations by defining a new legal standard of conduct for companies, applying to their whole value chain and enforceable in the courts. Unfortunately, this proposal was countered by a fierce corporate lobbying and never submitted to the vote.

Although the content of the LDV eventually enacted on 27 March 2017 differed from the initial proposal, the underlying principles remain similar. It introduced new provisions in the Commercial Code that require large French companies to

[48] S. Cossart, J. Chaplier, and T. B. de Loménie, 'The French Law on Duty of Care: A Historic Step Towards Making Globalization Work for All' (2017) 2 *Business and Human Rights Journal* 317–23.

[49] Proposition de loi relative au devoir de vigilance des sociétés-mères et entreprises donneuses d'ordre, enregistrée à la présidence de l'Assemblée nationale le 6 novembre 2013.

[50] S. Cossart and M.-L. Guislain, 'Le devoir de vigilance pour les entreprises multinationales, un impératif juridique pour une économie durable' (2017) 71 *Bulletin du Droit de l'Environnement Industriel*.

[51] O. Petitjean, *Devoir de vigilance—Une victoire contre l'impunité des multinationales* (2019).

[52] Assemblée nationale, 'Compte rendu des débats de la première séance du 11 mars 2015' <http:/www.assemblee-nationale.fr/14/cri/2014-2015/20150193.asp> accessed 4 June 2020.

[53] D. Potier, 'Rapport n°2628 sur la proposition de loi n° 2578 relative au devoir de vigilance des sociétés mères et des entreprises donneuses d'ordre' (11 March 2015) Assemblée nationale.

establish, publish, and effectively implement a vigilance plan.[54] This plan shall contain reasonable vigilance measures, adequate to identify risks and prevent serious violations of human rights, fundamental freedoms, the health and safety of individuals, and the environment. It applies not only to the company's activities but also to the activities of companies under its legal control as well as the activities of its suppliers and subcontractors with whom there is an 'established commercial relationship'.

The LDV therefore aims to create a new legal obligation in line with the realities of today's transnational value chains.[55] To a certain extent, it intends to rectify the dilution of liabilities caused by the multiplication of subsidiaries and chains of subcontractors in multinationals' value chains, by placing a duty of vigilance upon parent companies that extends beyond the corporate veil. However, in contrast with the proposal initially put forward by Sherpa and other NGOs, the existing legislation contains some vigilance measures that have been explicitly listed in the law (as a consequence of pressure by companies), which has led some to confuse the duty of vigilance with a mere compliance or reporting requirement.

Most importantly, the LDV's supporters managed to have inserted an express provision that a failure to respect these new obligations may trigger the company's civil liability, thereby creating a new cause of action in tort.

B. Judicial enforcement mechanisms

The LDV provides for two different judicial mechanisms. First, any interested person may request a judge to order a company to comply with the law, provided it first formally requested the company to comply and that the company failed to do so within three months. It is specified that periodic penalty payment may also be requested, that is, fines payable on a daily or per event basis until the defendant complies with the judicial order.[56]

This preventative mechanism aims, through an injunctive relief, to force compliance and avoid potential violations. The judge's powers under this provision could potentially be broad: a company could be judicially ordered to publish a vigilance plan, to take adequate vigilance measures, or to effectively implement measures stated in its vigilance plan. However, the extent to which judges will exercise this injunctive power, and in particular the specificity of the vigilance measures to be ordered, remains to be seen.

[54] Articles L. 225-102-4 and L. 225-102-5. This obligation only applies to companies with more than 5,000 employees in France or 10,000 worldwide (in both cases, including their subsidiaries).

[55] T. Beau de Loménie, S. Cossart, and P. Morrow, 'From Human Rights Due Diligence to Duty of Vigilance' in A. Bonfandi, *Business and Human Rights in Europe: International Law Challenges* (2018) 133–44.

[56] Commercial Code, art. L. 225-102-4 II.

The law specifies that these injunctions may be requested pursuant to the *référé* procedure, which empowers the judge to take interim or conservatory measures under certain conditions, including the need to prevent imminent damage or to stop overtly unlawful conduct.[57]

At the time of writing, several formal notices have already been sent to companies according to this first, preventative mechanism, requesting them to comply with the law. These cover a variety of legal issues: climate change (the first formal notice sent to Total), workers' fundamental rights (notices sent to Teleperformance and XPO Logistics) or indigenous rights (notice sent to EDF).[58]

The first judicial claim was brought against Total in the *Uganda* case, pursuant to the *référé* procedure. In a major backlash, the *Tribunal Judiciaire* (the first instance tribunal in civil matters) however declined jurisdiction and sent the case to the commercial court.[59] It found that the publication of a vigilance plan had a direct link with the management of the company and that this fell within the exclusive jurisdiction of the commercial courts. The Court of Appeal confirmed this decision. These first decisions are unfortunate because they rely on a fundamentally misguided understanding of the duty of vigilance: by all accounts, the duty of vigilance should be understood as a duty of care owed to third parties, aiming to protect their fundamental rights, not as a corporate management issue.

In fact, the second judicial case under the LDV was also brought against Total before the *Tribunal Judiciaire*—this time by 5 NGOs including Sherpa and 14 local authorities claiming that Total failed to take adequate measures to prevent climate change.[60] In this case, the *Tribunal Judiciaire* confirmed its jurisdiction in first instance, relying on the jurisdictional option offered to the claimants and the nature and purpose of the LDV.[61]

The civil nature of the duty is also made clear in the LDV, which expressly refers to civil liability provisions in the Civil Code in case of failures to comply with the law.[62]

Pursuant to this second judicial mechanism, a company is required to remedy any harm that due respect for its duty of vigilance would have prevented.[63] The duty of vigilance therefore creates a new standard of conduct placed upon parent

[57] Civil Procedure Code, arts 834 and 835.

[58] For an overview of these first formal notices, see E. Savourey and S. Brabant, 'All Eyes on France—Vigilance Law First Enforcement Cases' (*Cambridge Code Blog*, 24 January 2020) <https://www.cambridge.org/core/blog/2020/01/24/all-eyes-on-france-french-vigilance-law-first-enforcement-cases-1-2-current-cases-and-trends/#_edn13> accessed 1 June 2020.

[59] TJ Nanterre 30 January 2020 19/02833.

[60] A. Chrisafis, 'French NGOs and local authorities take court action against Total' (*The Guardian*, 27 January 2020) <https://www.theguardian.com/world/2020/jan/27/french-ngos-and-local-authorities-take-court-action-against-total> accessed 1 June 2020.

[61] TJ Nanterre 11 February 2021 20/00915.

[62] Civil Code, art. 1240 and 1241.

[63] Commercial Code, art. L. 225-102-5.

and instructing companies that, if not satisfied, can amount to the wrongful act or negligence necessary under French civil law to trigger civil liability.[64] For that reason, the duty of vigilance has sometimes been compared to a specific, statutory corporate duty of care in common law countries.[65]

C. Some unresolved legal issues

A number of legal issues raised by the LDV, however, remain and will probably give rise to important judicial decisions in the coming years.

i. Content of the duty of vigilance

First, the duty of vigilance is a relatively novel concept under French law.[66] Although the LDV spells out five specific categories of vigilance measures, it also makes clear that this list is not exhaustive and that it should not be read as a mere formalistic requirement. The adequacy of a risk-mapping in a company's vigilance plan, or the content of the prevention measures mentioned should therefore be subject to scrutiny.

In particular, faced with allegations that a company has failed to respect its duty of vigilance, judges will have to assess whether that company should have been able to identify a certain risk within its supply chain; whether the measures taken could be regarded as adequate; whether those measures were effectively implemented; and in short, whether a vigilant company placed in a similar situation would have acted the same way.[67] While not binding, soft law standards could have a crucial impact on the progressive construction of this new, general standard of conduct for companies regarding their supply chains.[68] Another difficulty here is ascertaining the extent of vigilance measures that are expected of a company as this may depend on the factual relationship between the defendant and other players involved, which in turn depends on access to internal information.

In addition, the unprecedented nature of the duty of vigilance will also prompt judges to determine how human rights law applies to corporate actors: while some human rights rules set forth absolute prohibitions (e.g. torture, slavery), most of human rights enshrined in international conventions involve balancing,

[64] S. Cossart, T.B. de Loménie, and A. Lubriani, 'L'extension du domaine de la vigilance' (2019) 16 *Revue des Juristes de Sciences Po* 88.

[65] B. Parance and E. Groulx, 'Regards croisés sur le devoir de vigilance et le duty of care' (2018) 145 *Journal du droit international* 21.

[66] Some vigilance requirements also exist in other legal areas, for instance in labour law (see Labour Code, art. L8222-1 ss; art. L8254-1; art. L4231-1).

[67] J. Lagoutte, 'Le devoir de vigilance des sociétés mères et des sociétés donneuses d'ordre ou la rencontre de la RSE et de la responsabilité juridique' (2015) 12 *Responsabilité civile et assurances* 11.

[68] Abadie (n 38).

proportionality tests that were primarily designed for States, even if they are already applied horizontally in domestic contexts.[69]

ii. Conflict of laws

Conflict of laws issues have not been expressly addressed in the new provisions introduced by the LDV, and civil liability cases introduced for damages caused abroad are likely to raise issues of applicable law.

The LDV explicitly refers to the articles governing civil liability under French law (Articles 1240 and 1241 of the Civil Code). However, according to the general rule laid out in Article 4.1 of Rome II Regulation, the law governing civil liability claims is 'the law of the country in which the damage occurs irrespective of the country in which the event giving rise to the damage occurred and irrespective of the country or countries in which the indirect consequences of that event occur'.[70] Following this logic, some may argue that the LDV may not be applicable in case of harm caused abroad by a French company's breach of its duty of vigilance.

In cases of environmental damage, Article 7 of Rome II Regulation provides the claimant with an option between the law of the country in which the damage occurred and the law of the country 'in which the event giving rise to the damage occurred'. This option should enable claimants to rely on the LDV where a French company's lack of vigilance caused environmental damage in another country.[71]

As far as other damages are concerned, applying the law of the country in which the damage occurs would seem contrary to the rationale of the LDV.[72] As Etienne Pataut explains:

> [S]ince the aim is to make parent and instructing companies accountable, the search for accountability is by nature focused on the behaviour of the authors. The applicability of the law of the event giving rise to the damage would therefore be particularly appropriate for torts of this nature.[73]

Given the objectives that the LDV pursues, as evidenced by the parliamentary works,[74] it could be regarded as an overriding mandatory provision under Article 16 of Rome II Regulation.[75] French law would therefore apply to civil liability

[69] D. Bilchitz, 'Corporate Obligations and a Business and Human Rights Treaty: a Constitutional Law Model?' in D. Bilchitz and S. Deva (eds), *Building a Treaty on Business and Human Rights: Context and Contours* (2017) 185–215.

[70] EU Regulation No. 864/2007 of 11 July 2007 on the law applicable to non-contractual obligations (Rome II).

[71] E. Pataut, 'Le devoir de vigilance—Aspects de droit international privé' (2017) 10 *Droit social* 833 ; O. Boskovic, 'Brèves remarques sur le devoir de vigilance et le droit international privé' (2016) 7 *Recueil Dalloz* 385.

[72] Ibid.

[73] Ibid., (our translation).

[74] *Assemblée nationale, Rapport* n° 2628 (11 March 2015) 30.

[75] A.-S. Epstein, 'La portée extraterritoriale du devoir de vigilance des sociétés mères et des entreprises donneuses d'ordre' (2018) 4 *Cahiers de droit de l'entreprise* 47.

cases triggered by a company's lack of vigilance even though the damage occurred abroad.

iii. Proving causation

Assuming the question of liability is governed by French law, claimants may be faced with other difficulties, including proving the three traditional elements of civil liability, that is, wrongful act, damage, and causation.[76] In the absence of reversal of the burden of proof (envisaged in the initial legislative proposal), the burden of proving these three elements falls on the claimant.

Proving causation means establishing that the defendant company's failure to respect the LDV requirements caused the damage suffered or, as laid out in the legal provision, that that damage 'would have been prevented' had that company respected its duty of vigilance.

This burden however seems difficult to meet.[77] In some cases causation may be considered multi-faceted: for example, damage directly caused by a subsidiary's action (e.g. violations of its employees' freedom of association, health, or safety), which would nonetheless have been avoided if the parent company had taken adequate mitigation and prevention measures. When human rights or environmental violations occur further along in the value chain or in the context of a suppliers or subcontractors' activities, this causal link may appear more difficult to establish, as such damage may have been the result of a number of causes, including—amongst others—the lack of vigilance of the instructing company.[78]

Requiring a stringent test of causation in those instances would be inconsistent with the objectives of the LDV, namely, preventing events like the collapse of the Rana Plaza, which indirectly supplied French garment companies. As some authors explain, in such instances, French judges should facilitate the burden of proof[79] or rely on a presumption of causation—as they do in cases in which the damage 'appears to be the normal and foreseeable realisation of a risk created out of imprudence'.[80]

Another familiar concept in civil liability law may also be relevant: the *perte de chance* (loss of chance).[81] In some cases the parent company's lack of vigilance would not directly cause the whole damage but rather impede an opportunity to prevent that damage.

[76] A. Danis-Fatôme and G. Viney, 'La responsabilité civile dans la loi relative au devoir de vigilance des sociétés mères et des entreprises donneuses d'ordre' (2017) 28 *Recueil Dalloz* 1610.

[77] Ibid., Lagoutte (n 67).

[78] C. Hannoun, 'Le devoir de vigilance des sociétés mères et entreprises donneuses d'ordre après la loi du 27 mars 2018' (2017) 10 *Droit social* 806.

[79] T. Sachs, 'La loi sur le devoir de vigilance des sociétés-mères et sociétés donneuses d'ordre: les ingrédients d'une corégulation' (2017) 6 *Revue de droit du travail* 380.

[80] Danis-Fatôme and Viney (n 76).

[81] Hannoun (n 78).

These legal difficulties show that, although the LDV has been an essential development, access to remedy remains far from being guaranteed in cases of corporate abuses. The introduction of absolute or strict liability and shifting the burden of proof, appears to be critical.[82] This is all the more so given that important procedural obstacles remain, calling for further legislative reforms.

IV. Procedural barriers

The use of litigation against multinational companies in human rights and environmental cases is obstructed by procedural rules that fail to take into account the fundamental imbalance between parties in those cases. These obstacles include rules on access to evidence (subsection IV.A); legal standing of NGOs (subsection IV.B), collective actions (subsection IV.C), and costs (subsection IV.D).

A. Access to evidence

The absence of discovery in French civil procedure, and its impact on victims' ability to present their claim, is undoubtedly an obstacle to the development of human rights and environmental litigation against corporate actors in France. As noted above, a large portion of the information needed to establish a company's liability is likely to rest within that company itself, creating a significant procedural imbalance. In addition, the recent development of legal privileges under French law, in particular the adoption of the 2018 Law on Trade Secrets, may further restrict access to evidence for victims of corporate abuses.[83]

The absence of discovery under French law is partly linked to the procedural structure of civil legal actions, where claimants are supposed to detail their claims already in the *assignation* (summons or statement of claim), adducing any necessary evidence to support their claims.[84] Party-controlled discovery—whereby a party would be able to collect a large amount of evidence directly from the other party through document requests, interrogatories, depositions or requests for admission—seems at odds with French civil procedure.

The Civil Procedure Code nonetheless provides for two different bases to obtain evidence in the other party's possession: the forced production of a document during judicial proceedings, and the request for investigative measures before any

[82] Lagoutte (n 67).

[83] Loi n° 2018-670 du 30 juillet 2018 relative à la protection du secret des affaires.

[84] R. Stürner, 'Transnational Civil Procedure: Discovery and Sanctions against Non-compliance' (2001) 6 *Uniform Law Review* 871.

trial (*référé probatoire in futurum*). Both procedures must be submitted to a judge who will decide whether to order the requested taking of evidence.

A party may indeed request the judge supervising a case to order the other party,[85] or a third party,[86] to produce some documents in its possession, potentially subject to a penalty payment.[87] Such applications are typically made in cases where a party has previous knowledge of a specific document in the possession of its opponent (e.g. a contract with a third party).

A party may also, before initiating any legal action on the merits, request a judge to order an investigative measure, including seizing another party's documents, 'if there is a legitimate reason to preserve or establish before any trial the evidence of facts on which the solution of a dispute may depend'.[88] That measure may be requested and ordered *ex parte* if the petitioner proves that there are valid reasons to do so, notably if giving the other party notice of the request may jeopardise the enforcement of the measure. The conditions controlled by the judge are, however, restrictive. A legitimate reason for requesting these documents is required: the petitioner must demonstrate the evidential value of such documents.[89] The judge must verify that a claim could be brought, that it is not purely artificial, and that the action is not clearly doomed to failure.

This mechanism, notably used in intellectual property cases, could prove particularly relevant to access to critical evidence in cases of corporate abuses. However, the case brought by Sherpa and its partner against the oil company Perenco illustrates some of the difficulties that victims may face when requesting such measures.[90]

The case relates to allegations of air, water, and land pollution, destruction of biodiversity, and health damages allegedly resulting from Perenco's activities in the Democratic Republic of Congo. The NGOs filed an *ex parte* request for investigative measures, to be enforced by a judicial officer, including the seizure of documents within the company's premises relating to its corporate structure and its claimed involvement in the alleged environmental damages. The request was granted by the judge, yet the company obstructed the enforcement of the court order, preventing the judicial officer from entering its corporate premises.[91] The

[85] Civil Procedure Code, art. 142.
[86] Civil Procedure Code, art. 138.
[87] Civil Procedure Code, art. 139.
[88] Civil Procedure Code, art. 145.
[89] Cass Civ 2 6 November 2008 07-17.398.
[90] J. Tilouine 'Perenco, boîte noire pétrolière et toxique en RDC' (*Le Monde*, 9 October 2019) <https://www.lemonde.fr/afrique/article/2019/10/09/perenco-boite-noire-petroliere-et-toxique-en-rdc_6014880_3212.html> accessed 1 June 2020. S. Cossart and L. Bourgeois, 'L'article 145 du Code de procédure civile: un outil insuffisant pour la preuve des violations économiques de droits fondamentaux', *Semaine sociale Lamy* (n°1923) <https://www.asso-sherpa.org/wp-content/uploads/2020/10/Larticle-145-CPC-un-outil-insuffisant-pour-la-preuve-violations-%C3%A9conomiques.pdf>.
[91] Tilouine, ibid.

NGOs filed another request under the same provision, in the presence of both parties. The claim was, however, rejected by both first instance and appeal judges, who requested that the claimants establish their legal standing pursuant to the foreign law that they deemed applicable while, as mentioned above, the conditions for such an investigative measure to be granted are only a *prima facie* case and a legitimate interest to access evidence. The NGOs have referred the case to the *Cour de Cassation*.

Some authors have traditionally justified the existence of broad discovery mechanisms in the United States because of the role of civil litigation in enforcing social norms: 'broad discovery seems critical in many situations in which private individuals in the United States use civil litigation to enforce rights', as opposed to other jurisdictions where comparable social norms would be enforced by the police or administrative authorities.[92] In the absence of adequate public regulation in matters of business and human rights, civil litigation today appears as one of the few enforcement mechanisms available for victims under French law—most notably via the LDV—which makes the lack of adequate mechanism on access to evidence all the more problematic.

B. Legal standing of NGOs

NGO action has proven to be crucial in initiating litigation against multinational companies. Under French law, NGOs (*associations*) cannot pursue claims on behalf of affected communities but they may have legal standing to defend and advocate for, on their own behalf, some of the collective interests that fall within their stated purpose. This right has, however, been challenged by recent judicial decisions and by the multiplication of special regimes.

In criminal matters, the ability of NGOs to trigger independent criminal investigations as 'civil parties' has been challenged in recent cases.[93] Authors seem to disagree on the legal significance of these decisions and whether they foreshadow a stricter approach on NGOs' legal standing.[94] Although the appeals against some of these decisions are still pending, this has undeniably affected the legal predictability of NGOs' judicial actions.

Sherpa has been facing such challenges in the above-mentioned *Lafarge* case in which it filed a criminal complaint against the cement company for various

[92] S. Subrin, 'Discovery in Global Perspectives: Are we Nuts?' (2002) 52(2) *DePaul Law Review* 299–318.

[93] Cass Crim 11 October 2017 16-86.868; Cass Crim 31 January 2018 17-80.659 (*Anticor* case)

[94] F. Fourment, 'Pro-CPP mais pas anti-corruption' (30 April 2018) 3214 *Gazette du Palais* 70; Raphaële Parizot, 'Fondement à la recevabilité de la constitution de partie civile d'une association de lutte contre la corruption: se limiter à l'article 2-23 ou admettre l'article 2 du code de procédure pénale?' (2018) *RSC* 136; D. Roets, 'Le ministère public bousculé par l'action associative—À propos de l'arrêt de la chambre criminelle rendu dans l'affaire dite des biens mal acquis' (2010) 357 *Gazette du Palais* 12.

offences purportedly committed in Syria, including complicity in crimes against humanity, financing of terrorism and endangerment. In October 2019, the Paris Court of Appeal declared Sherpa inadmissible for lack of standing.[95] In particular, it found that Sherpa's purpose included in its by-laws did not explicitly include seeking legal accountability for war crimes and crimes against humanity and only referred to human rights abuses.[96] An appeal has been brought before the *Cour de Cassation*, and Sherpa and its partner are challenging this restrictive approach. However, unfortunately, the challenges to Sherpa's legal standing in many of its cases goes hand in hand with a restrictive legislative movement against the participation of NGOs.

In civil matters, the principle applicable to the legal standing of NGOs was set out in 2008 by the *Cour de Cassation* after a general movement recognising the legitimacy of such legal actions: 'an association may take legal action on behalf of collective interests, as long as they fall within its purpose [*objet social*]'.[97] Some later decisions, however, appear more restrictive, declaring associations inadmissible because the purpose set out in their by-laws was found too vague.[98] In civil matters too, the admissibility of litigation initiated by NGOs therefore seems to be dependent on the interpretation of legislation by judges on a case by case basis, potentially affecting the predictability of court action.

C. Collective actions

The *Comilog* case mentioned above illustrated the inadequacies of the French civil procedure where there are multiple victims. In the absence of collective action under French law, 867 different cases had to be filed and handled by Sherpa and its lawyers, despite its limited resources. The courts had to proceed on an ad hoc basis, first deciding on six of the claimants' cases.[99]

Since then, collective actions have been introduced in French law, first in the area of consumer law in 2014,[100] before being extended to disputes relating to discrimination at work, health, environmental damage, and personal data in 2016.[101] It is available where 'several persons in a similar situation suffer damage caused by

[95] CA Paris 24 October 2019 2018/05060.

[96] Criminal Procedure Code, art. 2-4.

[97] Cass Civ 1 18 September 2008 06-22.038.

[98] N. Cuzacq, 'Premier contentieux relatif à la loi vigilance du 27 mars 2017, une illustration de l'importance du droit judiciaire privé' (2020) 17 *Recueil Dalloz* 970.

[99] This approach has been compared to the European Court of Human Rights pilot judgment procedure: E. Pataut, 'Le contentieux collectif des travailleurs face à la mondialisation—Réflexions à partir de l'affaire Comilog' (2016) 6 *Droit Social* 554.

[100] Loi n° 2014-344 du 17 mars 2014 relative à la consommation.

[101] Loi n° 2016-1547 du 18 novembre 2016 de modernisation de la justice du XXIe siècle.

the same person, having as a common cause a failure of that person to comply with its legal or contractual obligations'.[102]

These provisions are meant to create a general regime for collective actions in these five areas, relying on a two-step procedure. First, the collective action is introduced by an association or a trade union before the competent tribunal, which decides on the admissibility of the action, on the alleged breaches and, in case of liability, on the scope of the group and on the calculation of damages that will be awarded. It also orders the defendant to take the necessary measures to inform any person that could be part of the group as defined and sets a deadline to join that group. Secondly, once all remedies against that first decision have been exhausted, any person that joined the group may request compensation—on the basis of the judgment—directly to the defendant, or to the claimant organisation that may act on their behalf.

Although this mechanism may be relevant for some corporate abuse disputes, a number of human rights violations appear to fall outside the restricted scope of these five areas.[103]

While this mechanism is still recent, some have criticised its limited scope, its complexity, and its exclusive reliance on actors with limited resources (associations and trade unions)—which, together, are bound to restrict the number of cases. This could indeed explain why so few collective actions have been introduced so far, and for the most part in the area of consumer law.

D. Rules on costs

Financial issues, including rules on legal costs, may also constitute a serious hindrance for NGOs and victims' access to justice in cases of corporate abuses.

In criminal proceedings, after filing a *plainte avec constitution de partie civile*, the investigating judge may require the complainant to deposit a sum of money. The amount of the deposit is, in principle, determined in accordance with the complainant's income, and the deposit must be paid within a time limit set by the judge, failing which the complaint may be dismissed.[104] This sum is made to guarantee the payment of a possible fine imposed in the event the complaint proves to be abusive.[105] If the amount set is too high, this deposit may however be dissuasive and lead claimants to drop their action. For example, in the *Lafarge* case, the judge initially requested a €13,000 deposit, a sum clearly too high in light of the complainants' resources.[106]

[102] Loi n° 2016-1547 ibid., art. 62.
[103] M.J.A. Baud, 'Perspectives et pistes d'amélioration' (2019) 591 *Juris associations* 31.
[104] Criminal Procedure Code, art. 88.
[105] Criminal Procedure Code, arts 88–81.
[106] The judge finally reduced the amount of the deposit (€1,950).

In civil proceedings, costs are usually borne by the losing party.[107] Nevertheless, the judge is supposed to take account of equity and of the economic situation of the parties, so that a losing party will not necessarily have to pay for the other party's costs. In some cases, judges have relied on equity to allow NGOs not to support all the costs, as in the above-mentioned *Alstom* case, where the first instance judge considered that the NGO (whose claims were rejected) only had to pay for some of the costs.[108] However, decisions on the legal costs fall within the sole discretion of the courts and can give rise to unfair rulings, as courts may not pay sufficient heed to the principle of equity or to the economic situation of the parties. In the *Perenco–DRC* case, Sherpa and the other claimant have been ordered to pay the company's legal costs in addition to their own costs, despite an obvious financial imbalance between the parties and even though the company had previously blatantly refused to respect a judicial decision.

V. Conclusion

Existing legal mechanisms have proven unable to allow for remediation for victims, especially when applied in a transnational context, leading to situations of corporate impunity. The cases detailed above illustrate the array of practical and legal hurdles faced by human rights and environmental victims who seek remedy for corporate abuses.

Crucially, they also shed light on the fundamental imbalances between victims and corporations in legal proceedings. These include material imbalances (victims may lack access to crucial evidence or may not afford legal representation) but most importantly legal imbalances: doctrines such as the 'corporate veil', restrictions on collective actions, and limitations to extraterritorial jurisdiction often serve to shield parent companies and perpetuate impunity. While it remains to be seen how the LDV will be interpreted and applied, this promising legislation shows that legal imbalances may and need to be addressed and corrected in order to put an end to corporate impunity.

[107] Civil Procedure Code, arts 695 and 700.
[108] TGI Nanterre 30 May 2011 10/02629.

10

Human Rights Litigation against Multinational Companies in Germany

Miriam Saage-Maaß

I. Introduction

Historically human rights violations and environmental destruction committed by companies have been dealt with in continental Europe on the level of the nation State through labour, anti-discrimination, consumer protection, and environmental law. The regulations on these various areas of law relevant to the realisation of human rights are the result of political struggles and protests of respective civil society actors: unions, workers, women, lesbian, bisexual, gay, transexual, intersex, and queer/questioning (LBGTIQ) and environmental activists. Of course, litigation has always played a role in these struggles, including in a less litigious jurisdiction like Germany. With the growing globalisation of trade and production, these primarily national regulations reach a limit: companies that comply with labour and environmental standards in Germany may very well be involved in harmful business practices through their subsidiaries or suppliers abroad. As global networks of lawyers and human rights activist develop and as the interconnectedness between civil society actors worldwide grows, the resistance against the abuses of multinational companies is growing too. Starting with the cases in the United States under the Alien Torts Statute in the early 1990s against oil companies such as Unocal and Shell for the commission of international crimes in Myanmar and Nigeria until today, a wide range of civil litigation have been pursued by communities and individuals harmed by corporate behaviour. While the German legal system is more focused on the State as the actor to ensure the respect for human rights and environmental standards through administrative and criminal law, the debate on the duties of care that German companies bear with regard to their foreign subsidiaries and suppliers is growing and is accompanied by civil litigation. In the following I will outline the options and hurdles for claimants to bring civil compensation claims against German companies involved in human rights abuses abroad.

Miriam Saage-Maaß, *Human Rights Litigation against Multinational Companies in Germany* In: *Human Rights Litigation against Multinationals in Practice*. Edited by: Richard Meeran, Oxford University Press.
DOI: 10.1093/oso/9780198866220.003.0010

II. Jurisdiction

Whether German courts can exercise jurisdiction in tort-based proceedings concerning corporate human rights abuses in developing countries depends on the domicile of the corporate defendants.

In case of complaints against companies domiciled in Germany, jurisdiction is determined on the basis of Articles 4(1) and 63(1) of Regulation (EU) No. 1215/2012 of the European Parliament and of the Council of 12 December 2012 on jurisdiction and the recognition and enforcement of judgments in civil and commercial matters (Regulation 1215/2012), according to which companies with statutory seat, central administration, or principal place of business in a Member State shall be sued in the courts of that Member State. This implies that German courts can exercise jurisdiction in complaints filed against parent or buying companies involved in overseas human rights abuse that have their statutory seat, central administration, or principal place of business in Germany.[1] Applying these rules, courts have accepted jurisdiction in the cases *Jabbir et al. v. KiK Textilien- und Non-Food GmbH* as well as in *Lliuya v. RWE AG* as in both cases the defendant companies were headquartered in Germany.

In case of complaints against subsidiaries and suppliers domiciled outside the European Union, the German laws on civil jurisdiction apply.[2] According to section 17 of the Code of Civil Procedure (*Zivilprozessordnung*, ZPO), which regulates jurisdiction over judicial persons, German courts have jurisdiction over companies seated in Germany. The decisive factor in determining the location where a company is seated is its actual centre of administration, that is, the place where fundamental management decisions are taken and implemented.[3] Consequently, the German rules do generally not provide the courts with jurisdiction over non-EU subsidiaries or suppliers. However, there is some case law in which German courts exercised jurisdiction over companies incorporated outside of the European Union on the basis that their administration was actually carried out in Germany.[4] Similarly, there is jurisprudence on section 23 ZPO, in which courts assumed jurisdiction over foreign defendants that held assets in Germany.[5] Despite the fact, that in these cases the claimants were domiciled in Germany, the German Federal Court of Justice (*Bundesgerichtshof, BGH*) has taken a restrictive position.[6]

[1] The courts cannot halt proceedings on the basis of *forum non-conveniens* grounds (*Owusu v. Jackson* [2005] ECR 1383).

[2] Article 6, Regulation 1215/2012.

[3] BGHZ 97, 269, 272.

[4] BGH, Urteil vom 15.3.2010–II ZR 27/09; OLG Köln, Urteil vom 31.01.2006–22 U 109/05.

[5] M. Stürner, 'Zivilprozessuale Voraussetzungen für Klagen gegen transnationale Unternehmen wegen Menschenrechtsverletzungen' in M. Krajewski, F. Oehm, and M. Saage-Maaß (eds), *Zivil- und strafrechtliche Unternehmensverantwortung für Menschenrechtsverletzungen* (2018) 84 f.

[6] BGH RIW 2013, 399 Rn 13.

Another option to bring non-EU subsidiaries or suppliers under the jurisdiction of German courts is to sue them together with the German parent or buying company on the basis of section 32 ZPO, which provides jurisdiction over tortious acts and omissions committed in Germany, irrespective of where the harmful event occurred.[7] What makes this provision interesting is that under German law the contribution of each tortfeasor to a jointly committed tort is attributable to the other tortfeasors, not only in terms of damages but also in terms of establishing jurisdiction under section 32 ZPO.[8] On this basis, the German Supreme Court (*Bundesgerichtshof*, BGH) has exercised jurisdiction over non-EU companies that were allegedly involved in torts committed jointly with German nationals on German territory.[9] To establish jurisdiction, it is sufficient that the claimants present the court with conclusive facts substantiating their claim.[10]

III. Applicable law

While German courts can exercise jurisdiction over complaints against parent or buying companies domiciled in Germany, they usually do not apply German substantive tort law to these cases. This follows from Article 4(1) of Regulation (EC) 864/2007 of the European Parliament and of the Council of 11 July 2007 on the law applicable to non-contractual obligations (Rome II), according to which the applicable law in tort proceedings involving a conflict of laws is generally the law of the country where the damage occurred (*lex loci damni*). This has important implications for the feasibility of such cases as the applicable law governs, *inter alia*, (i) the basis and extent of liability; (ii) the existence, nature, and assessment of damage or the remedy claimed; (iii) liability for acts of other persons; (iv) limitation periods; and (v) the measures which a court may take to prevent or terminate injury or damage or to ensure the provision of compensation.[11]

In *Jabbir et al. v. KiK Textilien- und Non-Food GmbH* the claims were based on Pakistani law following Article 4(1) of the Rome II Regulation, which was accepted both by the defendant as well as the court.

However, there are a number of exceptions to the *lex loci damni* rule, which may be relevant in tort-litigation against German companies involved in overseas human rights abuse. Given short statute of limitations provisions in some countries like those in South Asia, German law could be favourable, but in terms of calculation of damages it is not, as will be explained below. First, in cases arising

[7] For relevant case law, see C. Heinrich, 'ZPO § 32 Besonderer Gerichtsstand der unerlaubten Handlung, Note 15' in H.G. Musielak (ed.), *Zivilprozessordnung* (2014).

[8] BGH, NJW 1995, 1225; BGH, NJW-RR 1990, 604.

[9] BGH, Urteil vom 9. 3. 2010–XI ZR 93/09; BGH, Urteilvom 29.6.2010–VI ZR 122/09.

[10] BGH, XI ZR 93/09, Urteil vom 9. 3. 2010; BGH, VI ZR 122/09, Urteil vom 29.6.2010.

[11] Article 15, Rome II.

out of environmental damage or damage sustained by persons or property as a result of such damage, claimants can choose to base their claims on the law of the country in which the conduct giving rise to the damage occurred.[12] This exception may be relevant in complaints concerning human rights abuses arising out of environmental harm if the conduct giving rise to such harm can be said to consist in a wrongful act or omission at the parent or buying company's seat in Germany, as was the case in *Lliuya v. RWE*. Here, both the defendant and the first-instance court as well as the appeals courts accepted the application of Article 7 Rome II, which is why the case is being argued under German law.

Second, the courts may apply German law instead of the *lex loci damni*, if they consider the case to be manifestly more closely connected to Germany.[13] However, in cases concerning human rights abuses that are primarily related to the operations of foreign companies, it seems unlikely that the courts will do so. Some scholars argue that Article 4(3) Rome II should, in particular, be applicable in case where the claimants are structurally disadvantaged as they typically are in the cases discussed here.[14]

In addition, there are a number of exceptions allowing the courts to apply or consider provisions of the law of the forum (German law) while applying the *lex loci damni*. First, the courts may disregard a provision of the *lex loci damni*, if its application would be manifestly incompatible with the public policy of the forum, and apply the law of the forum State instead.[15] There is some evidence that this exception may be invoked where provisions of foreign law are incompatible with the European Convention on Human Rights.[16] The German Constitutional rulings on Anti-Discrimination as an aspect of the personality rights in German tort law are seen as an exception to the *lex loci damni* rule.[17]

Second, overriding mandatory provisions of the law of the forum State remain applicable, irrespective of the law otherwise applicable to the dispute.[18] On this basis, it is conceivable that German courts may apply section 823(2) of the German Civil Code (*Bürgerliches Gesetzbuch*, BGB), which provides persons with a cause of action in tort for violations of statutory rules, in combination with provisions

[12] Article 7, Rome II.

[13] Article 4(3), Rome II.

[14] C.C. Thomale and L. Hübner, 'Zivilgerichtliche Durchsetzung völkerrechtlicher Unternehmensverantwortung' (2017) 72 *Juristenzeitung* 385, 386.

[15] Article 26 and Recital 32, Rome II. See also A. Junker, 'Verordnung (EG) Nr. 864/2007' in F.J. Säcker and R. Rixecker (eds), *Münchner Kommentar zum Bürgerlichen Gesetzbuch, Band 10* (2010).

[16] European Commission, 'Study of the Legal Framework on Human Rights and the Environment Applicable to European Enterprises Operating Outside the European Union. Report of a Study prepared by the University of Edinburgh for the European Commission' (2010); International Law Association, 'International Civil Litigation and the Interests of the Public. Final Report, Sofia Conference' (2012).

[17] A. Heinen, 'Auf dem Weg zu einem transnationalen Deliktsrecht?—Zur Begründung deliktischer Sorgfalts- und Organisationspflichten in globalen Wertschöpfungsketten' in M. Krajewski and M. Saage-Maaß (eds), *Durchsetzung menschenrechtlicher Sorgfaltspflichten von Unternehmen* (2018) 96 f.

[18] Article 16, Rome II.

of the German Criminal Code.[19] Laws establishing specific human rights due diligence obligations for companies regarding their (foreign) subsidiaries and suppliers, as they are currently being discussed in Germany and other EU countries,[20] would fall under this category and would therefore be directly applicable, even in cases that are otherwise governed by foreign law.[21]

Finally, in assessing the conduct of the person to be liable, the courts can take account of rules of safety and conduct which were in force at the place and time of the event giving rise to liability.[22] These include all regulations having any relation to safety from the fields of public and private law, including safety rules developed by jurisprudence.[23] While Article 17 does not allow courts to apply these rules, they may consider them in determining whether the respondent's factual conduct was consistent with the applicable standard of care of the *lex loci damni*.[24] Consequently, in tort cases that are based on the parent or buying company's own wrongful conduct in Germany, the courts may consider relevant German safety duties in determining whether the parent or buying company acted negligently.

IV. Substantive legal basis in the German law of delict

As the previous section has shown, German courts will usually determine tort complaints against companies for human rights abuse related to foreign subsidiaries and suppliers on the basis of the law of the country where these abuses occurred. However, to the extent that they may apply the German law of delict (in line with the exceptions provided in the Rome II Regulation), there are a number of causes of action that may be relevant in such litigation, in particular section 823(1) and (2) BGB. This section introduces these causes of action and then discusses their relevance in tort-litigation against parent or buying companies domiciled in Germany. Due to the lack of relevant case law, this discussion is rather hypothetical in nature.

A. Section 823(I) BGB

The most relevant legal basis for tort litigation concerning corporate human rights abuse is arguably section 823(I) BGB, which protects persons against

[19] A. Spickhoff, 'VO (EG) 864/2007 Art. 16, Rn 3' in H.G. Bamberger and H. Roth (eds) *Beck'scher Online Kommentar BGB* (2014).

[20] See Germany, Switzerland

[21] More, see C. Hartmann, 'Haftung von Unternehmen für Menschenrechtsverletzungen im Ausland aus Sicht des Internationalen Privat-und Zivilverfahrensrechts' in M. Krajewski and M. Saage-Maaß (eds), *Die Durchsetzung menschenrechtlicher Sorgfaltspflichten von Unternehmen* (2018) 301–5

[22] Article 17, Rome II.

[23] Junker (n. 15).

[24] H. Dörner, 'Rom II-VO Artikel 17 Sicherheits- und Verhaltensregeln' in R. Schulze (ed.), *Bürgerliches Gesetzbuch* (2014).

infringements of their life, body, freedom of movement, property, and personality rights.[25] Consequently, it protects persons against all human rights abuses involving damage to one or more of these protected interests. This includes abuses of a number of civil and political rights, such as the right to life, the right to bodily integrity, the right to liberty and security, or freedom from torture, which typically involve damage to life, body, and freedom of movement. Abuses of economic and social rights, such as the right to food and housing, are only covered to the extent that they involve damage to property. Abuses of core labour rights, such as freedom from forced or compulsory labour, the right to safe and healthy working conditions, or the right to rest and leisure, are covered to the extent that they have caused damage to life or body or restricted freedom of movement.[26] The general personality right protects privacy rights, freedom of association, and protects against discrimination on the basis of ethnicity, race, religion, and other matters.[27]

To hold a person liable for such infringements, the claimant must prove a number of requirements. These include (i) the violation of a codified normative rule, (ii) unlawfulness, (iii) fault, and (iv) causation.[28]

To establish the violation of a codified normative rule, the claimant must prove that the defendant infringed one of their protected rights through an act or omission. In the case of positive acts, conduct violating a codified normative rule is in principle unlawful. In the case of an omission, the claimant must prove that the conduct is unlawful (see further detail below).

The fault requirement is met when the defendants acted intentionally or negligently, which, according to section 276(II) BGB, is defined as conduct contrary to the care expected by society. With intentional conduct the defendant's intention to engage in conduct contrary to the care expected by society needs to be proved. Where it is alleged that the fault requirement is met as a result of negligent conduct, the court applies an objective test comparing the defendants' factual conduct with the conduct that can be expected from a person of average circumspection and capability. If the court concludes that the average careful person would have foreseen and prevented the damage and that the defendant's conduct falls short of this threshold, the defendant has acted negligently.[29] In *Lliuya v. RWE* the claimants define the relevant action causing the harm as the fact that the defendant has been

[25] According to section 823(1) German Civil Code, 'a person who, intentionally or negligently, unlawfully, injures the life, body, freedom, property or another right of another person is liable to make compensation to the other party for the damage arising from this'. In a long line of case law, the courts have established that the term 'other rights' includes general personality rights.

[26] Heinen (n. 17).

[27] Nordhues argues that forms of modern-day slavery are also protected under the general personality principle. S. Nordhues, *Die Haftung der Muttergesellschaft und ihres Vorstandes für Menschenrechtsverletzungen im Konzern* (2019) 109; G. Osieka, *Zivilrechtliche Haftung deutscher Unternehmen für menschenrechtsbeeinträchtigende Handlungen ihrer Zulieferer* (2014) 184.

[28] For an English-language introduction to section 823(I) BGB, see C. van Dam, *European Tort Law* (2nd edn, 2013) 73ff.

[29] Ibid., 231f. and 256.

and keeps on knowingly emitting greenhouse gas which has caused the threat to the claimants property.[30]

In addition to the infringement of a protected right, unlawfulness, and fault, the claimants must prove a causal relationship between the defendant's conduct and the infringement. In determining causation, the courts apply the *conditio sine qua non* test: when the damage would also have occurred if the defendant had not acted the way he did, he does not incur liability.[31]

i. Further detail on establishing a defendant's fault by omission

In case of omissions, the conduct of the defendant is only unlawful if it breached an affirmative duty to prevent the infringement. These duties are called safety duties (*Verkehrspflichten*) and are very similar to common law duties of care. As the concept of safety duties developed in case law, there are a large number of specific safety duties relevant, for example, to landowners, manufacturers, building contractors, or operators of mines and landfills.[32] In situations in which it is unclear whether the defendant incurred a safety duty, the courts determine the existence and extent of such a duty on the basis of general principles. In principle, safety duties exist where a person creates a source of danger, controls and profits from a source of danger, or voluntarily assumes a duty to ensure a source of danger is made safe.[33] Where a person is subject to a safety duty, the person has to take all possible and reasonable measures to prevent damage to third parties.[34] The courts determine the nature and extent of such measures on the basis of the specific facts of the case, balancing the benefits and costs associated with taking such measures. The defendant will be expected to have taken greater precautionary measures when the probability of potential infringements is high, the potential effects are more serious, and the costs of preventing such infringements are comparatively low.[35] In determining the nature of reasonable preventative measures, the courts can consider standards of public law, soft law as well as standards developed by private actors.[36] Potentially, soft law standards like the United Nations Guiding Principles on Business and Human Rights, the Organisation for Co-operation and Economic Development (OECD) Guidelines on Business and Human Rights or the OECD Guidance on Responsible Business Conduct as well as the standards of

[30] G. Wagner, *Klimahaftung vor Gericht. Eine Fallstudie* () 20.

[31] van Dam (n. 28) 310.

[32] For an overview of specific safety duties, see G. Spindler, '§823, Rn 227–232' in Bamberger and Roth (eds) n. 19).

[33] Ibid.

[34] H. Kötz and G. Wagner, *Deliktsrecht* (2010), 80f.

[35] BGH, VersR 2007, 72 Rn.11. For further criteria relevant for determining the nature and extent of reasonable preventative measures, see G. Spindler, '§823, Rn 233-258' in Bamberger and Roth (eds) (n. 19).

[36] G. Spindler, '§823, Rn 255' in Bamberger and Roth (eds) (n. 19).

multi-stakeholder initiatives can influence the courts determination of what reasonable precautionary measures are.[37] Also, standards set out by the company's own public-facing documents, like annual reports, and the voluntary corporate social responsibility codes it has signed up to, should be relevant in this regard.

In addition to proving the violation of a safety duty, in order to establish a defendant's fault by omission the claimant must also prove that the damage was foreseeable to the defendant.

B. Section 823(II) BGB

The second provision relevant in tort litigation concerning corporate human rights abuse is section 823(II) BGB, which protects persons against damages resulting from violations of statutory rules and thus opens up the field of tort law to other legal domains, such as administrative and criminal law. To the extent that human rights abuses involve violations of statutory rules, the provision provides claimants with a cause of action.

However, section 823(II), BGB, does not protect against violations of all forms of statutory rules, but only of those rules that are intended to protect individual interests (*Schutzgesetze*). In the field of criminal law these include, for example, section 229 of the Criminal Code (*Strafgesetzbuch*, StGB), which imposes a penalty for negligent conduct causing bodily harm.[38] In addition, section 823(II), BGB, contains two further requirements. First, the claimant must examine the relevant statutory rule to ensure they belong to the group of persons protected by the rule. Secondly, the infringement suffered by the claimant must fall within scope of protection of the rule.[39]

In order to establish liability, the claimant must prove that they satisfy the requirements of the specific statutory rule. The rule may prescribe a standard required to establish fault, in which case the claimant will have to prove that standard has been met. Where the rule does not provide for a fault requirement, the claimant still has to prove the defendant intentionally or negligently breached the statutory rule.[40]

German norms of criminal law are applicable to conduct occurring overseas provided that conduct constituted a criminal offence at the locality of its commission and that the offender was a German national at the time of the offence.[41] Of

[37] M.M. Saage-Maaß, *Labour Conditions in the Global Supply Chain—What is the extend of German corporate responsibility?* (2011) 11 ff.; M. Payandeh, 'Deliktische Haftung von Unternehmen für transnationale Menschenrechtsverletzungen' in K. Boele-Woelki (ed.), *Festschrift für Karsten Schmidt zum 80. Geburtstag*, Vol. II (2019) 131.

[38] G.G. Spindler, '§823, Rn 175' in Bamberger and Roth (eds) n. 19).

[39] van Dam (n. 28) 285.

[40] G. Spindler, '§823, Rn 163–165' in Bamberger and Roth (eds) n. 19).

[41] Section 7(2)(1) StGB.

course they are also applicable if the act or omission of the offender was committed on German territory.[42]

C. Section 1004 BGB and *Lliaya v. RWE*

If property is impaired or if there is a concrete risk that it will be negatively affected in the future, the owner may require the disturber to remove the interference or may seek an injunction from the court under section 1004 BGB prohibiting the interference. Section 1004 is directed at the elimination of an existing impairment so that it is removed for the future. It is not directed at restoring the previous status quo by eliminating or remedying the consequences of the impairment.

In the case of floods, it is recognised in this respect that the claim for removal of the consequences can be used to demand the removal of the cause of floods (including where flooding has not occurred previously).[43]

With regard to the impairment of property, the central problem is the distinction between the claim for elimination of consequences sought by the claimant and a claim for injunctive relief. Where damage or destruction to property has already occurred there is a clear route to satisfying the requirement of impairment. Where there is a threat of imminent impairment of property, the claimant can only claim injunctive relief to prevent pre-existing actions from continuing.[44]

The impairment must be attributable to the defendant and requires a proof of causality in the sense of condition *sine qua non* (i.e. if the defendant had not acted or omitted to act the way it did, the impairment would not have occurred).[45]

i. *Lliiuya v. RWE*

While the case is in the discovery phase before the first instance court, section 1004 BGB is the basis of *Lliuya v. RWE* as it gives a claim for both a removal of interference and injunction to prohibit further interference. In this case, the plaintiff, a Peruvian farmer was the owner of a plot of land in the city of Huaraz in Peru, which lay below a glacial lake at the foot of the Andes. The defendant, RWE AG, was registered in the German city of Essen and was the parent company of the energy group RWE, which owned various companies operating in the field of coal-based power generation. The plaintiff alleged that his home was acutely threatened by flooding as the glacial lake could break at any time due to the increased water level, which was a consequence of anthropogenic climate change.

42 Section 3 StGB, in conjunction with section 9(1) StGB.

43 O. Palandt, *Bürgerliches Gesetzbuch*, 73rd edn, section 1004 marginal no. 29: 'In the case of a dam burst, the source of the disturbance is the hole in the dam, its removal can be demanded, not the flood damage'.

44 Ibid., section 1004 marginal no. 27.

45 Wagner (n. 30) 23.

The plaintiff sought a declaration that the defendant should bear the costs of protective measures against a glacial flood of the plaintiff's property in proportion to its contribution to the impairment of global greenhouse gas emissions. It further argued that the defendant was jointly responsible for this anthropogenic climate change since it released large quantities of greenhouse gases throughout Europe, particularly through its subsidiaries which were active in the field of coal-fired power generation. The contribution of the defendant to global warming—including its legal predecessors—amounted to approximately 0.45 per cent. Total costs of approximately €3.5 million for remediation measure were incurred for this, which would correspond to a cost share of €17,000 for the defendant. The appeals court agreed with the argument of the plaintiffs that it was possible to regard even the high risk of a flood as an impairment as the use of the property in the potentially flooded area was restricted by this circumstance. It therefore allowed the case to proceed into the discovery phase.[46] The court ordered expert opinions on the question of causation and attribution.

D. Corporate liability and its relevance in transborder human rights

German tort law, if applicable under the Rome II Regulation, provides a cause of action to hold German companies liable for abuses directly caused by their employees. In general, there seem to be two potential approaches of establishing the liability of the German parent or buying company in these types of cases. The first approach is to argue that the foreign subsidiary or supplier, or its employees, were actually vicarious agents of the German company in the sense of section 831(I) BGB. If that were established, the German company would incur liability for their harmful acts or omissions if it failed to prove that it exercised reasonable care with regard to the instruction and supervision of its employees.

i. Vicarious liability

Section 831(I) BGB, constitutes a form of negligence liability with a reversed burden of proof. According to this provision, a person who uses another person to perform a task (*Geschäftsherr*, principal) is liable for damages unlawfully caused by that person (*Verrichtungsgehilfe*, vicarious agent) in performing the task, including damages covered by section 823 BGB (Duty to Compensate for Damage). However, the principal, which can also be a juridical person, does not incur liability if they can prove (i) that they exercised reasonable care in selecting, equipping, and supervising the vicarious agent or (ii) that the damage would also have

[46] OLG Hamm, I-5 U 15/17, Hinweis- und Beweisbeschluss vom 30.11.2017.

occurred if they had exercised such care.[47] Section 831(I) typically applies to employees working in the principal's small or medium-sized enterprise, rather than in relation to large corporate groups. However, as employment relationships have become more complicated, recent case law has addressed the question of whether independent companies, or employees working for independent companies, may qualify as vicarious agents under section 831(I) BGB.

The defining feature of vicarious agents is that they have to observe the instructions of the principal in carrying out the tasks with which they are entrusted. In order to qualify as a vicarious agent, the principal must be in a position to relieve the agent of their duties and control the nature and scope of his activities at any time, which has to be determined on the basis of the facts of the case.[48] On the basis of these principles, the German Supreme Court generally denies that affiliates within a corporate group,[49] or employees of affiliates,[50] qualify as vicarious agents of other companies of the group. In fact, the court applies these principles in a very strict way, which is biased towards legal criteria of independence. For example, in a case concerning an employee of one of the defendant company's affiliates, the court ruled that the employee could not be regarded as a vicarious agent of the defendant company, although he had previously worked for that company, had presented himself to the claimant as an employee of that company, and considered himself as being bound by the instructions of that company.[51] The court dismissed these arguments on the basis that his employment relationship with the defendant company had terminated before the relevant events, which would imply that he was no longer bound by its instructions. On the ground of the missing employment relationship, the court also criticised the appeal court's decision to shift the burden of proving that the employee was not a vicarious agent to the defendant. For these reasons, section 831(1) BGB appears to be of limited help in transnational human rights cases involving corporate group or supply chain structures.[52]

ii. Duty of care

The second, more promising approach is to argue that the German parent or buying company breached a safety duty to protect the claimants from the damages caused by the subsidiary's or supplier's operations under section 823(I) BGB. While there

[47] van Dam (n. 28)_503; G. Wagner, '§ 831' in J. von Hein, *Münchener Kommentar zum Bürgerlichen Gesetzbuch* (7th edn, 2017), para. 35 ff., 48.

[48] BGH, Urteil vom 10. 3. 2009–VI ZR 39/08 = NJW 2009, 1740; BGH, Urteil vom 12.6.1997–I ZR 36/95 = NJW 1998, 1078 L; BGH, Urteil vom 25.2.1988–VII ZR 348/86 = NJW 1988, 1380; BGH, Urteil vom 30.6.1966–VII ZR 23/65 = NJW 1966, 1807.

[49] BGH, Urteil vom 6. 11. 2012–VI ZR 174/11 = NJW 2013, 1002.

[50] BGH, Urteil vom 02.12.2014–VI ZR 520/13; BGH, Urteil vom 3.6.2014–VI ZR 394/13 = VersR 2014, 1018; BGH, Urteil vom 10.12.2013–VI ZR 534/12 = NJW-RR 2014, 614.

[51] BGH, Urteil vom 10.12.2013–VI ZR 534/12 = NJW-RR 2014, 614.

[52] M. Habersack and M. Ehrl, 'Verantwortlichkeit inländischer Unternehmen für Menschenrechtsverletzungen durch ausländische Zulieferer—de lege lata und de lege ferenda' (2019) *Archiv für civilistische Praxis* 219/ 2, 193; Thomale and Hübner (n. 14).

is a growing consensus in academic writing[53] and to some extent also in jurisprudence that accepts a duty of care of a parent company towards its subsidiaries,[54] there is no legal precedent on this question in cases of human rights abuses in the corporate group or in the supply chain. Courts would determine the existence of such a duty on the basis of general principles.[55] Thus, they would consider whether the parent or buying company has created, or controlled and profited from, the source of danger causing harm to the claimants, or whether it has assumed a duty to protect the claimants from that source of danger.

This may be the case where the parent or buying company effectively directs and administers the harmful operations in question or where it has assumed responsibility to manage the risks involved in these operations, for example by formulating and implementing health and safety standards at the subsidiary or supplier site. In the former situation, the parent or buying company could be considered as having created and controlled the source of danger causing harm to the claimants, while the latter situation could be treated as the subsidiary or supplier delegating their safety duties to the parent company. Where safety duties are delegated, which does not require a contract but can be inferred from the factual assumption of responsibility, the person assuming the duty becomes liable towards third parties for damages resulting from non-compliance with that duty.[56] The original duty holders would then be freed from responsibility if they had shown prudence in the selection of the delegate.[57] This does not mean that it would be possible for the parent company to avoid liability by simply refraining from any involvement in human rights issues in relation to the operations of a subsidiary or supplying producer. The original duty bearer will still have to ensure that his or her delegate was carrying out the necessary precautionary measures to avoid the potential harm.[58]

While a delegation of safety duties implies that the person assuming the duty becomes the main duty bearer, the person delegating the duty is not completely released of any responsibility. Instead, it has to ensure that the delegate complies with that duty by selecting a capable person and by adequately instructing and supervising that person.[59] The required extent of supervision increases with the

[53] G. Wagner, 'Haftung für Menschenrechtsverletzungen' (2015) *RabelZ* 717; G. Wagner, '§ 823' in J. von Hein, *Münchener Kommentar zum Bürgerlichen Gesetzbuch* (7th edn, 2017), para. 99; C. König, 'Delikthaftung von Konzernmuttergesellschaften' (2017) *Archiv für civilistische Praxis* 217/4, 611; A. Schall, 'Die Mutter-Verantwortlichkeit für Menschenrechtsverletzungen ihrer Auslandstöchter' (2018) *Zeitschrift für Unternehmens- und Gesellschaftsrecht* 479; Habersack and Ehrl, ibid.

[54] '*Neubürger Urteil*', LG München I, Urteil vom 10.12.2013—5HK O 1387/10.

[55] See Chapter B on section 823(I) BGB.

[56] OLG Frankfurt a. M., Urteil vom 19.2.2008–18 U 58/07; OLG Frankfurt a. M., Urteil vom 30.4.1998–24 U 61-96; BGH, Urteil vom 17.1.1989–VI ZR 186/88 (and case law cited there).

[57] BGH, Urteil vom 26.9.2006–VI ZR 166/05.

[58] Wagner, section 823 (n. 53), para. 469.

[59] BGH, Urteil vom 1.10.2013–VI ZR 369/12; BGH, Urteil vom 26.9.2006—VI ZR 166/05; BGH, Urteil vom 7.10.1975–VI ZR 43/74;

dangerousness of the delegated activity and with the likelihood that the other party will behave in an irresponsible manner.[60] On this basis, a parent or buying company may incur liability if it fails to adequately supervise a subsidiary or supplier responsible for a particularly dangerous aspect of its production process. While there is no case law concerning corporate groups, the German Supreme Court has convicted a petrochemical company for hazardous disposal of industrial waste by an independent contractor.[61]

iii. *Jabbir v. KiK*

The *KiK* case concerns a fire at the Ali Enterprises (AE) textile factory in Karachi in September 2012, Pakistan, in which 259 workers died and 32 were severely injured. The most notable customer of the factory was the German textile company KiK Textilien und Non-Food GmbH (KiK). According to its own statements KiK purchased at least 70 per cent of the production output of AE over a period of five years.[62] Four claimants, two fathers and one mother of deceased factory workers as well as one survivor, filed a civil lawsuit in March 2015 against KiK at the District Court of Dortmund (Landgericht Dortmund), demanding €30,000 per person as compensation for material damage.

In the KiK case, the claimants applied Pakistani common law, which is strongly influenced by Indian and UK jurisprudence.[63] Still, the negligence claim's reasoning on the defendant's duties of care towards its long-standing supplier's employees is also relevant to arguing a *Verkehrssicherungspflicht* under German law, as both require an obligation be breached by a negligent act or omission. Following the established English case law, the claimants argued that KiK breached its duty of care towards Ali Enterprises factory employees.[64] The duty of care requirements were largely based on the *Caparo v. Dickman* and *Chandler v. Cape* decisions, which establish a duty of care under the conditions: the harm that occurred was foreseeable and that there was sufficient proximity between the parties.[65] The *Chandler v. Cape* decision further details that a duty of care exists when (i) the businesses of the parent and subsidiary are in a relevant respect the same; (ii) the parent has, or ought to have, superior knowledge on some relevant aspect of health and safety in the particular industry; (iii) the subsidiary's system of work is unsafe as the parent knew, or ought to have known; and (iv) the parent knew or ought to

[60] BGH, Urteil vom 26.9.2006–VI ZR 166/05.

[61] BGH, Urteil vom 7.10.1975–VI ZR 43/74.

[62] H. Kazim and N. Klawitter, 'Zuverlässiger Lieferant' (*Der Spiegel*, 22 October 2012) <http://www.spiegel.de/spiegel/print/d-89234400.html> accessed on 30 July 2020.

[63] *Khan v. Haleem*, (2012) CLD (SC) 6 (2011), 8 (Khilji Arif Hssain, J., concurring) (Pak.); *Khanzada v. Sherin*, 1996 CLC 1440 (Peshwar) (Pak.), citing Indian law authoritatively in case alleging medical malpractice.

[64] C. Terwindt, S. Leader, A. Yilmaz-Vastardis, et al., 'Supply Chain Liability: Pushing the Boundaries of the Common Law?' (2018) 8(3) *Journal of European Tort Law* 276.

[65] *Caparo Industries plc v. Dickman* [1992] 2 AC 605; *Chandler v. Cape Plc* [2012] EWCA Civ 525 (25 April 2012).

have foreseen that the subsidiary or its employees would rely on its using that superior knowledge for the employee's protection.[66] The Dortmund District Court was asked to assess the relevant duty of care and thereby had to assess the nature of KiK and AE's relationship, applicable corporate social responsibility (CSR) industry standards, relevant standards for safety audits, and KiK's duty in relation to such audits.[67] The claimants argued that there was a clear economic dependence between KiK and AE. Since KiK factually controlled its supplier through economic dependence, KiK potentially had the possibility and power to dictate the terms and conditions under which AE ought to conduct its business in Pakistan. The claimants further constructed this obligation through a review of KiK's 2009 code of conduct,[68] and a statement by KiK's Managing Director weeks after the AE fire that '[t]he monitoring of adherence to safe and fire prevention [is] obligatory for us as a buyer'.[69] As the defendant's code of conduct was incorporated into the terms and conditions of every purchasing order,[70] the claimants argued that public pledges on safe and ethical working conditions created legal obligations: self-regulation must lead to self-obligation.[71]

The claimants also argued for vicarious liability, which provides for the strict liability of the employer or in a relationship 'akin to employment'.[72] The concept of vicarious liability under common law is more flexible than it is under German law as it is not necessarily based on a formal contractual relationship but instead

66 *Chandler v. Cape Plc* [2012] EWCA Civ 525 (25 April 2012), para. 80. The appeal's decision also clarifies that for the purpose of (iv), it is not necessary to show that the parent is in the practice of intervening in the health and safety policies of the subsidiary. The court will look at the relationship between the companies more widely. It may be enough to show the parent has a practice of intervening in the trading operations of the subsidiary, for example, production and funding issues. More recently this reasoning has been confirmed in the *Vedanta* UK Supreme Court decision, where the court held that 'everything depends on the extent to which, and the way in which, the parent availed itself of the opportunity to take over, intervene in, control, supervise or advise the management of the relevant operations (including land use) of the subsidiary. All that the existence of a parent subsidiary relationship demonstrates is that the parent had such an opportunity.' *Vedanta Resources PLC v. Lungowe* [2019] UKSC20, para. 49.

67 Terwindt, Leader, Yilmaz-Vastardis, et al. (n. 64) 268.

68 Here, KiK stated in the section 'Standard for Employment' in regards to 'Health and Safety at Work' in its supply chain that '[t]he workplace and the practice of the work must not harm the employees' or workers' health and safety. A safe and clean working environment shall be provided. Occupational health and safety practices shall be promoted, which prevent accidents and injury in the course of work or as a result of the operation of employer facilities. These safety practices and procedures must be communicated to the employees as well as the workers; they have to be trained in effective usage....' KiK Textilien und Non-Food GmbH, Code of Conduct, revised version, 1 August 2009, p. 3.

69 KiK Textilien und Non-Food GmbH, Statement on the Panorama Program of 06.12.2012.

70 Terwindt, Leader, Yilmaz-Vastardis, et al. (n. 64) 268.

71 A. Beckers, 'Legalization under the Premises of Globalization: Why and Where to Enforce Corporate Social Responsibility Codes' (2017) 15 *Indiana Journal of Global Legal Studies* 15. Interestingly, in the *Vedanta* case, the UK Supreme Court made the same point in stating that '[t]he parent may incur the relevant responsibility to third parties if, in published materials, it holds itself out as exercising that degree of supervision and control of its subsidiaries, even if it does not in fact do so. In such circumstances its very omission may constitute the abdication of a responsibility which it has publicly undertaken.' *Vedanta Resources PLC v. Lungowe* [2019] UKSC20, para. 53.

72 Terwindt, Leader, Yilmaz-Vastardis, et al. (n. 64) 269.

examines the overall circumstances of a business relationship between two parties through a five-factor lens.[73]

While the court in *Jabbir v. KiK* dismissed the case on the grounds that the limitation period has expired, it only dealt superficially with the question of which duties of care a buyer may owe towards the employees of a subsidiary.[74] The academic debate that followed the case shows that such as duty of care may well be argued[75] but that nevertheless a legislative approach would be favourable and help to give clarity to both claimants as well as defendants.[76] In July 2020, the German ministry of labour and social affairs has announced that it will present a legislative proposal that would introduce a mandatory human rights due diligence obligation for companies based in Germany.[77] Still, in the current election period such a law should be passed. From what is known so far of leaked government documents, such a law will foresee both administrative sanctions as well as provision for civil liability.

V. Practical and procedural factors

While substantive law does potentially provide causes of action to victims of human rights abuse, procedural provisions in German law also in principle allow for such claims. Nevertheless, there are several restrictions which pose severe obstacles to litigation.

A. Discovery and burden of proof

Litigation against transnational corporations is commonly characterised by a structural asymmetry of information. Before engaging in tort litigation against corporations for human rights abuses abroad it is worthwhile analysing how evidence can be collected. In particular, internal records of the defendant potentially contain information necessary for substantiating the legal claim, such as information

[73] *E v. English Province of Our Lady of Charity* [2012] EWCA (Civ) 938, [2013] 2 WLR 958, 19, 70 ff

[74] L.G. Dortmund, 7 O 95/15, Beschluss vom 10.1.2019

[75] Thomale and Hübner (n. 14); M. Weller and C. Thomale, 'Menschenrechtsklagen gegen deutsche Unternehmen' (2017) *Zeitschrift für Unternehmens- und Gesellschaftsrecht* 509; A. Schall, 'Die Mutter-Verantwortlichkeit für Menschenrechtsverletzungen ihrer Auslandstöchter' (2018) *Zeitschrift für Unternehmens- und Gesellschaftsrech* 479; König (n. 53) 611.

[76] Wagner (n. 53); H.-P. Mansel, 'Internationales Privatrecht de lege lata wie de lege ferenda und Menschenrechtsverantwortlichkeit deutscher Unternehmen' (2018) *Zeitschrift für Unternehmens- und Gesellschaftsrech* 439.

[77] Business Human Rights Resource Center, 'Commentary: Germany takes a step closer to mandatory human rights supply chain due diligence ' (*Business and Human Rights Resource Center*, 15 July 2020) <https://www.business-humanrights.org/en/latest-news/commentary-germany-takes-a-step-closer-to-mandatory-human-rights-supply-chain-due-diligence/ >, accessed 5 August 2020.

on the awareness of adverse human rights impacts associated with the company's activities, the lack of appropriate care and prudence in the management. In the German civil law system access to such evidence in the possession of the defendant party is comparatively difficult.

i. General principles of the burden of proof

The general standard of proof is effective certainty (*brauchbarer Grad an Gewissheit*), which means that the courts must be convinced by the facts presented and proved by the claimant beyond reasonable doubt.[78] Each party is responsible for producing the documentary evidence that will support its claims. Each party stating a fact favourable for the justification or the rejection of a claim is under an obligation to provide proof. Therefore the burden to prove the different requirements of section 823(I) and (II) generally rests on the claimants.

ii. Discovery

The ZPO does not provide for pre-trial discovery procedures. Also, in the trial phase the court is, in principle, under no duty to investigate the facts. It will accept all facts the claimant has substantiated as proved unless the defendant disputes them. For example, in the *KiK* case the defendant never disputed the intensity of the business relationship between the company and the supplying factory; the court therefore simply accepted the factual presentation of the claimants. If the defendant challenges the facts produced by the claimant, the claimant has to prove the disputed facts to the conviction of the court.[79] The court may also call expert witnesses into the proceedings or ask for expert opinions.

In both the *KiK* case as well as the *RWE* case (*Lliuya v. RWE*, see above), the respective courts commissioned expert opinions after declaring the cases admissible. In *KiK* the court asked for an expert opinion on Pakistani law as it wanted to first assess the legal questions of the case before going into the factual assessment.[80] In the *RWE* case the court ordered an expert opinion on the factual question of assessment of damages of the claimants and the causal link between damages and climate change and the actions of the defendant.[81]

The German Federal Court of Justice (BGH) has clarified that there is no general procedural duty of disclosure for a party not bearing the burden of proof.[82] This is also the prevailing view among civil law scholars today.[83] Such a duty to surrender documents can only arise pursuant to the special provisions of the Code

78 Section 286(1) ZPO. U. Foerste, '§ 286 Freie Beweiswürdigung, Rn 17-22' in H.J. Musielak (ed.), *Zivilprozessordnung mit Gerichtsverfassungsgesetz. Kommentar* (11th edn, 2014).

79 Ibid.

80 LG Dortmund, 7 O 95/15, Beschluss vom 29.08.2016.

81 OLG Hamm, I-5 U 15/17, Hinweis- und Beweisbeschluss vom 30.11.2017.

82 Beschluss des BGH vom 26.10.2006, III ZB 2/06, NJW 2007, 155.

83 H. Prütting, 'Discovery im deutschen Zivilprozess?' (2008) 3 *Anwaltsblatt* 153–9.

of Civil Procedure.[84] Such provisions are sections 422, 423 ZPO on the one hand and section 142(1) ZPO on the other, which contain potential entry points for an increasingly favourable legal position for the plaintiff.

If a record or document is in the hands of the opposing party, the other party can file a petition asking the court to direct the opponent to produce the said record or document (section 421 ZPO). The petition to produce must include (section 424 ZPO) a description of the document, details of the facts to be proven by the document, and a complete description of the contents of the document which needs to be as accurate as possible. Furthermore, the basis for the allegation that the opposing party possesses the document needs to be explained, and a description and *prima facie* justification of the grounds from which the obligation to produce the document arises has to be provided.[85] Unless the opposing party has itself referred to the document in the course of offering evidence (section 423 ZPO), the right to demand surrender or production must be founded on substantive private law (section 422 ZPO). Provision for such a statutory right to demand the production or surrender of documents is made in various German civil and commercial substantive laws.[86] The most relevant entitlement is contained in section 810 BGB.[87] Still, this provision is used very restrictively by courts as the BGH has outlined that a legitimate legal interest in inspecting a document is missing if the claimant demands inspection solely based on vague assumptions.[88] The court further clarified that section 810 BGB does not contain an entitlement to inspect a complete file but rather a concrete document which must be designated and its alleged content must be described.[89]

Also, section 142 ZPO is not designed as a means of disclosing a wide range of potentially relevant documents via the court.[90] Accordingly, the court is not allowed to order the disclosure of such documents for the purpose of a mere information retrieval but only if it can rely on conclusive references to concrete matters of fact provided by the defendant.[91] It is also important to note that a party cannot be forced (e.g. by means of an administrative fine or arrest) to comply with an order for disclosure.[92]

84 BGH, XI ZR 277/05, Urteil vom 26.06.07.

85 J. Holdsworth, 'Taking Evidence in Germany in Support of Foreign Action' <http://www.dh-resources.com/eng/04_publi/documents/discovery.01.PDF> accessed on 5 August 2020, p. 6.

86 Ibid.

87 'A person who has a legal interest in the examination of a document in the possession of another may demand from the possessor permission to examine it if the document is made in his interest or if in the document a legal relationship existing between himself and another is recorded or if the document contains the negotiations of any legal transaction that have been conducted between the person interested and another person or between one of them and a common intermediary.' Section 810 BGB.

88 BGH, XI ZR 264/13 Urteil vom 27.05.2014.

89 H.-T. Soergel, *Bürgerliches Gesetzbuch*, 13th edn, section 810 Rn. 18 mwN.

90 H.J. Musielak, Zivilprozessordnung (ZPO) (2002), section 142 ZPO at point 1.

91 BGH, Beschluss vom 15 Juni 2010, Az. XI ZR 318/09: Exploratory fact finding ('*Ausforschungsbeweis*') is prohibited.

92 K. Wach, M. Epping, U. Zinsmeister, et al., 'Germany Report' <http://ec.europa.eu/competition/antitrust/actionsdamages/national_reports/germany_en.pdf> accessed 18 November 2020, p. 13.

In conclusion, especially section 142 ZPO but also sections 422 ff. ZPO are applied very cautiously by German courts. While they provide an opportunity to obtain documents in the possession of the defendant corporation, this cannot be compared to the pre-trial or trial discovery of documents existing in many common law countries.

iii. Shifts in the burden of proof

The lack of pre-trial and far-reaching trial discovery is to some extent compensated for by the possibility for courts to ease or shift the burden of proof. With regard to negligence, the courts consider the actions that lead to a violation of a duty of care as *prima facie* evidence of whether the defendant was intentional, reckless, or negligent in their conduct, which implies that the claimants only have to prove that the defendants acted contrary to the standard of care required by society or in breach of a safety duty.[93] Where the claimants lack insight into the internal processes of the defendants, the courts also shift the burden of proof with regard to the state of mind of the defendant and whether they acted intentionally, recklessly, or negligently.[94] This is usually done in product liability litigation, where the courts presume that the defendants acted negligently once the claimants have established that their rights have been infringed by a product that was sold in an unsafe condition. The defendants then have to prove that they took reasonable precautionary measures in order to rebut this presumption.[95] The same principle also applies to environmental litigation where the operator of an industrial plant has to prove that they did not act negligently once it is established that the claimants' rights were infringed by the plant's emissions.[96] In addition to that, the courts ease the burden of proof with regard to the causal relationship between the defendant's conduct and the infringement. Where it is proven that the defendant acted in breach of a safety duty to prevent the kind of damage suffered by the claimant, this is considered as *prima facie* evidence of causation.[97] In cases concerning environmental liability, emissions above statutory limits indicate causation.[98]

As the claim against KiK was dismissed on grounds of statute of limitations, and in the absence of other relevant precedent regarding the extent and requirements of corporate human rights duties of care it is difficult to say at present, if and to what extent relaxation and shifts in the burden of proof will help overcome the lack of discovery.

93 BGHZ 80, 186, 199.
94 G. Spindler, '§823, Rn 27' in Bamberger and Roth (eds) (n. 19).
95 BGH, VI ZR 212/66, Urteil vom 26.11.1968.
96 BGH, VI ZR 223/82, Urteil vom 18.09.1984.
97 BGH, VI ZR 271/92, Urteil vom 14.12.1993.
98 BGH, VI ZR 223/82, Urteil vom 18.09.1984.

B. Collective actions

Further practical barriers to tort litigation against German companies involved in overseas abuse are the limitations on collective actions. German law of civil procedure does not generally provide for the possibility of joinder of claims in a group action, in the sense that all procedural motions can be done on behalf of the group as such. Nor is it possible to file class actions similar to those in some common law jurisdictions. Apart from certain types of consumer claims, where legislative reform was recently introduced and now allows for consumers to bring model declaratory action (*Musterfeststellungsklage*),[99] German law only provides for a joinder of claims that are based on the same, or an essentially similar, factual and legal cause.[100] In this case, the proceedings relating to each claim are joined; there is only one discovery procedure and only one judgment relevant to all claimants. However, each claimant is considered as an individual party and carries on the lawsuit independently, which implies that lawyers can usually not act in one petition on behalf of all claimants. Instead, they have to treat each claim as a separate lawsuit. This requires an advanced administrative infrastructure for claimants' law firms, which may not prove to be economically viable given the expected income in case of winning the litigation, as discussed in further detail below.

C. Limitation periods

According to the Rome II Regulation, limitation periods are generally governed by the *lex loci damni*. Under German law, the limitation period in civil claims is generally three years. It commences at the end of the year, in which the claim arose and the claimant was or should have been aware of all circumstances giving rise to the claim and the identity of the defendant.[101] There is a 30-year limitation period for intentional damages to life, body, health, physical freedom, and of sexual abuse.[102] The limitation period can be interrupted, for example, by sending a letter of claim or by starting negotiations over the claim.[103]

An important feature of German civil procedure is that the court will not on its own take the statute of limitation into account. It needs to be raised by one of the parties to the litigation, while it is also possible for the parties to agree to waive the statute of limitation.[104] While the claimants in the *KiK* case had negotiated a waiver on the statute of limitation in the pre-trial phase, the Dortmund court held that as

[99] BT-Drucks. 19/2439, 18.
[100] Section 59 ff. ZPO.
[101] Section 195, 199 BGB.
[102] Section 197(1) BGB.
[103] Section 203ff. BGB.
[104] H. Heinrichs, Überbl v section 194, in Palandt (n. 43) para. 13 f.

the case was governed by Pakistani law which does not provide for the possibility of such a waiver, this waiver was invalid. The claimants' argument that the waiver was governed by German law, as the representatives of the claimants and the defendant were both German lawyers using German legal language and therefore implicitly agreeing on the application of German law, did not succeed.

D. The damages awarded to the victims and the costs of civil proceedings

The conservative approach of German procedural law and its interpretation by German courts both on the damages awarded to victims as well as the lawyers' fee regulation may discourage lawyers from taking up the kind of cases discussed here.

i. Caps and ceilings and lack of punitive damages

German courts take a conservative approach to damages awarded to claimants. According to section 287 ZPO, German courts determine the amount based on their free discretion and conviction. Under the Rome II Regulation damages are in principle calculated according to applicable law. However, in reality German courts only grant moderate sums of compensation in line with inherent principles of German civil law, even if foreign law is applicable.

According to section 249 I BGB a person who is liable in damages must restore the position that would have existed if the circumstance obliging him to pay damages had not occurred (restoration of the status quo ante, *Naturalrestitution*).[105] Under section 249(2) BGB, when damages are to be paid for personal injury or material damage, the claimant may demand the required monetary amount in lieu of restitution. According to section 251 I BGB, monetary compensation is allowed if genuine restitution is impossible or if genuine restitution would be unreasonable (section 251 II BGB).[106] Under section 253 BGB, a monetary indemnification for non-economic losses requires an injury of the body or health, or an infringement of the victim's freedom or sexual self-determination.[107] It is therefore not surprising that in the *RWE* case (*Lliuya v. RWE*—see above) claimants asked for €17,000 and in the case against *KiK* (*Jabbir v. KiK*—) €30,000 per claimant for pain and suffering.

Punitive damages are not awarded, as German civil law does not aim at the punishment of the wrongdoer. In its landmark decision in 1992 BGH, the Federal Court of Justice dealt with the recognition and enforcement of a US judgment

[105] M. Tolani, 'U.S. Punitive Damages before German Courts—A Comparative Analysis with Respect to the Ordre Public' (2011) 17(1) *Annual Survey of International & Comparative Law* 193.

[106] Ibid.

[107] Jansen and L. Rademacher, 'Punitive Damages in Germany' in H. Koziol and V. Wilcox (eds), *Punitive Damages: Common Law and Civil Law Perspectives, Tort and Insurance Law* (2009) 75.

awarding punitive damages and denied punitive damages, primarily relying on the argument that the German law of damages is governed by the principles of compensation and restitution, while punishment is strictly reserved for criminal law.[108] In the opinion of the court, any higher amount would violate the principle of proportionality. The monopoly on penalisation rests with the State in which a judgment is to be recognised and enforced and punishment and deterrence are seen as unfamiliar concepts in the German civil law system. The prevention of wrongdoing is solely reserved to criminal law, while the function of civil law is to provide reparation for injury and the compensation for losses.[109]

However, elements and reasoning pertaining to the concept of punitive damages are not entirely unknown to German civil law. In fact, it has been argued that German civil law contains aspects that correspond to the intention of US punitive damages.[110] Punitive elements in assessing the amount of damages are considered to have an increasingly important role in legislation as well as in case law.[111] The developments in this area could potentially be catalyst towards reaching higher amounts of compensation in the long term.

ii. Costs and legal aid

Due to the restrictive court practice on damages, the costs of civil litigation in German courts are comparatively low. At the same time, the fact that the damages potentially awarded are relatively low, and that the recoverable lawyers' fees are limited by statutory provisions, mean that complex cases, such as those discussed in this chapter, are less financially viable for lawyers and law firms.

a) General rules governing the costs of litigation

Litigation costs in Germany can be divided into court fees and out-of-court costs.[112] The court fees cover the costs of court and its disbursements such as witnesses and experts, mail charges, and carriage costs.[113] Out-of-court costs are mainly the lawyers' fees and disbursements and pre-trial costs of expert opinions.[114]

The determination of the costs of legal proceedings is generally predictable, transparent, and comparatively low.[115] The costs of civil judicial proceedings are regulated by statutory law. Court fees as well as lawyers' fees are generally determined by three factors: (i) the value of the claim (value in dispute); (ii) the stage

108 BGHZ 118, 312 (343-344) = NJW 1992, 3096 (3104).
109 Ibid.
110 Tolani (n. 105) 185–207, 187.
111 V. Behr, 'Strafschadensersatz im deutschen Recht—Wiederauferstehung eines verdrängten Phänomens' (2010) 3 *Zeitschrift für das Juristische Studium* 292.
112 Wach, Epping, Zinsmeister, et al. (n. 92) p. 27.
113 H. Putzo, *Zivilprozessordnung* (2003) before section 91 at points 3, 4.
114 Wach, Epping, Zinsmeister, et al. (n. 92) 27.
115 Study on the Transparency of Costs of Civil Judicial Proceedings in the European Union, European Commission Country Report Germany, 30 December 2007, p. 7.

of proceedings (in particular whether the case is at first instance, appeal or final appeal stage); and (iii) the kind of proceeding.[116] All relevant laws and regulations include special schedules and tables by which court as well as lawyers' fees can be easily determined.

The losing party does not have to cover any costs other than those prescribed in the regulations.[117] According to the general rule in section 91 I 1 ZPO the losing party has to bear the costs of the litigation. If the plaintiff partly wins and partly loses its case, the costs will be compensated or proportionally allocated by reference to the degrees of success and loss.[118] Specific rules are contained in sections 91–107 ZPO regarding, for example, the costs of a settlement, costs in cases of immediate acknowledgements, and the costs of third parties having joined the proceedings.[119] The winning party may only recover those costs which were necessary for bringing or defending an action. The costs have to be kept as low as possible.[120] Court fees and disbursements are generally recoverable.[121] As regards lawyers' fees, the unsuccessful party is only liable to pay the opposing lawyer's statutory fees as set out by the Code of Lawyers' Fees (*Rechtsanwaltsvergütungsges etz*, RVG) and not any higher level of fees which the opponent may have agreed to pay to his lawyer.[122]

Plaintiffs who do not have their habitual place of living in a Member State of the European Union or in a signatory State of the Agreement on the European Economic Area have to provide security for the costs of the proceedings should this be requested by the defendant (section 110 ZPO). This means that the amount of money deposited has to include the estimated sum the defendant is likely going to spend. This means that claimants against a transnational corporation have to come up with the costs of the opposing side if they lose. Legal aid will cover their own lawyer's fees and the court fees, including all costs of expert opinions.

b) Lawyers' fees—Contingency fees

The main share of the costs of civil proceedings is determined by the lawyers' fees. The remuneration lawyers receive is governed by the RVG which regulates fees corresponding to the amount in dispute. Lawyers can also charge higher rates on the basis of negotiated fees which need to be contained in an express written agreement with the client.[123]

[116] Ibid.
[117] Ibid.
[118] Section 92 ZPO.
[119] Wach, Epping, Zinsmeister, et al. (n. 92) 27.
[120] Putzo (n. 113) section 91 at point 9; BGH MDR 10, 1286.
[121] Putzo (n. 113) section 91 at point 14.
[122] Putzo, (n. 113) section 91 at point 19.
[123] Section 3a RVG.

For claimants, contingency fees can facilitate access to justice for those encountering financial difficulties; described in the US context as 'the poor man's key to the courthouse door'.[124] An agreement on contingency fees is theoretically possible in Germany, however, the strict requirements in section 4a (1) RVG need to followed. section 4a (1) RVG affirms that the economic situation of the client is the decisive factor, whereas an unwillingness to take financial risks cannot be taken into account.[125] An exception justifying the conclusion of a contingency fee agreement may be made if the litigant is not eligible for legal aid.[126] This can be the case if exemption thresholds are exceeded, but the client would risk losing all his assets,[127] yet an agreement on contingency fees must prove comprehensible and plausible after objectively and reasonably acknowledging all circumstances of the individual case.[128] In practice, contingency fees are not common in Germany as they are frequently declared void by a court.[129]

c) Legal aid

Thus, foreigners unable to cover the costs of the proceedings are entitled to receive legal aid in Germany, even if they are domiciled outside Germany. Section 114 ZPO lists the prerequisites for legal aid. It is granted to any parties who, due to their personal and economic circumstances, are unable to pay the costs of litigation, provided that the action they intend to bring has sufficient prospects of success and does not seem frivolous.[130] Therefore, the court ruling on the legal aid application considers, apart from the economic situation of the claimants, the *prima facie* prospects of the lawsuit.[131] In the case of *Jabbir et al. v. KiK* the claimants were granted legal aid.[132]

The approval of legal aid means that the claimant's own lawyer's fees and the corresponding share of the court costs are partly or fully covered. Furthermore, the claimants are exempted from the obligation to provide a security deposit for the costs of the proceedings.[133] However, it is noteworthy that if approved, legal aid will not cover the claimant's obligation to reimburse the opponent for the costs it has incurred in the event the claimant loses.[134] Also, expenses arising during the

124 P. Corboy, 'Contingency Fees: The Individual's Key to the Courthouse Door' (1976) 2(4) *Litigation* 27–30.

125 H. Mayer and L. Kroiß, *Rechtsanwaltsvergütungsgesetz*, 4. Aufl. 2009, section 4a Rn 30; P. Hartmann, *Kostengesetze*, 40. Aufl. 2010, section 4a RVG Rn 18.

126 BVerfGE 117, 163 = NJW 2007, 979

127 Mayer and Kroiß, (n. 125), section 4a Rn 33.

128 W. Gerold and H. Schmidt, *Rechtsanwaltsvergütungsgesetz*, 19. Aufl. 2010, section 4a Rn 7 f.

129 LG Berlin, Urteil vom 2.12.2010–10 O 238/10.

130 Section 114 (1) ZPO.

131 European Commission, 'European Judicial Network in civil and commercial matters, Legal Aid—Germany' (*European Commission*, 8 November 2019) <http://ec.europa.eu/civiljustice/legal_aid/legal_aid_ger_en.htm> accessed 18 November 2020.

132 LG Dortmund, 7 O 95/15, Beschluss vom 29.08.2016.

133 Section 122 (1) ZPO.

134 Section 123 ZPO.

preparation of the often highly complex cases, especially the compilation of a substantial body of evidence, are not covered by the approved legal aid.[135]

VI. Conclusion

It is possible for victims of human rights abuses to use tort law as a means to gain redress and compensation from companies in Germany responsible for harm. Still, given that the German tort law system is not very litigious, claimants face serious hurdles. German courts have jurisdiction over the parent or buying company registered in Germany and possibly in exceptional cases also over the subsidiary.

Generally, German courts will generally determine these cases on the basis of the law of the country where the damage occurred, as they apply the Rome II regulation. Arguably, German law also provides a legal basis for parent company liability for human rights abuses involving harm to life, body, property, freedom of movement, and personality rights. The basic tort law principles seem quite similar to UK law. However, there is no solid case law on this issue as yet. In particular, the question how the existing duties of care should be interpreted with regard to subsidiaries and suppliers outside of the European Union is unresolved. While the existing standards including soft law standards, such as the OECD guidelines and guidance, give some indication and will help courts in the application of these standards, legislative reform seems necessary. As a German Value Chain Law (*Lieferkettengesetz*—a law on mandatory human rights due diligence for German companies and their supply chains will be passed in May 2020, but will not provide for civil remedies. Even German parliament will have to create a course of action under tort law implementing a currently debated EU Directive on mandatory Human Rights Due Diligence, which would clearly defining the duties of care of parent company towards their subsidiary and supplier were passed, the practical and procedural obstacles to tort law litigation in German would remain. The lack of a pre-trial discovery procedure and the absence of group or class actions are serious obstacles for victims of corporate human rights abuse, who often live in remote areas under precarious conditions. Therefore, the prospects of a legal claim to go forward depend to a large extent on the capacities and resources of the civil society organisations supporting the victims. While the costs of civil litigation in Germany are not comparatively high, the low amount of damages being granted by German courts and the prohibition on contingency fees strongly deter law firms from becoming routinely involved in these types of cases.

[135] C. Heydenreich, A. Paasch, and J. Kusch, *Globales Wirtschaften und Menschenrechte—Deutschland auf dem Prüfstand* (2014) 106.

11
Multinational Human Rights Litigation from the Perspective of Business

Rae Lindsay

I. Introduction

This chapter considers multinational human rights litigation from the perspective of business.[1] While no monolithic business perspective exists, the objective is to consider some of the challenges that confront organisations when sued for or threatened with claims of involvement in human rights abuse[2] and to attempt an evaluation of the extent to which the 2011 United Nations Guiding Principles on Business and Human Rights (UNGP)[3] are playing a role in recourse to and the conduct of multinational human rights litigation.

The chapter begins by defining 'multinational human rights litigation' for the purposes of this discussion. It offers an abbreviated and high-level overview of the recent history and evolution of this category of litigation, highlighting some characteristic themes to illustrate the challenges of multinational human rights litigation for business while proposing that such litigation is often a flawed route by which to pursue remedy for affected persons. The chapter next considers the interposition into the landscape of the UNGP and the ways in which their implementation might

[1] This chapter is intended to serve as a counterpoint to the claimant-focused perspectives that dominate most discussion of multinational human rights litigation. It is a non-comprehensive and abbreviated summary of some factors that may be relevant to or influence a business perspective. The intent is to present an objective overview and not necessarily to reflect the author's own personal views. Nothing in this chapter is attributable to the author's firm, any client, or other organisation. The author wishes to thank colleagues who assisted in research for this chapter and commented on earlier drafts and to acknowledge, in particular, the valuable insights of Anna Kirkpatrick.

[2] Discussions offering a business perspective include J.C. Drimmer and S.R. Lamoree, 'Think Globally, Sue Locally: Trends and Out-of-Court Tactics in Transnational Tort Actions' (2011) 29(2) *The Berkeley Journal of International Law* 456–527; J. Drimmer, 'Human Rights and the Extractive Industries: Litigation and Compliance Trends' (2010) 3(2) *Journal of World Energy Law & Business* 121–39; T.J. Boutrous, Jr, 'Ten Lessons from the Chevron Litigation: The Defense Perspective' (2013) 1(2) *Stanford Journal of Complex Litigation* 219–40.

[3] United Nations Office of the High Commissioner for Human Rights (OHCHR), *Guiding Principles on Business and Human Rights: Implementing the United Nations "Protect, Respect and Remedy' Framework* (2011), (hereafter UNGP) <https://www.ohchr.org/documents/publications/guidingprinciplesbusinesshr_en.pdf>, accessed 15 October 2020.

Rae Lindsay, *Multinational Human Rights Litigation from the Perspective of Business* In: *Human Rights Litigation against Multinationals in Practice*. Edited by: Richard Meeran, Oxford University Press. © The Several Contributors 2021.
DOI: 10.1093/oso/9780198866220.003.0011

be expected, on the one hand, to reduce the need for recourse to multinational human rights litigation and, on the other, to invigorate it. Finally, with an eye to the future, there is a brief discussion of the influence the UNGP are having to shape policy development and legal reform which in turn might encourage further multinational human rights litigation. The conclusion calls for inclusive dialogue that has regard to business' legitimate—indeed essential—voice in helping frame future regulation of corporate human rights risk management and the substance and processes of multinational human rights litigation.

II. What is 'multinational human rights litigation'?

This chapter adopts a basic and broad definition of multinational human rights litigation as encompassing court cases[4] against multinational corporations (MNCs)[5] seeking legal adjudication of claims alleging their involvement, direct or indirect, in infringements of human rights—whether those claims are framed in terms of human rights or not. A predominant category is 'foreign direct liability' cases, which seek to hold MNCs liable in the courts of their 'home State' (the State of incorporation or domicile of a parent or other core company in a transnational corporate group) under domestic civil laws for human rights harms suffered in a 'host State' (where a subsidiary within the same corporate group—or less commonly, a separately incorporated business partner such as a supplier—operates).[6] Some multinational human rights litigation is also pursued in host States, either instead of or as well as in a home State.[7] Civil litigation is a

[4] 'Litigation' is the process of taking a dispute between two or more parties to a court of law for determination. For purposes of this chapter, the discussion is confined to domestic court litigation. This necessarily excludes a growing body of practice connected with the pursuit of remedy through other State and non-State-based non-judicial mechanisms including, for present purposes, arbitration.

[5] 'Transnational corporations' is another term widely used. For purposes of this chapter, these terms are used interchangeably, along with others such as 'multinational enterprise'. Each of these terms implies an organisation or grouping of corporate entities operating within more than one country. Such groupings tend to have a management headquarters in one (sometimes more than one) country (home country) while also operating in other countries (host countries).

[6] For discussions of foreign direct liability cases see, for example, L. Enneking, *Foreign Direct Liability and Beyond: Exploring the Role of Tort Law in Promoting International Corporate Social Responsibility and Accountability* (2012); L. Enneking, 'The Future of Foreign Direct Liability? Exploring the International Relevance of the Dutch Shell Nigeria Case' (2014) 10(1) *Utrecht Law Review* 44–54; C. Bright, 'Vedanta v Lungowe Symposium: Foreign Direct Liability Cases in England After Vedanta' OpinioJuris, 26 April 2019, <http://opiniojuris.org/2019/04/26/vedanta-v-lungowe-symposium-foreign-direct-liability-cases-in-england-after-vedanta/>, accessed 15 October 2020.

[7] For example, proceedings in the United States and Ecuador against Texaco/Chevron concerning alleged liability for environmental damage and associated personal injuries from operations in Ecuador: as described in Drimmer and Lamoree (n. 2) 499–512; D. Khatan, 'Chevron and Ecuador Proceedings: A Primer in Transnational Litigation Strategies' (2017) 55(2) *Stanford Journal of International Law* 249–75. More recently, the collapse in 2015 in Brazil of a tailings dam operated by Samarco Mineração SA, a Brazilian joint venture company owned by Vale SA and BHP Billiton Brasil Ltda, led to litigation against BHP group companies in Brazil, Australia, the United States, and England. Claims in the English High Court on behalf of 202,600 claimants—asserted to be the most substantial

focus, but some factual contexts and legal systems give rise to possible criminal law exposures as well.[8]

The facts giving rise to multinational human rights litigation are extremely varied, as are the legal theories on which claims have been advanced. This chapter refers to a small sample of case law across a number of jurisdictions, with a main focus on the United Kingdom and United States. More detailed discussions of particular cases and jurisdictions are found in other chapters of this book.[9]

The range of cases falling under the umbrella of multinational human rights litigation includes the following (with some cases straddling more than one category):

- alleged corporate involvement in gross human rights abuses that could constitute international crimes, such as genocide, war crimes, and crimes against humanity;[10]
- impacts on individuals and communities associated with incidents of pollution or other significant environmental harm;[11]
- association with violence or oppression on the part of security, police, and armed forces and militias;[12]

ever brought in tort in an English court—were dismissed as an abuse of process in light of proceedings already taking place in Brazil: see *Municipo de Mariana & Ors v. BHP Group PLC (formerly BHP Billiton) & Ors* [2020] EWHC 2930 (TCC), (hereafter *BHP Group*). Permission to appeal this decision was granted on 27 July 2021 [2021] EWCA Civ 1156.

[8] Compilations of case studies and analysis include J. Zerk, 'Corporate liability for gross human rights abuses: Towards a fairer and more effective system of domestic law remedies' (OHCHR, 2013), <http://www.ohchr.org/Documents/Issues/Business/DomesticLawRemedies/StudyDomesticeLawRemedies.pdf>, accessed 15 October 2020; European Union (2019), Directorate-General for External Policies of the Union (European Parliament), '*Access to legal remedies for victims of corporate human rights abuses in third countries*' (February 2019) (hereafter the DROI Study), <https://www.europarl.europa.eu/RegData/etudes/STUD/2019/603475/EXPO_STU(2019)603475_EN.pdf>, accessed 15 October 2020.

[9] Studies of multinational human rights litigation include S. Joseph, *Corporations and Transnational Human Rights Litigation* (2004). The Corporate Legal Accountability portal hosted by the Business and Human Rights Resource Centre (BHRRC) contains information on multinational human rights litigation around the world: see <https://www.business-humanrights.org/en/big-issues/corporate-legal-accountability/>, accessed 15 October 2020. As noted, this chapter contains a sample of cases for illustrative purposes; it is not intended to be a comprehensive review nor to provide a complete litigation history of cases cited.

[10] See, for example, *Presbyterian Church of Sudan v. Talisman Energy, Inc.*, 582 F. 3d 244 (2d Cir. 2009), affirming grant of summary judgment in favour of Talisman (hereafter *Talisman*) (allegations of aiding and abetting Sudanese Government in committing acts of genocide, war crimes and crimes against humanity). See also case law discussed in R.C. Thompson, A. Ramasastry, and M.B. Taylor, 'Translating Unocoal: The Expanding Web of Liability for Business Entities Implicated in International Crimes' (2009) 40(4) *The George Washington International Law Review* 841–902.

[11] See, for example, litigation arising from a gas leak at a chemical plant in Bhopal, India, including: *Bano v. Union Carbide Corp.*, 361 F. 3d 696 (2d Cir. 2004) (hereafter *Union Carbide*). See also cases referenced at n. 7.

[12] For example, *Doe v. Drummond Co.*, 782 F. 3d 576 (11th Cir. 2015); *Doe I v. Unocal Corp.*, 395 F. 3d 932 (9th Cir. 2007); *Kadie Kalma & Ors v. African Minerals Ltd & Ors*, [2020] EWCA Civ 144 (hereafter *Kalma*).

- displacements, forced evictions, and other impacts of land acquisition for industrial or agricultural use or exploitation of natural resources;[13]
- various forms of labour exploitation,[14] including within global supply chains;[15]
- the human rights impacts of climate change's physical manifestations (and of corporate adaptation and transition strategies).[16] Given the urgent attention being paid to tackling climate change, these types of impact may be expected to feature more prominently in multinational human rights litigation in the future.

Certain business sectors tend to be more exposed to risk of association with severe human rights harms and consequently to multinational human rights litigation. This typically arises from operational contexts; for example, States in conflict, or those with weak governance, endemic corruption, and other systemic human rights issues. Consequently, natural resource extractive companies operating in challenging parts of the globe historically have made up a substantial proportion of defendants to multinational human rights litigation, although a wide range of sectors is represented.[17] One research project indicated that whilst most alleged human rights violations occur in South America, Africa, the Middle East, and South and South-east Asia, the majority of defendants sued in multinational human rights litigation tend to be Anglo-American headquartered.[18]

A broad summation of types of multinational human rights litigation might be:[19]

[13] For example, *Song Mao v. Tate & Lyle Sugar Industries Ltd* as described in 'Cambodian villagers defend their land rights', Jones Day, October 2011, <https://www.jonesday.com/en/practices/experience/2011/10/cambodian-villagers-defend-their-land-rights>, accessed 15 October 2020.

[14] For example, *Nevsun Resources Ltd v. Araya* [2020] SCC 5 (hereafter *Nevsun*) (alleged forced/conscripted labour at a mine in Eritrea operated by a subsidiary of the defendant Canadian company). This litigation has reportedly settled: 'Landmark settlement is a message to Canadian companies extracting resources overseas: Amnesty International', CBS News, 23 October 2020, <https://www.cbc.ca>, accessed 5 December 2020.

[15] Cases pursuant to the US Trafficking Victims Protection Act (TVPA) of 2000 and subsequent reauthorisations: see, for example, Amended Complaint, *Doe I v. Apple Inc.*, No. 19-cv-3737 (DDC 26 June 2020) (corporate defendants allegedly benefited from and aided and abetted abuse of children in cobalt mines in their supply chains) (hereafter *Doe v. Apple*). Although the TVPA provides liability for anyone who 'knowingly benefits, financially or by receiving anything of value, from participation in a venture which has engaged' in a violation of the TVPA, the scope and application of the TVPA remains uncertain. Compare *Bristline v. Parker*, 918 F. 3d 849, 873–76 (10th Cir. 2019) and *Ratha v. Phatthana Seafood Co.* No. 16-cv-4271, 2017 WL 8292391 (CD Cal. Dec. 21, 2017).

[16] For example, *Lliuya v. RWE AG*, Case No. 2 O 285/15 (Essen District Court 2015), a case founded in nuisance involving allegations that the defendant German electricity provider contributed to the harmful consequences of climate change suffered by a Peruvian farmer.

[17] R. Lindsay and A. Kirkpatrick. 'Human Rights and International Mining Disputes' in J. Fry and L.-A.Bret (eds), *The Guide to Mining Arbitrations* (2019), ch. 8; the *DROI Study* (n. 8); Drimmer (n. 2); C. van Dam, 'Enhancing Human Rights Protection: a Company Lawyer's Business' (Inaugural Lecture Rotterdam School of Management, Erasmus University, Rotterdam, The Netherlands, 18 September 2015), <https://repub.eur.nl/pub/78743/Professor-Cees-van-Dam-Inaugural-Lecture-EN.pdf>, accessed 15 October 2020 at p. 14.

[18] van Dam (n. 17) at pp. 13–14.

[19] The first four (slightly adapted) are listed in Zerk (n. 8) at 8.

- Businesses and their managers or other employees are accused as main perpetrators of abuse or other adverse human rights impacts;[20]
- Businesses provide support (e.g. through the supply of equipment or technology) in the context of a commercial relationship and that is then used abusively or repressively;[21]
- Businesses provide information, logistical, or financial assistance to human rights abusers and this is alleged to have facilitated or exacerbated the abuse;[22]
- Businesses are accused of being 'complicit' in (and having benefitted from) human rights abuse by virtue of investments in projects, joint ventures, or regimes with poor human rights records, or connections to known abusers;[23]
- Businesses are accused of culpable failures of control, oversight, or risk management with respect to activities of a related party (such as a subsidiary)[24] or an unrelated third party (e.g. suppliers, contractors or public authorities and their agents, security forces, or police) that have resulted in harm.[25]

It will be evident from these descriptions that it is not unusual for the MNC defendant to play a secondary role in any alleged human rights harm, rather than being the direct perpetrator or main causal actor. Indeed, this is the case in four of the five categories listed above. Part of the reason for this is that States, not corporations, are the duty bearers under international human rights law.[26] Indeed, there has been much debate over the extent to which non-State actors such as corporations are directly subject to international legal obligations with respect to human rights.[27] Often, therefore, in events giving rise to multinational human rights litigation the direct perpetrator of an alleged human rights violation is a State actor that, for a variety of reasons—for example, sovereign immunity—will not be a party to the eventual litigation in which the MNC is sued (and may not be susceptible

[20] For examples, see the case studies referred to in Zerk (n. 8) 17–18.

[21] For examples, see the case studies referred to in Zerk (n. 8) 18–19.

[22] For examples, see the case studies referred to in Zerk (n. 8) 20–3.

[23] For examples, see the case studies referred to in Zerk (n. 8) 23.

[24] For example, *Vedanta Resources Plc and another v. Lungowe and others* [2019] UKSC 20 (hereafter *Vedanta*). The litigation has reportedly settled: 'Vedanta Resources settles Zambia copper mine pollution claim', *Reuters* 19 January 2021, <https://www.reuters.com/article/us-zambia-mining-vedanta-idUSKBN29O1EL>, (accessed 4 February 2021); *Okpabi and others v. Royal Dutch Shell plc and another* [2021] UK SC 3 (hereafter *Okpabi*).

[25] Examples include *Kalma* (n. 12).

[26] For a discussion of the international human rights legal framework and the role of business within it, see L. Wendland, 'The International Human Rights Framework and the Role of Business: The Journey from the Universal Declaration of Human Rights to the UN Guiding Principles on Business and Human Rights' in R. Lindsay and R. Martella (eds), *Corporate Social Responsibility—Sustainable Business: Environmental, Social and Governance Frameworks for the 21st Century* (2020), ch. 19 at 457–8.

[27] See, for example, A. Clapham, *Human Rights Obligations of Non-state Actors* (2006); J.J. Paust, 'Human Rights Responsibilities of Private Corporations' (2002) 35 (3) *Vanderbilt Journal of Transnational Law* 801–25; P. Thielfbörger and T. Ackermann, 'A Treaty on Enforcing Human Rights Against Business: Closing the Loophole or Getting Stuck in a Loop?' (2017) 24(1) *Indiana Journal of Global Legal Studies* 43–79.

to action in any forum at all).[28] Secondary liability theories include, for example, that the MNC defendants allegedly aided and abetted abuses perpetrated by government actors in the host State,[29] although theories of vicarious liability or other direct duties of care to third parties also arise.[30] These types of cases can be challenging for many reasons, including if the absent party has sole access to key sources of information and witnesses.

Exact legal theories on which claims are advanced depend on the domestic laws of the relevant jurisdiction and the causes of action that may be available. Human rights law is generally a matter of public law, with enforcement and/or remedies routed through judicial review of State action, and the role played by international human rights law depends on the extent to which particular States have incorporated this into domestic causes of action litigable by private parties in their courts. International criminal law, offences under which often incorporate elements of human rights abuse, informs the content of some crimes incorporated into domestic laws that may or may not permit of corporate responsibility.[31]

Where an expressly human rights-centred claim is not possible, tort law is often invoked, making 'transnational tort litigation' a major subset of the genre. This can be unsatisfactory from a claimant's point of view as alleged international human rights abuses have to be translated into tort harms which may not convey the seriousness of the issues from the perspective of those affected.[32] Increasingly, statutory bases for civil claims are available in some jurisdictions allowing remedy against corporations that have benefitted from human rights abuses, as well as common law claims for unjust enrichment.[33] Other forms of litigation include claims under consumer protection legislation based on alleged failures to disclose labour abuses within a defendant's supply chain for its products.[34] Of course, these

[28] See, for example, B. Van Schaack, 'Unfulfilled Promise: The Human Rights Class Action' (2003) 1 *The University of Chicago Legal Forum* 279–352 at 295–7; D.J. Kochan, 'Legal Mechanization of Corporate Social Responsibility through Alien Tort Statute Litigation: A Response to Professor Branson with some Supplemental Thoughts' (2011) 9(1) *Santa Clara Journal of International Law* 251–60 at 258.

[29] See, for example, cases discussed in C.A. Bradley, 'State Action and Corporate Human Rights Liability' (2010) 85(5) *Notre Dame Law Review* 1823–38 at 1831–7.

[30] For example, *Kalma* (n. 12).

[31] W. Kaleck and M. Saage-Maaß, 'Corporate Accountability for Human Rights Violations Amounting to International Crimes: The Status Quo and its Challenges' (2010) 8(3) *Journal of International Criminal Justice* 699–724.

[32] In the US context see, for example, N.J. Miller, 'Human Rights Abuses as Tort Harms: Losses in Translation' (2016) 46(2) *Seton Hall Law Review* 505–63; R. Meeran, 'Tort Litigation against Multinational Corporations for Violation of Human Rights: An Overview of the Position Outside the United States' (Fall 2011) 3(1) *City University of Hong Kong Law Review* 1–41.

[33] For statutory frameworks see, for example, the TVPA and litigation thereunder; for example, *Doe v. Apple* (n. 15).

[34] See, for example, *Nike, Inc. v. Kasky*, 539 US 654 (2003); *Hodson v. Mars* 891 F 3d 857 (9th Cir. 2018); *Tomasella .v Nestlé USA* Nos 19-1130-19-1132 (1st Cir. 2020); *Dana v. Hershey Co.*, 730 F. App'x 460 (9th Cir. 2018); *Sud v. Costco Wholesale Corp.*, 731 F. App'x 719 (9th Cir 2018); *Wirth v. Mars, Inc.*, 730 F. App'x 468 (9th Cir 2018); *Barber v. Nestlé USA, Inc.*, 730 App'x 464 (9th Cir. 2018).

latter forms of litigation generally afford no direct remedy for immediate victims of any abuse.

By and large, claimants prefer to litigate in 'home' rather than 'host' States.[35] There are many reasons for this but, generally speaking, do so to avoid limiting factors within the 'host State'—such as ineffective or corrupt justice systems—and/or to seek advantages available within the 'home State'. Litigating in 'home States' can pose multiple jurisdictional challenges and an initial aim for claimants will be to identify an 'anchor' defendant; the attractiveness of the 'home State' is only increased if that defendant is likely to have a deep pocket and a significant interest in defending its reputation in the home State, helping overcome anticipated problems with judgments only against subsidiaries that have no or few assets.[36]

The pursuit of 'home' State litigation shines a spotlight on one of the endemic constraints on transnational business accountability: namely, the legal separation inherent in the corporate form coupled with limitations on the regulatory, enforcement, and adjudicatory jurisdiction of individual States. This has encouraged the development of claimant theories aimed at circumventing these limitations, given the difficulties of formally piercing the corporate veil.[37] One variant seeks to identify an independent duty of care to overseas third parties on the part of the 'home' State parent defendant (thus focusing on the parent's own alleged actions—or, potentially, omissions—with respect to operations conducted overseas by a subsidiary or related entity); others seek to hold 'home' State entities responsible for abuses or neglect by third parties, again through a direct duty of care or other theories of liability, such as agency.[38] Having identified an 'anchor' defendant within the jurisdiction, courts taking on cases against 'home' defendants will often also accept the claims against other parties allegedly involved in the abuse (in particular, related companies within the corporate group).[39] These and other factors combined mean there has been a preponderance of cases in jurisdictions where litigation is 'embedded in the national culture'.[40]

[35] van Dam (n. 17).

[36] See, for example, R.H. Weber and R. Baisch. 'Liability of Parent Companies for Human Rights Violations of Subsidiaries' (2016) 27(5) *European Business Law Review* 669–95; M. Weller and A. Pato, 'Local Parents as 'Anchor Defendants' in European Courts for Claims Against their Foreign Subsidiaries in Human Rights and Environmental Damages Litigation: Recent Case Law and Legislative Trends' June 2018) 23(2) *Uniform Law Review* 397–417; Joseph (n. 9) at 129; D.M. Branson, 'Holding Multinational Corporations Accountable? Achilles' Heels in Alien Tort Claims Act Litigation' (2011) 9(1) *Santa Clara Journal of International Law* 227–50 at 228–9.

[37] See, for example, Meeran (n. 32) at p. 5; Joseph (n. 9) at 129–32.

[38] In the English courts, cases include, for example, *AAA & Ors v. Unilever Tea Kenya Ltd* [2018] EWCA Civ 1532; *Okpabi* (n. 24); *Vedanta* (n. 24); *Kalma* (n. 12). For discussion of theories that may be deployed, such as joint liability or agency: see, for example, Joseph (n. 9) at 132–3.

[39] For example, *Okpabi* (n. 24), *Kalma* (n. 12), *Vedanta* (n. 24).

[40] van Dam (n. 17) at 14.

Since its origins in the 1980s, multinational human rights litigation has evolved dramatically.[41] For almost two decades, the US Alien Tort Statute[42] (ATS) was seen as the most promising route to remedy for victims of alleged corporate abuse and was 'a significant factor driving the global business and human rights agenda'.[43] A series of decisions by the US Supreme Court placed substantial limits on the viability of ATS litigation against corporations[44] and, at the time of writing, it remains to be seen whether a final death knell will be sounded on the key question of whether the ATS permits of corporate liability at all.[45] While multinational human rights litigation continues in the United States in State courts or under other federal statutes,[46] the curtailment of the ATS has encouraged claimants to look towards other potentially favourable jurisdictions as well.[47]

English courts have long offered a possible venue for transnational tort litigation and, with *forum non conveniens* in recent times playing a more limited role in

[41] The complex and long-running *Union Carbide* (n. 11) litigation that arose from the infamous Bhopal gas leak and that straddled the United States and India is often cited as a forerunner: see, for example, Joseph (n. 9) 140–1.

[42] 28 USC section 1350. The ATS provides that US federal district courts 'shall have original jurisdiction of any civil action by an alien for a tort only, committed in violation of the law of nations or a treaty of the United States'.

[43] J. Ruggie, *Just Business: Multinational Corporations and Human Rights* (2013) 197. The first ATS cases involving corporate defendants were filed in the 1990s: see, for example, *Beanal v. Freeport-McMoRan, Inc.*, 969 F. Supp. 362 (ED La. 1997), aff'd 197 F. 3d 161 (5th Cir. 1999); *Doe v. Unocal Corp.*, 963 F. Supp. 880 (CD Cal. 1997), vacated 403 F. 3d 708 (9th Cir. 2005). In Drimmer and Lamoree (n. 2) the authors calculated that 155 cases had to that point been filed against corporation (at 460); see also M.D. Goldhaber, 'Corporate Human Rights Litigation in Non-US Courts: A Comparative Scorecard' (2013) 3 *UC Irvine Law Review* 127.

[44] *Sosa v. Alvarez-Machain* 542 US 692 (2004) (albeit a case that did not involve a corporate defendant, the Court confirmed the types of international law norms, violations of which are justiciable, as only those that are 'specific, universal, and obligatory) (quoting *In re Estate of Marcos Human Rights Litigation*, 25 F. 3d 1467, 1475 (9th Cir. 1994); *Kiobel v. Royal Dutch Petroleum* 569 US 108 (2013) (confirming that the ATS was not intended to operate extraterritorially and that viable claims must 'touch and concern' the territory of the United States) (hereafter *Kiobel*); *Jesner v. Arab Bank plc* 1386 S Ct. 138 (2018) (excluding the possibility of claims against foreign corporations) (hereafter *Jesner*).

[45] Circuits have long been divided on the issue of corporate liability under the ATS, yet notwithstanding the centrality of the issue to the possibility of multinational human rights litigation under the ATS, it remains unresolved more than two decades after the first cases against corporations were filed. In July 2020, the US Supreme Court granted *certiorari* in *Nestlé USA Inc v. Doe I*, allowing an appeal from the Ninth Circuit: 906 F. 3d 1120 (9th Cir. 2018). Issues to be addressed are whether an aiding and abetting claim against a domestic (US) corporation under the ATS may overcome the extraterritoriality bar where the claim is based on allegations of general corporate activity within the United States; and whether liability may be imposed under the ATS against US corporations. See Petition for Writ of Certiorari, *Nestlé USA Inc v. Doe I*, Nos 19-416, 19-453 (US 25 September 2019).

[46] See, for example, P. Hoffman and B. Stephens, 'International Human Rights Cases under State Law and in State Courts' (2013) 3(1) *UC Irvine Law Review* 9–23; R. Davidson Raycraft, 'Bridging the Void in Transnational Corporate Accountability: *Jesner v. Arab Bank* as a Call to Action' (2020) 60(3) *Virginia Journal of International Law* 737–75 at 756–61; R. Chambers, 'Parent Company Direct Liability for Overseas Human Rights Violations: Lessons from the UK Supreme Court' (2020) *University of Pennsylvania Journal of International Law* (forthcoming) 13–22, available at <https://papers.ssrn.com/sol3/papers.cfm?abstract_id=3682273>, accessed 29 January 2021.

[47] J.A. Kirschner, 'A Call for the EU to Assume Jurisdiction over Extraterritorial Corporate Human Rights Abuses' (2015) 13(1) *Northwestern Journal of International Human Rights* 1–26; Chambers (n. 46).

courts' jurisdictional analyses,[48] have seen a growing share. This includes efforts over more than two decades to establish instances of parent company liability for breach of an alleged duty of care toward persons harmed by a subsidiary's overseas operations, with limited inroads being made.[49]

There has also been a cadre of important cases in Continental European courts[50] and, in Canada, encouragement of the possibility that international human rights law may be a source for common law tort claims against corporations.[51] This has evoked much interest given possible contrasts with the fate of claims based on violations of international law under the ATS.

Finally, across jurisdictions, an international focus on 'modern slavery' (including human trafficking) and other labour-related abuse has spawned a new wave of multinational human rights litigation involving efforts to impose liability on manufacturers, retailers, and others that source products from across complex global supply chains.[52] The 2013 Rana Plaza factory collapse notably led to claims against MNCs in several jurisdictions, including the United States and Canada.[53]

Multinational human rights litigation can be extremely protracted. Jurisdictional disputes, other preliminary motions, and interlocutory arguments on pivotal legal issues are often hotly contested and can take years to resolve, sometimes involving multiple references to appellate courts. This delays and ultimately may prevent cases advancing to an eventual examination of the merits.[54] It is

[48] Case C-281/02 *Owusu v. Jackson and Others* [2005] ECR I-1383 read alongside *Vedanta* (n. 24). The rules on jurisdiction post-Brexit are likely to reinvigorate *forum non conveniens* in multinational human rights litigation in English courts.

[49] The line of cases which began with *Connelly v. RTZ Corp* [1998] AC 854 is discussed, for example, in Meeran (n. 32). *Chandler v. Cape* [2012] EWCA Civ 525 was the first and, to date, only case in which a parent company has been held liable in English courts for breach of such a duty of care.

[50] See, for example, cases discussed in the DROI Study (n. 8). Referring to cases such as *Jabir* (n. 52) and *Akpan v. Royal Dutch Shell Plc*, No. 337050/HA ZA 09-1580 (District Court of the Hague, 30 January 2013; Appeals Court of the Hague, 17 December 2015), Chambers (n. 46) at 31–3 notes that, in relation to foreign directly liability cases in civil law jurisdictions, to date the 'distinctive trend' has involved the application of English common law precedent when the court has been called upon to apply 'host' State law to the claims. This 'trend' appears to have continued with a recent decision in litigation in the Netherlands relating to an oil well and pipelines in Nigeria involving Royal Dutch Shell and a Nigerian subsidiary: <https://nairametrics.com/2021/01/29/dutch-court-orders-shell-nigeria-to-pay-compensation-for-oil-spill/> accessed 10 February 2021.

[51] *Nevsun* (n. 14).

[52] See, for example, *Jabir and others v. KiK Textilien and Non-Food GmbH*, Landgericht Dortmund [LG] [Dortmund Regional Court], Case No. 7 O 95/15 (Ger.) (2019) (hereafter *Jabir*) (dismissed on statute of limitations grounds); *Doe I v. Wal-Mart Store, Inc.* 572 F. 3d 677 (9th Cir. 2009). Discussions of this form of litigation include C. Terwindt, S. Leader, A. Yilmaz-Vastardis, et al., 'Supply Chain Liability: Pushing the Boundaries of the Common Law?' (2017) 8(3) *Journal of European Tort Law* 261–96; P. Wesche and M. Saage-Maaß, 'Holding Companies Liable for Human Rights Abuses Related to Foreign Subsidiaries and Suppliers before German Civil Courts: Lessons from Jabir and others v Kik' (2016) 16(2) *Human Rights Law Review* 370–85.

[53] See, for example, *Rahaman v. J.C. Penney Corp.*, No. N15C-07-174 MMJ, 2016 WL 2616375 (Del. Super. Ct May 4, 2016); *Das v. George Weston Limited*, 2018 ONCA 1053 (which included claims against a social auditing firm).

[54] In *Nevsun* (n. 14), for example, litigation was commenced in 2014, made its way over several years through the Canadian courts on preliminary issues and only in 2020 was remanded to the lower courts for proceedings towards trial. The litigation has now settled (n. 14).

increasingly common for cases to settle;[55] very few culminate in a trial and only a handful of those that do have resulted in a judgment in favour of affected persons.[56] By its nature, litigation—involving the resolution of particular disputes between particular parties based on specific facts and the application of legal principles to them—can offer only incremental successes and normative shifts. In short: despite the dramatic increase in multinational human rights litigation worldwide over the last 35 years or so, it might be concluded that it remains 'a very rarefied form of legal struggle'.[57]

There is a fairly compelling view that home State litigation in foreign courts far removed from the place of harm is seldom the optimal route to remedy for affected persons resident in host States. It is costly, cumbersome, culturally alien, and courts cannot generally offer the gamut of remedial measures envisaged under international human rights law.[58] Critically, since it rarely succeeds, failed multinational human rights litigation might serve to exacerbate a sense of injustice on the part of affected people whose hopes have been raised and dashed.[59] According to one leading human rights lawyer, Helen Duffy, '[h]uman rights litigation is not a neutral enterprise that at worst does little good, while not doing any harm'.[60] Duffy proposes that further attention is needed to the potential impacts of litigation on those individuals in whose name cases are brought, and how the ethical, professional, and moral obligations to them are addressed in a 'medley of interests at play' in strategic litigation contexts.[61] She observes that victims 'often fare poorly in judicial processes';[62] litigation can be traumatising, with claimants feeling marginalised or disrespected within unfamiliar lawyer-led processes. Moreover, it deflects attention from the fundamental absence of capacity within host States, including with respect to judicial systems, local business regulation, and State actor accountability.

[55] See, for example, discussions in Drimmer and Lamoree (n. 2) 465; I. Wuerth, 'Wiwa v Shell: The $15.5 Million Settlement' (2009) 13(14) *ASIL Insights* <https://www.asil.org/insights/volume/13/issue/14/wiwa-v-shell-155-million-settlement>, accessed 15 October 2020; *Nevsun*, (n. 14); B. Bağlayan, I. Landau, M. McVey, et al., 'Good Business: The Economic Case for Protecting Human Rights', *BHR Young Researchers Summit, Frank Bold, International Corporate Accountability Roundtable* (December 2018) at p. 44, <https://corporatejustice.org/2018_good-business-report.pdf>, accessed 15 October 2020; the DROI Study (n. 8); L. Enneking, 'Judicial Remedies: The Issue of Applicable Law' in J.J. Álvarez Rubio and K. Yiannibas (eds), *Human Rights in Business: Removal of Barriers to Access to Justice in the European Union* (2017) 41–2.

[56] Drimmer and Lamoree (n. 2) 465 (commenting on outcomes in ATS litigation between 2007 and 2011). See also S. Khoury and D. Whyte, *Corporate Human Rights Violations: Global Prospects for Legal Action* (2017) 97.

[57] Ibid.

[58] As summarised in the UNGP (n. 3) commentary to principle 25, these would include apologies, restitution, rehabilitation, financial or non-financial compensation and punitive sanctions as well as preventive measures such as injunctions or guarantees of non-repetition.

[59] H. Duffy, *Strategic Human Rights Litigation: Understanding and Maximising Impact* (2018) 78.

[60] Duffy (n. 59) 5.

[61] Ibid., 45–7.

[62] Ibid., 270–5.

Proponents of multinational human rights litigation would argue that, to the contrary, it is a vital—and sometimes the only viable—tool amongst the options available to exert ongoing pressure on both multinational business and governments to improve protections for the rights of and remedy for harms to the most vulnerable groups and communities. Although the issues are complex, the persistent obstacles to accessing appropriate and effective remedy—particularly in host States and/or against the primary perpetrators of abuse—raise the question whether some of the vast resources and energy expended by all parties on long-running transnational litigation could not more valuably be redirected towards efforts to find innovative, expeditious, and constructive solutions to long-standing governance gaps that have been identified, including with respect to remedy.

III. Multinational human rights litigation—what are its particular challenges?

This era of increased multinational human rights litigation has played out against a backdrop of effective advocacy campaigns by NGOs, typically portraying multinational business as 'evil' or ruthlessly focused on profit and willing to use any loophole to avoid accountability.[63] Often portrayed as David pitted against Goliath,[64] the inequality of arms that may stem from the generally greater financial resources of business is at least partly offset in claimants' favour by the successful battles waged by those advocating for claimants in the court of public opinion. Corporate defendants therefore might be well advised to avoid the temptation to approach human rights litigation as no more than a legal fight, but rather as 'a battle for the hearts and minds of stakeholders'.[65]

In relation to the asserted inequality of arms between corporate defendants and claimants in multinational human rights litigation, this is not limited to monetary considerations but also includes access to information.[66] Advocates for reform seek ways to redress these perceived imbalances.[67] Although there are undoubtedly systemic obstacles to remedy for many, some of the asserted 'inequalities of arms' are mitigated in practice in some multinational human rights litigation

[63] See, for example, Amnesty International, *Injustice Incorporated: Corporate Abuse and the Human Right to Remedy* (2014) (2014) 192–6.

[64] Khoury and Whyte (n. 56) 81; see, for example, M. Carson and others, 'Gilberto Torres survived Colombia's death squads. Now he wants justice', *The Guardian*, 22 May 2015, <https://www.theguardian.com/world/2015/may/22/gilberto-torres-survived-colombias-death-squads-now-he-wants-justice>, accessed 15 October 2020.

[65] H.F. Garcia and A. Ewing, 'Defending corporate reputation from litigation threats' (2008) 36(3) *Strategy and Leadership* 41–5 at 42.

[66] See, for example, UNGP (n. 3), commentary to principle 26.

[67] See, for example, C. van Dam, F. Gregor with contribution from S. Brachotte and P. Morrow, 'Corporate Responsibility to Respect Human Rights, vis-a-vis legal duty of care', in Álvarez Rubio and Yiannibas (eds) (n. 55) 119–38.

where claimants are represented by teams of lawyers who specialise in the area and who have ample resources (in terms of finance and expertise) as well as a long track record of honing theories of liability—and tactical strategies—in sequential cases, and generally may have the benefit of the non-governmental organisation (NGO) community and media on their side.[68]

For businesses, '[i]t takes twenty years to build a reputation and five minutes to ruin it'.[69] An organisation's reputation—as also its brand—can be one of its most vital assets.[70] Even if strenuously denied, aggressively publicised allegations that an organisation has been involved in human rights abuse risk being perceived as fact by a public audience, long before they are tested in court. Such allegations are therefore extremely bad for image, if not for the bottom line.[71] For businesses that have striven to promote the image of good corporate citizen, a loss of trust in the company and its values can be very damaging,[72] all the more so in an era where sustainable business models with broader social purpose are highly valued.[73]

Claimants and their representatives are keenly aware of the sensitivity of corporations to damaging headlines. The deployment of a concerted publicity strategy across both traditional and social media can prove to be a company's Achilles heel.[74] When senior executives are implicated personally and named as defendants

[68] See, for example, Drimmer and Lamoree (n. 2) 520.

[69] Warren Buffett, as quoted by J. Berman, 'The Three Essential Warren Buffett Quotes to Live By', *Forbes Magazine*, 20 April 2014, <https://www.forbes.com/sites/jamesberman/2014/04/20/the-three-essential-warren-buffett-quotes-to-live-by/#2a9dc9866543>, accessed 15 October 2020.

[70] K.T. Jackson, 'Global Corporate Governance: Soft Law and Reputational Accountability' (2010) 35(1) *Brook Journal of International Law* 41–106 ('a company's reputation has become one of its most valuable assets') at 47.

[71] For a discussion of the correlation between reputational and financial impacts of litigation on US corporations (but not specifically examining multinational human rights litigation), see B. Aslem, I. Hutton, and A. Hoffmann Smith, 'How Much do Corporate Defendants Really Lose? A New Verdict on the Reputation Loss Induced by Corporate Litigation'(2017) 46(2) *Financial Management* doi:10.1111/fima.12171: 323–58; see also Garcia and Ewing (n. 65).

[72] M.M. Jennings, 'The Social Responsibility of Business is Not Social Responsibility: Assume That There Are No Angels and Allow the Free Market's Touch of Heaven' (2019) 16(2) *Berkeley Business Law Journal* 325–462, 365–6 notes that BP had achieved high ratings in corporate social responsibility (CSR) rankings before the Deepwater Horizon incident but that the spill indicated a discrepancy between rhetoric and reality, damaging BP's CSR credentials. See also the reported repercussions of the destruction of ancient Indigenous sites in Western Australia on Rio Tinto and senior members of its management: L. Albeck-Ripka, 'Executives to Step Down After Rio Tinto Destroys Sacred Australian Sites', *The New York Times*, 11 September 2020, <https://www.nytimes.com/2020/09/11/business/rio-tinto-indigenous-sites.html>, accessed 15 October 2020.

[73] See, for example, 'Big business is beginning to accept broader social responsibilities', *The Economist*, 22 August 2019, <https://www.economist.com/briefing/2019/08/22/big-business-is-beginning-to-accept-broader-social-responsibilities>, accessed 15 October 2020; O. Rodríguez-Vilá and S. Bharadwaj, 'Competing on Social Purpose' (Sept–Oct 2017) *Harvard Business Review* 94–101, <https://hbr.org/2017/09/competing-on-social-purpose>, accessed 15 October 2020; A. Edgecliffe-Johnson, 'Beyond the bottom line: should business put purpose before profit?', *Financial Times*, 4 January 2019, <https://www.ft.com/content/a84647f8-0d0b-11e9-a3aa-118c761d2745>, accessed 15 October 2020.

[74] Media tactics is one of the four main out-of-court tactics of claimants in transnational tort litigation identified in Drimmer and Lamoree (n. 2) 474–9 (others being community-organising, investment, and political efforts). See also Duffy (n. 59) 246–7. D.J. Kochan, 'Corporate Social Responsibility in a Remedy-Seeking Society: A Public Policy Perspective' (2014) 17(2) *Chapman Law Review* 413–76,

to proceedings, or when criminal prosecutions might materialise, this can further exacerbate the reputational impact as well as add to the complexities of defending litigation.[75]

An organisation's choice of defence strategy can also rebound against it. A strong defence—even if objectively sound in law and commercially prudent—can be turned on a corporate defendant as a form of hypocrisy when it simultaneously seeks to promote itself as a responsible business.[76] Moreover, companies that raise jurisdictional arguments or procedural defences such as limitation periods can be portrayed as cynically seeking to delay or sidestep accountability.[77] Critics will also decry any stance that smacks of 'hardball tactics'. There has, for example, been a very significant backlash against companies engaging in so-called SLAPP litigation (strategic litigation against public participation) which may be viewed as an effort to use legal proceedings to silence opposition.[78] While some corporate defendants and their lawyers have been criticised for tactics adopted in multinational human rights litigation, the claimants' bar is not immune from reports that some resort to questionable tactics.[79]

The power of social media to define the debate[80] and NGOs' skill at handling traditional media forms as well means businesses should approach the presentation of a counternarrative with care lest it backfire. Commentators decry a 'no comment' approach and hastily issued denials in the face of allegations of involvement in human rights harms can lead to subsequent retractions carrying damaging effect.[81] Equally, businesses' attempts to proactively respond to allegations can also

at 468 argues that much of the reputational damage to a corporate defendants occurs when a lawsuit is filed, meaning there are incentives to resolve matters without the need for formal proceedings.

[75] See, for example, reports of the imprisonment of two former executives for their role in the kidnapping and torture of a number of employees at a Ford Motor Company operation in Argentina (U. Goni, 'Argentina: two ex-Ford executives convicted in torture case', *The Guardian*, 11 December 2018, <https://www.theguardian.com/world/2018/dec/11/pedro-muller-hedro-sibilla-ford-executives-argentina-torture-case>, accessed 4 October 2020. Companies themselves may also be subject to prosecution: see, for example, 'Trafigura: A Toxic Journey', Amnesty International (2016), <https://www.amnesty.org/en/latest/news/2016/04/Trafigura-a-toxic-journey/>, accessed 4 October 2020.

[76] See, for example, A. Mehra and K. Shay, 'Shell, corporate responsibility and respect for the law', *Forbes*, EDT 3 October 2012, <https://www.forbes.com/sites/csr/2012/10/03/shell-corporate-social-responsibility-and-respect-for-the-law/#658b3de61a6f>, accessed 15 October 2020.

[77] Amnesty International (n. 63).

[78] See, for example, G.L. Skinner, 'Beyond Kiobel: Providing Access to Judicial Remedies for Violations of International Human Rights Norms by Transnational Businesses in A New (Post-Kiobel) World' (2014) 46(1) *Columbia Human Rights Law Review* 159–265, 234–6. For a discussion of the role of business in addressing risks to human rights defenders, issues of civic space and the rule of law, see <https://www.ohchr.org/en/issues/business/pages/hrdefenderscivicspace.aspx>, accessed 4 February 2021.

[79] See, for example, Boutros (n. 2).

[80] Jennings (n. 72) at p. 399 describes the power of social media to silence dissenting views in the wider CSR debate.

[81] See, for example, Garcia and Ewing (n. 65); J.W. Pitts III, 'Business, Human Rights & the Environment: The Role of the Lawyer in CSR & Ethical Globalization' (2008) 26(2) *Berkeley Journal of International Law* 479–502 at 499 who suggests that 'old-style blanket denials, circling the wagons, and

be met with scepticism: are these genuine attempts to understand and address issues, or hollow publicity stunts?[82] Sentiment across social media can be a compelling pressure point to influence a company's willingness to resolve claims even if it feels it has a strong case on the merits.[83] Meanwhile, business may make the judgment that the bad publicity and reputational damage associated with litigation may have a greater negative impact in the long term than the short-term costs of settling upfront.[84]

The popular public interest in outcomes is bolstered by courts' willingness to accept *amicus* input or third party intervention from NGOs and others on positions presented in multinational human rights litigation.[85] Third party interventions have long been a feature of ATS litigation in the United States with amicus briefs supporting both claimant and defence perspectives,[86] and such interventions are becoming a more regular feature in other jurisdictions.[87]

Evidently, multinational human rights litigation cannot be approached in the same way as commercial litigation. It should not necessarily be assumed, for example, that an adversary's main objective is the adjudication of liability for harm

aggressive refutations of claims are less likely to succeed (and could create greater risks) than human responses admitting imperfection but genuinely seeking to resolve issues in line with CSR principles'.

82 For example, following a wave of exposés into working conditions at its suppliers, Apple asked the Fair Labour Association to inspect its Foxconn factory near Shenzhen in China, which was hailed as a 'publicity stunt' by China Labour Watch: S. Foley, 'Apple admits it has a human rights problem', *The Independent*, 14 February 2012, <https://www.independent.co.uk/news/world/asia/apple-admits-it-has-human-rights-problem-6898617.html>, accessed 15 October 2020.

83 Jennings (n. 72) at p. 325 decries the 'issue resolution of social issues via Twitter. Businesses are responding to these activities by succumbing to demands without regard to the validity of those demands by external third parties.'

84 Bağlayan, Landau, McVey, et al. (n. 55) 50.

85 Duffy (n. 59) notes the increasing receptivity of courts to such interventions at p. 21.

86 Third party interventions supporting the business perspective in ATS litigation have emphasised matters such as the costs of litigation, increased insurance costs, difficulties accessing capital markets, negative effects on shareholder confidence and stock prices (see, for example, 'Supplemental Brief of Chevron Corp., Dole Food Co., Dow Chemical Co., Ford Motor Co., Glaxosmithkline PLC and Proctor & Gamble Co. as *Amici Curiae* in Support of Respondents' at pp. 2–3, *Kiobel v. Royal Dutch Petroleum* 569 US 108 (2013) (No. 10-1491), 2012 WL 3245485.

87 In Canada see, for example, 'Factum of the Intervenor, Amnesty International Canada' in *Choc v. Hudbay Minerals Inc., HMI Nickel Inc and Compañia Guartemalteca de Niquel SA* (Court File No. CV-11-435841), <https://www.amnesty.ca/sites/amnesty/files/imce/images/HudBay%20factum.20feb2013.pdf>, accessed 15 October 2020. In England see, for example, in *Vedanta* (n. 24): 'Draft Statement in Intervention, *Vedanta Resources Plc and another v. Lungowe and others*, Case No: A1/2016/2502 & 2504', <https://corporate-responsibility.org/wp-content/uploads/2019/01/Statement-in-Intervention-ICJ-CORE-.pdf>, (hereafter *Vedanta Intervention*) accessed 15 October 2020; in *Okpabi* (n. 24): CORE, 'RE: Rule 15 submission to the Supreme Court of the United Kingdom by CORE Coalition and Others on behalf of *Okpabi and others v. Royal Dutch Shell plc and another*, UKSC 2018/0068', <https://media.business-humanrights.org/media/documents/files/documents/CORE_Rule.15.Submission_UKSC_2018.0068.pdf>, (hereafter *Okpabi Intervention*) accessed 15 October 2020; and *Kalma* (n. 12): CORE, RAID, 'Re: Rule 15 submission in support of application for permission to appeal in *Kadie Kalma & others v. African Minerals Ltd and others*, [2020] EWCA Civ 144, Case No: UKSC 2020/0073'), <https://www.raid-uk.org/sites/default/files/raid-core_rule_15_submission_re_kalma_28_04_2020.pdf>, accessed 15 October 2020 (hereafter *Kalma Intervention*).

and compensation for the particular claimant(s) in question. The objective of many claimants will be settlement, with no appetite for adjudication of the claims at a trial.[88] For others, the proceedings may form part of a broader corpus of strategic human rights litigation, pursuing goals or concerning interests that extend beyond those of the parties to the dispute.[89] Such litigation is pursued to heighten public awareness, incentivise business improvements, and exert pressure towards regulatory change.[90] Indeed, claimants and their representatives may persevere with litigation that has little prospect of success in the hope that sequential cases or numerous cases of a particular genre will lead to corporate behavioural change.[91] A study of 40 foreign direct liability cases, for example, observed that litigation acted as an apparent incentive towards the adoption of human rights policies and/or additional measures to address human rights issues.[92] In cases such as these, the 'normal' drivers that shape the course of litigation are unlikely to determine outcomes.

The motivations behind multinational human rights litigation can be both complex and opaque.[93] Beyond accountability for particular alleged harms, another driver can be efforts to gain access to information not otherwise available to the claimants.[94] Another that lies behind much strategic human rights litigation is to seek establishment of favourable precedents that will lead to an expansion of liability.[95] Whilst adversarial litigation of its nature encourages parties to keep their cards close to their chest for fear of revealing weaknesses, defendants to multinational human rights litigation can find themselves answering seemingly hopeless claims that are nevertheless intractably difficult to resolve. Finding points of agreement or possible compromise can be much more difficult than in any commercial dispute where economic factors tend to dominate. Claimants in multinational human rights litigation may find it particularly difficult to walk away without issues of principle being acknowledged and might value a judgment of liability much more highly than an early monetary settlement (although on this, there is the possibility that the perspectives of individual claimants and of those backing them might diverge). Lawyers pursuing claims on behalf of affected persons make a significant monetary investment in preparing for, launching, and pursuing such litigation, with the consequent need to generate financial returns that exceed any financial sum that would compensate victims, a pressure that may

[88] See, for example, Kochan (n. 28) 258.
[89] Duffy (n. 59) with an introduction to the genre at 3–6.
[90] Kochan (n. 74) 413.
[91] Duffy (n. 59) 42–4.
[92] J. Schrempf-Stirling and F. Wettstein, 'Beyond Guilty Verdicts: Human Rights Litigation and its Impact on Corporations' Human Rights Policies' (October 2017) 145(3) *Journal of Business Ethics* 545–62.
[93] Generally, Duffy (n. 59).
[94] Ibid., 69–72; Khoury and Whyte (n. 56) 82.
[95] Kochan (n. 74) 456–7 describes NGO involvement in ATS litigation as a 'well-orchestrated campaign' attempting to create precedents and establish liability and remedy for harms.

form an obstacle to resolutions that might otherwise be possible and, even, operate in the better interests of the claimants themselves.[96] The situation is further complicated where there is a need to take account of the interests or wishes of third party sources of litigation funding, the implications of which will vary between jurisdictions.[97] Similarly, NGOs that support or encourage claims may have strategic concerns that do not exactly coincide with the immediate interests of claimants in particular cases.[98] From a broader strategic perspective, settlement might result in the issues that led to the litigation being buried; claimants and their representatives may worry that such outcomes offer limited deterrent impact on the individual defendant or the wider corporate sector.[99]

From the business perspective, one of the main attractions of settlement of litigation is that it should offer the possibility to draw a line under the dispute, providing finality, certainty, and (it would hope) an end to damaging media headlines.[100] In the context of business accused of liability for human rights abuses, however, settlement with individual claimants may instead activate additional demands for further accountability and compensation.[101] Sequential litigation involving the same issues is not unheard of.[102] Even settlements that are expressly without any admission of liability (which is the norm) might create real reputational difficulties for a corporate defendant that has been accused publicly of serious human rights violations. For many reasons, corporate defendants might regard confidentiality over some or all aspects of settlement terms as important, but this—as well as provisions aiming to achieve a 'full and final' settlement (including waivers of further legal claims)—may attract criticism from a remedy effectiveness and human rights compatibility perspective.[103]

[96] See, for example, Meeran (n. 32) pp. 18–19.

[97] In the US context, see, for example, Boutrous (n. 2) 238–9.

[98] Duffy (n. 59) 56–7. Some commentators observe that on occasion, some claimants' lawyers may be accused of an opportunistic approach to human rights litigation against corporations: Khoury and Whyte (n. 56) 81.

[99] See ibid., 97. Among discussions of some of the strategic dilemmas that may confront claimants in multinational human rights litigation see Duffy (n. 59) and, under the ATS, Kochan (n. 74) 462–43; N. Ela, 'Litigation Dilemmas: Lessons from the Marcos Human Rights Class Action' (2017) 42(2) *Journal of the American Bar Foundation Law & Social Inquiry* 479–508.

[100] Kochan (n. 74) suggests at 413 and 451 that when novel litigation theories start to survive motions to dismiss, corporate defendants will have more incentive to settle to avoid harm to reputation and potential adverse judgments.

[101] The remedial framework and settlements reached between Barrick Gold Corporation (Barrick) and survivors of rape involving workers at a Papua New Guinea mining site are instructive. While it was reported that the majority of survivors accepted compensation packages under the remedial framework that had been established, eleven secured a preferential settlement after filing a separate lawsuit against Barrick in the United States assisted by the organisation EarthRights International: R. Feneley, '200 girls and women raped: now 11 of them win better compensation from the world's biggest gold miner', *Sydney Morning Herald*, 4 April 2015, <https://www.smh.com.au/world/200-girls-and-women-raped-now-11-of-them-win-better-compensation-from-the-worlds-biggest-gold-miner-20150325-1m7ibq.html>, accessed 15 October 2020.

[102] Consider the lawsuits brought against BHP group entities following the collapse of the Samarco dam (n. 7) and (n. 11).

[103] See, in the context of company-led remedial processes, n. 211 below.

On occasion, a corporate defendant may feel compelled to continue to trial where precedential issues of principle are at stake that could expand liability thresholds for the future. The corresponding risk for claimants is that there is a consolidation of jurisprudence that limits liability theories or pressure for clarifying legislation that could further restrict substantive rights.[104]

For reasons such as these, multinational human rights litigation can be a strategic quagmire which the corporate defendant can only navigate by first developing an understanding of the broader agenda from which the litigation has emerged and to try to understand its contextual drivers.[105] This can better equip defendants to anticipate the underlying strategies and likely tactics of claimants and their representatives but also help avoid drawing early lines in the sand that can prove difficult to retract from, perpetuating conflict and impeding resolutions that might be in the overall interests of both parties.[106]

Aside from the serious reputational risk that accompanies multinational human rights litigation, there are also significant financial risks for business. Most obviously, there is the tangible financial cost when exposed to a damages award following an adverse judgment in litigation or the payment of significant sums in settlement of claims.[107] These are compounded by the possibility of class actions in various forms. Added to this is the exposure to possible penalties and fines if governmental attention is drawn to issues for which the organisation may be held to account under applicable law.[108]

Significant events involving tragic human impacts may receive so much media attention that a company's share price is affected, particularly if the potential financial liabilities of the company are substantial.[109] Corporate defendants may find

[104] The risk for claimants of the limiting effects of jurisprudence is demonstrated by recent experience with respect to claims against corporations under the ATS: see the Supreme Court rulings in *Kiobel* (n. 44) and *Jesner* (n. 44).

[105] See Garcia and Ewing (n. 65) 42; Drimmer and Lamoree (n. 2) 522–6.

[106] See, for example, Pitts (n. 81) 496–502. In some jurisdictions, civil procedure frameworks encourage early mediation and settlement efforts which facilitate early identification of key issues between the parties and aim to unclog overburdened court systems. For example, the Civil Procedure Rules (CPR) in England and Wales encourage parties to settle disputes without litigation proceedings (CPR, Practice Direction—Pre-action Conduct and Protocols, 3(c)); and to pursue alternative dispute resolution (ADR) means to achieve an early settlement (CPR, Practice Direction—Pre-action Conduct and Protocols, 3(d)).

[107] Bağlayan, Landau, McVey, et al. (n. 55) 44–6; Drimmer and Lamoree (n. 2); Drimmer (n. 2). The risks associated with adverse judgments may be compounded in US jurisdictions that offer jury trials in civil actions and the potential for awards of punitive, as well as compensatory, damages.

[108] See *Union Carbide* (n. 11) and reported criminal prosecutions and convictions in India: 'Ex-Union Carbide officials sentenced over Bhopal leak', *Reuters* (7 June 2010); Amnesty International (n. 75): 'Trafigura found guilty of toxic waste offence', *The Independent*, 24 July 2010, <https://www.independent.co.uk/news/world/europe/trafigura-found-guilty-toxic-waste-offence-2034313.html>, accessed 15 October 2020.

[109] For example, the BHP share price suffered in the immediate aftermaths of the Samarco tailings dam collapse in Brazil in 2015 discussed in n. 7, as reported in R. Hoyle and A. MacDonald, 'BHP Slips as Brazil Troubles Mount', *Wall Street Journal*, 30 November 2015, <https://www.wsj.com/articles/bhp-shares-plunge-as-brazil-files-suit-against-dam-owners-1448885093>, accessed 15 October 2020; 'BHP Billiton shares drop after Samarco accusations in Brazil', *Sydney Morning Herald*, 10 June 2016, <https://

themselves targets of concerted campaigns calling for divestment.[110] Conversely, there may be pressure on the corporate defendant to extricate itself from its business relationships associated with the litigation.[111] The existence of multinational human rights litigation—even if contested and unproven—can be taken as an indicator of a poor human rights record. This can lead to 'blacklisting' by investors, including influential market participants such as sovereign wealth funds.[112] Similarly, access to capital may be constrained when financial institutions, export credit agencies, and other finance providers factor human rights issues into credit processes and broader due diligence.[113]

Leading brands may be particularly susceptible to these types of risk, particularly if consumers are encouraged to boycott their goods.[114] There may be other commercial impacts, such as exclusion from procurement processes, including those offered by government clients.[115] Involvement in multinational human

www.smh.com.au/business/companies/bhp-billiton-shares-drop-after-samarco-accusations-in-brazil-20160610-gpg8ek.html>, accessed 15 October 2020. In June 2020, reports of low pay at factories supplying a 'fast fashion' retailer preceded a sharp drop in share price for the retailer: Labour Behind The Label, 'Boohoo & Covid-19: The people behind the profits', June 2020, <https://labourbehindthelabel.net/wp-content/uploads/2020/06/LBL-Boohoo-WEB.pdf>, accessed 15 October 2020. G. Mantilla, 'Emerging International Human Rights Norms for Transnational Corporations' (2009) 15(2) *Global Governance* 279–98, 284 reports that human rights scandals in the 1990s were reflected in share price drops and divestments. A review of studies of the effects of human rights incidents and litigation on stock performance is in Bağlayan, Landau, McVey, et al. (n. 55) 51, 59.

110 In 7 of 25 transnational tort matters reviewed in Drimmer and Lamoree (n. 2), claimants had unsuccessfully pressured investors to divest. However, those companies then received negative ratings from the funds that rated on ethical performance.

111 This occurred in relation to *Talisman* (n. 10). See Drimmer and Lamoree (n. 2) 521–2. Following pressure from human rights groups and others, in 2003 Talisman sold its stake in the Greater Nile Petroleum Company Limited in Sudan to India's State-run Oil and Natural Gas Corporation: 'Talisman pulls out of Sudan', BBC, 10 March 2003, <http://news.bbc.co.uk/1/hi/business/2835713.stm>, accessed 15 October 2020.

112 For a discussion of the role and influence of sovereign wealth funds, see J. Slawotsky, 'Corporate liability for violating international law under the Alien Tort Statute: the corporation through the lens of globalisation and privatisation'(2013) 6 *International Review of Law* 2–7.

113 Drimmer (n. 2); Shift, 'OECD Includes Human Rights Due Diligence in Recommendations for Export Credit Agencies', (Shift, April 2016) <https://shiftproject.org/oecd-includes-human-rights-due-diligence-in-recommendations-for-export-credit-agencies/>, accessed 15 October 2020; 'UK Export Finance (UKEF)—the UK's Export Credit Agency—takes account of factors 'beyond the purely financial and of relevant government policies in respect of ESHR impacts on individual transaction'': 'Policy and practice on Environmental, Social and Human Rights due diligence and monitoring', *UKEF*, 26 August 2020, <https://www.gov.uk/government/publications/uk-export-finance-environmental-social-and-human-rights-policy/policy-and-practice-on-environmental-social-and-human-rights-due-diligence-and-monitoring#fn:1>, accessed 15 October 2020. For a critique of CSR screening, rating, and rankings, see Jennings (n. 72) 355–71.

114 Jennings (n. 72) 329 observes that '[t]he ubiquity of social media ... has produced fast moving waves of business boycotts and banishment. In the blink of an eye, a company is paralyzed.' Amidst the Covid-19 crisis, the NHS reportedly was asked to avoid PPE gloves made by Malaysian manufacturer Top Glove, following allegations of modern slavery in their factories: P. Pattison, 'NHS urged to avoid PPE gloves made in 'slave-like' conditions', *The Guardian*, 23 April 2020, <https://www.theguardian.com/global-development/2020/apr/23/nhs-urged-to-avoid-ppe-gloves-made-in-slave-like-conditions-coronavirus>, accessed 15 October 2020.

115 See, for example, Danish Institute for Human Rights, 'Driving Change through Public Procurement: A Toolkit on Human Rights for Procurement Policy Makers and Practitioners'

rights litigation might also hamper progress of commercial opportunities with potential counterparties deterred by a company's exposure to claims or relationship with abusive regimes and, in the context of merger and acquisition (M&A) transactions, involvement in multinational human rights litigation may be seen as a deal breaker or at least a factor in pricing.[116]

Multinational human rights litigation also can take a toll on an organisation's personnel, including at senior executive level, particularly when individuals are specifically identified, or when the litigation is long-running and involves multiple strands.[117] Defending claims on several fronts, and sequential claims over a number of years, even decades, can be a strain on management time and morale.[118] Dealing with personnel who had oversight of activities giving rise to claims and the potential that they may be named individually in litigation or even subject to prosecution requires sensitive attention, particularly if disciplinary action may be warranted. Meanwhile, their cooperation is likely to be important for the conduct of the litigation. Claims implicating powerful interests within host States may not only threaten the corporate defendant commercially but could also result in serious concerns around the safety and security of personnel in that State, or others coming forward as witnesses in the litigation. Finally, reputational exposure through multinational human rights litigation may have an impact on the organisation's recruitment of new talent.[119]

(DIHR, March 2020), <https://www.hrprocurementlab.org/wp-content/uploads/2020/03/DIHR_Toolkit_public-procurement_2020.pdf>, accessed 15 October 2020. The BP Deepwater Horizon incident and BP's guilty plea to felony charges reportedly led to BP temporarily being suspended from entering contracts with the US federal government: C. Liu, 'Escaping Liability via Forum Non Conveniens: ConocoPhillips's Oil Spill in China' (2014) 17(2) *University of Pennsylvania Journal of Law and Social Change* 137–8, 138.

[116] D. Hasselback, 'Corporate social responsibility adherence now key to deals', *National Post's Financial Post and FP Investing*, 30 July 2015, <https://www.pressreader.com/canada/calgary-herald/20150730/282136405117899>. accessed 15 October 2020. A. Triponel, 'What Do Human Rights Have to Do With Mergers and Acquisitions?', *Shift*, January 2016, <https://shiftproject.org/wp-content/uploads/2016/01/Shift_MAarticle_Jan2016.pdf>, accessed 15 October 2020 (see the three examples set out at p. 2).

[117] Most legal systems have rules aimed at ensuring that parallel proceedings do not proceed against the same defendant on the same factual and legal bases at the same time, but litigation—particularly if mounted in more than one forum—can be costly, time-consuming, and lead to uncertainty. C. Kenney, 'Disaster in the Amazon: Dodging 'Boomerang Suits' in Transnational Human Rights Litigation' (June 2009) 97(3) *California Law Review* 873–83, <https://heinonline.org/HOL/Page?public=true&handle=hein.journals/calr97&div=26&start_page=857&collection=journal&set_as_cursor=0&men_tab=srchresults>, accessed 15 October 2020.

[118] For example, *Nestlé USA Inc v. Doe I* is (n. 45) currently pending before the US Supreme Court was commenced in 2005. *Kiobel* (n. 44) lasted 11.5 years without trial in the US (and continued in a different form before Dutch courts).

[119] H. Tuttle, 'Corporate Reputation Drastically Impacts Talent Acquisition, Salary Costs', *Risk Management Monitor*, 7 November 2014, <https://www.riskmanagementmonitor.com/corporate-reputation-drastically-impacts-talent-acquisition-salary-costs>, accessed 15 October 2020: referencing a study from *Corporate Responsibility Magazine* and talent acquisition firm Alexander Mann Solutions.

These are a few of the manifold ways in which multinational human rights litigation promises a rocky ride for the corporate defendant even outside the confines of the proceedings themselves. However, as noted, multinational human rights litigation is often an imperfect vehicle for claimants as well, not least because litigation—including the strategic variety—'rarely resolves human rights problems'.[120]

For their part, many multinational businesses with global interests have come to recognise that there is good business sense in not only avoiding involvement in the types of harm that can result in multinational human rights litigation but also in engaging proactively with organisational changes that support sustainable business models and society more broadly: it is part of their social licence to operate. These recognitions have been reinforced and accelerated by the UNGP.

IV. The UN Guiding Principles on Business and Human Rights (UNGP)

The UNGP[121] are 'the global authoritative standard' on business and human rights.[122] Approaching a decade since their endorsement by the UN Human Rights Council, this chapter offers a brief examination of ways in which effective implementation of the UNGP might be expected to lead to a reduction in multinational human rights litigation, or a shift in its contours. The role of business is the main focus here, but States' duties with respect to regulation and remedial structures are fundamental.

It is important to recall that the UNGP involved a rejection of prior initiatives that sought to impose the same human rights obligations on corporations that apply to States.[123] Instead, a three-pillar 'Protect, Respect and Remedy' framework was conceived of[124] which the UNGP were then designed to 'operationalise'.[125] This

[120] Duffy (n. 59) 273.

[121] UNGP (n. 3).

[122] Z.R. Al Hussein, 'Ethical Pursuit of Prosperity', *The Law Society Gazette*, 23 March 2015, <https://www.lawgazette.co.uk/comment-and-opinion/ethical-pursuit-of-prosperity/5047796.article>, accessed 15 October 2020. The unanimous endorsement of the UNGP by the UN Human Rights Council in 2011 followed extensive and widespread multistakeholder consultation and research during the course of the mandate of the UN Special Representative of the Secretary-General on the Issue of Human Rights and Transnational Corporations and Other Business Enterprises, Professor John Ruggie. For an overview of the mandate and access to resources and documents relating to it, see OHCHR, *Special Representative of the Secretary-General on human rights and transnational corporations and other business enterprises* ohchr.org/EN/Issues/Business/Pages/SRSGTransCorpIndex.aspx, accessed 15 October 2020.

[123] UNHRC, 'Interim report of the Special Representative of the Secretary-General on the issue of human rights and transnational corporations and other business enterprises' (2006), UN Doc E/CN.4/2006/97 at paras 64–69.

[124] UNHRC, 'Report of the Special Representative of the Secretary-General on the issue of human rights and transnational corporations and other business enterprises—Protect, Respect and Remedy: A Framework for Business and Human Rights' (2008), UN Doc A/HRC/8/5.

[125] UNHRC, 'Report of the Special Representative of the Secretary-General on the issue of human rights and transnational corporations and other business enterprises, John Ruggie—Business and

recognises, first, that States have existing legal obligations to protect against human rights abuses by business, through effective policies, legislation, regulation, and adjudication;[126] second, above and beyond the requirement on business enterprises to comply with laws applicable to them,[127] they also have a responsibility to respect human rights, which is rooted in a 'transnational social norm' that they should act with due diligence to avoid infringing on the rights of others and address adverse impacts with which the business is or may become involved;[128] and third, those whose rights are infringed should have access to effective remedy for business-related harm.[129]

Core components of the corporate responsibility to respect human rights are a policy commitment meeting UNGP expectations;[130] human rights due diligence (HRDD) processes integrated across business functions to identify, prevent, mitigate, and account for how the enterprise addresses impacts on human rights;[131] as well as processes to enable remediation of any adverse human rights impacts.[132]

Once a business enterprise has deployed HRDD to identify potential and actual adverse impacts, the factors that dictate appropriate action depend on the nature of the business enterprise's 'involvement' with them. Businesses should take steps to avoid causing or contributing to adverse human rights impacts through their own activities and should seek—through the exercise of 'leverage'[133]—to prevent or mitigate adverse impacts that are directly linked to their operations, products, or services by their business relationships, even if they do not contribute to those impacts.[134] Direct linkage and the expectation to exercise leverage are blind to the existence of legal relationships (such as by way of contract) between the business enterprise that identifies an adverse impact, and the entity that causes the impact.

The concept of 'leverage' forms the basis for business' management of human rights risks through their value chain, but the existence of leverage does not of itself entail responsibility. Assessing when and by what means to exercise leverage can be one of the most challenging features of HRDD, combined with the dynamic nature of HRDD and the need to re-evaluate impacts, appropriate responses, and their effectiveness over time,[135] whereby the nature of the business' involvement may also

human rights: further steps toward the operationalization of the "protect, respect and remedy" framework', (2010) UN Doc A/HRC/14/27, leading to UNHRC Resolution 17/4, 'Human rights and transnational corporations and other business enterprises' (2011), UN Doc A/HRC/RES/17/4.

[126] UNGP (n. 3) principles 1–10.
[127] Ibid., principle 23.
[128] Ibid., principles 11–24.
[129] Ibid., principles 25–31.
[130] Ibid., principles 15(a) and 16.
[131] Ibid., principles 15(b) and 17–21.
[132] Ibid., principle 15(c).
[133] 'Leverage' is defined as 'the ability to effect change in the wrongful practices of an entity that causes a harm': ibid., principle 19 commentary.
[134] Ibid., principles 13 and 19.
[135] Ibid., principles 17(c) and 18 commentary.

evolve.[136] Crucially, HRDD is focused on risks to rightsholders,[137] and thus goes beyond identifying and managing risks to the business itself.[138] HRDD is fact- and context-specific, and not a 'one-size-fits-all' endeavour, but the most severe risks should receive priority attention[139] and the risk of causing or contributing to gross human rights abuses should be treated as a legal compliance issue.[140]

The UNGP are exactly what they say they are: guiding principles. While the responsibility to respect human rights applies to all business enterprises across all sectors, the UNGP acknowledge the vast array of organisational structures, sizes, operational activities, geographical spread, and resources, and the contextual factors that can affect both risk and the practicalities of addressing impacts.[141] They conceive of governance of human rights risks within a framework of policies and processes tailored to each organisation's particular circumstances, while also providing decision-making frameworks for the determination of appropriate action in a principles-based and outcomes-oriented fashion that respects internationally recognised human rights.[142] They prescribe 'practical ways of integrating human rights concerns within enterprise-wide risk management systems'[143] and provide authoritative guidance for how to manage the risks of adverse impacts. For good reason, their approach was characterised by their author as 'principled pragmatism'.[144]

Much of the focus of the HRDD provisions of the UNGP are on prevention and mitigation of adverse impacts. Actual impacts—those that have already occurred—should be addressed in accordance with UNGP 22 which states that '[w]here business enterprises identify that they have caused or contributed to adverse impacts, they should provide for or cooperate in their remediation through legitimate processes'. Businesses should have operational level grievance mechanisms (OLGMs)

[136] The different forms of involvement in adverse human rights impacts and the way in which involvement can shift over time is discussed in 'OHCHR response to request from BankTrack for advice regarding the application of the UN Guiding Principles on Business and Human Rights in the context of the banking sector' (OHCHR, 12 June 2017), ohchr.org/Documents/Issues/Business/InterpretationGuidingPrinciples.pdf accessed 15 October 2020.

[137] UNGP (n. 3) principle 17 commentary.

[138] The UNGP (n. 3) build on the ways in which businesses have always sought to address social issues in a meaningful way: reliance on accurate information and its input into risk analysis: see Jennings (n. 72) 325. Jennings urges businesses to address human rights impacts based on rationality (not emotional factors driven by short term stakeholder pressure) and long-term responses and solutions.

[139] UNGP (n. 3) principle 24.

[140] Ibid., principle 23.

[141] Ibid., principle 17(b) and commentary.

[142] It should involve appropriate engagement with and input from stakeholders external to the organisation and the organisation's monitoring and tracking of its performance will enable it to account for its impacts and human rights risk management. Ibid., principles 18–21.

[143] Ruggie (n. 43) at 189.

[144] UNHRC (n. 123) at paras 70–81. At para. 81, Professor Ruggie encapsulates principled pragmatism as 'an unflinching commitment to the principle of strengthening the promotion and protection of human rights as it relates to business, coupled with a pragmatic attachment to what works best in creating change where it matters most—in the daily lives of people'.

in place to enable remediation as appropriate.[145] Where adverse impacts have occurred that the business enterprise has not caused or contributed to, but which are directly linked to its operations, products, or services by a business relationship, the responsibility to respect human rights does not require that the enterprise itself provide for remediation, although it may play a role in doing so.[146] The UNGP acknowledge that—as is the case with any form of risk management—even with the best policies and practices, a business enterprise may cause or contribute to an adverse human rights impact that it has not foreseen or been able to prevent.[147]

Multinational human rights litigation—the focus of this chapter—occurs within State-based judicial mechanisms and these are addressed in the third pillar of the UNGP (access to remedy).[148] Judicial mechanisms may be resorted to, for example, where allegations relating to adverse human rights impacts or abuse are contested.[149]

V. Implications of the UNGP for multinational human rights litigation

There are several intersecting ways in which it might be expected that the UNGP, operationalising the three-pillar framework, could influence the occurrence or conduct of multinational human rights litigation.

A. State regulatory intervention

It might be expected that there would be increased State regulatory intervention to protect against business-related human rights harms and that this in turn might lead to either a reduction in litigation (through more effective regulation of business behaviour or deterrence of poor behaviour), or, by State-led reforms, an increase in and/or streamlining of litigation through more expansive access to—and more effective forms of—remedy. The direction of regulatory innovation is discussed in section VI below, including by reference to litigation.

145 UNGP (n. 3) principle 29. If integrated into the business' enterprise risk management systems, OLGMs can act as a filter to alert the business at an early stage to emerging issues, supporting 'feedback loops' to trigger appropriate action with respect to activities and their impacts, prevent or mitigate impacts and so avoid escalation to serious harms. OLGMs should meet the effectiveness criteria set out in UNGP (n. 3) principle 31.

146 Ibid., principle 22 commentary.

147 Ibid., principle 22 commentary.

148 Ibid., principle 26.

149 Ibid., principle 22 is limited to situations in which the business enterprise itself recognises that it has caused or contributed to an adverse human rights impact: see UN OHCHR '*The Corporate Responsibility to Respect Human Rights, An Interpretive Guide*' (2012) HR/PUB/12/02, Q63 and Q68.

B. Publicly stated commitments by business and their implementation

There should be an increase in publicly stated commitments to human rights by business enterprises and the effective integration of HRDD processes within their global operations. Meaningful policy commitments and effective HRDD processes should, in principle, result in many adverse human rights impacts of business being identified, avoided, and/or mitigated.[150] If there are fewer adverse impacts, and if businesses are better equipped to avoid involvement in or association with human rights abuse, a decline in multinational human rights litigation might follow. Moreover, it might be expected that where adverse impacts do come to light through due diligence or otherwise, there would be prompt action to address and/or remediate harms when appropriate and consequently, a reduced need for litigation.

A number of MNCs do now publicly commit to respect human rights consistently with the UNGP[151] and/or other standards aligned with the UNGP[152] including acceptance of remedial responsibilities, either expressly or by implication (through wholesale alignment with the UNGP).[153] Factors driving increased business alignment with the UNGP include States' expectations,[154] regulatory, investor,[155] and other pressures[156]—such as conditionality of demonstrating a

150 Mantilla (n. 109) describes the impetus behind a growing number of voluntary codes and initiatives that accelerated in the 1990s and predated the UNGP. In its 2018 report to the UN General Assembly, the UN Working Group on Business and Human Rights highlighted key features of HRDD, gaps and challenges in practice and emerging good practice, and how key stakeholders can contribute to the scaling up of effective HRDD. See UNGA, 'Working Group on the issue of human rights and transnational corporations and other business enterprises' (2018), UN Doc A/73/163, and companion papers I and II, <https://digitallibrary.un.org/record/1639520?ln=en>, accessed 15 October 2020 (hereafter UNWG). The development of due diligence guidance by the OECD in support of the OECD 'Guidelines for Multinational Enterprises' (hereafter OECD MNE Guidelines) (OECD Publishing, 2011), <https://www.oecd.org/corporate/mne/>, accessed 15 October 2020, has also contributed to the development of practice and effective integration: see, for example, OECD 'Due Diligence Guidance for Responsible Business Conduct', (OECD, 2018) <https://mneguidelines.oecd.org/OECD-Due-Diligence-Guidance-for-Responsible-Business-Conduct.pdf>, accessed 15 October 2020 and other sector- and issue specific guidance.

151 UNWG (n. 150) at para. 23. 'Company statements of policy on human rights: Examples', BHRRC, <https://media.business-humanrights.org/media/documents/files/reports-and-materials/Company-policies-Examples.htm>, accessed 15 October 2020.

152 Prominent examples include the 'Ten Principles of the UN Global Compact', *UN Global Compact*, <http://www.unglobalcompact.org/what-is-gc/mission/principles>, accessed 15 October 2020; OECD MNE Guidelines (n. 150); and the Voluntary Principles Initiative, *The Voluntary Principles on Security and Human Rights*, <https://www.voluntaryprinciples.org/the-principles/>, accessed 15 October 2020.

153 Consider statements available in the compilation hosted by the BHRRC (n. 151).

154 See, for example, national action plans on implementation of the UNGP, such as that of the United Kingdom: *The UK National Action Plan on implementing the UN Guiding Principles, Progress Report* (May 2020), <http://www.gov.uk/government/publications/implementing-the-un-guiding-principles-on-business-and-human-rights-may-2020-update/uk-national-action-plan-on-implementing-the-un-guiding-principles-on-business-and-human-rights-progress-update-may-2020>, accessed 29 January 2021; UNWG (n. 150) para. 20.

155 See, for example, ibid., paras 85–91.

156 Some of these influences are described in ibid., at paras 20–22.

human rights policy and risk management framework for access to capital or to government procurement processes, contractual requirements included within supply chains and even as a necessary element of qualifying as 'environmentally sustainable'.[157] Public reporting is an element of HRDD[158] and businesses do disclose information about risk assessment, identified impacts, and other relevant data generated through due diligence processes.[159]

Public reporting—whether voluntary or mandated[160]—brings a level of transparency that enhances accountability and provides an additional incentive for businesses to improve their human rights risk management.[161] Reporting frameworks aligned with the UNGP encourage a common approach that supports meaningful disclosures as well as external assessment.[162] Analyses and commentary by academic researchers, civil society, and government-sponsored reviews further facilitate critical assessment of the effectiveness of these steps as do an increasing number of human-rights focused benchmarks that seek to shine a light on both best practice and on areas for improvement.[163] When disclosures reveal identified adverse human rights impacts or indicate HRDD shortcomings, these might be used by third parties to encourage improvements in performance but also, potentially, as evidence for use in mounting claims and, eventually, litigation.[164] Record

[157] Regulation (EU) No. 2020/852 of the European Parliament and of the Council of 18 June 2020 on the establishment of a framework to facilitate sustainable investment, OJ L198, 27.6.2020, pp. 13–43, Articles 3(c) and 18.

[158] UNGP (n. 3) principle 21 and commentary.

[159] Shift, as part of the Human Rights Reporting and Assurance Frameworks Initiative (RAFI)—a multistakeholder consultative initiative designed to support the development of the UNGP: 'Human Rights Reporting and Assurance Frameworks Initiative' (Shift 2012), <https://shiftproject.org/resource/human-rights-reporting-and-assurance-frameworks-initiative/>, accessed 15 October 2020—hosts a database and analysis of a number of companies reporting on human rights in line with the responsibility to respect as articulated in the UNGP: <https://www.ungpreporting.org/database-analysis/#:~:text=%E2%80%9CThe%20UNGP%20Reporting%20Database%20helps,human%20rights%20on%20companies'%20performance.&text=Shift%20has%20created%20an%20agile,integration%20in%20investment%20decision%2Dmaking>, accessed 15 October 2020.

[160] See, for example, laws referenced at n. 228 below.

[161] The public reporting expectations on business enterprises contained in the UNGP are explained in more detail in the UNGP Interpretive Guide (n. 149), Q54–61.

[162] See, for example, the UN Guiding Principles Reporting Framework, <https://www.ungpreporting.org/framework-guidance/>, developed through RAFI (n. 159). See also the disclosure database hosted by Shift (n. 159).

[163] UNWG (n. 150) at paras 25–30. See, for example, the Corporate Human Rights Benchmark (CHRB), World Benchmarking Alliance, <https://www.worldbenchmarkingalliance.org/corporate-human-rights-benchmark/>, accessed 29 January 2021. The CHRB, based only on public information, has examined and assessed 230 publicly traded companies across five sectors (agricultural producers, apparel, extractive, ICT manufacturing, and automotive) by reference to matters such as their human rights policy commitments, due diligence, and remedy.

[164] Nestlé reportedly conducted an investigation into forced labour and other human rights abuses in its seafood supply chain in Thailand, publishing a report in 2015: Associated Press, 'Nestlé admits to forced labour in its seafood supply chain in Thailand', *The Guardian*, <https://www.theguardian.com/global-development/2015/nov/24/nestle-admits-forced-labour-in-seafood-supply-chain>, accessed 15 October 2020. Nestlé was one of several US retailers sued (unsuccessfully) in California in class action lawsuits based on consumer protection laws in connection with sourcing of seafood from Thailand in circumstances of alleged forced labour within their supply chains: see *Barber v. Nestlé* (n. 34); *Sud v. Costco Wholesale Corp.* (n. 34).

keeping expectations associated with HRDD or gaps in reporting might form a hook for disclosure requests when litigation is commenced.

Critics of voluntary measures and those cynical towards corporate endeavours in this area point to an absence of empirical evidence of tangible benefits to vulnerable people. Others observe good and improving practices but lament that the provision of prompt and effective redress for those adversely impacted appears to lag.[165] Of course, HRDD policies and processes inevitably take time to design and embed throughout transnational organisations and their supply chains. Multinational enterprises with truly global operations spread across numerous and diverse business divisions may source raw materials, components and services from tens of thousands of first-tier suppliers who in turn rely on multiple lower tier suppliers within their supply chains.[166] The practical challenges of mapping those supply chains and implementing HRDD through them cannot be overstated.

There has not yet been an obvious downturn in multinational human rights litigation notwithstanding the increased prevalence of corporate human rights policies and HRDD implementation since the adoption of the UNGP in 2011. It is debatable how quickly tangible reductions might materialise, given inevitable delays between impacts and proceedings. It is possible that instances of improved outcomes are not yet sufficiently widespread—by way of impact avoidance and/or prompt remediation—but are also counterbalanced by intense external scrutiny and the ability to more readily identify and substantiate impacts. Certainly, the landscape and the operative influences are complex and much more research and analysis are needed to understand the true picture.

C. 'Legalisation' of the responsibility to respect

The UNGP do not place new, legally binding obligations on business enterprises,[167] but they do not operate in a 'law-free zone'.[168] Their implementation was recognised to call for a 'smart mix of measures' to foster business respect for human rights that would necessarily include developments of both a practical and regulatory nature.[169] Since 2011, there has been a somewhat inevitable 'legalisation' of aspects of the UNGP, and this evolution, while accelerating, remains fluid. It is yet

[165] For example, commenting on the mining sector, C. Hill, and S. Lillywhite, 'The United Nations 'Protect, Respect and Remedy' Framework: Six Years on and What Impact Has it Had?' (2015) 2(1) *The Extractive Industries and Society* 4.

[166] UNWG (n. 150) 13, para. 48. Unilever, for example, has reported that its ultimate supply chain includes 1.5 million smallholder farmers: Unilever, 'Mapping our farmer programmes', <https://www.unilever.com/sustainable-living/enhancing-livelihoods/inclusive-business/connecting-with-smallholder-farmers-to-enhance-livelihoods/mapping-our-farmers-programmes/>, accessed 30 October 2020.

[167] UNGP (n. 3), principle 12 commentary.

[168] UNHCR (n. 125) at para. 66.

[169] UNGP (n. 3), principle 3 commentary. For further discussion, see section VI below.

to be seen just how extensively UNGP expectations will be transposed into hard law, in what forms, and whether this will be achieved effectively to promote beneficial outcomes for affected persons or could in practice stifle inroads that may only be practicable with the latitude that voluntary initiates provide. Suffice to say that where aspects of the corporate responsibility to respect human rights articulated in the UNGP are transposed into legal obligation, litigation for non-fulfilment might be expected to follow.

The most obvious form of 'legalisation' is States' drive toward more formal regulation, already referenced in section VA and elaborated further in section VI below.

Another strand of 'legalisation' is driven by business itself. Commercial relationships with third parties are typically governed by contracts as well as other less formal arrangements (such as expected adherence to corporate codes of conduct or specific supplier codes of conduct).[170] Through transactional and other commercial documentation, businesses seek to ensure that they will not themselves cause or contribute to adverse impacts and also aim to increase leverage with counterparties to encourage or incentivise respect for human rights by including appropriate human-rights focused provisions within business relationships (including cascading expectations about HRDD through supply chains to parties with whom they have no contractual nexus).[171] As businesses seek to translate their policy commitments into practice by using contractual provisions to facilitate management of human rights risks, there could be a further 'hardening' of the UNGP within contractual terms and in modes of performance of them (including, for example, provisions governing how the parties should seek to ensure that adverse human rights impacts are identified and addressed, responses monitored and remedial action taken, collaboration, and capacity building encouraged).[172] Principles of privity of contract may be expected generally to limit potential litigation exposure to commercial counterparties but the possibility of claims by third parties (if not eventual liability) cannot be ruled out. Such arrangements may encourage litigation

[170] See, generally, A. Beckers, 'Regulating Corporate Regulators through Contract Law? The Case of Corporate Social Responsibility Codes of Conduct', *EUI Working Papers Max Weber Programme 2016/12* (2016), <https://papers.ssrn.com/sol3/papers.cfm?abstract_id=2789360>, accessed 15 October 2020. By way of example, see the supplier code of conduct published by Apple containing detailed provisions on matters such as safe and hygenic working conditions, the right to collective bargaining, a commitment to living wages and prohibitions on child labour (among other things): Apple (2020), *Apple Supplier Code of Conduct*, <https://www.apple.com/supplier-responsibility/pdf/Apple-Supplier-Code-of-Conduct-January.pdf>, accessed 15 October 2020.

[171] UNWG (n. 150) paras 53 and 54. An ABA Section of Business Law has developed model clauses aimed at protecting workers in international supply chains that take account of the UNGP. Published in April 2021, these are available at <https://americanbar.org/groups/human_rights/business-human-rights-initiative/contractual-clauses-project/> accessed 17 May 2021.

[172] J.G. Ruggie and J.F. Sherman III 'Adding Human Rights Punch to the New *Lex Mercatoria*: The Impact of the UN Guiding Principles on Business and Human Rights on Commercial Legal Practice' (2015) 6 *Journal of International Dispute Settlement* 455–61; R. Lindsay, R. McCorquodale, A. Sheppard, et al., 'Human Rights Responsibilities in the Oil and Gas Sector: Applying the UN Guiding Principles' (2013) 6(1) *Journal of World Energy Law & Business* 2–66, <https://doi.org/10.1093/jwelb/jws033>, accessed 15 October 2020.

in the future asserting that the company's contractual requirements—designed in particular to ensure that rights of workers in supply chains are not impacted negatively—implicitly confer enforceable third party rights.[173]

There might also be 'legalisation' of aspects of the responsibility to respect human rights through multinational human rights litigation itself and incremental developments in case law.

Evidently, there are potential intersections between the implementation of HRDD by business enterprises and legal standards and risks.[174] Albeit 'the responsibility of business enterprises to respect human rights (of which human rights due diligence is an integral part) is theoretically distinct from issues of legal liability, there are many ways in which the two concepts can interact in practice'.[175]

It is self-evident that systematic information gathering and analysis of human rights risks and actions taken (or not taken) in response will generate records, including details of the information available to various parts of a business, reports to and reactions by management, and other material of use to claimants seeking to evidence legal liability. While on the one hand, '[c]onducting appropriate human rights due diligence should help business enterprises address the risk of legal claims against them by showing that they took every reasonable step to avoid involvement with an alleged human rights abuse',[176] on the other, it might become easier to demonstrate when failings have occurred. Combined with the practicalities of transnational business organisation management forms,[177] 'knowing and showing'[178] in accordance with the UNGP could potentially increase exposure to litigation.

173 There have been a few instances of courts addressing the question of whether employees alleging worker violations in a supply chain might benefit from contracts between a retailer and their empoyer (its suppliers): for example, *Doe I v. Wal-Mart Stores, Inc.* (n. 52) at 681–2.

174 UNWG (n. 150) companion note I, 'Corporate human rights due diligence—Background note elaborating on key aspects', at 4–6.

175 OHCHR, 'Improving accountability and access to remedy for victims of business-related human rights abuse: The relevance of human rights due diligence to determinations of corporate liability: Report of the United Nations High Commissioner for Human Rights' (A/HRC/38/20/Add.2) (2018) para. 43.

176 UNGP (n. 3) principle 17 commentary. J.G. Ruggie and J.F. Sherman III, 'The Concept of 'Due Diligence' in the UN Guiding Principles on Business and Human Rights: A Reply to Jonathan Bonnitcha and Robert McCorquodale' (2017) 28(3) *European Journal of International Law* 921–8, <https://academic.oup.com/ejil/article/28/3/921/4616676>, accessed 15 October 2020, at p924: 'Simply put, without conducting human rights due diligence, companies can neither know nor show that they respect human rights and, therefore, cannot credibly claim that they do'.

177 For example, organisations may operate on a 'matrix' model, employing 'a multiple command system that includes not only a multiple command structure but also related support mechanisms and an associated organizational culture and behavior pattern': S.M. Davis, P.R. Lawrence, H. Kolodny, et al., *Matrix* (1997), 3. Matrix organisations may structure reporting and accountability processes across functional and business groups or by reference to particular projects; they include horizontal as well as vertical structures. This can facilitate risk management, including with respect to human rights but could also potentially add complexity to legal risk management.

178 UNGP (n. 3) principle 15 commentary; Ruggie and Sherman (n. 176).

For some time, it has been suggested that the responsibility to respect human rights as articulated in the UNGP—and in particular HRDD—may be invoked within domestic laws of tort, as supporting the existence of a duty of care and evidencing standards by which to judge when due care has (or has not) been exercised.[179] Such theories are now being articulated in some multinational human rights litigation.

The legal barriers to accountability that stem from the separate personality of corporate entities were studied closely in the development of the UNGP which specifically were not intended to 'establish a global enterprise legal liability model'.[180] Nevertheless, as noted in section II, multinational human rights litigation has included the development of theories aimed at circumventing restrictions on liability associated with the corporate veil. The UK Supreme Court has acknowledged the possibility of parent company liability to third parties with respect to overseas operations of a subsidiary, emphasising that this is not dependent on a novel or controversial extension of the tort of negligence and does not signify a new species of liability.[181] The precise contours of this genre of legal risk—which are centred on demonstrating a sufficient level of intervention by the parent in the conduct of operations of the subsidiary, through modes of control, oversight, and/or management of particular risks—are still in flux but the direction of travel augurs increased litigation (if not liability) risk. The basic conditions for liability are familiar but the circumstances in which a duty might be held to arise in practice remain uncertain.

Claimants alleging parent company liability for harms associated with overseas operations of a subsidiary have invoked group-wide policies concerning aspects of corporate governance and risk management.[182] Although courts have been reticent to accord undue significance to corporate statements of policy, particularly when earmarked as a feature of 'corporate social responsibility',[183] businesses are expected

[179] See, for example, A. Sanders, 'The Impact of the 'Ruggie Framework' and the United Nations Guiding Principles on Business and Human Rights on Transnational Human Rights Litigation' in J. Martin and K.R. Bravo (eds), *The Business and Human Rights Landscape: Moving Forward, Looking Back* (2015), exploring the consequences of analogising the responsibility to respect human rights with 'ordinary' tort laws and foreseeing a possible argument that there is a duty of care on business enterprises to act with due diligence to avoid infringing on the human rights of others. Also, P.T. Muchlinski, 'Implementing the New UN Corporate Human Rights Framework: Implications for Corporate Law, Governance and Regulation' (2012) 22 *Business Ethics Quarterly* 145.

[180] Ruggie (n. 43) 189; J.G. Ruggie, 'Global governance and new governance theory: lessons from Business and Human Right's (2014) 20(1) *Global Governance* 14.

[181] *Vedanta* (n. 24) at [54], [60].

[182] Voluntary Principles (n. 152); *Okpabi* (n. 24).

[183] In the *Tahoe v. Garcia* litigation, for example, both at first instance and on its subsequent appeal, the claimants relied on Tahoe's CSR intiatives to argue that it had a direct responsibility for the conduct of security personnel at its Guatemalan subsidiary but the courts did not engage with those assertions: (2015) BCSC 2045, [67], [78], and (2017) BCCA 39, [20]. This litigation was settled in 2019 following the acquisition of Tahoe Resources by Pan American Silver Corp.: see 'Pan American Silver Announces Resolution of Garcia v Tahoe Case', *CISION PRNewswire* 30 July 2019, <https://www.prnewswire.com/news-releases/pan-american-silver-announces-resolution-of-garcia-v-tahoe-case-300893365.html>, accessed 15 October 2020.

to do more than pay lip-service to standards to which they say they adhere[184] and, in English courts at least, it has been clarified that group-wide corporate policies concerning particular areas of activity may be a pertinent consideration in appropriate cases.[185] Alongside modes of implementation through corporate groups, such policies may be argued to offer evidence of a parent company's assumption of responsibility on particular matters rising to the level of a duty of care to third parties and, if a duty were established, it would no doubt also be argued that they reflect standards of care to which the relevant business should be held to account.[186]

Although the UNGP occasionally have been referenced in litigation,[187] they have not yet been widely invoked as a foundational element of claimants' legal cases. Developments in recent litigation may signify a shift towards this in the future.[188] Efforts may intensify to persuade courts not only to consider specific corporate policies that include commitments to the UNGP but also to consider the UNGP as a widely accepted and therefore generally applicable standard of business management of human rights risk.[189] It seems, therefore, that the UNGP could now be invoked in support of legal consequences even if it was not the intention of the UNGP to create them.

It is unclear how far this will advance claimants' cases in practice. Judicial examination will be subject to relevant evidential standards and courts' rigorous scrutiny of the facts presented to substantiate the requisite elements of liability in particular cases. Given that '[t]here is no limit to the models of management and control which may be put in place within a multinational group of companies',[190] each case will depend on its particular facts. The UNGP themselves assume widespread variation in the process-driven governance frameworks that might be adopted to address particular risks in particular contexts. They are not a 'toolkit' that can be taken off the shelf, plugged in, and an answer given: they are a principles-based framework' rather than a rules-based system.[191] Indeed, HRDD 'is an art more

[184] *Vilca v. Xtrata Ltd & Ors.*, [2016] EWHC 2757 (QB), Foskett J. at [25] (in relation to the Voluntary Principles (n. 152)).

[185] *Vedanta* (n. 24) at [52]–[53].

[186] For a consideration of the relevance of the Voluntary Principles in one case, see the Court of Appeal's observations in *Kalma* (n. 12) at [149–151].

[187] See, for example, *Choc, et al. v. HudBay Minerals Inc*, 2013 ONSC 1414 (Can.) and third party intervention (n. 87).

[188] See the *Okpabi Intervention* and the *Vedanta Intervention* (n. 87) urging an expansive approach to imposing a duty of care on parents, invoking various international legal developments as well as international standards such as the UNGP. Similarly, the *Kalma Intervention* (n. 87) argued that the UNGP and other international standards (in particular in that case, the Voluntary Principles), supported the existence of a duty of care and indicated the relevant standard of care.

[189] Ibid (n. 188). Similarly, it is possible that the more granular guidance provided in the more targeted due diligence guidelines developed under the OECD MNE Guidelines (n. 150) could also be argued to inform the relevant standard of care in particular circumstances.

[190] *Vedanta* (n. 24) at [51].

[191] 'Business and Human Rights: Interview with John Ruggie', *Business Ethics* 30 October 2011, <https://www.business-ethics.com/2011/10/30/8127-un-principles-on-business-and-human-rights-interview-with-john-ruggie/>, accessed 4 February 2021.

than a science',[192] with outcomes contingent on the bespoke design and application of organisations' HRDD processes, overlayed with judgments exercised in the course of business—and on infinitely variable factors in given cases.

Recognising that corporate efforts to implement the UNGP might feature in multinational human rights litigation, it is important to avoid the temptation to equate concepts deployed in the UNGP with those prevalent within domestic legal systems or under international law: to try to 'fit everything into, or render compatible with, traditional legal forms'.[193] The UNGP could all too easily be misinterpreted as a 'template liability framework', depending on the significance accorded various aspects of the principles articulated in them, particularly with respect to HRDD.[194]

An example is the cause, contribute, and direct linkage forms of involvement in human rights impacts and associated guidance to address them outlined in the UNGP. HRDD does not shift responsibility from an entity that causes harm to an entity linked to the harm by [reason of] a business relationship, and care is needed to avoid legal extrapolations that are inconsistent with the nature and intent of the UNGP.[195] Particularly with respect to impacts linked to their operations, products, or services by a business relationship, businesses will often take steps seeking to prevent or mitigate such impacts that are above and beyond any legal requirement (as acknowledged within the UNGP). Indeed, the factual ability to exercise leverage that could help mitigate or prevent adverse human rights impacts in remote tiers of a supply chain can in practice encourage businesses to act in ways that exceed both legal duty and even the defined contours of responsibility expressed by the UNGP.[196] Unless great care is exercised, seeking to impose legal liabilities in connection with impacts to which a business is linked across multiple tiers of supply chains—including in relation to efforts to address them—could risk creating

[192] UNWG (n. 150) para. 42.

[193] Ruggie and Sherman (n. 176) 925.

[194] OHCHR (n. 175); OHCHR, *UN Human Rights Issues Paper on legislative proposals for mandatory human rights due diligence by companies*, <https://www.ohchr.org/Documents/Issues/Business/MandatoryHR_Due_Diligence_Issues_Paper.pdf>, accessed 15 October 2020.

[195] Y. Aftab and A. Mocle, *Business and Human Rights as Law: Towards Justiciability of Rights, Involvement, and Remedy* (2019 at ch. 4 discusses 'Involvement' and concludes at p. 129 that '[i]nvolvement may be the clearest indicator of paradigm incompatibility between the [UNGP] as voluntary corporate responsibility norms and their emerging role as bases of legal liability'. John Ruggie has observed that 'my main concern with regard to the cause/contribute/linked discussion is to stress the critical difference between further operationalising elements of the GPs [Guiding Principles] and GLs [OECD MNE Guidelines] for particular sectors and contexts, which is both desirable and necessary, and introducing entirely new premises and terminology that misconstrue and diminish the actual intended meaning of the two texts'. *Letter from John Ruggie to Working Group for Responsible Business of the OECD* (6 March 2017), <https://media.business-humanrights.org/media/documents/files/documents/OECD_Workshop_Ruggie_letter_-_Mar_2017_0.pdf>, accessed 15 October 2020.

[196] Thus, businesses with economic or other leverage in particular situations might be able to influence the behaviour of third parties (such as remotely positioned suppliers) with respect to human rights impacts of the latter that are completely unconnected with (and not directly linked to) the business' operations, products, or services.

'perverse incentives' (discouraging businesses from actively engaging with difficult human rights issues) and/or render the most responsible companies 'the architects of their own legal risk'.[197]

It is therefore important for business to understand the points at which efforts to respect human rights in alignment with the UNGP may engage potential legal risk, not to discourage implementation of the UNGP but to enable appropriate management of all relevant risks. Businesses are bound to be wary, if it becomes evident that good faith efforts to embrace the UNGP through enterprise-wide HRDD—including disclosures—are likely to be used against them to found litigation. At its most extreme, this could backfire into a retraction from the most meaningful and effective forms of HRDD encouraged by the UNGP[198] and cancel out gains that accompany their widespread implementation in practice.[199] As efforts intensify to incentivise business to carry out meaningful HRDD—including by new legal requirements on them, supported in principle by some businesses themselves (see section VI)—it will be crucial to design measures that are 'smart', and this will necessarily involve a nuanced reflection on the interface between HRDD and potential legal liabilities.

D. Grievance mechanisms

There might be a diversion of complaints and grievances to less formal mechanisms by which issues can be resolved and impacts remediated, obviating the need for full-scale multinational human rights litigation.[200] OLGMs, for example, can serve a unique function in both helping prevent the escalation of human rights-related disputes and in providing access to remedy in ways that are sensitive to the particular context and affected persons. OLGMs should complement rather than seek to usurp judicial processes or other non-judicial mechanisms to which affected people would otherwise wish to refer complaints.[201] There has also been increased recourse to other non-judicial processes with respect to human rights

[197] Aftab and Mocle (n. 195) 29.

[198] It has been noted that this could be the defensive reaction by some to the Supreme Court's decision in *Vedanta* (n. 24), leading to a retraction of parent companies from their involvement in putting in place group-wide risk management frameworks. See, for example, R. McCorquodale, 'Vedanta v Lungowe Symposium: Duty of Care of Parent Companies', 18 April 2019, <https://opiniojuris.org/2019/04/18/symposium-duty-of-care-of-parent-companies/>, accessed 15 October 2020.

[199] Thus, the UNGP are expressly not a framework for legal liability and applying them in this way would be antithetical to their aims and to the wider cause of corporate social responsibility: see van Dam (n. 17), p. 4.

[200] Skinner (n. 78) 176–7 notes that the UNGP have encouraged the use of internal grievance mechanisms and other non-judicial proceedings to address issues. They are quicker and cheaper than litigation (and also circumvent some common jurisdictional factors that augur against speedy and satisfactory outcomes).

[201] UNGP (n. 3) principle 25 commentary and principle 17 commentary. Skinner (n. 78) cautions that they may in practice limit access to judicial remedies.

issues.[202] A prime example has been National Contact Points (NCPs) established to receive specific instance complaints of alleged breaches of the OECD Guidelines for Multinational Enterprises (OECD MNE Guidelines), which include due diligence provisions and a human rights chapter that closely track the UNGP.[203]

From a business perspective, willingness to engage in some such processes will inevitably be accompanied by a residual concern that they can also be used as a stepping stone towards multinational human rights litigation where complainants access them not with the primary aim of resolving grievances but rather to secure admissions, generate information, or elicit findings that can then facilitate such litigation. Unlike State-based judicial mechanisms, there are often few formalised and enforceable protections concerning matters such as confidentiality of disclosed material.[204] Businesses may find it difficult to balance their willingness to engage—to resolve human rights complaints at an early stage, satisfy stakeholder expectation, and meet their stated commitments—with their concern to limit eventual litigation exposure.[205]

Unless carefully and sensitively managed, resolution by way of non-State based grievance mechanisms can rebound on MNCs. In a relatively undeveloped field of practice, efforts to construct processes to address adverse human rights impacts—in particular serious abuses—may attract widespread critical scrutiny.[206] A business whose objectives are to enable remediation consistent with its commitments to human rights but wishing also to draw a line under grievances is likely to want an assurance that resolution reached by agreement is truly the end of the matter. To achieve finality, it is likely to prefer to seek confirmation of a full and final settlement, including a waiver of any rights or claims

[202] Many non-State based and/or non-judicial mechanisms are neither designed nor appropriate to provide remedy for serious infringements of human rights harms, in particular abuses that may amount to crimes.

[203] The OECD MNE Guidelines were revised in 2011 to incorporate a human rights chapter aligned with the UNGP, as well as due diligence provisions reflecting the UNGP approach. Annual Reports discuss the activities of NCPs undertaken to promote the effectiveness of the OECD MNE Guidelines. See 'Annual Reports on the OECD Guidelines for Multinational Enterprises', <https://www.oecd.org/daf/inv/mne/annualreportsontheguidelines.htm>, accessed 15 October 2020.

[204] OECD, *Guide for National Contact Points on Confidentiality and Campaigning when handling Specific Instances*, (OECD 2019) at p. 6. The UK NCP provides quite detailed guidance on confidentiality expectations at various points in its process: *UK national contact point: procedures for complaints brought under the OECD guidelines for multinational enterprises* (2011, updated 2014), <https://www.gov.uk/government/publications/uk-national-contact-point-procedures-for-complaints-brought-under-the-oecd-guidelines-for-multinational-enterprises>, accessed 15 October 2020.

[205] Some claimants also have concerns regarding perceived limitations of the NCP processes see, for example, OECD Watch, 'The State of Remedy under the OECD Guidelines: Understanding NCP cases concluded in 2019 through the lens of remedy' (June 2020), <https://www.oecdwatch.org/the-state-of-remedy-under-the-oecd-guidelines-in-2019/>, accessed 15 October 2020.

[206] Consider the scrutiny over a considerable period of time accorded Barrick Gold Corporation's involvement in the creation and implementation of remedial mechanisms in connection with abuses at the Porgera Joint Venture in Papua New Guinea, referenced and discussed in M. Jungk, O. Chichester, and C. Fletcher, *In Search of Justice: Pathways to Remedy at the Porgera Gold Mine*, Report, *BSR*, San Francisco (2018), <https://www.bsr.org/reports/BSR_In_Search_of_Justice_Porgera_Gold_Mine.pdf>, accessed 15 October 2020.

relating to the same subject matter.[207] By so doing, it may well find itself accused of having reduced claimants' access to effective remedy because the waiver (assuming effective) would preclude court action.[208] Further study is needed to identify ways to achieve a fair balance between a business' interest in ensuring it is not called upon to remedy the same harm multiple times and ensuring claimants' access to effective remedy is not curtailed.[209] It remains unclear what a 'full and final' settlement agreement compatible with all UNGP expectations would look like.[210] Nevertheless, in the sphere of multinational human rights litigation, settlement expectations have moved in some cases beyond the payment of monetary compensation to the particular claimants. One recent settlement agreement, for example, reportedly included not only a monetary payment but also the establishment of a new and independent operational grievance mechanism, as advocated by the UNGP.[211] Alignment with the UNGP can only encourage further advances in this regard.

E. Conduct of litigation

Multinational human rights litigation is conducted within State-based judicial mechanisms; the applicable frameworks, substantive causes of action, processes, and rules are established by the State. Litigants need to navigate systems that have evolved over centuries, reflecting international legal rules on the limits of State jurisdiction and with entrenched features that may be ineffective by reference to aspects of the State's duty to protect human rights. States are uniquely positioned to address such systemically entrenched features of domestic legal systems that could better serve the interests of all parties to multinational human rights litigation—including, as appropriate, through redefinition of jurisdictional requirements, causes of action, and the contours of liability. When multinational human rights litigation is threatened or pursued, however, business should aim to approach it consistently with the responsibility to respect human rights.

[207] Jennings (n. 72), discussing Barrick Gold's establishment of the mechanism referenced at n.206, notes the concern that individuals passing through this had to sign a waiver against legal proceedings, and so were required to relinquish their rights in order to achieve any sort of remedy. MiningWatch Canada criticised settlement conditions whereby claimants had to agree not to pursue any further claim for compensation, or civil action, opining that such terms were contrary to the UNGP: OHCHR, 'Re: Allegations regarding the Porgera Joint Venture remedy framework', (July 2013), <https://media.business-humanrights.org/media/documents/files/media/ohchr-porgera-joint-venture-letter-aug-2013.pdf>, (hereafter *OHCHR—Porgera*), accessed 15 October 2020.

[208] Jennings (n. 72). Skinner (n. 78) at 181–2. *OHCHR—Porgera* (n. 207) 6–9.

[209] See the Jungk, Chichester, and Fletcher (n. 206) and Aftab and Mocle (n. 195) at ch. 5.

[210] Difficulties are compounded where claimants are representatives of a wider class of affected rightsholders who may not have been included within particular litigation proceedings: see Van Schaack (n. 28) 329.

[211] Gemfields, 'Gemfields Press Statement' (29 January 2019), <https://mining.com/wp-content/uploads/2019/01/gemfields-press-announcement-jan29-2019.pdf>, accessed 15 October 2020.

Critics of MNCs sometimes perceive a 'disconnect' between corporate social responsibility and actual corporate behaviour in the context of choices of litigation strategy and legal positions adopted.[212] In the non-transparent area of litigation strategy development,[213] it is perhaps not surprising that public discourse on this subject has been limited and the implications of the responsibility to respect human rights within a litigation context remain largely unexplored. In situations where a company has choices about the grounds on which to defend itself, the question has been posited whether it should seek to avoid adopting positions that go further than is necessary, if they might lead to negative consequences from the broader perspective of victims' access to remedy.[214] Although there is much scope for debate around the parameters of UNGP expectations in this context, it is possible that some cases could present a true tension between mounting a robust legal defence and a strategy that might negatively impact rights. While no-one would question a business' entitlement to contest claims it believes to be unmeritorious or inflated, some cases could call for careful consideration of an array of legally defensible options—jurisdictional, substantive, procedural—to navigate a course that both reflects the interests of the business and its stakeholders while demonstrating consistency with stated human rights commitments. Given that the outcome of any litigation is inherently uncertain, some cases might call for difficult judgements by businesses and their advisers, particularly in jurisdictions where the stakes are high.[215]

Of course businesses, in common with other actors, should respect the rule of law and participate in good faith in judicial processes[216] and not act in ways that might weaken the integrity of such processes.[217] In these respects, a human-rights

[212] Mehra and Shay (n. 76) have argued that adopting a position that seeks to limit recourse for victims of human rights abuses is fundamentally incompatible with CSR initiatives and statements, asserting an 'alarming disconnect between corporate social responsibility practices and actual corporate behaviour, including the choice of litigation strategy and legal position'.

[213] Legal professional privilege will protect lawyer-client communications on that subject in common law jurisdictions.

[214] The issues were raised for discussion by John Ruggie's intervention in the public debate about the *Kiobel* litigation in the United States in which the US Supreme Court ultimately restricted the scope of potential application of the ATS (n. 44). Professor Ruggie had filed an amicus brief in the litigation and also published an 'issues brief' in which he acknowledged that companies must be able to defend themselves but should also consider the consequences of the legal arguments they advance. He posed a number of rhetorical questions concerning the extent of expectation that might be placed on businesses and the lawyers advising them, including with respect to strategies that could result in the elimination of judicial means by which victims of gross human rights abuses could otherwise seek remedy, where other legal arguments were available to the corporation. J. Ruggie, 'Kiobel and Corporate Social Responsibility: An Issues Brief', 4 September 2012, <https://www.business-humanrights.org/en/latest-news/pdf-kiobel-and-corporate-social-responsibility-an-issues-brief/>, accessed 15 October 2020.

[215] Certain features of the US litigation model that are particularly challenging have been mentioned (see, for example, n. 107).

[216] A/HRC/RES/44/15, Resolution adopted by the Human Rights Council on 17 July 2020. The Resolution refers to other issues that may be relevant in some multinational human rights litigation, including the position of human rights defenders.

[217] UNGP (n. 3), principle 11 commentary.

respecting litigation strategy could form one facet of a broader 'ethical' litigation approach. For businesses, such approaches would be supported by well-integrated HRDD processes incorporating effective feedback loops (including from grievance processes). Coordination between business functions—including the in-house legal department—from the earliest identification of issues can facilitate non-escalation into fully fledged grievances and eventual litigation, allowing the business to monitor developments and gain an early understanding of affected persons' concerns.[218] If litigation becomes inevitable, such processes will have helped businesses prepare and plan productively, aiming to adopt a stance that both respects its human rights responsibilities and defends its legitimate legal interests.

Where in-house teams depend heavily on external counsel for litigation support, it is important to ensure that counsel fully understands the client's commitments to respect human rights and, in alignment with applicable professional duties, is able to reflect this within advice on the merits of claims as well as on strategic efforts to defend and resolve disputes.[219]

Litigation is a dynamic process that depends on the shifting aims, priorities, and choices of at least two opposing sides and, in some adversarial systems, the traditional 'battle' or 'game' stance has historically promoted strategies towards winning at all costs.[220] Adversarial systems by their nature inhibit the cultivation of consultative and rightsholder-focused approaches, at least prior to the point at which a defendant company has identified it caused or contributed to a harm, the court has adjudicated liability, or settlement negotiations have commenced in earnest. Perhaps there is a mutual interest shared by claimants and defendants to consider how the litigation process can more readily embrace approaches that are 'responsible' even if the specific expectations of the UNGP within the conduct of litigation are few.

It was observed in sections II and III that multinational human rights litigation can be an unsatisfactory model for the effective resolution of human rights-related claims. Even in the absence of State-led reform, there is some urgency to confront its particular features that may compound this. It is possible that progress could be made through a recalibration of the typical dynamics within adversarial multinational human rights litigation. Where procedural rules themselves do not so require, this could include the parties seeking to define the contours of the litigation

[218] van Dam (n. 17) 8 and 9.

[219] The application of the responsibility to respect human rights as articulated in the UNGP to lawyers has received considerable attention. The responsibility extends to the lawyer's own business and to the lawyer/client relationship, in which context it operates alongside and does not abridge a lawyer's professional duties to act in a client's best interests and to uphold the administration of justice. See, for example, A4ID, *The UN Guiding Principles on Business and Human Rights A guide for the legal profession* (2013), <http://www.a4id.org/wp-content/uploads/2016/04/A4ID-Business-and-Human-Rights-Guide-2013-web.pdf>, accessed 15 October 2020; International Bar Association, *IBA Practical Guide on Business and Human Rights for Business Lawyers* (2016), <https://www.ibanet.org/LPRU/Business-and-Human-Rights-for-the-Legal-Profession.aspx>, accessed 10 February 2021.

[220] See, for example, Pitts (n. 81) 489–3.

narrowly, promoting early identification of the factual and legal issues in dispute, aiming for a streamlined process[221] and not engaging in wasteful or antagonistic tactics designed to wear the other side down rather than confront the merits of claims. All parties could demonstrate due sensitivity to the challenges that may confront claimants and witnesses within a system that may appear intimidating as well as geographically remote. It is perhaps worth injecting within the various proposals for reform that focus on barriers to access to remedy[222] a more systematic focus on the potential benefits that could accompany mandatory mediation or other forms of alternative dispute resolution (ADR) as a precondition to litigation or requirements on parties to consider ADR at various points in litigation to seek to minimise conflict and find appropriate outcomes short of a trial.[223]

Commitment to respectful (as well as rights-respecting) approaches to multinational human rights litigation by the parties involved in it could be powerful influences in minimising collateral damage to all parties while supporting fairer and more effective judicial processes. Meaningful progress would require appropriate reflection and commitment on all sides, as well as a fair degree of trust. If feasible, it may be timely to seek to build coalitions across the claimant-defendant divide with a mutual aim to identify constructive approaches to resolving disputed multinational human rights litigation in ways that support the implementation of the UNGP.

VI. The future: regulation, legal liability models, and multinational human rights litigation

In his final report to the UN Human Rights Council in 2011, John Ruggie emphasised that endorsement of the UNGP would not by itself bring business and human rights challenges to an end. Rather it marked 'the end of the beginning: by establishing a common global platform for action, on which cumulative progress can be built, step-by-step, without foreclosing any other promising longer-term developments'.[224]

[221] For an example of a court's admonishment of lawyers for failing to promote the overriding objective of enabling the court to deal with cases justly and at proportionate cost, see *Lungowe v. Vedanta Resources Plc & Ors* [2020] EWHC 749 (TCC).

[222] See, for example, the proposals for a business and human rights treaty under the auspices of the Open-ended working group on transnational corporations and other business enterprises with respect to human rights, <https://ohchr.org/en/hrbodies/hrc/wgtranscorp/pages/igwgontnc.aspx>, accessed 17 May 2021; and the OHCHR, Accountability and Remedy Project : Improving accountability and access to remedy in cases of business involvement in human rights abuses, <https://ohchr.org/EN/Issues/Business/Pages/OHCHRaccountabilityandremedyproject.aspx>, accessed 17 May 2021.

[223] Relevant mediation processes and other forms of alternative dispute resolution should also be compatible with the UNGP.

[224] OHCHR, 'Report of the Special Representative of the Secretary General on the issue of human rights and transnational corporations and other business enterprises, John Ruggie—Guiding Principles

In the intervening years, States have published national action plans setting out their domestic agendas on business and human rights confirming the expectation that business will operate in accordance with the responsibility to respect human rights as articulated in the UNGP.[225] The UNGP have proven invaluable in equipping business to confront multiple pressing issues, including most recently the challenges of addressing the Covid-19 pandemic.[226] Meanwhile, after circumspect beginnings, movements toward future regulation have accelerated and intensified.

A variety of legal measures recently adopted or proposed by governments and international organisations encourage or require more effective management of human rights risks and transparency around this. Although measures vary in their content and focus, individually and collectively they generally tend to support the effective management of human rights risks consistently with the UNGP, even if they do not expressly require it.

Mandatory disclosure requirements were the initial policy tool of choice for governments,[227] attracting critical evaluation by civil society and others who question the effectiveness of disclosure alone to generate meaningful shifts in corporate behaviours and positive outcomes for affected people.[228] In particular, although such laws incentivise the implementation of HRDD—if not implicitly requiring it—a general view has been that progress towards this has been slow and more specific mandatory measures should be adopted.[229]

There has been a surge in enthusiasm among States and other stakeholders (including some businesses)[230] for mandatory HRDD (mHRDD)—defined as 'the use of law to compel companies to take proactive steps to identify, prevent, mitigate and account for how they address their adverse human rights impacts'.[231] However,

on Business and Human Rights: Implementing the United Nations 'Protect, Respect and Remedy' Framework' (2011) UN Doc A/HRC/17/31, para. 13.

225 See OHCHR, 'State national action plans on business and human rights', <https://www.ohchr.org/en/issues/business/pages/nationalactionplans.aspx>, accessed 15 October 2020.

226 OHCHR, 'Ensuring that business respects human rights during the Covid-19 crisis and beyond: The relevance of the UN Guiding Principles on Business and Human Rights', statement by the UN Working Group on Business and Human Rights', <https://www.ohchr.org/EN/NewsEvents/Pages/DisplayNews.aspx?NewsID=25837&LangID=E>, accessed 15 October 2020.

227 For example UK Modern Slavery Act 2015 (2015 c. 30); Modern Slavery Act 2018 (Cth) (AUS); California Transparency in Supply Chains Act 2012 (Senate Bill 657); R. Lindsay, A. Kirkpatrick, and J.E. Low, 'Hardly Soft Law: The Modern Slavery Act 2015 and the Trend Toward Mandatory Reporting on Human Rights' (2017) 18(1) *Business Law International* 29–50.

228 BHRRC, *FTSE 100 and The UK Modern Slavery Act: From Disclosure to Action* (BHRRC 2018), <https://www.business-humanrights.org/en/from-us/briefings/ftse-100-the-uk-modern-slavery-act-from-disclosure-to-action/>, accessed 15 October 2020.

229 There have been manifold calls for States to take additional measures to encourage or require businesses to undertake HRDD: see, for example, Council of Europe, 'Human rights and business—Recommendation' CM/Rec (2016) 3 of the Committee of Ministers to Member States (2016) at para. 20, <https://edoc.coe.int>, accessed 15 October 2020.

230 See reports of companies, including investors, indicating support as compiled on the BHRRC website: https://business-humanrights.org, accessed 29 January 2021.

231 OHCHR (n. 194) 1. Shift, 'Fulfilling the State Duty to Protect: A Statement on the Role of Mandatory Measures in a 'Smart Mix'', *Shift* (2019), <https://shiftproject.org/

'when it comes to translating the ideas set out in the UNGPs into a legally binding regime, there are many different variants', so that discussions of mHRDD regimes potentially encompass 'a wide range of legal and regulatory possibilities'.[232] A number of governments and the European Union have either introduced[233] or announced their consideration of[234] legislative regimes to encourage or require companies and corporate groups to carry out mHRDD. It is also a key element of the proposed business and human rights treaty, discussed below.[235] Legislators taking the opportunity to introduce mHRDD requirements seem inclined to include equivalent due diligence requirements in relation to environmental issues (including climate change) within the relevant measures.[236] The introduction of mHRDD regimes are likely to be accompanied by broadened exposure to legal liability for companies with compliance obligations, although the exact parameters are unclear pending selection of particular legislative models.[237] There has

fulfilling-the-state-duty-to-protect-a-statement-on-the-role-of-mandatory-measures-in-a-smart-mix/>, accessed 15 October 2020; John Ruggie, letter dated 19 September 2019 addressed to the Business and Human Rights Resource Centre in connection with communications relating to the Swiss Responsible Business Initiative, <https://www.business-humanrights.org/pt/%C3%BAltimas-not%C3%ADcias/john-ruggie-responds-to-letter-from-swiss-business-associations-raising-concerns-it-misconstrues-foundational-elements-of-ungps/>, accessed 15 October 2020.

232 OHCHR (n. 194); OHCHR (n. 175).

233 The French Law related to Duty of Vigilance of Parent Companies and Commissioning Companies, Code de Commerce Art. L 225-102-4 (2017), as discussed in A. Triponel and J. Sherman, 'Legislating human rights due diligence: opportunities and potential pitfalls to the French Duty of Vigilance Law,' (IBA 17 May 2017), <https://www.ibanet.org/Article/Detail.aspx?ArticleUid=E9DD87DE-CFE2-4A5D-9CCC-8240EDB67DE3>, accessed 15 October 2020; Regulation (EU) 2017/821 of the European Parliament and of the Council of 17 May 2017 laying down supply chain due diligence obligations for Union importers of tin, tantalum and tungsten, their ores, and gold originating from conflict-affected and high-risk areas.

234 The European Union has begun a process towards the adoption of mandatory human rights and environmental due diligence requirements on business: see the Commission's consultation on sustainability in corporate governance as discussed in Global Business Initiative on Human Rights/Clifford Chance, 'What will an EU-level mandatory human rights and environmental due diligence law mean for business?' (January 2021), <https://gbihr.org/updates/what-will-an-eu-level-mandatory-human-rights-and-environmental-due-diligenc>, accessed 29 January 2021; Clifford Chance, 'European Parliament adopts position on corporate due diligence and accountability, now hands baton to Commission' (March 2021), <https://www.cliffordchance.com/insights/resources/blogs/business-and-human-rights-insignts/european-parliament-adopts-position-on-corporate.html>, accessed 14 May 2021. The German government's official proposal for a mHRDD law entered the parliamentary procedure on 22 April 2021. See 'Germany: Cabinet passes mandatory due diligence proposal; Parliament now to consider and strengthen', <https://www.business-humanrights.org/en/latest-news/german-due-diligence-law/>, accessed 14 May 2021.

235 See n. 224. At time of writing, the current draft Legally Binding Instrument to Regulate, in International Human Rights Law, the Activities of Transnational Corporations and Other Business Enterprises is the OEIGWG Chairmanship Second Revised Draft 06.08.2020 ('Second Revised Draft Treaty'), Article 6 ('Prevention') of which provides that State Parties shall require business enterprises to undertake human rights due diligence. The Second Revised Draft Treaty includes other relevant provisions that include Access to Remedy (Article 7), Legal Liability (Article 8), and Adjudicative Jurisdiction (Article 9).

236 See, for example, the French Duty of Vigilance Law (n. 235) and the proposed EU-wide mandatory due diligence legislation (n. 236).

237 Aftab and Mocle (n. 195) 46.

already, for example, been litigation pursuant to the French Duty of Vigilance Law of 2017.[238]

In parallel, there has been a specific focus internationally and regionally on the third pillar of the UNGP, access to remedy.[239] Just three years after endorsement of the UNGP, the Human Rights Council approved two parallel (but potentially complementary) tracks of activity. The first set in course discussions towards a possible treaty, which are ongoing,[240] and the second mandated an Accountability and Remedy Project (ARP) under the auspices of the OHCHR with the aim to contribute to a fairer and more effective system of domestic law remedies in cases of business involvement in severe human rights abuses.[241] The ARP in particular has sought to identify and analyse existing barriers to access to remedy for victims of business-related human rights abuse and to make recommendations to States how to address these, including within judicial systems.[242] Both the ARP and the treaty processes are bringing to the fore significant themes for the future of multinational human rights litigation.

Prominent among these are efforts within the various initiatives and policy pronouncements to address the 'governance gaps' facilitated by the corporate form and limitations on home State regulation. Some proposals favour broad measures that impose responsibility on parents with respect to subsidiaries and beyond, to suppliers.[243] On jurisdiction, some propose that accountability gaps should also be addressed by ensuring expanded access to remedy in home courts.[244] As for 'equality of arms,' some proposals favour reforms that would include a reversal of the burden of proof in civil litigation on certain issues, and increased access to documents.[245]

[238] See, for example, 'Legal action based on the French Vigilance Law triggered by a windfarm project in Mexico,' Clifford Chance 2021, <https://www.cliffordchance.com/insights/resources/blogs/business-and-human-rights-insights/legal-action-based-on-the-french-vigilance-law-triggered-by-a-wind-farm-project-in-mexico.html>, accessed 3 February 2021.

[239] At the European level see, for example, Council of the European Union, 'Council Conclusions on EU Priorities in UN Human Rights Fora in 2020,' (17 February 2020) no. 5982/20 (the Council committed to continuing to promote the implementation of the UNGP, including through access to remedy for victims of corporate abuses) <http://www.consilium.europa.eu/media/42570/st05982-en20.pdf>, accessed 15 October 2020.

[240] See the Second Revised Draft Treaty (n. 224 and n. 237).

[241] See n. 224. The ARP has spanned several phases pursuant to the UNHRC's mandate and at time of writing in in phase IV.

[242] See OHCHR at n. 224, in particular the work under ARP I culminating in the UN High Commissioner for Human Rights 2016 report to the UN General Assembly (A/HRC/32/19).

[243] The EU's consultation questionnaire proposed a definition of due diligence that would impose a duty on companies that extends to their subsidiaries and subcontractors, and in relation to their supply chain. The European Parliament's March 2021 Resolution proposing a draft directive prefers a due diligence requirement that encompasses an undertaking's value chain: see n. 236.

[244] It remains to be seen what forms of civil liability or other remedial requirements may be incorporated within the EU's proposed legislation on mHRDD (see n. 236). The Second Revised Draft Treaty provides for Access to Remedy, Legal Liability and Adjudicative Jurisdiction in draft Articles 7, 8 and 9 respectively (see n. 224, n. 237).

[245] See, for example, Second Revised Draft Treaty, draft Articles 7(6) and Articles 4(1) and 7(2) respectively (n. 224, n. 237).

From a business perspective, some generalised considerations may be observed. One is the importance of policy coherence and harmonisation. There are immense practical challenges to comply with multiple overlapping and inconsistent regulatory requirements; this can be costly and inefficient. There is also the concern that there should be a level playing field. Businesses are not generally opposed to legal requirements per se: what is important is certainty, clarity, and not being placed at a competitive disadvantage with organisations operating in less onerous regulatory environments.[246] All stakeholders would also surely agree that regulation should be 'smart': carefully designed to achieve positive and beneficial outcomes.[247] Some legal requirements are onerous and costly to implement and might even carry draconian enforcement risk yet offer no or minimal associated benefits for individuals and communities whose rights are impacted.[248] Over-regulation or poorly designed regulation risks discouraging proactive corporate behaviours that can have the greatest practical impact on the ground and engender 'tick box' compliance practices that comply in form but not substance.[249]

VII. Conclusion

One of the key factors behind the successful development and universal uptake of the UNGP was the consultative approach followed and the consideration of the views and perspectives of all relevant constituencies, including business.[250] While many current initiatives actively seek to adopt a similar approach, it can be challenging for policy-makers to include the business perspective in a representative and meaningful way.[251] It can be equally challenging for large numbers of vastly diverse

[246] Business respondents to a mHRDD study commissioned by the EU reportedly noted that the 'voluntary' UNGP lead to a competitive disadvantage and that a legal requirement would be expected to level the playing field as well as increase leverage with third parties in the value chain, reducing reputational risks: European Commission, *Study on due diligence requirements through the supply chain* (January 2020), <https://op.europa.eu/en/publication-detail/-/publication/8ba0a8fd-4c83-11ea-b8b7-01aa75ed71a1/language-en>, accessed 15 October 2020, pp. 67, 97, 146–7.

[247] L.C. Backer and F. Sapio, 'Emancipating the Mind in the New Era' (2019) 14(2) *Bulletin of the Coalition for Peace & Ethics* 270, 279, highlights potentially counterproductive features of the draft business and human rights treaty.

[248] OHCHR (n. 194) has noted the need for States to consider the extent to which proposed mandatory requirements are likely to drive effective implementation by business. See n. 231 and UNWG (n. 150).

[249] OHCHR (n. 175), [13], [17].

[250] Ruggie (n. 43) 80; OHCHR, '*Report of the Special Representative—Protect, Respect and Remedy*' (n. 124).

[251] Attempts at broad consultation are generally made but the scale and scope of outreach may be constrained by resources and accessibility. Efforts have been made to inject a business perspective into the deliberations around the proposed Treaty: see, for example, the IOE, Business at OECD and BusinessEurope, *Joint business response to the Revised Draft Legally Binding Instrument to Regulate, in International Human Rights Law, the Activities of Transnational Corporations and Other Business Enterprises ('Draft Treaty—Joint business response')* (October 2019), <https://www.businesseurope.eu/sites/buseur/files/media/position_papers/social/2019-10-11_joint_business_response_-_revised_draft_treaty_-_un_treaty_process_on_business_human_rights.pdf>, accessed 29 January 2021.

businesses to develop or present a consensus view. Certainly, however, 'smart' regulation requires development by reference to business' perspective on what is feasible and capable of delivering meaningful results.

There are clear indications that mandatory human rights due diligence will be a reality for swathes of multinational business in the relatively near future. Laws imposing such requirements are likely to permit and, in practice, stimulate, new forms of human rights litigation. Policies aimed at easier access to remedy for affected persons in European courts may facilitate this, which many will celebrate. Increased multinational human rights litigation in home States by affected persons may not do much, however, to encourage inroads with respect to existing limitations on access within host States, associated forms of impunity, and the imperfections of this remedial option for victims. Indeed, it could operate to decelerate efforts towards reform and capacity-building in host jurisdictions.

An idealist might call for a more expansive exploration of innovative models that do not rely so heavily on traditional litigation structures and processes since these are often inherently ill-equipped to encourage effective dispute resolution and remedial approaches that both respect the rights and interests of affected persons in particular cases, while acknowledging legitimate business concerns. Clearly, judicial processes will always have a key role in cases of serious human rights abuse, but there are manifold forms of adverse human rights impacts associated with business that are not well served by multinational human rights litigation in its existing forms, pursued within existing judicial structures. A mutual acknowledgement between claimants and business—and their lawyers—of the vital need to develop litigation practice in ways that respect rights while never occasioning adverse impacts as a by-product might be a sound starting point within a next era of multinational human rights litigation.

12

Litigation Funding

Practical Aspects

Susan Dunn and Felix Curtis

I. Introduction

'Litigation funding' is now a widely used term and has become an important tool in enabling human rights matters to proceed, providing access to justice for those who would otherwise be unable to pay their own legal fees. Third party litigation funders provide funding for the costs of a case in return for a pre-agreed amount of the proceeds in the event the case is successful *and* compensation is paid by the defendant. Litigation funding is particularly suited to mass tort claims, rather than individual or small group claims, in jurisdictions which permit multiparty actions. It is also useful where public funding such as legal aid is unavailable, or where lawyers are unable to act on a *pro bono* basis.

The principal focus of this chapter is on third party funders, and specifically on funding claimant group actions for damages claims in the courts of England and Wales.[1] It also considers funding options for lawyers in a number of other jurisdictions in which similar considerations apply.

This chapter will address:

- the legality of third party funding arrangements
- what cases might be suitable for funding (and how those cases might vary depending on costs, jurisdiction, levels of adverse costs payable on a loss, and amount of funding required);
- particular considerations in claims against multinationals;
- overall viability assessment and typical pricing terms for funding;
- what to look for in a funder;
- jurisdictional variations in the rules where lawyers act as the funder (e.g. by deferring their fees in return for either an uplift on their hourly rate payable

[1] While funding is available for defendants in certain circumstances (typically funding the defendant to help avoid a liability rather than recovering monies), this chapter is focused on funding for claimants.

Susan Dunn and Felix Curtis, *Litigation Funding: Practical Aspects* In: *Human Rights Litigation against Multinationals in Practice*. Edited by: Richard Meeran, Oxford University Press. © The Several Contributors 2021.
DOI: 10.1093/oso/9780198866220.003.0012

if the client succeeds (a 'conditional fee') or a share of the proceeds (a 'contingency fee')); and
- human rights cases which have benefitted from funding.

II. Legality of third party funding arrangements

A. The doctrines of maintenance and champerty

The doctrines of maintenance and champerty were previously impediments to third party litigation funding in common law jurisdictions, but developments in the law now mean that third party funding of litigation is possible.

The law of maintenance can be defined as the 'support of litigation by a stranger without just cause. Champerty is an aggravated form of maintenance whose distinguishing feature is the support for litigation by a stranger, in return for a share of the proceeds.'[2]

There was just reason for the prohibition against third party investors taking a stake in litigation in 11th-century English law, whereby wealthy barons would otherwise corrupt the judicial process by backing baseless claims to land. However, by the 18th and 19th centuries, a more rigorous legal system, supported by the Industrial Revolution, provided the framework to realise the benefit of a third party investor providing access to justice for the common man.[3] The doctrines of Maintenance and Champerty ceased to be criminal offences since the Criminal Law Act 1967, since which time the legitimate purpose of third party funding has been increasingly recognised by the courts of England and Wales.

In the *Factortame* case[4] the Court of Appeal stated that only third party funding arrangements that tended to 'undermine the ends of justice'[5] would breach the modern doctrines of Maintenance and Champerty. English case law has developed in a way in which 'litigation funding is an accepted and judicially sanctioned activity perceived to be in the public interest'[6] so long as the funding arrangement does not remove 'control' of the litigation away from the claimant and in the hands of the funder, and the funder is prepared and able to pay any adverse costs, including costs awarded on an indemnity basis.[7] Tomlinson LJ went on to credit the Association of Litigation Funders and its members as conducting themselves responsibly, without danger of being characterised as champertous.[8]

2 *Giles v. Thompson* [1993] UKHL 2, [1993] 3 All ER 321 (26 May 1993).

3 Martin Kenney, 'Third Party Funding of Litigation and Arbitration in the BVI' (*IFC*, 27 August 2019) <https://www.ifcreview.com/articles/2019/august/third-party-funding-of-litigation-and-arbitration-in-the-bvi/> accessed 12 May 2020.

4 Factortame (No. 8) [2002] EWCA Civ 932.

5 Ibid., [36].

6 *Excalibur [2016] EWCA Civ 1144*, [31].

7 Ibid.

8 Ibid.

B. The importance of control

The claimant should retain control of the claim to uphold the modern approach to the doctrines of Maintenance and Champerty that have been moulded in the interest of access to justice. Clearly, however, the funder will expect to be kept informed about what is going on with its investment in the claim, so there has to be an appropriate balance between the claimant retaining conduct and the funder being apprised of developments.

III. Which cases will a litigation funder fund?

As with the claimants and their lawyers, a funder will consider four key elements in any case to determine whether they are able to it:

A. The ability of the defendant to pay the amount being claimed;
B. The realistic minimum value of the claim;
C. The amount of funding being sought; and
D. The strengths and weaknesses of the legal merits of the case.

These four key elements are further explored below. In addition, third party funders will examine the competence, experience, and reputation of the lawyers litigating the claims, focusing on the lawyers' historic success in building books of claimants, that is in attracting instructions from a significant proportion of the victims of a particular occurrence; on average the amounts paid in past cases, on settlement, versus the initial claim value determined by the lawyers; the typical duration of cases, by jurisdiction; and the lawyers' record of accuracy in forecasting budgets versus the actual costs incurred in a given case.

A. The ability of the defendant to pay the amount being claimed

There is sometimes a mistaken assumption that funders have special additional means of locating assets of defendants. In reality, they are equipped with the same resources as the claimants' lawyers in determining whether a defendant can pay. Therefore, before the merits of a claim are investigated, the funder will want to see that the claimants and their lawyers have a clear enforcement strategy which identifies (i) the specific defendants who are being sued (especially relevant where there are complex corporate structures involved); (ii) the basis on which the defendants are being sued; (iii) that the defendants have sufficient assets to satisfy the value of the claim; (iv) that the defendants' assets are located in a jurisdiction which will recognise a judgment from the courts in the jurisdiction in which proceedings are brought; (v) that the fact of the case having been funded will not frustrate enforcement of the judgment; and (vi) clear strategies for preventing the defendants from avoiding the claim by sequestering assets by way of corporate restructuring, etc.

In the human rights context, accurately identifying defendants and the basis on which they are sued, can be difficult for claimants and their lawyers. This is because human rights claims against multinationals tend to concern harmful acts or omissions perpetrated by corporate entities within complex corporate structures or supply chains. It is important for claimants and their lawyers to demonstrate to a funder their grasp of those corporate structures and/or supply chains and to be as clear as possible as to the extent of any involvement of particular entities within that structure. This will give a funder confidence in the claimants' enforcement strategy.

In toxic tort cases, liability might attach to different companies, over different periods of time, or even across different incarnations of a particular business, where liabilities might vary or have been assigned away over the years.

When establishing which entity is most likely to have caused the harm, it may be useful to consider the following:

- Does the entity even still exist or has corporate reorganisation or sale meant that there is no succession in title of liability?
- Has the company been sold in the past, if so to whom, and did the vendor indemnify the purchaser against claims or not?

As mentioned above, it is important for the claimants' lawyers to be clear with a funder as to how a judgment-debt may be enforced against a defendant's assets. The claimants' lawyers should have clear answers to issues such as whether the defendant has sufficient assets to satisfy the amount claimed and the assets are located in a jurisdiction which will recognise a judgment from the courts where proceedings are brought without complex enforcement procedures. Funders are understandably sensitive about this since although confident in assessing and taking litigation risk (i.e. the risk that litigation will not succeed), funders will seek to avoid enforcement risk. They will therefore require a clear enforcement strategy which considers the various political and legal challenges of each jurisdiction where enforcement action may need to be taken.

This is all the more important given that in practice, very few lawyers have meaningful enforcement experience. Ninety-five per cent of issued claims are resolved before trial and of those which go to trial, only a small percentage are not paid. Most lawyers know the theory of enforcement, but few have actually had to take enforcement action. It is very costly and time-consuming if a defendant does not pay. The defendant may seek to frustrate enforcement by:

- challenging the judgment;
- seeking to have it overturned in the country of enforcement (where the defendant's assets are located);
- transferring assets to other jurisdictions to try to hide them; or
- by putting companies into liquidation to avoid liabilities.

A clear enforcement strategy should therefore include options such as seeking to freeze or preserve assets before (or as soon as) a claim is issued. It may be necessary to consider working alongside a firm in the same jurisdiction as the defendant's assets and which has particular expertise and local knowledge in relation to the local court enforcement processes. Incorporating this into an enforcement strategy will demonstrate to funders that the claimants' lawyers have carefully considered how the claimants and the funder will be paid.

The value of the claim in relation to the assets of the putative defendant is also an important strategic consideration. Will the survival of the defendant depend on the outcome of the case? If so, they will inevitably be inclined to fight the claim harder. The costs budget should take into account strategy for a long, drawn out case which considers all possible outcomes. For planning purposes, it can typically be assumed that companies which commit human rights violations may be less concerned about damage to their reputation and therefore less likely to settle cases at an early stage.

The claimants' enforcement strategy could envisage the use of investigators. From the funder's perspective, this can have some value in identifying assets where appropriate, but the limitations and accuracy of such investigations should be understood as well as the fact that such information can quickly change. Fixed assets such as property are much easier to identify and secure than cash.

It is therefore critical for claimants' lawyers to show the funder that they will continue to monitor the financial position of the defendant on a periodic basis throughout the case. There are a number of services and alerts which can be set up to monitor share prices and news about defendants to ensure that information is kept up to date.

Most funders will be content to work in certain jurisdictions but there will be many in which they will not consider operating, so it is sensible to ask the funder about this upfront. Important considerations will include:

- the legality of litigation funding in the jurisdiction. Funding is legal in most jurisdictions but it is important to ascertain any limitations on its use;
- the typical duration of cases in a jurisdiction;
- the certainty about the integrity of the jurisdiction and how it ranks in corruption indices;

- the precedent for successful outcomes of the case under consideration; and
- the level of costs of running cases and extent of adverse costs exposure.

B. The realistic minimum value of the claim

Once the claimants' lawyers have been able to satisfy the funder that the defendant has sufficient assets to cover the amount claimed, and that there is a demonstrable enforcement strategy for getting paid, the funder will next want to focus on the realistic minimum value of the claim.

This will break down into a number of factors in human rights matters, which, in common law jurisdictions, are typically (but not always) group or class actions.

i. Size of cohort

The first number the funder will be interested in is the size of the claimant cohort, the assumed total number of claimants it is alleged are affected by the wrongdoing of the defendant. The funder will also want to know the geographic spread of the cohort to understand how likely it is that the claimant group might be assembled, and at what cost. In addition, the funder will want to be satisfied that there is a workable strategy for sign up, and for updating and communicating with the claimant group.

ii. Value per claim

Funders recognise that human rights claims can raise complex or novel legal theories and that assigning an accurate value to each claim is difficult; they will therefore seek to determine an initial value from similar cases. Funders like to see a conservative approach to valuation and good funders will work with lawyers to agree what assumptions are being made to determine the value of the claim. These might include:

- Statutory bases for compensation under the governing law of the case. Some jurisdictions have statutory scales for injuries, where relevant.
- Case law, which can help to provide guidance about the likely range of values for a given claim.

If, for example, a claim relates to underpayment for work done, or loss of income because the claimant was unable to work due to injury caused by the acts or omissions of the defendant, income information should be available. Where this information is not available, claimants' lawyers would need to consider comparable data in similar industries, for example farmers' wages might be compared with those of tea pickers.

C. Amount of funding required

Since return on its investment is contingent on success, the funder will wish to ensure that sufficient funding is available to achieve this result. At the same time, as a commercial business a funder is required to operate to a budget and avoid unnecessary overspending. It is therefore crucial from the perspective of both the funder and the claimants that a reliable budget and time frames for various phases of the case are formulated from the outset and kept under constant review.

The funder will want to know how much of each of the following categories of cost lawyers will need in order to take the case to a successful conclusion:

- *Claimants' lawyers' costs*—are they proposing to work on any kind of discounted fee? If so, how much of a discount and what is the proposal for any uplift on success?
- *Experts' fees*—are technical experts required to prove the claim? This might include medical, toxicology, and financial experts.
- *Issue costs/arbitrators' fees where applicable*
- *Anticipated costs in dealing with defendants' lawyers*—human rights lawyers typically find that they repeatedly encounter the same representatives acting for defendants. This can provide useful insight into their likely behaviour and tactics and can inform budgeting decisions when factoring in what costs might be incurred in arguing the case.
- *Provision for adverse costs*—the rules that govern the amount of adverse costs payable on a loss will need to be clarified. While the claim might be brought in one jurisdiction, the governing law (where different) might prescribe a tariff of costs payable. The likelihood of a security for costs application will need to be considered as well as the possibility of securing a one-way costs shifting order—as in the United Kingdom, for example, where a personal injury claimant is generally exempt from the normal 'loser pays' rule. Further consideration should be given to whether the jurisdiction in question has, in previous cases, deemed after the event insurance to be adequate security for costs.

D. Strengths and weaknesses of the legal claim

i. General approach

Many applicants for funding wrongly assume that legal merits are the first consideration for a funder. Instead, a funder will not review the legal merits of a case in detail until elements one to three (outlined above) have been evaluated.

In order to be convinced of the merits of a claim, the funder will require a legal opinion containing reasoned analysis to be submitted by the claimants' lawyers. The legal opinion should detail the strengths and (crucially) the weaknesses of the claim. In particular, funders will want to understand whether the weaknesses are terminal for the claim in question or whether they can be addressed with additional work. Although funders will seek out cases which are more likely than not to succeed, they are also used to examining complex cases. Some funders might require a percentage chance of success set out in the legal opinion, but most are equipped to review an opinion and form their own view based on the information provided.

Where a claim shows promise at an early stage, some funders will provide what is known as 'seed funding' to help develop crucial aspects of the claim; this is typically for valuation reports and a more detailed analysis of the legal merits. If the lawyers believe they have a strong claim, they should not be afraid to ask a funder if they could work together on the case theory so that it can be developed sufficiently for submission as a formal request for funding.

IV. Particular considerations in claims against multinationals

A. Provision for the likelihood of the defendant's vigorous defence of the claims

As already touched on, corporations accused of committing human rights violations typically mount vigorous defences to claims concerning such violations. They tend to be able to afford to engage large, expensive law firms to conduct their defences. Such firms are highly experienced in deploying a diversity of tactics to frustrate or defeat the claim.

Therefore, when applying to a funder, claimants' lawyers should be able to demonstrate that they have a strategy for technical, jurisdictional, limitation and substantive issues that might arise and be used by the defendant's lawyers. This includes the likelihood that the defendant will appeal every decision in order to drag out the case and cause the claimants and their funder to run out of funds. As part of this, claimants' lawyers must be able to show they have considered in their own budget every provision for dealing with what will most likely be the defendant's 'scorched earth' approach to the case.

B. Jurisdiction, applicable law, and the effect of those on the recoverability of funder's fees

In its assessment of a case for funding, the funder will want to know where the claim is to be brought. It is becoming more common for claims to be brought in the English courts while governed by the law of the place where the harm occurred.

It is therefore important for claimants' lawyers to demonstrate to the funder that they have considered the jurisdictional elements and are able to provide written advice about the key elements of the applicable law. If the claimants' lawyers are seeking to assert why English law should apply to the valuation of the claim, they should explain why that is the case, providing as much case law in support as possible.

Funders will also want to know:

- whether there is a requirement that the funder's fee has to be approved by the court and if so at what stage (if it is only approved at the end of the case this may be a deterrent to funders for lack of certainty)
- when the fee is payable to the funder, for example from gross or net proceeds or even only from monies unclaimed by the claimants
- what the local precedents are for typically acceptable funders' fees
- whether the class itself has to be approved by the court (regardless of whether it is funded), for example does a Group Litigation Order or Representative Action need to be approved by the judge?

If the claim is to be pursued in the country in which the harmful act or omission occurred or where the claimants are domiciled, it is critical that claimants' lawyers are able to demonstrate their experience in that jurisdiction and that they have confidence in its integrity. Funders are particularly interested in how long cases take to reach conclusion in a given jurisdiction.

C. Recovery of the funder's fee more generally

At the conclusion of a successful claim, the funder will seek to establish the following in relation to the recovery of its fee:

- That the defendant can pay;
- That the monies will be paid to the law firm for distribution to the claimants and the funder;
- That the claimants sign an irrevocable undertaking with the claimant law firm for the payment of any monies to which they are entitled, so that they can be properly distributed to claimant and funder;

- That the funding agreement provides for prioritised repayment first of the amounts the funder has spent;

Once the funder is satisfied that the above criteria have been met, repayment of the remaining monies would typically be in the following order:

- payment to the law firm of the amount of their hourly rate fee which was on risk;
- payment of the funder's success fee;
- payment of the law firm's success fee (which should expect to be *pari passu* to the funder's fee in the event of a shortfall); and
- payment of the balance to the claimant.

V. Overall commercial viability assessment of a case from the funder's perspective and typical pricing terms for funding

To state the obvious, funders will only fund cases where they are going to secure a return on their investment (accepting that they may lose all their funding if the case is not successful). In broad terms, funders seek cases where the claim value is roughly ten times the amount of funding required. This is not what they charge but is the proportion they look for between claim value and total envisioned costs. Lawyers running the case can assist with this metric if they agree to go on risk for some of their fees but not all funders insist that lawyers do so; it does, however, indicate a level of confidence in the likelihood of success of a case, which in turn increases the funder's confidence in the viability of the claim.

There are no standard terms for the pricing of funder's fees for providing funds, but claimants might expect to pay to the funder 15–40 per cent of the proceeds of their claim. This will vary based on case size, budget, and likely duration of the claim. Most funders do not charge on the basis of perceived risk but rather according to the ratio of the envisioned budget required for the case to the value of the claim. That said, in some cases, the amount charged by the funder is lower at the start of a claim than at the end to reflect the fact that the longer the case goes on, the greater the risk is for the funder.

A. Book building

In order to be viable for the funder, the claim must be equal to or exceed a minimum value threshold to be determined by the funder. In determining that threshold, the funder will take into account the likely value of each claim and the number of claimants that are likely to sign up to the proposed action given the number of potentially affected individuals (the cohort). Consequently, the funder will want to see that a 'book' of claimants is being built.

In addition to the value per claim and the size of the cohort, it is critical that claimants' lawyers can demonstrate the following:

- Where that cohort is located and the logistics of and costs (e.g. travel costs) associated with ensuring those claimants can sign up to the proposed action;
- The assumptions made about how much of that cohort is expected to sign up and the cost per claimant in procuring their sign up. Most funders assume that a maximum of 50 per cent of a cohort will be signed up but if the claimants' lawyers believe a higher number would need to sign up in order for the case to be viable, they should explain why that is the case and whether signing up that higher number is likely to be achieved;
- What local resources are to be used to carry out the sign up and the costs associated with that;
- What plan is in place for maximising the numbers signed up, for example arranging townhall meetings and liaising with central aggregators (e.g. prominent local figures such as heads of villages);
- What fee agreements (e.g. conditional fee agreements, damages-based agreements, funding agreements) are expected to be put in place between lawyers and claimants;
- Whether there is applicable distance-selling legislation which claimants' lawyers will need to comply with, including any mandatory cooling-off periods.[9] Compliance with such legislation is crucial since failure to do so can invalidate agreements between lawyers and claimants;
- How communication with the group is to occur on an ongoing basis;
- How the lead claimant is to be identified and any others who might form a sample group for the purposes of providing evidence in the case.

[9] In the United Kingdom, the Consumer Protection (Distance Selling) Regulations 2000 (SI 2000/2334) (as amended by the Consumer Protection (Distance Selling) (Amendment) Regulations 2005 (SI 2005/689). Subject to certain exceptions, the Regulations apply to contracts for goods or services to be supplied to a consumer where the contract is made exclusively by means of distance communication, that is any means used without the simultaneous physical presence of the consumer and the supplier. The Regulations require certain information to be provided to the consumer prior to the conclusion of the contract, for example the main characteristics of the service, the delivery costs, the rights of cancellation, and any conditions and procedures for exercising cancellation rights. The Regulations also provide for a cooling-off period to enable the consumer to cancel the contract by giving notice of cancellation to the supplier. The effect of giving notice of cancellation under the Regulations is that the contract is treated as if it had not been made. The length of cooling-off period depends on when the supplier provided the information required by the Regulations to the consumer: if the information is provided on or before the day the contract is concluded, the period is seven days (beginning with the day after the day on which the contract was concluded); if the information has not been provided at all, the period is three months and seven days beginning with the day after the day on which the contract was concluded), etc.

Crucially, claimants' lawyers will need to be able to show how they plan to use technology both to manage the data of those being signed up and to communicate with the claimants. Where townhall style meetings are required, claimants' lawyers should demonstrate how they plan to communicate electronically via local resources as opposed to requiring always to meet with the group in person. Funders will be unimpressed if there is no clear plan in place for the use of technology in the management of data relating to the claim.

B. Adverse costs

Adverse costs, whereby the loser in litigation is required to pay a proportion of the winner's costs, are a feature of all litigation in common law jurisdictions (save for the United States) and therefore a crucial part of the budget to be considered for funding. Claimants' lawyers should therefore make sensible provision for this in their budget. The funder will usually buy After the Event (ATE) insurance to cover adverse costs exposure in the event of a loss at trial of the funded claim. However, sums payable in respect of ATE insurance do not need to be provided for specifically in the claimants' costs budget since the cost of the ATE insurance will form part of the Funder's total investment amount. The typical cost of ATE insurance is around 35 per cent of the amount of cover, that is £100,000 of cover will typically cost £35,000. There are, however, products which have deferred elements to the premium, meaning a lower up-front payment in exchange for a higher amount being payable from proceeds on success. Funders will tend to know good brokers who are able to conduct a genuine search of the market for the appropriate policy, rather than simply opting for the insurer who pays the highest commission.

VI. What to look for in a funder

The key questions to ask when dealing with a funder are as follows:

- How long have they been funding and how experienced are they in particular types of cases?
- How much do they have in funds and what is the source of those funds? Are the funds permanent or are they subject to withdrawal at short notice?
- Is the funder regulated and if so by whom? Each jurisdiction has a different approach to funding, for example by statute, by the development of case law, or a combination of the two.
- In England, are they a member of the Association of Litigation Funders? If they are not, is there a good reason for this?

- Do they ringfence the entire budget for each new claim they fund, thereby removing the risk of funds running out before the claim concludes?
- Do they commit the same monies to more than one claim? If the funder is relying on one case to successfully conclude in order to fund the next, could funds run out or could there be a delay in funds being advanced?
- How many cases is the funder currently committed to and will the applicant have a dedicated point of contact with whom they will be able to communicate throughout the case?
- What other human rights cases are they funding and what understanding and experience do they have of funding large claims?
- What is their process for approving the funding of your claim?
- What is their reputation in the market for how they interact with lawyers and their clients during the claim?

VII. Options for lawyers to risk share—legal frameworks in various jurisdictions

It is a positive sign as to the merits of the case where the acting lawyers are willing to put some or all of their fees at risk. To be clear though, not all funders demand that lawyers go on risk for their fees, albeit there are a number of options to do so in different jurisdictions.

A. England and Wales

Conditional Fee Agreements (CFAs) and Damages Based Agreements (DBAs) are both risk-sharing agreements between lawyers and their clients.

Since 1 April 2013, DBAs (also known as contingency fees), have been permitted for contentious work (i.e. litigation or arbitration proceedings) in England and Wales. This means that lawyers can conduct litigation and arbitrations in this jurisdiction in return for a share of any damages.

Under CFAs, if the lawyers succeed in litigating the claim, they are entitled to a success fee in addition to their normal fee (of up to 100 per cent of the normal fee). If the claim is not successful the lawyers may not be entitled to their fees or may only be entitled to a proportion of their fees.[10]

[10] The material in this section is derived from the following website: Herbert Smith Freehills, 'Contingency Fees or Damages-Based Agreements (DBAs)' (*HSF Litigation Notes*, 30 April 2019), <https://hsfnotes.com/litigation/jackson-reforms/contingency-fees-or-damages-based-agreements-dbas/>, accessed 30 May 2020.

A DBA potentially entitles the lawyer to a greater return from the claim. However, the *quid pro quo* is that the lawyers could be liable for any adverse costs if the case is not successful, and few law firms have the appetite or financial capacity for this kind of exposure.

i. What fees are recoverable from a losing defendant?

The claimant's *recoverable* costs will be assessed in the conventional way using the proportionality test, based on how many lawyers' hours are deemed to be reasonable for the case in question and at what rate. If the DBA fee agreed between the claimant and the lawyer is higher than recoverable costs ordered, then the claimant will be required to pay the shortfall out of the proceeds recovered. Thus, if the contingency fee is lower than the figure arrived at through traditional cost assessment, the losing defendant will only be liable to pay the lower amount and nothing at all if the claim against the defendant is unsuccessful.

ii. Does the defendant have to be notified of the existence of a DBA?

Since 2013, additional costs resulting from CFAs and the costs of putting in place an ATE insurance policy are not recoverable from the losing party. As a result, there is no obligation to notify the defendant of any such arrangements or that a DBA that might be in place.

This is consistent with the position for third party funders, where there is generally no obligation to notify the defendant or the court of the funding arrangement. There are some exemptions to this rule under some arbitral rules but those are unlikely to apply to the types of cases we are discussing here. It is always prudent to check the situation for each forum so as not to run the risk of the funding agreement being subsequently deemed void for failure to disclose.

There is nothing to preclude lawyers offering a DBA and a funder offering a separate funding agreement to cover certain specified costs. This allows law firms to receive part payment on an hourly basis as the case proceeds together with a share of a contingency fee in the event of success. Such arrangements offer law firms some of the benefits of contingency fee work but with a funder taking on some of the risk.

B. Canada

Alternative fee arrangements are becoming increasingly common in Canadian commercial matters, including:

- Fixed fee by phase (where the matter is broken down into phases and a fee for each phase is agreed based on relevant assumptions).

- Fixed fee or fee cap with collar. A fixed fee is agreed for each phase, and if the fee amount is above or below the target, the lawyer will share in the savings or cost overage, based on a predetermined split of difference.
- Risk-sharing arrangements, based on a predetermined definition of success.

Contingency fee arrangements are also permitted in all Canadian jurisdictions, subject to the applicable rules and regulations. Third parties can fund the cost of litigation and can do so by providing loans or funds on contingency. In class actions, a third party funder can provide funds to indemnify class counsel for their disbursements and the representative claimant for adverse costs awards.

In relation to class actions, the publicly funded Class Proceedings Fund provides an indemnity for adverse costs for those lawyers who run their claims on a contingency fee basis.[11] However, it is not necessary for a representative of a class action to approach the Class Proceedings Fund before considering funding from a third party funder.

In common law provinces, notably Ontario, third party funding agreements for class actions require the approval of the court. The merits of the case need not be considered at this point; however, the court will consider the financial position of the third party funder before ordering any security for costs that the defendant may request. The court, along with considerations as to the legality and necessity of the third party funding arrangement, will assess the termination and promise provisions in the funding agreement to ensure that the they do 'not interfere with the lawyer–client relationship, the lawyer's duties of loyalty and confidentiality, or the lawyer's professional judgment and carriage of the litigation on behalf of the representative plaintiff or class members'.[12] The court will also be very mindful that the funder is not to be overcompensated to the extent that class members would receive little or no benefit in the event of a success in proceedings, while recognising that funders take the risk when information about a case is inevitably imperfect and incomplete at the outset of a case.

In Ontario, lawyers may accept a contingency fee in certain circumstances,[13] but not in criminal or quasi-criminal matters. Lawyers must assess their pricing of the contingency fee by looking at various elements including the likelihood of success, expense, and risk associated with pursuing the claim and the likely claim value. The ultimate amount payable to the lawyers is invariably assessed, in class actions,

[11] The Law Foundation of Ontario, 'About the Class Proceedings Fund' (*For lawyers & paralegals*), <https://lawfoundation.on.ca/for-lawyers-and-paralegals/class-proceedings-fund/>, accessed 21 May 2020.

[12] *Drynan v. Bausch Health Companies Inc.*, 2020 ONSC 4379, [50].

[13] Rule 3.6-2—Rules of Professional Conduct (lawyers' Rules) referred to in Law Society of Ontario, 'Contingency Fees' (*Contingency Fees—Lawyer*), <https://lso.ca/getdoc/e6b83846-07d7-43f4-9865-da7e7a2755ac/contingency-fees>, accessed 22 May 2020.

at the conclusion of the case and might be varied depending on the actual amount recovered.

In litigation matters where contingency fees are permitted, the agreement must be in writing and, when between a lawyer and client, must comply with the Solicitors Act[14] and the accompanying regulation, O. Reg. 195/04 Contingency Fee Agreements. In any event, much like a third party funder's terms, the arrangement must be approved by the judge overseeing the claim, who will assess whether the terms are 'fair and reasonable'.[15]

C. The United States

Fees in the United States are not specifically regulated in that no tariff system is established, nor is any specific fee required or set by any State or oversight agency.

Under the Model Rules of Professional Conduct,[16] lawyers are required to charge and/or collect only a reasonable fee and a reasonable amount for expenses. There are a number of factors to be considered in determining whether a fee is reasonable, including (Model Rule 1.5(a)):

- The time and labour involved;
- The novelty of the issues;
- The skill required to perform the service;
- Prevention of other employment;
- Customary fees for similar services;
- The amount at issue and the results obtained;
- Time limitations;
- The nature of the fee, whether fixed, contingency, or other.[17]

Contingency fees (referred to as contingent fees in the United States) are permitted, except in family and criminal cases.[18] Fees may generally be divided between lawyers who are not in the same firm, as long as:

- The overall fee is reasonable;
- The client consents to the division;
- The division is either in proportion to the services provided by each lawyer, or each lawyer assumes joint responsibility for the representation.[19]

[14] Solicitors Act, RSO 1990 referred to in *Law Society of Ontario* (n 13).
[15] Rule 3.6-2—Rules of Professional Conduct (lawyers' Rules) referred to in *Law Society of Ontario* (n. 13).
[16] The ABA Model Rules of Professional Conduct.
[17] Ibid., Model Rule 1.5(a).
[18] Ibid., Model Rule 1.5(d)(1)–(2).
[19] Ibid., Model Rule 1.5(e).

Legal fees may not be shared with non-lawyers, except, to a limited extent, in the District of Columbia.

The formal requirements for fee agreements vary somewhat from State to State, although most States have adopted some version of the Model Rules. It is prudent to check the specific rules that apply on a State-by-State basis.

Many States limit the percentage of the outcome that may be charged in a contingency fee agreement. The agreement must notify the client of expenses the client will bear if the client does not prevail. In many States, when a contingent fee matter is concluded, the lawyer must provide a written statement setting out the calculations of the fee.[20]

D. Australia

Under current regulations in States other than Victoria, lawyers are restricted to offering 'conditional' billing where they charge no fee, or a lower fee (much like CFAs in the United Kingdom, save they are not entitled to charge an uplift on their hourly rate on success), if the case is lost but can charge an uplift based on normal rates (rather than a share of damages) if the case is successful. This uplift is capped at 25 per cent of the normal fee. However, in Victoria, the Supreme Court Act 1986 as amended by the Justice Legislation Miscellaneous Amendments Act 2020 (Vic) at section 33ZDA allows the court to make an order in class actions for plaintiff law firms to charge their fees on a contingent basis as a percentage of the amount recovered. The Act does not limit the percentage amount of the recovered sum that can be charged as a contingency fee, but the court will determine at any time during the proceeding what this will be and is subject to change at any time.[21] This may lead to lawyers and funders working together more closely to share risk on cases.

E. Germany

Contingency fee arrangements between a client and lawyer are prohibited under German law due to the underlying concern that contingency or success fees might lead to lawyers trying to win or settle a case in their own interests which could lead

[20] K.L. Basner, W. Wen Yun Chang, C.E. Chivers, et al., 'Regulation of the Legal Profession in the United States: Overview' (*Practical Law*, 1 April 2018), <https://uk.practicallaw.thomsonreuters.com/2-633-6340?transitionType=Default&contextData=(sc.Default)&firstPage=true>, accessed 18 November 2020.

[21] Clyde & Co, 'Victoria: First Australian State to Permit Contingency Fees in Class Actions' (*Clyde & Co*, 2 July 2020), <https://www.clydeco.com/en/insights/2020/07/victoria-first-australian-state-to-permit-continge>, accessed 20 August 2020.

to tampering with evidence, influencing witnesses, etc.[22] There is, however, one exception which is if the client would otherwise be barred from pursuing their rights due to their financial circumstances.[23] Alternatively, the Lawyer's Fees Act[24] allows for individual fee agreements, such as the agreement of hourly rates, whilst also providing for a regulated tariff system which calculates the fees due for a lawyer's services in a certain case which is proportionate to the value of the case.[25] On a successful outcome of a case, the client's recoverable costs are limited to the amount as stated in the statutory tariff fees, regardless of the actual costs.[26]

F. France

Whilst 'no win, no fee' agreements are prohibited in France, it is possible for clients to negotiate and enter into a fee agreement with the lawyer whereby a contingency or success fee is combined with more traditional hourly rates or task-based fees.[27]

G. Netherlands

In the Netherlands, lawyers are not allowed to work on a pure contingency fee basis, but alternative arrangements are permitted. This can include, a limited upside percentage sharing arrangement, so long as the lawyer also receives payments which cover the costs of the fees, independent from the outcome.[28]

H. South Africa

Contingency fee arrangements are permitted in South Africa as a result of the Contingency Fee Agreement Act 1997, which introduced 'no win, no fee' agreements and agreements which allow the lawyer to be entitled to fees higher than

22 Bernhard Schmeilzl, 'No Win No Fee Agreements are Void in Germany' (*Cross Channel Lawyers: the experts on Anglo-German law*, 26 July 2016), <https://www.crosschannellawyers.co.uk/no-win-no-fee-agreements-are-void-in-germany/>, accessed 05 April 2020.

23 *Rechtanwaltsvergütungsgesetz* (The Lawyer's Fees Act) section 4.

24 Ibid.

25 Ibid., section 3(a).

26 J. Lehmann, 'Regulation of the Legal Profession in Germany: Overview' (*Practical Law*, 1 November 2018), <https://uk.practicallaw.thomsonreuters.com/2-638-8145?transitionType=Default&contextData=(sc.Default)&firstPage=true#co_anchor_a194508>, accessed 5 April 2020.

27 A. Bailly and X. Haranger, 'Litigation and Enforcement in France: Overview' (*Practical Law*, 1 February 2020), <https://uk.practicallaw.thomsonreuters.com/9-502-0121?transitionType=Default&contextData=(sc.Default)#co_anchor_a836037>, accessed 5 April 2020.

28 R. Philips, 'Netherlands' in L. Perrin (ed.), *Third Party Litigation Funding Law Review* (3rd edn, 2019).

normal fees if the case is successful. Agreements not permitted by the Act will be considered illegal. The uplift in the event of a successful outcome, 'may not exceed the normal fees of the legal practitioner by more than 100 per cent and in the case of claims sounding in money this fee may not exceed 25 per cent of the total amount awarded or any amount obtained by the client in consequence of the proceedings, excluding costs'.[29] It was established that these agreements would be monitored by the courts to ensure the rights of the clients in litigation are protected and not compromised by aggressive arrangements put in place by lawyers.[30]

VIII. Case studies

Set out below are two examples of cases which have benefitted from funding. Both involved challenging book builds of claimants spread over wide geographic areas. In both cases it would not have been possible to bring the claims in the absence of funding.

A. *Indonesian seaweed farmers v. PTTEP Australasia*

More than 13,000 seaweed farmers, whose livelihoods were decimated by an avoidable oil spill on the Montara oil field west of Darwin, launched an Australian class action against PTTEP Australasia (Ashmore Cartier) Pty Ltd, the oil giant responsible for operating the Montara Well Head Platform, the rig that leaked.

The class action was brought by Daniel Sanda on behalf of himself and other Indonesian seaweed farmers. On 21 August 2009, the Montara oil rig began uncontrollably spewing oil and gas into the Timor Sea, about 250 kilometres southeast of Rote Island, Indonesia, for more than 70 days. It is estimated that in excess of 300,000 litres of oil per day contaminated the sea. The Australian Maritime Safety Authority sprayed more than 180,000 litres of dispersants into the water. The result was devastating for thousands of Indonesian seaweed farmers located in the area, many of whom had successfully moved from being subsistence farmers to having enough money to send children to university.

The claim was run by Maurice Blackburn in New South Wales. On 19 March 2021, Justice Yates found that the oil company did owe a legal duty of care to the seaweed farmers in its operation of the Montara oil well. It was found that as a result of the company's negligent operation of the oil well, oil reached the coastal areas of the districts of Rote and Kupang and caused or materially contributed to

29 *Price Waterhouse Coopers Inc and Others v. National Potato Co-operative Ltd* 2004 (9) BCLR 930 (SCA).

30 *Masango v. Road Accident Fund* 2016 (6) SA 508 (GJ).

the death and loss of local seaweed crops.[31] It is yet to be determined how much compensation is owed to the rest of the group members.[32]

B. *Children and Women of the Kabwe District of Zambia v. Anglo American South Africa Ltd*

The claim was issued in the Guateng division of the South African High Court on behalf of more than 100,000 claimants against Anglo American South Africa Ltd for the mismanagement of their lead mining operations in Zambia, which it is alleged has resulted in in multi-generational lead poisoning.[33]

The lead poisoning causes a range of significant conditions, from psychological, intellectual, and behavioural damage, to serious damage to bodily organs as well as neurological and fertility problems. In some cases, serious brain damage and death occurs. Lead poisoning can also impact pregnant women, whereby the unborn child will be subject to the same concentrations of lead as the mother, leading to complications when the baby is born and before that the mother experiences a higher risk of pre-eclampsia, gestational hypertension, and miscarriage.[34] Kabwe was the world's largest lead mine. It operated from 1915 until its closure in 1994.[35] It is alleged that from 1925 to 1974, its most productive period, Anglo American South Africa Ltd played a key role in controlling, managing, supervising, and advising on the medical, technical, and safety aspects at the mine, and that it failed to take reasonable steps to prevent lead poisoning of the local residents. The mine is in close proximity to the surrounding communities in Kabwe, where tens of thousands of Kabwe residents are estimated to have developed high levels of lead in their blood, mainly through ingestion of dust contaminated by emissions from the mine smelter and waste dumps.[36]

The purpose of this class action is to secure compensation for victims of the lead poisoning, including the cost of an effective medical monitoring system for blood lead levels among the community.[37] The claim is that Anglo American, as

[31] <https://www.mauriceblackburn.com.au/class-actions/current-class-actions/montara-oil-spill-class-action/>, accessed 12 May 2021.

[32] *Sanda v. PTTEP Australia (Ashmore Cartier) Pty Ltd (No 7)* [2021] FCA 237 (19 March 2021).

[33] <https://www.leighday.co.uk/latest-updates/cases-and-testimonials/cases/anglo-american-lead-poisoning/>, accessed 17 May 2021.

[34] <https://www.leighday.co.uk/latest-updates/news/2020-news/anglo-american-sued-on-behalf-of-children-and-women-poisoned-by-the-worlds-most-toxic-lead-mine/>, accessed 17 May 2021.

[35] <https://www.business-humanrights.org/de/neuste-meldungen/zambia-international-law-firm-leigh-day-prepares-a-class-action-case-against-anglo-american-ltd-on-behalf-of-zambian-communities-living-near-kabwe-mine-and-suffering-from-lead-exposure/>, accessed 17 May 2021.

[36] <https://www.leighday.co.uk/latest-updates/cases-and-testimonials/cases/anglo-american-lead-poisoning/>, accessed 17 May 2021.

[37] <https://www.business-humanrights.org/de/neuste-meldungen/zambia-international-law-firm-leigh-day-prepares-a-class-action-case-against-anglo-american-ltd-on-behalf-of-zambian-communities-living-near-kabwe-mine-and-suffering-from-lead-exposure/>, accessed 17 May 2021.

the company which it holds itself out as a responsible corporate, should provide that compensation because of the overwhelmingly significant role it played in the cause of the damage to the victims. The case continues.

IX. Conclusion

Inevitably a chapter such as this can only provide the overview of considerations when seeking funding for a human rights claim. The considerations are generally the same, irrespective of whether third party funding is sought or whether the claimant's lawyers will fund the case by foregoing legal fees.

Provided claimants' lawyers:

- follow the guidance set out here in assessing whether a case is suitable for funding;
- keep in mind the considerations for dealing with the claimant or claimant group;
- are clear on how the group will be paid in the event of success;
- assess the value of the claim in a realistic manner; and
- provide a conservative budget for running the claim;

they are likely to secure funding for the claim. On a broader level, third party funding is a crucial element in increasing the accountability of MNCs for human rights abuses, as so many of these cases rely on funding to succeed.

Index